The Pre-Raphaelites

AND THEIR CIRCLE

Dante Gabriel Rossetti

Christina Rossetti

William Michael Rossetti

Frederic George Stephens

John Everett Millais

Thomas Woolner

William Holman Hunt

William Morris

Edward Burne-Jones

Ford Madox Brown

Algernon Charles Swinburne

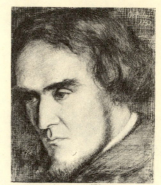

William Bell Scott

George Meredith

John Ruskin

The Pre-Raphaelites

and Their Circle

Edited with an Introduction and Notes by

CECIL Y. LANG
University of Virginia

SECOND EDITION

The University of Chicago Press
Chicago and London

The University of Chicago Press, Chicago 60637
The University of Chicago Press, Ltd., London

Library of Congress Cataloging in Publication Data

Lang, Cecil Y   comp.
  The Pre-Raphaelites and their circle.

  Bibliography: p.
  Includes index.
  1.   English poetry—19th century.   I.   Title.
PR1223.L3   1975   821'.8'08   75–12233
ISBN 0–226–46866–6

PREFACE

This volume is meant to fill an obvious and urgent need—it is a textbook with generous selections from several poets nearly always short-changed, in the anthologies, in favor of the Victorian Trinity, Tennyson, Browning, and Arnold. The selections represent the whole range of each poet's achievement and include for each one a major work complete: D. G. Rossetti's *The House of Life*, Christina Rossetti's "Goblin Market" and "Monna Innominata," Morris's whole volume *The Defence of Guenevere*, Swinburne's *Atalanta in Calydon*, and Meredith's "Modern Love" and "The Woods of Westermain." In order to admit so much I have had to exclude much, and, though I regret the absence of the minor poets, I confess that with more space I would have added more Morris, Swinburne, and Meredith.

The choice of pictures was incomparably more difficult than the choice of poems. For the Frontispiece I have done my best to present The Pre-Raphaelites and Their Circle as young rebels in their spring tide. In his late portraits Rossetti tends to look like a jaded Borgia, Holman Hunt like an octogenarian returned from beyond life. William Michael Rossetti lived to be ninety and, though his opinions remained steadfast, his appearance did not. As for Swinburne, one's imagination reels in trying to see the putative satyr of the sixties in the pursy nursling of Putney — or would reel but for the saving Comic Spirit.

Apart from portraits, some of the standard pieces, as in any anthology, had to be included; otherwise, the illustrations would not illustrate, least of all illuminate. But I hope some of the portraits and pictures will not seem hackneyed to the initiate, and I know that a few of them are here reproduced for the first time in book form. They are not necessarily my own taste. Rossetti's work I like very much indeed, and at least one of his paintings, "Ecce Ancilla Domini," seems to me to approach greatness. And I am aware that as there are people who like folk dancing and "good" jazz there are people who like Holman Hunt. So I have done the best I could by him, but fastidiousness requires me to record that my own response is merely a discrimination among revulsions. The recent appearance on B.B.C. television of his "Light of the World," "in which the mouth of the picture spoke words advertising paraffin" (*The Times*, February 17, 1967, p. 2) perfectly expresses my own feeling.

I owe large debts of gratitude to many people for help and advice, and I only wish I could be as happy with my other debts as I am with these. Helen Rossetti Angeli, Morton N. Cohen, Imogen Dennis, William E. Fredeman, Rosalie Glynn Grylls, Robert Langbaum, Jerome McGann, Richard L. Purdy, Mark L. Reed, and Richard N. Swift have been especially generous and helpful, and I am also obliged to James S. Dearden, Shirley Hazzard, C. K. Hyder, Leslie Marchand, John Mayfield, Douglas North, W. D. Paden, Gordon Ray, Graham Reynolds, Bernard Schilling, David Smith, Francis Steegmuller, Virginia Surtees, Helen Willard, and Marjorie Wynne. Most of all I am indebted, as always, to my wife.

C. Y. L.

This reissue incorporates a few slight corrections and additions, drops FitzGerald's *Rubáiyát,* which is readily available elsewhere, and adds two Swinburne poems, "The Leper" and "Anactoria," both first rate, which show an aspect of Swinburne not before represented here and are not, I believe, included in any anthology, or any selection of Swinburne's poetry, in print in the United States.

C. Y. L.
February, 1975

CONTENTS

William Morris

George Meredith

Algernon Charles Swinburne

viii • *Contents*

ILLUSTRATIONS

INTRODUCTION

Pre-Raphaelitism, though we cannot do without it, is meaningless as a literary term. We cannot dispense with it, because economy of discussion depends on it. It is meaningless as a literary term because, properly, it belongs to the history of painting and, unlike such words as *impressionism,* say, or *neo-classicism* or *mannerist* or *dada* or *surrealism,* does not in itself say something about both arts. Confusion is further confounded by the fact that neither the writers and painters nor their propagandists show much agreement about what the Pre-Raphaelites were doing or, for that matter, in their latter years, when the world, having blamed the living man, was ready enough to applaud the hollow ghost, about what they had done. Nonetheless, if one does not insist on semantic niceties or legal exactitudes, it is possible to discriminate various applications of the word as useful verbal counters for discussing a particular literary and artistic phenomenon.

Pre-Raphaelitism had, in one of its senses, a definite beginning and end in the Pre-Raphaelite Brotherhood. The only feature that distinguishes this organization from dozens, or hundreds, of others is perhaps the one that makes it worth writing about today — it was not born of students in a university but of actual painters in an artist's studio. The story has been recounted in too many places to require a detailed narrative here. The bare facts are that in September, 1848, three talented students, William Holman Hunt (1827–1910), Dante Gabriel Rossetti (1828–81), and John Everett Millais (1829–96), who had almost nothing in common except an insularity and ignorance more than counterbalanced by vigor, enthusiasm, talent, and sound instincts — they were, in short, young rebels — agreed that British painting of their own day required drastic reformation. One evening, in Millais's home, they happened to look through a folio volume of Carlo Lasinio's engravings after the frescoes, by Benozzo Gozzoli and others, of the Campo Santo at Pisa (where Liszt had been inspired to compose his "Totentanz"). In them they saw the very qualities they could not find in painting after the time of Raphael, especially not in British painting — strength, freshness, originality, independence. In other words, they were ready to reject the kind of tradition enshrined in the *Discourses* of Sir Joshua Reynolds ("Sir Sloshua," they of course called him), President of the Royal Academy, the academic tradition perfectly caricatured in Sir George Beaumont's question to Constable:

"Do you not find it very difficult to determine where to place your *brown tree?*" (Their error, though it is of no importance, lay in equating freedom from rules with "emotional sincerity" or, to put it another way, in confusing decorum and conformity.) All painting *after* Raphael, they thought, had been so dominated by the great master that the very art had stagnated, and they therefore resolved to break free, in order to paint, not according to rules, like the imitators of Raphael (the "Raphaelites"), but according to nature. Thus, they organized the Pre-Raphaelite Brotherhood and to their signatures began to add the secret, and therefore mysterious, initials "P.R.B." which indeed attracted some of the attention they sought and needed. The three became seven with the addition of Rossetti's brother, William Michael Rossetti (1829–1919), who, his gifts being scholarly and critical rather than artistic, was their natural scribe and historian; Thomas Woolner (1825–92), a sculptor; James Collinson (1825–81), a painter; and F. G. Stephens (1828–1907), an artist and critic. Of these four, little need be said except that "flat characters," in E. M. Forster's sense of the phrase, are as necessary in life as in fiction. Two others, though closely associated with Pre-Raphaelitism, were not asked to join — Ford Madox Brown (1821–93), an excellent artist who had been giving lessons to Rossetti and became his lifelong friend as well as his brother's father-in-law; and Christina Rossetti (1830–94), partly because of her sex, it seems, and partly because of her shyness.

Today, a viewer of the early (much less the later) paintings of Rossetti, Hunt, and Millais would not necessarily suppose they had any significant common denominator. Their pictures are literary and anecdotal, but, as George Levine's great epigram has it, "all Victorian art aspired to the condition of fiction," and, moreover, painting had always tended to be literary, and even anecdotal, when not exclusively decoration or portraiture. (Only in the last hundred years has subject-matter in painting yielded its pride of place to other considerations.) Their pictures tend, also, to be heavily symbolic and moralistic, but the same can be said of medieval, renaissance, and English neo-classic art. They have in common, however, a definiteness of contour, an avoidance of *chiaroscuro,* and a deliberately novel use of color, applied on a luminous ground, that often struck contemporary viewers as harsh or raw — certainly no common greyness silvers all — and, what is much more important, they all show an overmastering concern for proliferated, minute detail as scrupulously defined in background as in foreground. Reducing, or even eliminating, tensions, this technique tends to create a kind of democracy of components in which every part of a picture vies for attention with all the other parts, so that the effect — quite different from the so-called naïveté of the early painters — is of a manipulated artificiality. In addition, some of them brought the outdoors into the studio — more literally, they set up their easels *en plein air* — to an extent hardly yet acknowledged. Fidelity to nature was their rubric, though *nature,* in this case, meant the visible world, not "Mother Nature" or "external nature," and *fidelity* a self-conscious effort to render faithfully what their eyes saw — color, shape, and number, leaves on a tree, blades of grass, threads in a carpet, words on the spine of a book or on a sheet of music or in a newspaper. The traditional admonition to a young student learning to draw a cross-section under the microscope — "Don't draw every cell you see, but see every cell you draw" — could have been their own motto.

It was precisely the technique implied by such a motto that attracted the attention of John Ruskin (1819–1900), who, perceiving in works by Hunt and Millais the exemplification of some of his own cardinal tenets, wrote two letters to *The Times* in May, 1851, in defense of the Pre-Raphaelites. The support of the most powerful art critic in England in the most influential paper was not to be taken lightly, even in face of the clear fact that Ruskin either did not really understand what Pre-Raphaelitism was or had emphasized one feature of it at the expense of others.

Origins and influences can only be mentioned here. In Rome, in the early 1840's, Ford Madox Brown, who struggled to instil in Rossetti some few principles of the painter's craft, had visited and seen the work of the so-called "Early Christians" or Nazarenes, also known as the German Pre-Raphaelites, Peter von Cornelius (1783–1867), Johann Friedrich Overbeck (1789–1869), and others. Holman Hunt had actually read the second volume of Ruskin's *Modern Painters,* published in 1846. Rossetti had absorbed, with passionate admiration, the poetry of Keats. What is more, he had noted Keats's response to the same Campo Santo engravings in the same book that within a month were to excite himself, Millais, and Hunt. The works of Walter Scott, which had already had something to do with the medieval orientation of tractarianism, the poetry of Blake, Coleridge, and Chatterton, the old ballads, in the revival of which so much had been accomplished in the last half-century or so, and even the early poetry of Tennyson, which, in 1857, Woolner, Hunt, Millais, and Rossetti, with many others, were to collaborate in illustrating in the great Moxon edition — all these things, and many more, flowed together in such a way as to predispose these people to paint pictures and compose poems in ways that have come to be known as Pre-Raphaelite.

As a sort of house organ, the Pre-Raphaelite Brotherhood had a "little magazine" that lasted four months. Beginning in January, 1850, it was called *The Germ: Thoughts towards Nature in Poetry, Literature, and Art* in the first two numbers, *Art and Poetry, Being Thoughts towards Nature, Conducted Principally by Artists* in the latter two. It printed poems by Dante Gabriel Rossetti (most notably "The Blessed Damozel") and Christina and a lovely little poem, "The Seasons" (later called "The Year"), by Coventry Patmore. For lack of nourishment *The Germ* perished, but it is no exaggeration to say that its posthumous life has been more vigorous than its first incarnation was. The original issue has become a collector's item. Two reprints of it appeared half a century after its demise, one in 1898, the other, a facsimile edition with an authoritative history by William Rossetti, in 1901, a third one was issued in 1965, and others are promised.

As early as January, 1851, the Brotherhood, hardly lustier than *The Germ*, was "sinking into desuetude," as William Rossetti put it, and in its expiration God and Mammon literally played the parts that later on they may be said to have played symbolically. In May, 1850, James Collinson, having become a Roman Catholic, found it necessary to withdraw because of religious scruples, his defection being followed by that of Woolner, who, in the summer, 1852, withdrew to Australia, lured by gold. Millais was elected to the Royal Academy in November, 1853, a premonitory celebration of the death of the artist. "So now," wrote Dante Gabriel Rossetti to his sister, "the whole Round Table is dissolved," and P.R.B., which, according to their old jest, had designated the successors to Sir Joshua Reynolds, P.R.A., needed revising now to P.R.Z., as Christina recognized in the sonnet she extemporized in answer:

> The P.R.B. is in its decadence:
>   For Woolner in Australia cooks his chops,
>   And Hunt is yearning for the land of Cheops;
>   D. G. Rossetti shuns the vulgar optic;
> While William M. Rossetti merely lops
>   His B's in English disesteemed as Coptic;
> Calm Stephens in the twilight smokes his pipe,
>   But long the dawning of his public day;
>   And he at last the champion great Millais.
> Attaining academic opulence,
>   Winds up his signature with A.R.A.
> So rivers merge in the perpetual sea;
>   So luscious fruit must fall when over-ripe;
>   And so the consummated P.R.B.

In the event, God and Mammon once more played their usual roles. To an amateur who said that painting was a passion with him, Constable is said to have retorted, "And a very bad passion." And though neither would have admitted it, to Millais popular acclaim, and to Holman Hunt religious conviction, were clearly passions. In each case our comment today would be Constable's. Millais sought success and found it. He was created a baronet in 1885, served as President of the Royal Academy for a few brief months before his death in 1896, and died England's most famous painter, and perhaps her richest. His retrogression from P.R.B. to P.R.A. was not merely alphabetical. Holman Hunt's "bad passion" for authentic and too meticulous detail took him four times to the Holy Land to paint the pictures that his religious commitment required of him. He died in 1910, aged but by no means mellowed, even by the ritual conscience-money that society pays to success — high prices for his pictures, the Order of Merit, an Oxford honorary degree. Like Millais, he was interred in the crypt of St. Paul's. His failure, as we now see it, was that what he took to be realism was in fact atomism. All his life his painting was as atomistic as his religion was holistic. Bunyan is realistic without being atomistic and so are the Dutch painters of the seventeenth century. Much of Browning's poetry is atomistic and so is much of Defoe's fiction, as are all truly impressionistic paintings, but their atomism, self-governing and self-contained, is essentially vitalistic, whereas Hunt's, subservient and propagandist, is (like that of his only disciple, Ivan Albright) essentially necrophiliac. "Let me warn the world," he wrote late in life (*Pre-Raphaelitism and the Pre-Raphaelite Brotherhood*, II, 490), "that the threat to modern art, menacing nothing less than its extinction, lies in 'Impressionism' as a dogma without any regard to its limitations . . . . the greater part is childishly drawn and modelled, ignorantly coloured and handled, materialistic and soulless. Let it be clearly known that it is so, in being destitute of that spirit of vitality and poetry in nature which every true master, ancient or modern, painter, sculptor, or architect, has given to his simplest work, this supermundane spirit coming from his responsible soul, whether he intended or not to teach any special lesson."

II

The narrative from now on will be dominated, as the people concerned were dominated, by Dante Gabriel Rossetti. His presence, as so many have testified, was commanding. He was (Whistler's word) a "king." Younger admirers, disciples all, stood round him like "a guard of honor." With the publication of his letters we can now at last see him plain, not (in the words of Oswald Doughty, their co-editor) as "a darkly brooding, mysterious, mystical, poet recluse, a Byronic hero who was also a *vates sacer*, a Poet-Seer." His own brother's description, as Doughty observes, was of a very different man. "I have more than once," wrote William Rossetti, introducing his volume *Praeraphaelite Diaries and Letters* (1900), "had occasion to confute a current misconception that Dante Rossetti could be adequately described as a sentimentalist, a dreamer, a mystic, an aesthete, and the like, without allowance being made for a considerable counterbalance of attributes of a very opposite character. Certainly he had some sentiment; he dreamed several dreams, asleep and awake; he may have been a mystic . . . and he had a passion for art in various forms. . . . But it is not the less true that he was full of vigour and buoyancy, full of *élan*, well alive to the main chance, capable of enjoying the queer as well as the grave aspects of life, by no means behindhand in contributing his quota to the cause of high spirits — and generally a man equally natural and genial. . . .whatever else Dante Rossetti may have been, he was a quick-blooded, downright-speaking man, with plenty of will and an abundant lack of humbug. People who take an interest in him may depend upon it that the more they learn about him . . . the more will the masculine traits of his character appear in evidence, and the less will room be left for the notion of a pallid and anaemic 'aesthete,' a candidate for the sunflowers of a Du Maurier design. He did not 'yearn.' "

The facts of Rossetti's life are so accessible that the limited space available here can be put to better use than those of a biographical narrative. To put it succinctly, he married a woman he did not love, he loved a woman he could not marry, and he lived with a woman whom he neither loved nor married. Abnormally sensitive to criticism as he grew older, he became, in his brother's words, "not entirely sane" and "an actual monomaniac," a condition exacerbated by overdoses of chloral rendered palatable by whiskey. He died, a month short of his 54th year, in 1882, a pitiful wreck of a man, by no means unhonored, but alienated from many old friends, and he was buried, not with funeral pomp in a great cathedral, but in a lonely churchyard over-looking the sea, remote from metropolitan acclaim.

Rossetti's wife was Elizabeth Siddal, described by his brother as a "most beautiful creature . . . tall, finely formed, with a lofty neck, and regular somewhat uncommon features, greenish-blue unsparkling eyes, large perfect eyelids, brilliant complexion, and a lavish heavy wealth of coppery-golden hair." They first met in 1850 and became en-gaged in a year or so. She served as model for Hunt and Millais (and others), as well as for Rossetti, and herself produced a few poems and pictures of tenuous merit. The word for her artistic gifts, as for her beauty, was *talent*, and Rossetti reserved his hushed obeisance, "Beauty like hers is genius," years later, for physical endowments of another order. For nearly a decade they prolonged the engagement, only subconsciously realizing, if at all, how ill-matched they were, and finally, in the spring, 1860, decided to formalize their misery in mar-riage. Mrs. Rossetti committed suicide less than two years later, and Rossetti, overwhelmed by remorse, thrust into her coffin his manu-script poems. Melodramatic though this immolation may seem, it certainly did his heart credit rather than his head, for some of the in-humed selves were unique transcriptions. Later on, time having dulled repentance and begun its erosion of body and soul, it was neces-sary for Rossetti, a sick man preparing to publish his first volume of original poems, to have the manuscripts exhumed.

The other two women so important in Rossetti's life entered it about the same time. One, Fanny Cornforth, whom he first met in 1856 or 1857, was taken on as non-resident "housekeeper" in the early sixties, the harvest of an intimacy that had been maturing for several years. She was low-born, ill-bred, illiterate, voluptuous and gorgeous. As a widower, Rossetti made no attempt to hide her or conceal the rela-tionship, except of course from the ladies, and their loyal devotion to each other endured till his death. The contemporary who could not see what her "overpowering attractions" were must have been blind if not totally insensate. To William Rossetti, who took no special pleasure in praising his brother's whore, "she was a pre-eminently fine woman, with regular and sweet features, and a mass of the most lovely blond hair — light golden or 'harvest yellow.' *Bocca Baciata,* which is a most faithful portrait of her, might speak for itself." A worthy com-plement of the picture is Rossetti's poem "The Song of the Bower."

The third affair is more complex. The lady was Jane Burden. Ros-setti met her in Oxford in 1857 and introduced her to his friends, among them William Morris, who married her in April, 1859. How-ever much reason there is to believe that Rossetti loved her from the beginning, he neither would, nor could, in that day, break off the engagement to Elizabeth Siddal in favor of a rival. Janey Morris walked in beauty. On this point all who saw her, including Swinburne, Burne-Jones, William Rothenstein, and Shaw, who wrote that when "she came into a room in her strangely beautiful garments, looking at least eight feet high, the effect was as if she had walked out of an Egyptian tomb at Luxor" — all are at one. That beauty like hers was indeed genius there can be no doubt, though one may prefer the evidence of poems like Morris's "Praise of My Lady" and Rossetti's "Her Gifts" and "The Portrait" to the mannered, rather intimidating portraits that survive in Rossetti's oils, which make it appear too rich for use. Everything in Rossetti's life seems to fall into symbolic patterns that one has to resist, but it would require a scholarship of uncommon severity to believe that Rossetti was oblivious of ironies in painting her as Pandora, Persephone, and, above all, as Oswald Doughty observes, La Pia, "Dante's ill-starred lady of Siena, condemned by a cruel husband to perish amidst the pestilential exhalations of the Maremma marshes." Rossetti was in love with Mrs. Morris, perhaps from the late fifties, certainly from the late sixties, and we can hardly doubt that the affair was not only known to but also — in an exercise of principle that would seem otherworldly in a man less noble — countenanced by her husband. Even if the monitions of his heart had been stilled, the evidence of his eyes and mind could not be ignored. What seems obvious to us in Rossetti's paintings and is all but incontrovertible in so many of the sonnets in *The House of Life* would not have been lost on the man involved as profoundly and as painfully, if not as intimately, as the two unhappy lovers.

The second flowering of Pre-Raphaelitism, though superficially similar, was very different from the first. Their common ground was the person and personality of Dante Gabriel Rossetti. At Oxford, in the mid-fifties, a small group of undergraduates, mostly Pembroke men from Birmingham, clustering round two Exeter College men, William Morris (1834–96) and Edward Jones (1833–98), himself from Birmingham, formed "The Brotherhood" and produced a review, *The Oxford and Cambridge Magazine,* in twelve numbers, from January to December, 1856. Morris and Burne-Jones (to use the name, adopted decades later, that he is known by) had seen and admired Pre-Raphaelite pictures in Oxford. The latter sought Rossetti's advice and, following it, abandoned Oxford to become a painter. Morris, too, apprenticed to an architect, well-to-do, and already dabbling in poetry and painting, was stirred by Rossetti's commanding authority, and partly under his influence the two moved to London and, as Rossetti said, "turned artists instead of taking up any other career to which the University generally leads, and both," he added, "are men of genius." Late in 1857 all three of them, in company with half a dozen others, none with more than elementary competence for such work, undertook to paint frescoes on the walls and ceiling of the Debating Hall of the Oxford Union Society. But since neither enthusiasm, good-will, camaraderie, nor even their "reckless self-confidence" was an adequate substitute for knowledge and skill, most of the pictures were never completed and all of them deteriorated, rapidly and to such a degree that William Rossetti, writing in 1895, had to admit that "for many years past the painted surface of the Union walls has been a confused hybrid between a smudge and a blank."

Of Burne-Jones not much more need be said for the present. His painting was influenced early and strongly by Rossetti, he was taken up by Ruskin, and, as will be seen, he is very clearly the link between Pre-Raphaelitism and estheticism, or art for art's sake, and *art nouveau*. The work of Aubrey Beardsley, of the *Yellow Book* period, has been described as "Burne-Jones with acid," and the old quip scores not only in telling us something central about Beardsley and the nineties but also in calling our attention to something central about Burne-Jones. Rossetti's influence lingered (it never disappeared), and it would not be an exaggeration to say that in his work the decorative, poetic, literary, fantastic, and medieval aspects owe to Rossetti at least their early nourishment and upbringing, if not their actual paternity. Rossetti, however, gave ground to others, especially Botticelli, who began to be rediscovered in England in the sixties and seventies, and a French contemporary recognized Burne-Jones as "the poor man's Mantegna." A versatile and learned man, within fairly narrow confines, Burne-Jones also turned his hand to interior decoration, cartoons for stained glass, designs for tapestry, needlework, and mosaics, not to mention books (especially the great Kelmscott Chaucer), and achieved worldly success before the end of the seventies. He was elected to membership of the Royal Academy in 1885 (but resigned a few years later), was created a baronet in 1894, and on his death in 1898 was honored with a memorial service in Westminster Abbey. Now that he is regaining some of his former popularity, scholarship is very much in need of some critical studies of his work. The biography and edition of his letters that we also need are less likely to be forthcoming, since there is a blot in the 'scutcheon (presumably, infidelity leading to actual desertion of his wife) that familial alertness has so far suppressed.

William Morris's first published volume, *The Defence of Guenevere and Other Poems* (1858), is generally described as the first, as well as the most, Pre-Raphaelite volume of poems. It was also his last, for his later poetry became Chaucerian narrative, as in *The Life and Death of Jason* (1867) and *The Earthly Paradise* (3 vols., 1868–70); Middle-English alliterative verse, in *Love Is Enough* (1873); Nordic epic, in *The Story of Sigurd the Volsung* (1877); and more or less conventional lyrics, as in much of *Poems by the Way* (1891). He also translated the *Odyssey* and the *Aeneid* and he wrote a good deal of prose, including *A Dream of John Ball* (1888) and prose romances (*The House of the Wolfings*, 1889; *The Roots of the Mountains*, 1890; *The Story of the Glittering Plain*, 1890; *The Wood beyond the World*, 1894; *Child Christopher*, 1895; *The Well at the World's End*, 1896; *The Water of the Wondrous Isles*, 1897; and *The Story of the Sundering Flood*, 1898). These, though they repel some readers, are curiously hypnotic in themselves and fascinating as a reflection of Morris's mind. In 1864 Morris was instrumental in founding a decorating firm, Morris, Marshall, Faulkner, & Co. (among the partners were at first numbered Rossetti, Burne-Jones, and Ford Madox Brown), and from this date forward his concern was for applied art — interior decoration, furniture, wallpaper, tapestry, embroidery, carpets, weaving, dyeing, and even the manufacture of utensils. He designed type and, after founding the Kelmscott Press in 1890, issued books that merit a chapter in the history of printing. He was too multifarious a man to be summed up in an essay, or in a book, least of all in a paragraph, and in any case his activities as a Socialist, in themselves enough for a normal man's lifetime, sit uneasily in an anthology of Pre-Raphaelitism.

If Rossetti is the most interesting of the Pre-Raphaelites, Morris is the most elusive. For Morris was not a normal man, he was a kind of superman. He did all things and did them well. It may be true, as has been said, that he loved people without caring very much for persons, but he was so admirable in every department of his genius that we distrust our own humanness in finding his a trifle remote or chilly, as we admire his nobility without quite liking it or desiring to emulate it. That he could be admired by such worldly disparates as Yeats and Shaw says it all. Both knew him personally, both revered him. To Yeats he was "my chief of men," to Shaw "our one acknowledged Great Man," and it is instructive and amusing to compare their accounts of him, Yeat's in an essay, "The Happiest of Poets" (1902) and in his autobiography, Shaw's in "William Morris as I Knew Him," in *William Morris, Artist, Writer, Socialist*, II, ix-xl.

The connection of Algernon Charles Swinburne (1837–1909) and George Meredith (1828–1909) with the Pre-Raphaelites ranges from adventurous to adventitious. Swinburne, himself at Balliol, met Rossetti, Morris, and Burne-Jones at Oxford in 1857 during the disastrous festival of the frescoes in the Oxford Union Society. Falling, like so many others, under the spell of Rossetti's personality, he too began to manufacture Pre-Raphaelite verses, but the mode was alien to him and he quickly abandoned it to follow his own very different genius. It is not fanciful to see in an occasional sharply limned detail or the uncommonly definite positioning of a character a certain debt to this early tutelage — one finds such features principally in his work up to *Poems and Ballads* (1866) and, later, in the medieval narratives, *Tristram of Lyonesse* (1881) and *A Tale of Balen* (1896), though hardly elsewhere — but the truth is that neither Swinburne's Pre-Raphaelite phase nor its general influence on his poetry is really significant. His real relevance here lies in his sovereign authority in the development of estheticism, stemming from his early prose style, his art criticism, his interpretations of Blake, refracted (and thus both distorted and concentrated) through the prism of his own genius, which had already taken some of its shape from contemporary French sources, notably Gautier, Baudelaire, and Hugo. Equally interesting is his personal relationship with the Rossettis, Morris, and Burne-Jones, especially Dante Gabriel Rossetti, who was for fifteen years his most intimate friend. Rossetti and his wife had dined out with Swinburne on the very evening when, later on, she was found a suicide. In October, 1862, Rossetti moved into Tudor House, Chelsea, on the still unembanked Thames, with Swinburne as joint tenant and William Rossetti and Meredith as paying guests for a night or so a week — the sort of household one would rather dream or read about than share. Neither Rossetti nor Meredith had been able to cope with a conventional ménage, and Swinburne was a precocious youth on the verge of, and bent on, making a splash in London literary life. Obviously, the arrangement was doomed. Meredith never spent much time there and Rossetti managed to ease Swinburne off without damaging their affectionate relations, which nonetheless, came to an abrupt end in 1872, yet another casualty of Rossetti's breakdown.

Meredith's genius was less remote from Pre-Raphaelitism than Swinburne's. Only the over-zealous would call his poetry Pre-Raphaelite, since the whole tendency and final impression of the two modes are diametrically opposed, but it would not be unreasonable to perceive something of Rossetti either in its sharp pictorial detail or in its occasional sense of brooding mystery.

III

Pre-Raphaelitism has never been satisfactorily defined either as a literary or a pictorial term. Obviously, the components of the term itself have no meaning at all in poetry and, except for drawing attention to a state of mind, very little relevance to actual practice in painting. William Michael Rossetti, discussing the Brotherhood in 1895 (*Dante Gabriel Rossetti, His Family-Letters with a Memoir*, I, 135), said this:

> That the Praeraphaelites valued moral and spiritual ideas as an important section of the ideas germane to fine art is most true, and not one of them was in the least inclined to do any work of a gross, lascivious, or sensual description; but neither did they limit the province of art to the spiritual or the moral. . . . the bond of union among the Members of the Brotherhood was really and simply this: 1, To have genuine ideas to express; 2, to study Nature attentively, so as to know how to express them; 3, to sympathize with what is direct and serious and heartfelt in previous art, to the exclusion of what is conventional and self-parading and learned by rote; and 4, and most indispensable of all, to produce thoroughly good pictures and statues.

One's objection to this pronouncement is not that it is false but that it is worthless. The same claims could be made for virtually any serious painter in the whole history of western art before the twentieth century. "We can dismiss at once the aim to 'return to Nature,'" Mr. Graham Reynolds (*Victorian Painting*, London, 1966, p. 60) points out, "because this is the parrot-cry of every new generation of artists, and means a different thing to each one — Romantic, Barbizon, Impressionist, Cubist, Abstract Expressionist." Other attempts at definition are no more helpful.

The Pre-Raphaelitism of Hunt and Millais was a meticulous rendering of detail that, if the word did not imply parentage or a specific indebtedness, could as well be described as "Ruskinism" laden with a heavy weight of symbolic objects. No matter what scholarship and criticism suggest, this is assuredly the common understanding of the term, and it is the sense that will prevail. If the Pre-Raphaelitism of painting and that of poetry have any common denominator, however, it must be inferred from the practice of the only major figure in the group. Rossetti added another ingredient, and it is his work, and the very fact that he worked in two arts, that make the definition elusive — and the redefinition necessary.

What he added to Hunt's and Millais's "representational fidelity" crossed with symbolism can be called "romance" or "strangeness" or "a sense of wonder" or "mystery" or even "fantasy" or "poetry" or "evocativeness." It can be described as "visionary" or "irrational" or even "oneirocritical." The distinction is crucial, for it also shows us by what means he created Pre-Raphaelite poetry. This is the quality that moves us in his "Girlhood of Mary Virgin" or "Ecce Ancilla Domini." And, though we must admire the dazzling technique of Millais's works of the same period (and may even admire Hunt's), the highest compliment we can pay them is the most devastating adjective in the vocabulary of praise, they are (or may be) *interesting*. They are never, to use Rossetti's word for a quality he sought in certain kinds of poetry, "amusing" (except in the conventional sense of the word).

Millais, in 1849–50, painted "Christ in the House of His Parents" as Rossetti portrayed Mary Virgin as a girl in the house of *her* parents. Millais chose his own father for the head of Joseph (for the body, the authentic musculature of an actual carpenter was required), Rossetti his own mother for St. Anne. Both paintings spill over with symbolic props, and in both the symbolism also emerges from the governing cruciform design. They are, in fact, in every way comparable; yet the difference between them is approximately the difference between the implications of Glendower's claim that he could call up spirits from the vasty deep and the pragmatic retort, "Why so can I or so can any man. But will they come when you do call for them?"

Rossetti always endeavored to call up spirits, always grasped after both the human and divine. His vision was poetic, Millais's prosaic. Where Millais asserts, Rossetti suggests or evokes. The ritualistic gestures and postures of "Christ in the House of His Parents" are studied and even stagey. Rossetti's truer instinct led him to expressive color and design. "Ecce Ancilla Domini" is dominated by an expanse of whiteness enclosed with red, blue, and gold, all with their time-honored associations, but the lily, from which the awakened Virgin seems to shrink, its whiter whiteness intensified against the Marian blue of the bed-hanging, receives the full focus of the viewer's gaze and returns to it all the kinds of value, cognitive, affective, and esthetic, that a representational painting can encompass. "The Girlhood of Mary Virgin," on the other hand, dominated by green, the color of life and growth, accented by red, appropriately draws our minds to the human aspects of the story, so that the very cross, central in pattern as in force, is intertwined with vine tendrils.

It is fair to ask, now, why the paintings of the Pre-Raphaelites have declined in critical esteem. The vagaries and whimsicalities of fashion can never be definitively accounted for, but there is evidence, as Paul Oppé and others have suggested, that the invention of the daguerreotype had something to do not only with the birth of Pre-Raphaelite representationalism but also, by rendering it superfluous, with its demise. Moreover, these talented young men had the hard luck to be the contemporaries, more or less, of some of the greatest geniuses in the whole panorama of art, geniuses who, forming a "movement" or "school" and producing works of an originality, quality, and quantity hardly equaled and not definitely surpassed in history, changed the course of art. Nonetheless, if we ask why their popularity has declined, we must also ask why they have held on to whatever extent they can be said to have done so. Though negligible outside the Anglo-Saxon world, within it, and especially in England, the Pre-Raphaelites' place is assured, partly, no doubt, because of mere antiquarianism, but partly, also (though this does not apply to Rossetti), because of their very Englishness. In its persistent imitation of art the visible world continues to accommodate itself to the forms of those who render it, and we see Hampstead or the Heath, an English autumn or autumn leaves, a rainbow in a Winchelsea summer or Magdalen Tower, as we have been taught to see them by Ford Madox Brown (incomparably the greatest landscapist of the group) and by Hunt and Millais and the lesser painters associated with them.

The importance of Pre-Raphaelitism is another matter. Its primacy among the influences on estheticism, *art nouveau,* and symbolism is indisputable. The point is familiar from having been reiterated so often since 1890, when Burne-Jones, exhibiting in the Parisian salons, became known to the French *avant garde,* and the line of descent is visible and easily recognizable — Rossetti to Burne-Jones to Wilde and Beardsley, etc.; Rossetti to Burne-Jones to Gustave Moreau, the French painter, honored with a retrospective at the Louvre a few years ago, so admired by Huysmans' Des Esseintes. T. H. Robsjohn-Gibbings traced some of these trends in *Mona Lisa's Moustache* (1947). His book rests on valid premises, though their effect, already diminished by the frivolous and even silly presentation, is virtually vitiated by the perverse conclusions. Recent attention has been more scholarly. Rossetti's "Girlhood of Mary Virgin," according to Robert Schmutzler (*Art Nouveau,* London, 1964, p. 62), "started a movement in London which leads uninterruptedly and logically through half a century to Art Nouveau, thus marking a turning point in art history. For the first time the latent tendencies that were to be realized in Art Nouveau made their existence known and emerged from pre-history into a historically comprehensive phase which deserves to be called 'Early Art Nouveau.'" Maurice Rheims, an even more recent historian of the movement, traces to the Pre-Raphaelites' minute representation of nature and to their skill in blending the rational and irrational the decisive role in the evolution of symbolism. "En réalité," he says (*L'art 1900 ou le style Jules Verne*, Paris, 1965, p. 140), "l'icono-graphie préraphaélite vouée apparemment à la piété et à la révélation mystique, se consacre plus volontiers au culte de la sensualité, abolie des textes et de l'illustration romantique depuis bientôt un demi-siècle." By way of the "Rose-Croix du Temple et du Graal" Erik Satie comes into the picture (his letter to *Gil Blas* denying a debt to the Rosicrucians is itself a marvelous piece of pseudo-Pre-Raphaelitism); and Edward Lockspeiser, the distinguished musicologist, can trace an influence on Debussy, who based "La Demoiselle Elue" on Sarrazin's translation and began a piece based on "Willowwood" — an "impor-tant work and written in the light of my latest discoveries in musical chemistry," Debussy said of it (Lockspeiser, *Debussy*, London and New York, 1963, p. 62). James MacNeill Whistler, born in Lowell, Massachusetts, and educated (I use the word merely for convenience) at West Point for three years before his expulsion, but more English than American and more French than English, may have been the most important link between English and French estheticism, and Rosalie Glynn Grylls (*Portrait of Rossetti*, London, 1964, p. 103) has suggested that if he and Rossetti had met sooner each could have been a healthy influence on the other. (If Rossetti had only visited the continental galleries with Whistler instead of Holman Hunt!) Nikolaus Pevsner can title a book *Pioneers of the Modern Movement from William Morris to Walter Gropius* (London, Faber and Faber, 1936). Yeats's father, himself a Pre-Raphaelite painter for a while, brought up his son in such a way that, in the much-quoted phrase from the *Autobiographies*, he was "in all things romantic and in all things Pre-Raphaelite" — so much so that a poem, he said, should be a "painted and bepictured argosy." His earliest master was Rossetti, and nothing is more obvious than the influence on his early verse of both Rossetti, whom he never met, and (in a different way) Morris, at whose feet he sat. As we learn more about Yeats, especially about the sources of his inspiration and some of the techniques of his craft, it becomes more certain that Rossetti's authority, both directly and by way of imitators and disciples, can be discerned even in the great poems of the last phase. No one who has made his own the dense subtleties of Rossetti's sonnet "Ardour and Memory" (*The House of Life*, 64) could deny that, at his best, Rossetti is in the line of sover-eigns, and not Yeats himself, of whose very fiber this poem seems wrought and who might have owned it with pride, could have brought it into being with more "warranty and majesty." It is no mean thing to have been one of the masters of the greatest poet writing in English after that second (and greater) renaissance, the romantic.

In the history of Pre-Raphaelitism a whole world of supplementary detail and anecdote — from Burne-Jones's designs for ballet to Proust's "Little actress," mentioned by Schmutzler (p. 62), who "made her appearances holding a lily and wearing a gown copied from Rossetti's 'Ecce Ancilla Domini' " — lies waiting for the investigator, but since the present survey must not explode into a history of everything in the world, it will suffice to observe that a movement whose importance can hardly be overestimated is in no danger of being overlooked by historians.

IV

Pre-Raphaelite poetry has generated even more critical vagueness than the painting. Indeed, loose and flaccid conceptions have prevailed so long and so largely that some clear-cut assertions are required. Pre-Raphaelite poetry is not necessarily medieval, and it is not "picture poetry" in the commonly understood sense of the phrase. In English verse, from Chaucer or Spenser to Tennyson or Yeats, as in English vocal music from Handel's choruses to W. S. Gilbert's, the tendency to be pictorial always swells as with a strong tidal urge. No one would say, however, that "See, from his post Euphrates flies" is Pre-Raphaelite and (waiving a few isolated passages) no careful speaker would say so of "The Palace of Art." The Squire and Yeoman and Prioress and Monk of the *General Prologue* are not Pre-Raphaelite conceptions nor are the figures in Spenser's verbal tapestries. Charles Reade's novel *The Cloister and the Hearth* (1861), though both late-medieval and pictorial, is not really Pre-Raphaelite: the real Pre-Raphaelite novels — though only the brave deserve this fare — are *Jane Eyre* and *Wuthering Heights, The Marble Faun* and *The Turn of the Screw.*

If the term *Pre-Raphaelite* refers, as it usually does, to poetry written by the Pre-Raphaelites, their associates and disciples, it has a certain utility in literary history but does not belong to criticism. If it refers to poetry written by Rossetti, of whatever kind, late love sonnets as well as early poems in *The Germ* and *The Oxford and Cambridge Magazine,* its historical value diminishes as its critical significance increases. If, however, it is to be used as a strictly critical term, it has to mean something like "visualized poetry of fantasy" or "fantasy crossed with realism." So defined, the term obviously admits Coleridge's

"Christabel," Keats's "La Belle Dame Sans Merci," and Tennyson's "The Lady of Shalott," for instance, and it is a fact that any purely descriptive definition will have to include these and other such poems. Wordsworth's Lucy poems, for instance, are nearly as Pre-Raphaelite in this sense as Rossetti's "My Sister's Sleep" and "The Woodspurge," and the differences between these poems and the "Willowwood" sonnets in *The House of Life* (49–51) are of manner — or mannerism! — rather than of essence or substance. It seems to me equally obvious that the definition excludes nearly all the poetry of Christina Rossetti (Queen of the Pre-Raphaelites, so called), though "Goblin Market" might be said to qualify, all the poetry of William Morris after *The Defence of Guenevere* (1858), and, to some extent, most of the poetry of Rossetti after the fifties, except a quartet of late narratives. In short, though the definition is nearly self-annihilating, so it must be if it is to serve any useful critical function. Nuances of appreciation are more rewarding when based on nice discriminations, and it is of course such nuances, not the definition, that make the game worth the candle.

All romanticism is, in a sense, "natural supernaturalism," however; so, at the risk of appearing too ponderous for so frail a vessel, it is necessary to insist on the special qualities that distinguish Pre-Raphaelitism. Fortunately, the matter can be summed up simply, lucidly, and finally, though not at first, perhaps, helpfully. In its purest form, romantic "supernaturalism," positing a higher order of reality within us all, denies philosophic dualism. Pre-Raphaelitism — and this is at once its characteristic strength and its mortal weakness — strives, impossibly, to accept and reject it simultaneously: matter and spirit are not quite different and not quite identical, they are "the same and not the same." Pre-Raphaelite fantasy affirms the dichotomy, Pre-Raphaelite particularity repudiates it.

Roger Fry, writing in *The Burlington Magazine,* June, 1916, of Rossetti's watercolors, said that "passionate desire was the central point of this world but that passion was not enough, it must rage in a curiosity shop, amid objects which had for him peculiarly exciting associations." The sarcastic quip of a nineteenth-century critic that Rossetti ought to have painted his poems and written his pictures points to something similar. Fry's "curiosity shop" calls to mind the "definiteness of sensible imagery" found by Pater to be the distinctive feature of the poetry. The "passion" that Fry spoke of is the equivalent of "strangeness added to beauty" or of what Rossetti was getting at in saying that poetry must be "amusing," as Keats's urn must "tease us out of thought."

Rossetti thought and felt visually and painted poetically, though the "fundamental brainwork," to use his own phrase, that always preceded his artistic composition was a necessary condition of the intellectual subtlety that always characterized it. Like the Dadaists, though without their built-in, self-destroying irony, he may have been striving, deliberately or unconsciously, to synthesize the arts but he was assuredly not confounding them. What concerned him in his poetry, as in his painting, was the creation of a symbolic atmosphere, an atmosphere always invested with his apprehension of (and revulsion from) the mystery informing the immedicable opposition of sense and spirit, soul and body, objects and emotions, Beatrice and Guenevere:

> Lady, I fain would tell how evermore
> Thy soul I know not from thy body, nor
> Thee from myself, neither our love from God.

So, though the Damozel is blessed and in heaven, the gold bar she leans on, indubitably metal, is warmed by her bosom. As Keats's Knight-at-Arms shut the wild, wild eyes of the Belle Dame Sans Merci with "kisses four" and Tennyson's Lady of Shalott made "three paces thro' the room," so the Blessed Damozel has three lilies in her hand and seven stars in her hair, not only because she could scarcely be visualized with an indefinite number but also because such precision is a necessary component of the factuality, of the senses mixed in the spirit's cup. Her lover on earth *sees* her smile and *hears* her tears, reminding us of the great scene between Jane Eyre and Rochester (chap. 23) that rises to this climax: "I am not talking to you now through the medium of custom, conventionalities, or even of mortal flesh: — it is my spirit that addresses your spirit, just as if both had passed through the grave, and we stood at God's feet, equal, — as we are!" Catherine Earnshaw's dream of being miserable in heaven (chap. 9) is even more striking. "Heaven did not seem to be my home," she declares to Nelly, in one of the crucial scenes, "and I broke my heart with weeping to come back to earth, and the angels were so angry that they flung me out, into the middle of the heath on the top of Wuthering Heights." The apocalyptic finale, Heathcliff and Cathy united in and beyond the grave, is vouchsafed only to the incorrupt or the unsophisticated, those whose spiritual perceptions have not been or are no longer veiled by mortality, the very young, the very old, and the fearful sheep.

In "The Blessed Damozel" Rossetti may have been writing fiction, but in *The House of Life* experience compelled his profoundest and most authentic poetic intuitions to confront, first, "Youth and Change," and then "Change and Fate," and in this world there were no incorrupt or unsophisticated, only the triumph of life (in Shelley's sense) rather than the triumph of time (in Swinburne's).

We can talk about the *history* of art and literature because all artists build on their predecessors. Without Milton, neither Wordsworth nor Keats would have become the poet we know. Without Mozart, Beethoven would have been different — and the Ninth Symphony changed the course of Wagner's life. Louis H. Sullivan was Frank Lloyd Wright's master. But artists rise also from their own dead selves: *Madame Bovary* came out of Flaubert's early novel *Novembre;* the Minuet of Beethoven's great Septet is an outgrowth of the Minuet of the G Major piano sonata (Op.49. No.2); and the stunning tripartite Picasso exhibition in Paris has shown us, step by step, that master's evolution as we had never seen it before.

Rossetti built upon Pre-Raphaelitism, and it has never been observed to what a degree both "Willowwood" and "The One Hope," the final sonnet of *The House of Life,* are a kind of eidolon of "The Blessed Damozel" — incomparably more subtle, profound, and sombre, but the same poem, nonetheless, with a difference. The images are the poetry instead of the vehicle of a poetic effect. The lovers who, hand in hand, bathe in God's sight in "The Blessed Damozel" have become, in "The One Hope," "vain desire" and vain regret, "going hand in hand to death." The falling autumn leaves of "The Blessed Damozel," which energize and particularize the scene with such precision and originality, are, as dropping rose petals, actually woven into the very integrity of the fabric of "Willowwood," and, as the hyacinthine petals of "The One Hope" scriptured with "Ai, Ai," are as complex and condensed as any symbol in Blake or Shelley. The "deep wells of light" of "The Blessed Damozel" are darkened to the "woodside well" of "Willowwood" and are mocked by the "sunk stream" and "Sweet life-fountain" of "The One Hope," as the mound of tree and earth on which the earthbound lover leans his head in "The Blessed Damozel" — implied in the poem, explicit in the painting — becomes the grim pillow of "Willowwood," the "bitter banks" wan with that most hallucinogenic of surrealistic flora, the "tear-spurge." In either case the contact with nature suggests not — as with Gautama Buddha, Newton, and Rousseau, or the poet of *The Prelude,* Vernon Whitford, or Walter Morel — a life-enhancing epiphany or renewal but rather, as with the poet under the chestnut tree in "The Triumph of Life" or Keats's Knight-at-Arms on the cold hill side, a vision of thralldom to our own nature, an imprisonment from which there is no release, unless the "One Hope's one name be there" — and if that one name is not "Wanhope."

The Pre-Raphaelites

AND THEIR CIRCLE

Raphael no longer looking at things individually. Return to realism (outside) Couldn't reconcile sensual with spiritual (SOUL/BODY SPLIT) Equated human love with God. Used religion as device (atmosphere). Man's happiness depends on exalted view of women (thru love). Precise language.

Dante Gabriel Rossetti

worried more about eagle than Truth True to experience not ideas notorious asceticism. Love in heaven longing for love on earth

THE BLESSED DAMOZEL

THE blessed damozel leaned out
 From the gold bar of Heaven;
Her eyes were deeper than the depth
 Of waters stilled at even;
She had three lilies in her hand,
 And the stars in her hair were seven.

Her robe, ungirt from clasp to hem,
 No wrought flowers did adorn,
But a white rose of Mary's gift,
 For service meetly worn;   **10**
Her hair that lay along her back
 Was yellow like ripe corn.

Herseemed she scarce had been a day
 One of God's choristers;
The wonder was not yet quite gone
 From that still look of hers;
Albeit, to them she left, her day
 Had counted as ten years.

LOVER : (To one, it is ten years of years.
 . . . Yet now, and in this place," *Body/Soul" separation* **20**
Surely she leaned o'er me — her hair
 Fell all about my face. . . .

1

Nothing: the autumn-fall of leaves.
  The whole year sets apace.)

It was the rampart of God's house
  That she was standing on;
By God built over the sheer depth
  The which is Space begun;
So high, that looking downward thence
  She scarce could see the sun. 30

It lies in Heaven, across the flood
  Of ether, as a bridge.
Beneath, the tides of day and night
  With flame and darkness ridge
The void, as low as where this earth
  Spins like a fretful midge.

Around her, lovers, newly met
  'Mid deathless love's acclaims,
Spoke evermore among themselves
  Their heart-remembered names; 40
And the souls mounting up to God
  Went by her like thin flames.

And still she bowed herself and stooped
  Out of the circling charm;
Until her bosom must have made
  The bar she leaned on warm,
And the lilies lay as if asleep
  Along her bended arm.

From the fixed place of Heaven she saw
  Time like a pulse shake fierce 50
Through all the worlds. Her gaze still strove
  Within the gulf to pierce
Its path; and now she spoke as when
  The stars sang in their spheres.

The sun was gone now; the curled moon
  Was like a little feather
Fluttering far down the gulf; and now
  She spoke through the still weather.
Her voice was like the voice the stars
  Had when they sang together. 60

(Ah sweet! Even now, in that bird's song,
  Strove not her accents there,
Fain to be hearkened? When those bells
  Possessed the mid-day air,
Strove not her steps to reach my side
  Down all the echoing stair?)

"I wish that he were come to me,
  For he will come," she said.   *Catholicism*
"Have I not prayed in Heaven? — on earth,
  Lord, Lord, has he not pray'd?   70
Are not two prayers a perfect strength?
  And shall I feel afraid?

                                        halo
"When round his head the aureole clings,
  And he is clothed in white,
I'll take his hand and go with him
  To the deep wells of light; *(then love)*
As unto a stream we will step down,
  And bathe there in God's sight.

"We two will stand beside that shrine,
  Occult, withheld, untrod, *(virginity held in abeyance)*   80
Whose lamps are stirred continually
  With prayer sent up to God;
And see our old prayers, granted, melt
  Each like a little cloud.

"We two will lie i' the shadow of
  That living mystic tree
Within whose secret growth the Dove
  Is sometimes felt to be,
While every leaf that His plumes touch
  Saith His Name audibly.   90

                                   sure he's gonna show up
"And I myself will teach to him,
  I myself, lying so,
The songs I sing here; which his voice
  Shall pause in, hushed and slow,
And find some knowledge at each pause,
  Or some new thing to know."

(Alas! We two, we two, thou say'st!
  Yea, one wast thou with me

That once of old. But shall God lift
    To endless unity
The soul whose likeness with thy soul
    Was but its love for thee?)

100

"We two," she said, "will seek the groves
    Where the lady Mary is,
With her five handmaidens, whose names
    Are five sweet symphonies,
Cecily, Gertrude, Magdalen,
    Margaret and Rosalys.

"Circlewise sit they, with bound locks
    And foreheads garlanded;
Into the fine cloth white like flame
    Weaving the golden thread,
To fashion the birth-robes for them
    Who are just born, being dead.

110

"He shall fear, haply, and be dumb:
    Then will I lay my cheek
To his, and tell about our love,
    Not once abashed or weak:
And the dear Mother will approve
    My pride, and let me speak.

120

"Herself shall bring us, hand in hand,
    To Him round whom all souls
Kneel, the clear-ranged unnumbered heads
    Bowed with their aureoles:
And angels meeting us shall sing
    To their citherns and citoles.

"There will I ask of Christ the Lord
    Thus much for him and me: —
Only to live as once on earth
    With Love, — only to be,
As then awhile, for ever now
    Together, I and he."

130

She gazed and listened and then said,
    Less sad of speech than mild, —
"All this is when he comes." She ceased.
    The light thrilled towards her, fill'd

With angels in strong level flight.
    Her eyes prayed, and she smil'd.

(I saw her smile.) But soon their path
    Was vague in distant spheres: 140
And then she cast her arms along
    The golden barriers,
And laid her face between her hands,
    And wept. (I heard her tears.)
[1847]   [*1850; 1870*]

MY SISTER'S SLEEP*

SHE fell asleep on Christmas Eve:
    At length the long-ungranted shade
    Of weary eyelids overweigh'd
The pain nought else might yet relieve.

Our mother, who had leaned all day
    Over the bed from chime to chime,
    Then raised herself for the first time,
And as she sat her down, did pray.

Her little work-table was spread
    With work to finish. For the glare   10
    Made by her candle, she had care
To work some distance from the bed.

Without, there was a cold moon up,
    Of winter radiance sheer and thin;
    The hollow halo it was in
Was like an icy crystal cup.

Through the small room, with subtle sound
    Of flame, by vents the fireshine drove
    And reddened. In its dim alcove
The mirror shed a clearness round.   20

* This little poem, written in 1847, was printed in a periodical at the outset of 1850. The metre, which is used by several old English writers, became celebrated a month or two later on the publication of *"In Memoriam."* [ROSSETTI]

I had been sitting up some nights,
   And my tired mind felt weak and blank;
   Like a sharp strengthening wine it drank
The stillness and the broken lights.

Twelve struck. That sound, by dwindling years
   Heard in each hour, crept off; and then
   The ruffled silence spread again,
Like water that a pebble stirs.

Our mother rose from where she sat:
   Her needles, as she laid them down,   30
   Met lightly, and her silken gown
Settled: no other noise than that.

"Glory unto the Newly Born!"
   So, as said angels, she did say;
   Because we were in Christmas Day,
Though it would still be long till morn.

Just then in the room over us
   There was a pushing back of chairs,
   As some who had sat unawares
So late, now heard the hour, and rose.   40

With anxious softly-stepping haste
   Our mother went where Margaret lay,
   Fearing the sounds o'erheard — should they
Have broken her long watched-for rest!

She stooped an instant, calm, and turned;
   But suddenly turned back again;
   And all her features seemed in pain
With woe, and her eyes gazed and yearned.

For my part, I but hid my face,
   And held my breath, and spoke no word: 50
   There was none spoken; but I heard
The silence for a little space.

Our mother bowed herself and wept:
   And both my arms fell, and I said,
   "God knows I knew that she was dead."
And there, all white, my sister slept.

Then kneeling, upon Christmas morn
   A little after twelve o'clock
   We said, ere the first quarter struck,
"Christ's blessing on the newly born!"   60
  [1847–49]   [*1850;* 1870]

MARY'S GIRLHOOD

(For a Picture)

I

THIS is that blessed Mary, pre-elect
   God's Virgin. Gone is a great while, and she
   Dwelt young in Nazareth of Galilee.
Unto God's will she brought devout respect,
Profound simplicity of intellect,
   And supreme patience. From her mother's knee
   Faithful and hopeful; wise in charity;
Strong in grave peace; in pity circumspect.

So held she through her girlhood; as it were
   An angel-watered lily, that near God   10
   Grows and is quiet. Till, one dawn at home
She woke in her white bed, and had no fear
   At all, — yet wept till sunshine, and felt awed:
   Because the fulness of the time was come.
  [1848]   [*1849;* 1870]

II

THESE are the symbols. On that cloth of red
   I' the centre is the Tripoint: perfect each,
   Except the second of its points, to teach
That Christ is not yet born. The books — whose head
Is golden Charity, as Paul hath said —
   Those virtues are wherein the soul is rich:
   Therefore on them the lily standeth, which
Is Innocence, being interpreted.

The seven-thorn'd briar and the palm seven-leaved
   Are her great sorrow and her great reward.   10
     Until the end be full, the Holy One

Abides without. She soon shall have achieved
  Her perfect purity: yea, God the Lord
    Shall soon vouchsafe His Son to be her Son.
[1849]   [*1849;* 1882, 1886]

AVE

Mother of the Fair Delight,
Thou handmaid perfect in God's sight,
Now sitting fourth beside the Three,
Thyself a woman-Trinity, —
Being a daughter born to God,
Mother of Christ from stall to rood,
And wife unto the Holy Ghost: —
Oh when our need is uttermost,
Think that to such as death may strike
Thou once wert sister sisterlike!   10
Thou headstone of humanity,
Groundstone of the great Mystery,
Fashioned like us, yet more than we!

  Mind'st thou not (when June's heavy breath
Warmed the long days in Nazareth,)
That eve thou didst go forth to give
Thy flowers some drink that they might live
One faint night more amid the sands?
Far off the trees were as pale wands
Against the fervid sky: the sea   20
Sighed further off eternally
As human sorrow sighs in sleep.
Then suddenly the awe grew deep,
As of a day to which all days
Were footsteps in God's secret ways:
Until a folding sense, like prayer,
Which is, as God is, everywhere,
Gathered about thee; and a voice
Spake to thee without any noise,
Being of the silence: — "Hail," it said,   30
"Thou that art highly favourèd;
The Lord is with thee here and now;
Blessed among all women thou."

Ah! knew'st thou of the end, when first
That Babe was on thy bosom nurs'd? —
Or when He tottered round thy knee
Did thy great sorrow dawn on thee? —
And through His boyhood, year by year
Eating with Him the Passover,
Didst thou discern confusedly   40
That holier sacrament, when He,
The bitter cup about to quaff,
Should break the bread and eat thereof? —
Or came not yet the knowledge, even
Till on some day forecast in Heaven
His feet passed through thy door to press
Upon His Father's business? —
Or still was God's high secret kept?

Nay, but I think the whisper crept
Like growth through childhood. Work and play,   50
Things common to the course of day,
Awed thee with meanings unfulfill'd;
And all through girlhood, something still'd
Thy senses like the birth of light,
When thou hast trimmed thy lamp at night
Or washed thy garments in the stream;
To whose white bed had come the dream
That He was thine and thou wast His
Who feeds among the field-lilies.
O solemn shadow of the end   60
In that wise spirit long contain'd!
O awful end! and those unsaid
Long years when It was Finishèd!

Mind'st thou not (when the twilight gone
Left darkness in the house of John,)
Between the naked window-bars
That spacious vigil of the stars? —
For thou, a watcher even as they,
Wouldst rise from where throughout the day
Thou wroughtest raiment for His poor;   70
And, finding the fixed terms endure
Of day and night which never brought
Sounds of His coming chariot,
Wouldst lift through cloud-waste unexplor'd
Those eyes which said, "How long, O Lord?"

Then that disciple whom He loved,
Well heeding, haply would be moved
To ask thy blessing in His name;
And that one thought in both, the same
Though silent, then would clasp ye round   80
To weep together, — tears long bound,
Sick tears of patience, dumb and slow.
Yet, "Surely I come quickly," — so
He said, from life and death gone home.
Amen: even so, Lord Jesus, come!

But oh! what human tongue can speak
That day when Michael came* to break
From the tir'd spirit, like a veil,
Its covenant with Gabriel
Endured at length unto the end?   90
What human thought can apprehend
That mystery of motherhood
When thy Beloved at length renew'd
The sweet communion severèd, —
His left hand underneath thine head
And His right hand embracing thee? —
Lo! He was thine, and this is He!

Soul, is it Faith, or Love, or Hope,
That lets me see her standing up
Where the light of the Throne is bright?   100
Unto the left, unto the right,
The cherubim, succinct, conjoint,
Float inward to a golden point,
And from between the seraphim
The glory issues for a hymn.
O Mary Mother, be not loth
To listen, — thou whom the stars clothe,
Who seëst and mayst not be seen!
Hear us at last, O Mary Queen!
Into our shadow bend thy face,   110
Bowing thee from the secret place,
O Mary Virgin, full of grace!
[1847]   [1870]

---

* A Church legend of the Blessed Virgin's Death. [ROSSETTI]

JENNY

chastity vs. promiscuity

"Vengeance of Jenny's case! Fie on her! Never name her,
child!" — (*Mrs. Quickly.*)

LAZY laughing languid Jenny,
Fond of a kiss and fond of a guinea,
Whose head upon my knee to-night
Rests for a while, as if grown light
With all our dances and the sound
To which the wild tunes spun you round:
Fair Jenny mine, the thoughtless queen
Of kisses which the blush between
Could hardly make much daintier;
Whose eyes are as blue skies, whose hair   10
Is countless gold incomparable:
Fresh flower, scarce touched with signs that tell
Of Love's exuberant hotbed: — Nay,
Poor flower left torn since yesterday
Until to-morrow leave you bare;
Poor handful of bright spring-water
Flung in the whirlpool's shrieking face;
Poor shameful Jenny, full of grace
Thus with your head upon my knee; —
Whose person or whose purse may be   20
The lodestar of your reverie?

    This room of yours, my Jenny, looks
A change from mine so full of books,
Whose serried ranks hold fast, forsooth,
So many captive hours of youth, —
The hours they thieve from day and night
To make one's cherished work come right,
And leave it wrong for all their theft,
Even as to-night my work was left:
Until I vowed that since my brain   30
And eyes of dancing seemed so fain,
My feet should have some dancing too: —
And thus it was I met with you.
Well, I suppose 'twas hard to part,
For here I am. And now, sweetheart,
You seem too tired to get to bed.

It was a careless life I led
When rooms like this were scarce so strange
Not long ago. What breeds the change, —
The many aims or the few years?   40
Because to-night it all appears
Something I do not know again.

The cloud's not danced out of my brain —
The cloud that made it turn and swim
While hour by hour the books grew dim.
Why, Jenny, as I watch you there, —
For all your wealth of loosened hair,
Your silk ungirdled and unlac'd
And warm sweets open to the waist,
All golden in the lamplight's gleam, —   50
You know not what a book you seem,
Half-read by lightning in a dream!
How should you know, my Jenny? Nay,
And I should be ashamed to say: —
Poor beauty, so well worth a kiss!
But while my thought runs on like this
With wasteful whims more than enough,
I wonder what you're thinking of.

If of myself you think at all,
What is the thought? — conjectural   60
On sorry matters best unsolved? —
Or inly is each grace resolved
To fit me with a lure? or (sad
To think!) perhaps you're merely glad
That I'm not drunk or ruffianly
And let you rest upon my knee.

For sometimes, were the truth confess'd,
You're thankful for a little rest, —
Glad from the crush to rest within,
From the heart-sickness and the din   70
Where envy's voice at virtue's pitch
Mocks you because your gown is rich;
And from the pale girl's dumb rebuke,
Whose ill-clad grace and toil-worn look
Proclaim the strength that keeps her weak
And other nights than yours bespeak;
And from the wise unchildish elf,

To schoolmate lesser than himself,
Pointing you out, what thing you are: —
Yes, from the daily jeer and jar,   80
From shame and shame's outbraving too,
Is rest not sometimes sweet to you? —
But most from the hatefulness of man
Who spares not to end what he began,
Whose acts are ill and his speech ill,
Who, having used you at his will,
Thrusts you aside, as when I dine
I serve the dishes and the wine.

    Well, handsome Jenny mine, sit up:
I've filled our glasses, let us sup,   90
And do not let me think of you,
Lest shame of yours suffice for two.
What, still so tired? Well, well then, keep
Your head there, so you do not sleep;
But that the weariness may pass
And leave you merry, take this glass.
Ah! lazy lily hand, more bless'd
If ne'er in rings it had been dress'd
Nor ever by a glove conceal'd!

    Behold the lilies of the field,   100
They toil not neither do they spin;
(So doth the ancient text begin, —
Not of such rest as one of these
Can share.) Another rest and ease
Along each summer-sated path
From its new lord the garden hath,
Than that whose spring in blessings ran
Which praised the bounteous husbandman,
Ere yet, in days of hankering breath,
The lilies sickened unto death.   110

    What, Jenny, are your lilies dead?
Aye, and the snow-white leaves are spread
Like winter on the garden-bed.
But you had roses left in May, —
They were not gone too. Jenny, nay,
But must your roses die, and those
Their purfled buds that should unclose?
Even so; the leaves are curled apart,

Still red as from the broken heart,
And here's the naked stem of thorns.   120

Nay, nay, mere words. Here nothing warns
As yet of winter. Sickness here
Or want alone could waken fear, —
Nothing but passion wrings a tear.
Except when there may rise unsought
Haply at times a passing thought
Of the old days which seem to be
Much older than any history
That is written in any book;
When she would lie in fields and look   130
Along the ground through the blown grass,
And wonder where the city was.
Far out of sight, whose broil and bale
They told her then for a child's tale.

Jenny, you know the city now.
A child can tell the tale there, how
Some things which are not yet enroll'd
In market-lists are bought and sold
Even till the early Sunday light,
When Saturday night is market-night   140
Everywhere, be it dry or wet,
And market-night in the Haymarket.
Our learned London children know,
Poor Jenny, all your pride and woe;
Have seen your lifted silken skirt
Advertise dainties through the dirt;
Have seen your coach-wheels splash rebuke
On virtue; and have learned your look
When, wealth and health slipped past, you stare
Along the streets alone, and there,   150
Round the long park, across the bridge,
The cold lamps at the pavement's edge
Wind on together and apart,
A fiery serpent for your heart.

Let the thoughts pass, an empty cloud!
Suppose I were to think aloud, —
What if to her all this were said?
Why, as a volume seldom read
Being opened halfway shuts again,
So might the pages of her brain   160

Be parted at such words, and thence
Close back upon the dusty sense.
For is there hue or shape defin'd
In Jenny's desecrated mind, sewers
Where all contagious currents meet,
A Lethe of the middle street?
Nay, it reflects not any face,
Nor sound is in its sluggish pace,
But as they coil those eddies clot,
And night and day remember not.   170

Why, Jenny, you're asleep at last! —
Asleep, poor Jenny, hard and fast, —
So young and soft and tired; so fair,
With chin thus nestled in your hair,
Mouth quiet, eyelids almost blue
As if some sky of dreams shone through!

Just as another woman sleeps!
Enough to throw one's thoughts in heaps
Of doubt and horror, — what to say
Or think, — this awful secret sway,   180
The potter's power over the clay!
Of the same lump (it has been said)
For honour and dishonour made,
Two sister vessels. Here is one.

My cousin Nell is fond of fun,
And fond of dress, and change, and praise.
So mere a woman in her ways:
And if her sweet eyes rich in youth
Are like her lips that tell the truth,
My cousin Nell is fond of love.   190
And she's the girl I'm proudest of.
Who does not prize her, guard her well?
The love of change, in cousin Nell,
Shall find the best and hold it dear;
The unconquered mirth turn quieter
Not through her own, through others' woe:
The conscious pride of beauty glow
Beside another's pride in her,
One little part of all they share.
For Love himself shall ripen these   200
In a kind soil to just increase
Through years of fertilizing peace.

Of the same lump (as it is said)
For honour and dishonour made,
Two sister vessels. Here is one.

It makes a goblin of the sun.

So pure, — so fall'n! How dare to think
Of the first common kindred link?
Yet, Jenny, till the world shall burn
It seems that all things take their turn;   210
And who shall say but this fair tree
May need, in changes that may be,
Your children's children's charity?
Scorned then, no doubt, as you are scorn'd!
Shall no man hold his pride forewarn'd
Till in the end, the Day of Days,
At Judgment, one of his own race,
As frail and lost as you, shall rise, —
His daughter, with his mother's eyes?

How Jenny's clock ticks on the shelf!   220
Might not the dial scorn itself
That has such hours to register?
Yet as to me, even so to her
Are golden sun and silver moon,
In daily largesse of earth's boon,
Counted for life-coins to one tune.
And if, as blindfold fates are toss'd,
Through some one man this life be lost,
Shall soul not somehow pay for soul?

Fair shines the gilded aureole   230
In which our highest painters place
Some living woman's simple face.
And the stilled features thus descried
As Jenny's long throat droops aside, —
The shadows where the cheeks are thin,
And pure wide curve from ear to chin, —
With Raffael's, Leonardo's hand
To show them to men's souls, might stand,
Whole ages long, the whole world through,
For preachings of what God can do.   240
What has man done here? How atone,
Great God, for this which man has done?
And for the body and soul which by

Man's pitiless doom must now comply
With lifelong hell, what lullaby
Of sweet forgetful second birth
Remains? All dark. No sign on earth
What measure of God's rest endows
The many mansions of his house.

Can't know from living point of view

If but a woman's heart might see   250
Such erring heart unerringly
For once! But that can never be.

Like a rose shut in a book
In which pure women may not look,

"book" closing flower

For its base pages claim control
To crush the flower within the soul;
Where through each dead rose-leaf that clings,
Pale as transparent Psyche-wings,
To the vile text, are traced such things
As might make lady's cheek indeed   260
More than a living rose to read;
So nought save foolish foulness may
Watch with hard eyes the sure decay;
And so the life-blood of this rose,
Puddled with shameful knowledge, flows
Through leaves no chaste hand may unclose;
Yet still it keeps such faded show
Of when 'twas gathered long ago,
That the crushed petals' lovely grain,
The sweetness of the sanguine stain,   270
Seen of a woman's eyes, must make
Her pitiful heart, so prone to ache,
Love roses better for its sake: —
Only that this can never be: —
Even so unto her sex is she.

Yet, Jenny, looking long at you,
The woman almost fades from view.
A cipher of man's changeless sum
Of lust, past, present, and to come,
Is left. A riddle that one shrinks   280
To challenge from the scornful sphinx.

Like a toad within a stone
Seated while Time crumbles on;
Which sits there since the earth was curs'd

For Man's transgression at the first;
Which, living through all centuries,
Not once has seen the sun arise;
Whose life, to its cold circle charmed,
The earth's whole summers have not warmed;
Which always — whitherso the stone   290
Be flung — sits there, deaf, blind, alone
Aye, and shall not be driven out
Till that which shuts him round about
Break at the very Master's stroke,
And the dust thereof vanish as smoke,
And the seed of Man vanish as dust: —
Even so within this world is Lust.

Come, come, what use in thoughts like this?
Poor little Jenny, good to kiss, —
You'd not believe by what strange roads   300
Thought travels, when your beauty goads
A man to-night to think of toads!
Jenny, wake up. . . . Why, there's the dawn!

And there's an early waggon drawn
To market, and some sheep that jog
Bleating before a barking dog;
And the old streets come peering through
Another night that London knew;
And all as ghostlike as the lamps.

So on the wings of day decamps   310
My last night's frolic. Glooms begin
To shiver off as lights creep in
Past the gauze curtains half drawn-to,
And the lamp's doubled shade grows blue, —
Your lamp, my Jenny, kept alight,
Like a wise virgin's, all one night!
And in the alcove coolly spread
Glimmers with dawn your empty bed;
And yonder your fair face I see
Reflected lying on my knee,   320
Where teems with first foreshadowings
Your pier-glass scrawled with diamond rings:
And on your bosom all night worn
Yesterday's rose now droops forlorn
But dies not yet this summer morn.

And now without, as if some word
Had called upon them that they heard,
The London sparrows far and nigh
Clamour together suddenly;
And Jenny's cage-bird grown awake   330
Here in their song his part must take,
Because here too the day doth break.

And somehow in myself the dawn
Among stirred clouds and veils withdrawn
Strikes greyly on her. Let her sleep.
But will it wake her if I heap
These cushions thus beneath her head
Where my knee was? No, — there's your bed,
My Jenny, while you dream. And there
I lay among your golden hair   340
Perhaps the subject of your dreams,
These golden coins.
                    For still one deems
That Jenny's flattering sleep confers
New magic on the magic purse, —
Grim web, how clogged with shrivelled flies!
Between the threads fine fumes arise
And shape their pictures in the brain.
There roll no streets in glare and rain,
Nor flagrant man-swine whets his tusk;
But delicately sighs in musk   350
The homage of the dim boudoir;
Or like a palpitating star
Thrilled into song, the opera-night
Breathes faint in the quick pulse of light;
Or at the carriage-window shine
Rich wares for choice; or, free to dine,
Whirls through its hour of health (divine
For her) the concourse of the Park.
And though in the discounted dark
Her functions there and here are one,   360
Beneath the lamps and in the sun
There reigns at least the acknowledged belle
Apparelled beyond parallel.
Ah, Jenny, yes, we know your dreams.

For even the Paphian Venus seems
A goddess o'er the realms of love,

When silver-shrined in shadowy grove:
Aye, or let offerings nicely plac'd
But hide Priapus to the waist,
And whoso looks on him shall see   370
An eligible deity.
  Why, Jenny, waking here alone
May help you to remember one,
Though all the memory's long outworn
Of many a double-pillowed morn.
I think I see you when you wake,
And rub your eyes for me, and shake
My gold, in rising, from your hair,
A Danaë for a moment there.

  Jenny, my love rang true! for still   380
Love at first sight is vague, until
That tinkling makes him audible.

  And must I mock you to the last,
Ashamed of my own shame, — aghast
Because some thoughts not born amiss
Rose at a poor fair face like this?
Well, of such thoughts so much I know:
In my life, as in hers, they show,
By a far gleam which I may near,
A dark path I can strive to clear.   390

  Only one kiss. Good-bye, my dear.
[1848, 1858–69]   [1870]

THE PORTRAIT

THIS is her picture as she was:
  It seems a thing to wonder on,
As though mine image in the glass
  Should tarry when myself am gone.
I gaze until she seems to stir, —
Until mine eyes almost aver
  That now, even now, the sweet lips part
  To breathe the words of the sweet heart: —
And yet the earth is over her.

Alas! even such the thin-drawn ray 10
    That makes the prison-depths more rude. —
The drip of water night and day
    Giving a tongue to solitude.
Yet only this, of love's whole prize,
Remains; save what in mournful guise
    Takes counsel with my soul alone, —
    Save what is secret and unknown,
Below the earth, above the skies.

In painting her I shrined her face
    'Mid mystic trees, where light falls in 20
Hardly at all; a covert place
    Where you might think to find a din
Of doubtful talk, and a live flame
Wandering, and many a shape whose name
    Not itself knoweth, and old dew,
    And your own footsteps meeting you,
And all things going as they came.

A deep dim wood; and there she stands
    As in that wood that day: for so
Was the still movement of her hands 30
    And such the pure line's gracious flow.
And passing fair the type must seem,
Unknown the presence and the dream.
    'Tis she: though of herself, alas!
    Less than her shadow on the grass
Or than her image in the stream.

That day we met there, I and she
    One with the other all alone;
And we were blithe; yet memory
    Saddens those hours, as when the moon 40
Looks upon daylight. And with her
I stooped to drink the spring-water,
    Athirst where other waters sprang:
    And where the echo is, she sang, —
My soul another echo there.

But when that hour my soul won strength
    For words whose silence wastes and kills,
Dull raindrops smote us, and at length
    Thundered the heat within the hills.
That eve I spoke those words again 50

Beside the pelted window-pane;
    And there she hearkened what I said,
    With under-glances that surveyed
The empty pastures blind with rain.

Next day the memories of these things,
    Like leaves through which a bird has flown,
Still vibrated with Love's warm wings;
    Till I must make them all my own
And paint this picture. So, 'twixt ease
Of talk and sweet long silences,   60
    She stood among the plants in bloom
    At windows of a summer room,
To feign the shadow of the trees.

And as I wrought, while all above
    And all around was fragrant air,
In the sick burthen of my love
    It seemed each sun-thrilled blossom there
Beat like a heart among the leaves.
O heart that never beats nor heaves,
    In that one darkness lying still,   70
    What now to thee my love's great will
Or the fine web the sunshine weaves?

For now doth daylight disavow
    Those days, — nought left to see or hear.
Only in solemn whispers now
    At night-time these things reach mine ear;
When the leaf-shadows at a breath
Shrink in the road, and all the heath,
    Forest and water, far and wide,
    In limpid starlight glorified,   80
Lie like the mystery of death.

Last night at last I could have slept,
    And yet delayed my sleep till dawn.
Still wandering. Then it was I wept:
    For unawares I came upon
Those glades where once she walked with me:
And as I stood there suddenly,
    All wan with traversing the night,
    Upon the desolate verge of light
Yearned loud the iron-bosomed sea.   90

Even so, where Heaven holds breath and hears
  The beating heart of Love's own breast, —
Where round the secret of all spheres
  All angels lay their wings to rest, —
How shall my soul stand rapt and awed,
When, by the new birth borne abroad
  Throughout the music of the suns,
  It enters in her soul at once
And knows the silence there for God!

Here with her face doth memory sit   100
  Meanwhile, and wait the day's decline,
Till other eyes shall look from it,
  Eyes of the spirit's Palestine,
Even than the old gaze tenderer:
While hopes and aims long lost with her
  Stand round her image side by side
  Like tombs of pilgrims that have died
About the Holy Sepulchre.

[1846–69]   [1870]

uncovered, came "back to life"

THE BURDEN OF NINEVEH

IN our Museum galleries
To-day I lingered o'er the prize
Dead Greece vouchsafes to living eyes, —
Her Art for ever in fresh wise
  From hour to hour rejoicing me.
Sighing I turned at last to win
Once more the London dirt and din;
And as I made the swing-door spin
And issued, they were hoisting in
  A wingèd beast from Nineveh.   10

*juxtaposition of
spiritual artifact
and decadent society*

A human face the creature wore,
And hoofs behind and hoofs before,
And flanks with dark runes fretted o'er.
'Twas bull, 'twas mitred Minotaur,
  A dead disbowelled mystery:
The mummy of a buried faith

Stark from the charnel without scathe,
Its wings stood for the light to bathe, —
Such fossil cerements as might swathe
    The very corpse of Nineveh.   20

The print of its first rush-wrapping,
Wound ere it dried, still ribbed the thing.
What song did the brown maidens sing,
From purple mouths alternating,
    When that was woven languidly?
What vows, what rites, what prayers preferr'd,
What songs has the strange image heard?
In what blind vigil stood interr'd
For ages, till an English word
    Broke silence first at Nineveh?   30

Oh when upon each sculptured court,
Where even the wind might not resort, —
O'er which Time passed, of like import
With the wild Arab boys at sport, —
    A living face looked in to see: —
Oh seemed it not — the spell once broke —
As though the carven warriors woke,
As though the shaft the string forsook,
The cymbals clashed, the chariots shook,
    And there was life in Nineveh?   40

On London stones our sun anew
The beast's recovered shadow threw.
(No shade that plague of darkness knew,
No light, no shade, while older grew
    By ages the old earth and sea.)
Lo thou! could all thy priests have shown
Such proof to make thy godhead known?
From their dead Past thou liv'st alone;
And still thy shadow is thine own,
    Even as of yore in Nineveh.   50

That day whereof we keep record,
When near thy city-gates the Lord
Sheltered His Jonah with a gourd,
This sun, (I said) here present, pour'd
    Even thus this shadow that I see.
This shadow has been shed the same
From sun and moon, — from lamps which came

For prayer, — from fifteen days of flame,
The last, while smouldered to a name
    Sardanapalus' Nineveh.   60

Within thy shadow, haply, once
Sennacherib has knelt, whose sons
Smote him between the altar-stones:
Or pale Semiramis her zones
    Of gold, her incense brought to thee,
In love for grace, in war for aid: . . . .
Ay, and who else? . . . . till 'neath thy shade
Within his trenches newly made
Last year the Christian knelt and pray'd —
    Not to thy strength — in Nineveh.°   70

Now, thou poor god, within this hall
Where the blank windows blind the wall
From pedestal to pedestal,
The kind of light shall on thee fall   *drab London*
    Which London takes the day to be:
While school-foundations in the act
Of holiday, three files compact,
Shall learn to view thee as a fact   *gonna be seen as*
Connected with that zealous tract: *merely a religious*
    "ROME, — Babylon and Nineveh."   *fact.*   80

Deemed they of this, those worshippers,
When, in some mythic chain of verse
Which man shall not again rehearse,
The faces of thy ministers
    Yearned pale with bitter ecstasy?
Greece, Egypt, Rome, — did any god
Before whose feet men knelt unshod
Deem that in this unblest abode
Another scarce more unknown god
    Should house with him, from Nineveh?   90

Ah! in what quarries lay the stone
From which this pillared pile has grown
Unto man's need how long unknown,
Since thy vast temples, court and cone,
    Rose far in desert history?

° During the excavations, the Tiyari workmen held their services in the
shadow of the great bulls. (*Layard's "Nineveh,"* ch. ix.) [ROSSETTI]

Ah! what is here that does not lie
All strange to thine awakened eye?
Ah! what is here can testify
(Save that dumb presence of the sky)
    Unto thy day and Nineveh?   100

Why, of those mummies in the room
Above, there might indeed have come
One out of Egypt to thy home,
An alien. Nay, but were not some
    Of these thine own "antiquity"?
And now, — they and their gods and thou
All relics here together, — now
Whose profit? whether bull or cow,
Isis or Ibis, who or how,
    Whether of Thebes or Nineveh?   110

The consecrated metals found,
And ivory tablets, underground,
Winged teraphim and creatures crown'd
When air and daylight filled the mound,
    Fell into dust immediately.
And even as these, the images
Of awe and worship, — even as these, —
So, smitten with the sun's increase,
Her glory mouldered and did cease
    From immemorial Nineveh.   120

The day her builders made their halt,
Those cities of the lake of salt
Stood firmly 'stablished without fault,
Made proud with pillars of basalt,
    With sardonyx and porphyry.
The day that Jonah bore abroad
To Nineveh the voice of God,
A brackish lake lay in his road,
Where erst Pride fixed her sure abode,
    As then in royal Nineveh.   130

The day when he, Pride's lord and Man's,
Showed all the kingdoms at a glance
To Him before whose countenance
The years recede, the years advance,
    And said, Fall down and worship me: —
'Mid all the pomp beneath that look,

Then stirred there, haply, some rebuke,
Where to the wind the Salt Pools shook,
And in those tracts, of life forsook,
    That knew thee not, O Nineveh!   140

Delicate harlot! On thy throne
Thou with a world beneath thee prone
In state for ages sat'st alone;
And needs were years and lustres flown
    Ere strength of man could vanquish thee:
Whom even thy victor foes must bring,
Still royal, among maids that sing
As with doves' voices, taboring
Upon their breasts, unto the King, —
    A kingly conquest, Nineveh!   150

. . . Here woke my thought. The wind's slow sway
Had waxed; and like the human play
Of scorn that smiling spreads away,
The sunshine shivered off the day:
    The callous wind, it seemed to me,
Swept up the shadow from the ground:
And pale as whom the Fates astound,
The god forlorn stood winged and crown'd:
Within I knew the cry lay bound
    Of the dumb soul of Nineveh.   160

And as I turned, my sense half shut
Still saw the crowds of kerb and rut
Go past as marshalled to the strut
Of ranks in gypsum quaintly cut.
    It seemed in one same pageantry
They followed forms which had been erst;
To pass, till on my sight should burst
That future of the best or worst
When some may question which was first,
    Of London or of Nineveh.   170

For as that Bull-god once did stand
And watched the burial-clouds of sand,
Till these at last without a hand
Rose o'er his eyes, another land,
    And blinded him with destiny: —
So may he stand again; till now,
In ships of unknown sail and prow,

Some tribe of the Australian plough
Bear him afar, — a relic now
   Of London, not of Nineveh!   180

Or it may chance indeed that when
Man's age is hoary among men, —
His centuries threescore and ten, —
His furthest childhood shall seem then
  More clear than later times may be:
Who, finding in this desert place
This form, shall hold us for some race
That walked not in Christ's lowly ways,
But bowed its pride and vowed its praise
   Unto the god of Nineveh.   190

The smile rose first, — anon drew nigh
The thought: . . . Those heavy wings spread high,
So sure of flight, which do not fly;
That set gaze never on the sky;
  Those scriptured flanks it cannot see;
Its crown, a brow-contracting load;
Its planted feet which trust the sod: . . .
(So grew the image as I trod:)
O Nineveh, was this thy God, —
   Thine also, mighty Nineveh?   200
[1850]   [*1856;* 1870]

THE STAFF AND SCRIP

"Who rules these lands?" the Pilgrim said.
  "Stranger, Queen Blanchelys."
"And who has thus harried them?" he said.
  "It was Duke Luke did this:
    God's ban be his!"

The Pilgrim said: "Where is your house?
  I'll rest there, with your will."
"You've but to climb these blackened boughs
  And you'll see it over the hill,
    For it burns still."   10

"Which road, to seek your Queen?" said he.
  "Nay, nay, but with some wound

You'll fly back hither, it may be,
    And by your blood i' the ground
      My place be found."

"Friend, stay in peace. God keep your head,
    And mine, where I will go;
For He is here and there," he said.
    He passed the hill-side, slow,
      And stood below.   20

The Queen sat idle by her loom:
    She heard the arras stir,
And looked up sadly: through the room
    The sweetness sickened her
      Of musk and myrrh.

Her women, standing two and two,
    In silence combed the fleece.
The pilgrim said, "Peace be with you,
    Lady;" and bent his knees.
      She answered, "Peace."   30

Her eyes were like the wave within;
    Like water-reeds the poise
Of her soft body, dainty thin;
    And like the water's noise
      Her plaintive voice.

For him, the stream had never well'd
    In desert tracts malign
So sweet; nor had he ever felt
    So faint in the sunshine
      Of Palestine.   40

Right so, he knew that he saw weep
    Each night through every dream
The Queen's own face, confused in sleep
    With visages supreme
      Not known to him.

"Lady," he said, "your lands lie burnt
    And waste: to meet your foe
All fear: this I have seen and learnt.
    Say that it shall be so,
      And I will go."   50

She gazed at him. "Your cause is just,
  For I have heard the same,"
He said: "God's strength shall be my trust.
  Fall it to good or grame,
    'Tis in His name."

"Sir, you are thanked. My cause is dead.
  Why should you toil to break
A grave, and fall therein?" she said.
  He did not pause but spake:
    "For my vow's sake."   60

"Can such vows be, Sir — to God's ear,
  Not to God's will?" "My vow
Remains: God heard me there as here,"
  He said with reverent brow,
    "Both then and now."

They gazed together, he and she,
  The minute while he spoke;
And when he ceased, she suddenly
  Looked round upon her folk
    As though she woke.   70

"Fight, Sir," she said: "my prayers in pain
  Shall be your fellowship."
He whispered one among her train, —
  "To-morrow bid her keep
    This staff and scrip."

She sent him a sharp sword, whose belt
  About his body there
As sweet as her own arms he felt.
  He kissed its blade, all bare,
    Instead of her.   80

She sent him a green banner wrought
  With one white lily stem,
To bind his lance with when he fought.
  He writ upon the same
    And kissed her name.

She sent him a white shield, whereon
  She bade that he should trace

His will. He blent fair hues that shone,
    And in a golden space
      He kissed her face.   90

Born of the day that died, that eve
    Now dying sank to rest;
As he, in likewise taking leave,
    Once with a heaving breast
      Looked to the west.

And there the sunset skies unseal'd,
    Like lands he never knew,
Beyond to-morrow's battle-field
    Lay open out of view
      To ride into.   100

Next day till dark the women pray'd:
    Nor any might know there
How the fight went: the Queen has bade
    That there do come to her
      No messenger.

The Queen is pale, her maidens ail;
    And to the organ-tones
They sing but faintly, who sang well
    The matin-orisons,
      The lauds and nones.   110

Lo, Father, is thine ear inclin'd,
    And hath thine angel pass'd?
For these thy watchers now are blind
    With vigil, and at last
      Dizzy with fast.

Weak now to them the voice o' the priest
    As any trance affords;
And when each anthem failed and ceas'd,
    It seemed that the last chords
      Still sang the words.   120

"Oh what is the light that shines so red?
    'Tis long since the sun set;"
Quoth the youngest to the eldest maid:
    " 'Twas dim but now, and yet
      The light is great."

Quoth the other: " 'Tis our sight is dazed
    That we see flame i' the air."
But the Queen held her brows and gazed,
    And said, "It is the glare
        Of torches there."   130

"Oh what are the sounds that rise and spread?
    All day it was so still;"
Quoth the youngest to the eldest maid:
    "Unto the furthest hill
        The air they fill."

Quoth the other: " 'Tis our sense is blurr'd
    With all the chants gone by."
But the Queen held her breath and heard,
    And said, "It is the cry
        Of Victory."   140

The first of all the rout was sound,
    The next were dust and flame,
And then the horses shook the ground:
    And in the thick of them
        A still band came.

"Oh what do ye bring out of the fight,
    Thus hid beneath these boughs?"
"Thy conquering guest returns to-night,
    And yet shall not carouse,
        Queen, in thy house."   150

"Uncover ye his face," she said.
    "O changed in little space!"
She cried, "O pale that was so red!
    O God, O God of grace!
        Cover his face."

His sword was broken in his hand
    Where he had kissed the blade.
"O soft steel that could not withstand!
    O my hard heart unstayed,
        That prayed and prayed!"   160

His bloodied banner crossed his mouth
    Where he had kissed her name.

"O east, and west, and north, and south,
　Fair flew my web, for shame,
　　To guide Death's aim!"

The tints were shredded from his shield
　Where he had kissed her face.
"Oh, of all gifts that I could yield,
　Death only keeps its place,
　　My gift and grace!"　　　　　　　　　170

Then stepped a damsel to her side,
　And spoke, and needs must weep:
"For his sake, lady, if he died,
　He prayed of thee to keep
　　This staff and scrip."

That night they hung above her bed,
　Till morning wet with tears.
Year after year above her head
　Her bed his token wears,
　　Five years, ten years.　　　　　　　180

That night the passion of her grief
　Shook them as there they hung.
Each year the wind that shed the leaf
　Shook them and in its tongue
　　A message flung.

And once she woke with a clear mind
　That letters writ to calm
Her soul lay in the scrip; to find
　Only a torpid balm
　　And dust of palm.　　　　　　　　　190

They shook far off with palace sport
　When joust and dance were rife;
And the hunt shook them from the court;
　For hers, in peace or strife,
　　Was a Queen's life.

A Queen's death now: as now they shake
　To gusts in chapel dim, —
Hung where she sleeps, not seen to wake
　(Carved lovely white and slim),
　　With them by him.　　　　　　　　　200

Stand up to-day, still armed, with her,
    Good knight, before His brow
Who then as now was here and there,
    Who had in mind thy vow
      Then even as now.

The lists are set in Heaven to-day,
    The bright pavilions shine;
Fair hangs thy shield, and none gainsay;
    The trumpets sound in sign
      That she is thine.   210

Not tithed with days' and years' decease
    He pays thy wage He owed,
But with imperishable peace
    Here in His own abode,
      Thy jealous God.
[1851–52]   [*1856;* 1870]

SISTER HELEN

"WHY did you melt your waxen man,
    Sister Helen?
To-day is the third since you began."
"The time was long, yet the time ran,
    Little brother."
      (*O Mother, Mary Mother,*
Three days to-day, between Hell and Heaven!)

"But if you have done your work aright,
    Sister Helen,
You'll let me play, for you said I might."   10
"Be very still in your play to-night,
    Little brother."
      (*O Mother, Mary Mother,*
Third night, to-night, between Hell and Heaven!)

"You said it must melt ere vesper-bell,
    Sister Helen;
If now it be molten, all is well."

"Even so, — nay, peace! you cannot tell,
    Little brother."
            (*O Mother, Mary Mother,*   20
O what is this, between Hell and Heaven?)

"Oh the waxen knave was plump to-day,
    Sister Helen;
How like dead folk he has dropped away!"
"Nay now, of the dead what can you say,
    Little brother?"
        (*O Mother, Mary Mother,*
What of the dead, between Hell and Heaven?)

"See, see, the sunken pile of wood,
    Sister Helen,   30
Shines through the thinned wax red as blood!"
"Nay now, when looked you yet on blood,
    Little brother?"
        (*O Mother, Mary Mother,*
How pale she is, between Hell and Heaven!)

"Now close your eyes, for they're sick and sore,
    Sister Helen,
And I'll play without the gallery door."
"Aye, let me rest, — I'll lie on the floor,
    Little brother."   40
        (*O Mother, Mary Mother,*
What rest to-night, between Hell and Heaven?)

"Here high up in the balcony,
    Sister Helen,
The moon flies face to face with me."
"Aye, look and say whatever you see,
    Little brother."
        (*O Mother, Mary Mother,*
What sight to-night, between Hell and Heaven?)

"Outside it's merry in the wind's wake,   50
    Sister Helen;
In the shaken trees the chill stars shake."
"Hush, heard you a horse-tread as you spake,
    Little brother?"
        (*O Mother, Mary Mother,*
What sound to-night, between Hell and Heaven?)

"I hear a horse-tread, and I see,
   Sister Helen,
Three horsemen that ride terribly."
"Little brother, whence come the three,   **60**
   Little brother?"
  (*O Mother, Mary Mother,*
Whence should they come, between Hell and Heaven?)

'They come by the hill-verge from Boyne Bar,
   Sister Helen,
And one draws nigh, but two are afar."
"Look, look, do you know them who they are,
   Little brother?"
  (*O Mother, Mary Mother,*
Who should they be, between Hell and Heaven?) **70**

"Oh, it's Keith of Eastholm rides so fast,
   Sister Helen,
For I know the white mane on the blast."
"The hour has come, has come at last,
   Little brother!"
  (*O Mother, Mary Mother,*
Her hour at last, between Hell and Heaven!)

"He has made a sign and called Halloo!
   Sister Helen,
And he says that he would speak with you." **80**
"Oh tell him I fear the frozen dew,
   Little brother."
  (*O Mother, Mary Mother,*
Why laughs she thus, between Hell and Heaven?)

"The wind is loud, but I hear him cry,
   Sister Helen,
That Keith of Ewern's like to die."
"And he and thou, and thou and I,
   Little brother."
  (*O Mother, Mary Mother,* **90**
And they and we, between Hell and Heaven!)

"Three days ago, on his marriage-morn,
   Sister Helen,
He sickened, and lies since then forlorn."

"For bridegroom's side is the bride a thorn,
  Little brother?"
  (*O Mother, Mary Mother,*
Cold bridal cheer, between Hell and Heaven!)

"Three days and nights he has lain abed,
  Sister Helen,
And he prays in torment to be dead."
"The thing may chance, if he have prayed,
  Little brother!"
  (*O Mother, Mary Mother,*
If he have prayed, between Hell and Heaven!)

"But he has not ceased to cry to-day,
  Sister Helen,
That you should take your curse away."
"*My* prayer was heard, — he need but pray,
  Little brother!"
  (*O Mother, Mary Mother,*
Shall God not hear, between Hell and Heaven?)

"But he says, till you take back your ban,
  Sister Helen,
His soul would pass, yet never can."
"Nay, then shall I slay a living man,
  Little brother?"
  (*O Mother, Mary Mother,*
A living soul, between Hell and Heaven!)

"But he calls for ever on your name,
  Sister Helen,
And says that he melts before a flame."
"My heart for his pleasure fared the same,
  Little brother."
  (*O Mother, Mary Mother,*
Fire at the heart, between Hell and Heaven!)

"Here's Keith of Westholm riding fast,
  Sister Helen,
For I know the white plume on the blast."
"The hour, the sweet hour I forecast,
  Little brother!"
  (*O Mother, Mary Mother,*
Is the hour sweet, between Hell and Heaven?)

100

110

120

130

"He stops to speak, and he stills his horse,
                    Sister Helen;
But his words are drowned in the wind's course."
"Nay hear, nay hear, you must hear perforce,
                    Little brother!"
            (*O Mother, Mary Mother,*
What word now heard, between Hell and Heaven?)   **140**

"Oh he says that Keith of Ewern's cry,
                    Sister Helen,
Is ever to see you ere he die."
"In all that his soul sees, there am I,
                    Little brother!"
            (*O Mother, Mary Mother,*
The soul's one sight, between Hell and Heaven!)

"He sends a ring and a broken coin,
                    Sister Helen,
And bids you mind the banks of Boyne."   **150**
"What else he broke will he ever join,
                    Little brother?"
            (*O Mother, Mary Mother,*
No, never joined, between Hell and Heaven!)

"He yields you these and craves full fain,
                    Sister Helen,
You pardon him in his mortal pain."
"What else he took will he give again,
                    Little brother?"
            (*O Mother, Mary Mother,*   **160**
Not twice to give, between Hell and Heaven!)

"He calls your name in an agony,
                    Sister Helen,
That even dead Love must weep to see."
"Hate, born of Love, is blind as he,
                    Little brother!"
            (*O Mother, Mary Mother,*
Love turned to hate, between Hell and Heaven!)

"Oh it's Keith of Keith now that rides fast,
                    Sister Helen,   **170**
For I know the white hair on the blast."

"The short short hour will soon be past,
                Little brother!"
            (*O Mother, Mary Mother,*
Will soon be past, between Hell and Heaven!)

"He looks at me and he tries to speak,
                Sister Helen,
But oh! his voice is sad and weak!"
"What here should the mighty Baron seek,
                Little brother?"   180
            (*O Mother, Mary Mother,*
Is this the end, between Hell and Heaven?)

"Oh his son still cries, if you forgive,
                Sister Helen,
The body dies, but the soul shall live."
"Fire shall forgive me as I forgive,
                Little brother!"
            (*O Mother, Mary Mother,*
As she forgives, between Hell and Heaven!)

"Oh he prays you, as his heart would rive,   190
                Sister Helen,
To save his dear son's soul alive."
"Fire cannot slay it, it shall thrive,
                Little brother!"
            (*O Mother, Mary Mother,*
Alas, alas, between Hell and Heaven!)

"He cries to you, kneeling in the road,
                Sister Helen,
To go with him for the love of God!"
"The way is long to his son's abode,   200
                Little brother."
            (*O Mother, Mary Mother,*
The way is long, between Hell and Heaven!)

"A lady's here, by a dark steed brought,
                Sister Helen,
So darkly clad, I saw her not."
"See her now or never see aught,
                Little brother!"
            (*O Mother, Mary Mother,*
What more to see, between Hell and Heaven?)   210

"Her hood falls back, and the moon shines fair,
                Sister Helen,
On the Lady of Ewern's golden hair."
"Blest hour of my power and her despair,
                Little brother!"
        (*O Mother, Mary Mother,*
Hour blest and bann'd, between Hell and Heaven!)

"Pale, pale her cheeks, that in pride did glow,
                Sister Helen,
'Neath the bridal-wreath three days ago."   220
"One morn for pride and three days for woe,
                Little brother!"
        (*O Mother, Mary Mother,*
Three days, three nights, between Hell and Heaven!)

"Her clasped hands stretch from her bending head,
                Sister Helen,
With the loud wind's wail her sobs are wed."
"What wedding-strains hath her bridal-bed,
                Little brother?"
        (*O Mother, Mary Mother,*   230
What strain but death's, between Hell and Heaven?)

"She may not speak, she sinks in a swoon,
                Sister Helen, —
She lifts her lips and gasps on the moon."
"Oh! might I but hear her soul's blithe tune,
                Little brother!"
        (*O Mother, Mary Mother,*
Her woe's dumb cry, between Hell and Heaven!)

"They've caught her to Westholm's saddle-bow,
                Sister Helen,   240
And her moonlit hair gleams white in its flow."
"Let it turn whiter than winter snow,
                Little brother!"
        (*O Mother, Mary Mother,*
Woe-withered gold, between Hell and Heaven!)

"O Sister Helen, you heard the bell,
                Sister Helen!
More loud than the vesper-chime it fell."

"No vesper-chime, but a dying knell,
            Little brother!"   250
(O Mother, Mary Mother,
His dying knell, between Hell and Heaven!)

"Alas! but I fear the heavy sound,
            Sister Helen;
Is it in the sky or in the ground?"
"Say, have they turned their horses round,
            Little brother?"
(O Mother, Mary Mother,
What would she more, between Hell and Heaven?)

"They have raised the old man from his knee,   260
            Sister Helen,
And they ride in silence hastily."
"More fast the naked soul doth flee,
            Little brother!"
(O Mother, Mary Mother,
The naked soul, between Hell and Heaven!)

"Flank to flank are the three steeds gone,
            Sister Helen,
But the lady's dark steed goes alone."
"And lonely her bridegroom's soul hath flown.   270
            Little brother."
(O Mother, Mary Mother,
The lonely ghost, between Hell and Heaven!)

"Oh the wind is sad in the iron chill,
            Sister Helen,
And weary sad they look by the hill."
"But he and I are sadder still,
            Little brother!"
(O Mother, Mary Mother,
Most sad of all, between Hell and Heaven!)   280

"See, see, the wax has dropped from its place,
            Sister Helen,
And the flames are winning up apace!"
"Yet here they burn but for a space,
            Little brother!"
(O Mother, Mary Mother,
Here for a space, between Hell and Heaven!)

"Ah! what white thing at the door has cross'd,
                    Sister Helen?
Ah! what is this that sighs in the frost?"   290
"A soul that's lost as mine is lost,
                    Little brother!"
          (*O Mother, Mary Mother,*
Lost, lost, all lost, between Hell and Heaven!)
[1851]   [*1854;* 1870]

THE WOODSPURGE

THE wind flapped loose, the wind was still,
Shaken out dead from tree and hill:
I had walked on at the wind's will, —
I sat now, for the wind was still.

Between my knees my forehead was, —
My lips, drawn in, said not Alas!
My hair was over in the grass,
My naked ears heard the day pass.

My eyes, wide open, had the run
Of some ten weeds to fix upon;   10
Among those few, out of the sun,
The woodspurge flowered, three cups in one.

From perfect grief there need not be
Wisdom or even memory:
One thing then learnt remains to me, —
The woodspurge has a cup of three.
[1856]   [1870]

EVEN SO

So it is, my dear.
All such things touch secret strings
For heavy hearts to hear.
So it is, my dear.

Very like indeed:
Sea and sky, afar, on high,
Sand and strewn seaweed, —
Very like indeed.

But the sea stands spread
As one wall with the flat skies,   10
Where the lean black craft like flies
Seem well-nigh stagnated,
Soon to drop off dead.

Seemed it so to us
When I was thine and thou wast **mine,**
And all these things were thus,
But all our world in us?

Could we be so now?
Not if all beneath heaven's pall
Lay dead but I and thou,   20
Could we be so now!
[1859]   [1870]

THE SONG OF THE BOWER

Say, is it day, is it dusk in thy bower,
Thou whom I long for, who longest for me?
Oh! be it light, be it night, 'tis Love's hour,
Love's that is fettered as Love's that is free.
Free Love has leaped to that innermost chamber,
Oh! the last time, and the hundred before:
Fettered Love, motionless, can but remember,
Yet something that sighs from him passes the door.

Nay, but my heart when it flies to thy bower,
What does it find there that knows it again?   10
There it must droop like a shower-beaten flower,
Red at the rent core and dark with the rain.
Ah! yet what shelter is still shed above it, —
What waters still image its leaves torn apart?
Thy soul is the shade that clings round it to love it,
And tears are its mirror deep down in thy heart.

What were my prize, could I enter thy bower,
  This day, to-morrow, at eve or at morn?
Large lovely arms and a neck like a tower,
  Bosom then heaving that now lies forlorn.   20
Kindled with love-breath, (the sun's kiss is colder!)
  Thy sweetness all near me, so distant to-day;
My hand round thy neck and thy hand on my shoulder,
  My mouth to thy mouth as the world melts away.

What is it keeps me afar from thy bower, —
  My spirit, my body, so fain to be there?
Waters engulfing or fires that devour? —
  Earth heaped against me or death in the air?
Nay, but in day-dreams, for terror, for pity,
  The trees wave their heads with an omen to tell;   30
Nay, but in night-dreams, throughout the dark city,
  The hours, clashed together, lose count in the bell.

Shall I not one day remember thy bower,
  One day when all days are one day to me? —
Thinking, "I stirred not, and yet had the power!" —
  Yearning, "Ah God, if again it might be!"
Peace, peace! such a small lamp illumes, on this highway,
  So dimly so few steps in front of my feet, —
Yet shows me that her way is parted from my way. . . .
  Out of sight, beyond light, at what goal may we meet?   40
[1860, 1869]   [1870]

THE STREAM'S SECRET

    WHAT thing unto mine ear
Wouldst thou convey, — what secret thing,
O wandering water ever whispering?
  Surely thy speech shall be of her.
Thou water, O thou whispering wanderer,
    What message dost thou bring?

    Say, hath not Love leaned low
This hour beside thy far well-head,
And there through jealous hollowed fingers said
  The thing that most I long to know, —   10

Murmuring with curls all dabbled in thy flow
    And washed lips rosy red?

        He told it to thee there
    Where thy voice hath a louder tone;
But where it welters to this little moan
    His will decrees that I should hear.
Now speak: for with the silence is no fear,
        And I am all alone.

        Shall Time not still endow
    One hour with life, and I and she
Slake in one kiss the thirst of memory?
    Say, stream; lest Love should disavow
Thy service, and the bird upon the bough
        Sing first to tell it me.

        What whisperest thou? Nay, why
    Name the dead hours? I mind them well:
Their ghosts in many darkened doorways dwell
    With desolate eyes to know them by.
That hour that must be born ere it can die, —
        Of that I'd have thee tell.

        But hear, before thou speak!
    Withhold, I pray, the vain behest
That while the maze hath still its bower for quest
    My burning heart should cease to seek.
Be sure that Love ordained for souls more meek
        His roadside dells of rest.

        Stream, when this silver thread
    In flood-time is a torrent brown,
May any bulwark bind thy foaming crown?
    Shall not the waters surge and spread
And to the crannied boulders of their bed
        Still shoot the dead drift down?

        Let no rebuke find place
    In speech of thine: or it shall prove
That thou dost ill expound the words of Love,
    Even as thine eddy's rippling race
Would blur the perfect image of his face.
        I will have none thereof.

20

30

40

O learn and understand
That 'gainst the wrongs himself did wreak
Love sought her aid; until her shadowy cheek
And eyes beseeching gave command;
And compassed in her close compassionate hand
My heart must burn and speak.

For then at last we spoke
What eyes so oft had told to eyes
Through that long-lingering silence whose half-sighs
Alone the buried secret broke,
Which with snatched hands and lips' reverberate stroke
Then from the heart did rise.

But she is far away
Now; nor the hours of night grown hoar
Bring yet to me, long gazing from the door,
The wind-stirred robe of roseate grey
And rose-crown of the hour that leads the day
When we shall meet once more.

Dark as thy blinded wave
When brimming midnight floods the glen, —
Bright as the laughter of thy runnels when
The dawn yields all the light they crave;
Even so these hours to wound and that to save
Are sisters in Love's ken.

Oh sweet her bending grace
Then when I kneel beside her feet;
And sweet her eyes' o'erhanging heaven; and sweet
The gathering folds of her embrace;
And her fall'n hair at last shed round my face
When breaths and tears shall meet.

Beneath her sheltering hair,
In the warm silence near her breast,
Our kisses and our sobs shall sink to rest;
As in some still trance made aware
That day and night have wrought to fulness there
And Love has built our nest.

And as in the dim grove,
When the rains cease that hushed them long,

'Mid glistening boughs the song-birds wake to song, —
So from our hearts deep-shrined in love,
While the leaves throb beneath, around, above,
    The quivering notes shall throng.   90

    Till tenderest words found vain
Draw back to wonder mute and deep,
And closed lips in closed arms a silence keep,
    Subdued by memory's circling strain, —
The wind-rapt sound that the wind brings again
    While all the willows weep.

    Then by her summoning art
Shall memory conjure back the sere
Autumnal Springs, from many a dying year
    Born dead; and, bitter to the heart,   100
The very ways where now we walk apart
    Who then shall cling so near.

    And with each thought new-grown,
Some sweet caress or some sweet name
Low-breathed shall let me know her thought the same;
    Making me rich with every tone
And touch of the dear heaven so long unknown
    That filled my dreams with flame.

    Pity and love shall burn
In her pressed cheek and cherishing hands;   110
And from the living spirit of love that stands
    Between her lips to soothe and yearn,
Each separate breath shall clasp me round in turn
    And loose my spirit's bands.

    Oh passing sweet and dear,
Then when the worshipped form and face
Are felt at length in darkling close embrace;
    Round which so oft the sun shone clear,
With mocking light and pitiless atmosphere,
    In many an hour and place.   120

    Ah me! with what proud growth
Shall that hour's thirsting race be run;
While, for each several sweetness still begun
    Afresh, endures love's endless drouth;

Sweet hands, sweet hair, sweet cheeks, sweet eyes, sweet mouth,
    Each singly wooed and won.

     Yet most with the sweet soul
    Shall love's espousals then be knit;
For very passion of peace shall breathe from it
    O'er tremulous wings that touch the goal,   130
As on the unmeasured height of Love's control
    The lustral fires are lit.

     Therefore, when breast and cheek
    Now part, from long embraces free, —
Each on the other gazing shall but see
    A self that has no need to speak:
All things unsought, yet nothing more to seek, —
    One love in unity.

     O water wandering past, —
    Albeit to thee I speak this thing,   140
O water, thou that wanderest whispering,
    Thou keep'st thy counsel to the last.
What spell upon thy bosom should Love cast,
    Its secret thence to wring?

     Nay, must thou hear the tale
    Of the past days, — the heavy debt
Of life that obdurate time withholds, — ere yet
    To win thine ear these prayers prevail,
And by thy voice Love's self with high All-hail
    Yield up the amulet?   150

     How should all this be told? —
    All the sad sum of wayworn days; —
Heart's anguish in the impenetrable maze;
    And on the waste uncoloured wold
The visible burthen of the sun grown cold
    And the moon's labouring gaze?

     Alas! shall hope be nurs'd
    On life's all-succouring breast in vain,
And made so perfect only to be slain?
    Or shall not rather the sweet thirst   160
Even yet rejoice the heart with warmth dispers'd
    And strength grown fair again?

Stands it not by the door —
Love's Hour — till she and I shall meet;
With bodiless form and unapparent feet
   That cast no shadow yet before,
Though round its head the dawn begins to pour
     The breath that makes day sweet?

    Its eyes invisible
Watch till the dial's thin-thrown shade   170
Be born, — yea, till the journeying line be laid
   Upon the point that wakes the spell,
And there in lovelier light than tongue can tell
     Its presence stand array'd.

    Its soul remembers yet
Those sunless hours that passed it by;
And still it hears the night's disconsolate cry,
   And feels the branches wringing wet
Cast on its brow, that may not once forget,
     Dumb tears from the blind sky.   180

    But oh! when now her foot
Draws near, for whose sake night and day
Were long in weary longing sighed away, —
   The hour of Love, 'mid airs grown mute,
Shall sing beside the door, and Love's own lute
     Thrill to the passionate lay.

    Thou know'st, for Love has told
Within thine ear, O stream, how soon
That song shall lift its sweet appointed tune.
   O tell me, for my lips are cold,   190
And in my veins the blood is waxing old
     Even while I beg the boon.

    So, in that hour of sighs
Assuaged, shall we beside this stone
Yield thanks for grace; while in thy mirror shown
   The twofold image softly lies,
Until we kiss, and each in other's eyes
     Is imaged all alone.

    Still silent? Can no art
Of Love's then move thy pity? Nay,   200

To thee let nothing come that owns his sway:
Let happy lovers have no part
With thee; nor even so sad and poor a heart
As thou hast spurned to-day.

To-day? Lo! night is here.
The glen grows heavy with some veil
Risen from the earth or fall'n to make earth pale;
And all stands hushed to eye and ear,
Until the night-wind shake the shade like fear
And every covert quail.   210

Ah! by a colder wave
On deathlier airs the hour must come
Which to thy heart, my love, shall call me home.
Between the lips of the low cave
Against that night the lapping waters lave,
And the dark lips are dumb.

But there Love's self doth stand,
And with Life's weary wings far-flown,
And with Death's eyes that make the water moan,
Gathers the water in his hand: 220
And they that drink know nought of sky or land
But only love alone.

O soul-sequestered face
Far off, — O were that night but now!
So even beside that stream even I and thou
Through thirsting lips should draw Love's grace,
And in the zone of that supreme embrace
Bind aching breast and brow.

O water whispering
Still through the dark into mine ears, —   230
As with mine eyes, is it not now with hers? —
Mine eyes that add to thy cold spring,
Wan water, wandering water weltering,
This hidden tide of tears.

[1869–70]   [1870]

AFTER THE FRENCH LIBERATION OF ITALY

As when the last of the paid joys of love
  Has come and gone; and with a single kiss
  At length, and with one laugh of satiate bliss,
The wearied man a minute rests above
The wearied woman, no more urged to move
  In those long throes of longing, till they glide,
  Now lightlier clasped, each to the other's side,
In joys past acting, not past dreaming of: —

So Europe now beneath this paramour
  Lies for a little out of use, — full oft   10
Submissive to his lust, a loveless whore.
  He wakes, she sleeps, the breath falls slow and soft.
Wait: the bought body holds a birth within,
An harlot's child, to scourge her for her sin.
[1859]   [1904]

THREE TRANSLATIONS FROM
FRANÇOIS VILLON, 1450

I

THE BALLAD OF DEAD LADIES

TELL me now in what hidden way is
  Lady Flora the lovely Roman?
Where's Hipparchia, and where is Thais,
  Neither of them the fairer woman?
  Where is Echo, beheld of no man,
Only heard on river and mere, —
  She whose beauty was more than human? . . .
But where are the snows of yester-year?

Where's Héloise, the learned nun,
  For whose sake Abeillard, I ween,   10
Lost manhood and put priesthood on?
  (From Love he won such dule and teen!)
  And where, I pray you, is the Queen

Who willed that Buridan should steer
    Sewed in a sack's mouth down the Seine? . . .
But where are the snows of yester-year?

White Queen Blanche, like a queen of lilies,
    With a voice like any mermaiden, —
Bertha Broadfoot, Beatrice, Alice,
    And Ermengarde the lady of Maine, —   20
    And that good Joan whom Englishmen
At Rouen doomed and burned her there, —
    Mother of God, where are they then? . .
But where are the snows of yester-year?

Nay, never ask this week, fair lord,
    Where they are gone, nor yet this year,
Save with thus much for an overword, —
    But where are the snows of yester-year?
[1869]   [*1869;* 1870]

II

TO DEATH, OF HIS LADY

DEATH, of thee do I make my moan,
    Who hadst my lady away from me,
    Nor wilt assuage thine enmity
Till with her life thou hast mine own;
For since that hour my strength has flown.
    Lo! what wrong was her life to thee,
                  Death?

Two we were, and the heart was one;
    Which now being dead, dead I must be,
    Or seem alive as lifelessly   10
As in the choir the painted stone,
                  Death!
[1869]   [*1869;* 1870]

III

HIS MOTHER'S SERVICE TO OUR LADY

LADY of Heaven and earth, and therewithal
    Crowned Empress of the nether clefts of Hell,—
I, thy poor Christian, on thy name do call,

Commending me to thee, with thee to dwell,
  Albeit in nought I be commendable.
But all mine undeserving may not mar
Such mercies as thy sovereign mercies are;
  Without the which (as true words testify)
No soul can reach thy Heaven so fair and far.
  Even in this faith I choose to live and die.   10

Unto thy Son say thou that I am His,
  And to me graceless make Him gracious.
Sad Mary of Egypt lacked not of that bliss,
  Nor yet the sorrowful clerk Theophilus,
  Whose bitter sins were set aside even thus
Though to the Fiend his bounden service was.
Oh help me, lest in vain for me should pass
  (Sweet Virgin that shalt have no loss thereby!)
The blessed Host and sacring of the Mass.
  Even in this faith I choose to live and die.   20

A pitiful poor woman, shrunk and old,
  I am, and nothing learn'd in letter-lore.
Within my parish-cloister I behold
  A painted Heaven where harps and lutes adore,
  And eke an Hell whose damned folk seethe full sore:
One bringeth fear, the other joy to me.
That joy, great Goddess, make thou mine to be, —
  Thou of whom all must ask it even as I;
And that which faith desires, that let it see.
  For in this faith I choose to live and die.   30

O excellent Virgin Princess! thou didst bear
King Jesus, the most excellent comforter,
Who even of this our weakness craved a share,
  And for our sake stooped to us from on high,
Offering to death His young life sweet and fair.
Such as He is, Our Lord, I Him declare,
  And in this faith I choose to live and die.
[1870]   [1870]

THE BRIDE'S PRELUDE

"SISTER," said busy Amelotte
    To listless Aloÿse;
"Along your wedding-road the wheat
Bends as to hear your horse's feet,
And the noonday stands still for heat."

Amelotte laughed into the air.
    With eyes that sought the sun:
But where the walls in long brocade
Were screened, as one who is afraid
Sat Aloÿse within the shade.   10

And even in shade was gleam enough
    To shut out full repose
From the bride's 'tiring-chamber, which
Was like the inner altar-niche
Whose dimness worship has made rich.

Within the window's heaped recess
    The light was counterchanged
In blent reflexes manifold
From perfume-caskets of wrought gold
And gems the bride's hair could not hold,   20

All thrust together: and with these
    A slim-curved lute, which now,
At Amelotte's sudden passing there,
Was swept in somewise unaware,
And shook to music the close air.

Against the haloed lattice-panes
    The bridesmaid sunned her breast;
Then to the glass turned tall and free,
And braced and shifted daintily
Her loin-belt through her côte-hardie.   30

The belt was silver, and the clasp
    Of lozenged arm-bearings;
A world of mirrored tints minute
The rippling sunshine wrought into 't,
That flushed her hand and warmed her foot.

At least an hour had Aloÿse —
   Her jewels in her hair —
Her white gown, as became a bride,
Quartered in silver at each side —
Sat thus aloof, as if to hide.   40

Over her bosom, that lay still,
   The vest was rich in grain,
With close pearls wholly overset:
Around her throat the fastenings met
Of chevesayle and mantelet.

Her arms were laid along her lap
   With the hands open: life
Itself did seem at fault in her:
Beneath the drooping brows, the stir
Of thought made noonday heavier.   50

Long sat she silent; and then raised
   Her head, with such a gasp
As while she summoned breath to speak
Fanned high that furnace in the cheek
But sucked the heart-pulse cold and weak.

(Oh gather round her now, all ye
   Past seasons of her fear, —
Sick springs, and summers deadly cold!
To flight your hovering wings unfold,
For now your secret shall be told.   60

Ye many sunlights, barbed with darts
   Of dread detecting flame, —
Gaunt moonlights that like sentinels
Went past with iron clank of bells, —
Draw round and render up your spells!)

"Sister," said Aloÿse, "I had
   A thing to tell thee of
Long since, and could not. But do thou
Kneel first in prayer awhile, and bow
Thine heart, and I will tell thee now."   70

Amelotte wondered with her eyes;
   But her heart said in her:

"Dear Aloÿse would have me pray
    Because the awe she feels to-day
Must need more prayers than she can say."

So Amelotte put by the folds
    That covered up her feet,
And knelt, — beyond the arras'd gloom
And the hot window's dull perfume, —
Where day was stillest in the room.   **80**

"Queen Mary, hear," she said, "and say
    To Jesus the Lord Christ,
This bride's new joy, which He confers,
New joy to many ministers,
And many griefs are bound in hers."

The bride turned in her chair, and hid
    Her face against the back,
And took her pearl-girt elbows in
Her hands, and could not yet begin,
But shuddering, uttered, "Urscelyn!"   **90**

Most weak she was; for as she pressed
    Her hand against her throat,
Along the arras she let trail
Her face, as if all heart did fail,
And sat with shut eyes, dumb and pale.

Amelotte still was on her knees
    As she had kneeled to pray.
Deeming her sister swooned, she thought,
At first, some succour to have brought;
But Aloÿse rocked, as one distraught.   **100**

She would have pushed the lattice wide
    To gain what breeze might be;
But marking that no leaf once beat
The outside casement, it seemed meet
Not to bring in more scent and heat.

So she said only: "Aloÿse,
    Sister, when happened it
At any time that the bride came
To ill, or spoke in fear of shame,
When speaking first the bridegroom's name?"   **110**

A bird had out its song and ceased
    Ere the bride spoke. At length
She said: "The name is as the thing: —
Sin hath no second christening,
And shame is all that shame can bring.

"In divers places many an while
    I would have told thee this;
But faintness took me, or a fit
Like fever. God would not permit
That I should change thine eyes with it.   **120**

"Yet once I spoke, hadst thou but heard: —
    That time we wandered out
All the sun's hours, but missed our way
When evening darkened, and so lay
The whole night covered up in hay.

"At last my face was hidden: so,
    Having God's hint, I paused
Not long; but drew myself more near
Where thou wast laid, and shook off fear,
And whispered quick into thine ear   **130**

"Something of the whole tale. At first
    I lay and bit my hair
For the sore silence thou didst keep:
Till, as thy breath came long and deep,
I knew that thou hadst been asleep.

"The moon was covered, but the stars
    Lasted till morning broke.
Awake, thou told'st me that thy dream
Had been of me, — that all did seem
At jar, — but that it was a dream.   **140**

"I knew God's hand and might not speak.
    After that night I kept
Silence and let the record swell:
Till now there is much more to tell
Which must be told out ill or well."

She paused then, weary, with dry lips
    Apart. From the outside
By fits there boomed a dull report

From where i' the hanging tennis-court
The bridegroom's retinue made sport.   150

The room lay still in dusty glare,
    Having no sound through it
Except the chirp of a caged bird
That came and ceased: and if she stirred,
Amelotte's raiment could be heard.

Quoth Amelotte: "The night this chanced
    Was a late summer night
Last year! What secret, for Christ's love,
Keep'st thou since then? Mary above!
What thing is this thou speakest of?   160

"Mary and Christ! Lest when 'tis told
    I should be prone to wrath, —
This prayer beforehand! How she errs
Soe'er, take count of grief like hers,
Whereof the days are turned to years!"

She bowed her neck, and having said,
    Kept on her knees to hear;
And then, because strained thought demands
Quiet before it understands,
Darkened her eyesight with her hands.   170

So when at last her sister spoke,
    She did not see the pain
O' the mouth nor the ashamèd eyes,
But marked the breath that came in sighs
And the half-pausing for replies.

This was the bride's sad prelude-strain: —
    "I' the convent where a girl
I dwelt till near my womanhood,
I had but preachings of the rood
And Aves told in solitude   180

"To spend my heart on: and my hand
    Had but the weary skill
To eke out upon silken cloth
Christ's visage, or the long bright growth
Of Mary's hair, or Satan wroth.

"So when at last I went, and thou,
    A child not known before,
Didst come to take the place I left, —
My limbs, after such lifelong theft
Of life, could be but little deft   190

"In all that ministers delight
    To noble women: I
Had learned no word of youth's discourse,
Nor gazed on games of warriors,
Nor trained a hound, nor ruled a horse.

"Besides, the daily life i' the sun
    Made me at first hold back.
To thee this came at once; to me
It crept with pauses timidly;
I am not blithe and strong like thee.   200

"Yet my feet liked the dances well,
    The songs went to my voice,
The music made me shake and weep;
And often, all night long, my sleep
Gave dreams I had been fain to keep.

"But though I loved not holy things,
    To hear them scorned brought pain, —
They were my childhood; and these dames
Were merely perjured in saints' names
And fixed upon saints' days for games.   210

"And sometimes when my father rode
    To hunt with his loud friends,
I dared not bring him to be quaff'd,
As my wont was, his stirrup-draught,
Because they jested so and laugh'd.

"At last one day my brothers said,
    'The girl must not grow thus, —
Bring her a jennet, — she shall ride.'
They helped my mounting, and I tried
To laugh with them and keep their side.   220

"But breaks were rough and bents were steep
    Upon our path that day:

My palfrey threw me; and I went
Upon men's shoulders home, sore spent,
While the chase followed up the scent.

"Our shrift-father (and he alone
    Of all the household there
Had skill in leechcraft,) was away
When I reached home. I tossed, and lay
Sullen with anguish the whole day.   230

"For the day passed ere some brought
    To mind that in the hunt
Rode a young lord she named, long bred
Among the priests, whose art (she said)
Might chance to stand me in much stead.

"I bade them seek and summon him:
    But long ere this, the chase
Had scattered, and he was not found.
I lay in the same weary stound,
Therefore, until the night came round.   240

"It was dead night and near on twelve
    When the horse-tramp at length
Beat up the echoes of the court:
By then, my feverish breath was short
With pain the sense could scarce support.

"My fond nurse sitting near my feet
    Rose softly, — her lamp's flame
Held in her hand, lest it should make
My heated lids, in passing, ache;
And she passed softly, for my sake.   250

"Returning soon, she brought the youth
    They spoke of. Meek he seemed,
But good knights held him of stout heart.
He was akin to us in part,
And bore our shield, but barred athwart.

"I now remembered to have seen
    His face, and heard him praised
For letter-lore and medicine,
Seeing his youth was nurtured in
Priests' knowledge, as mine own had been."   260

The bride's voice did not weaken here,
 Yet by her sudden pause
She seemed to look for questioning;
Or else (small need though) 'twas to bring
Well to her mind the bygone thing.

Her thought, long stagnant, stirred by speech,
 Gave her a sick recoil;
As, dip thy fingers through the green
That masks a pool, — where they have been
The naked depth is black between.   270

Amelotte kept her knees; her face
 Was shut within her hands,
As it had been throughout the tale;
Her forehead's whiteness might avail
Nothing to say if she were pale.

Although the lattice had dropped loose,
 There was no wind; the heat
Being so at rest that Amelotte
Heard far beneath the plunge and float
Of a hound swimming in the moat.   280

Some minutes since, two rooks had toiled
 Home to the nests that crowned
Ancestral ash-trees. Through the glare
Beating again, they seemed to tear
With that thick caw the woof o' the air.

But else, 'twas at the dead of noon
 Absolute silence; all,
From the raised bridge and guarded sconce
To green-clad places of pleasaùnce
Where the long lake was white with swans.   290

Amelotte spoke not any word
 Nor moved she once; but felt
Between her hands in narrow space
Her own hot breath upon her face,
And kept in silence the same place.

Aloÿse did not hear at all
 The sounds without. She heard
The inward voice (past help obey'd)

Which might not slacken nor be stay'd,
But urged her till the whole were said.   300

Therefore she spoke again: "That night
        But little could be done:
My foot, held in my nurse's hands,
He swathed up heedfully in bands,
And for my rest gave close commands.

"I slept till noon, but an ill sleep
        Of dreams: through all that day
My side was stiff and caught the breath;
Next day, such pain as sickeneth
Took me, and I was nigh to death.   310

"Life strove, Death claimed me for his own
        Through days and nights: but now
'Twas the good father tended me,
Having returned. Still, I did see
The youth I spoke of constantly.

"For he would with my brothers come
        To stay beside my couch,
And fix my eyes against his own,
Noting my pulse; or else alone,
To sit at gaze while I made moan.   320

"(Some nights I knew he kept the watch,
        Because my women laid
The rushes thick for his steel shoes.)
Through many days this pain did use
The life God would not let me lose.

"At length, with my good nurse to aid,
        I could walk forth again:
And still, as one who broods or grieves,
At noons I'd meet him and at eves,
With idle feet that drove the leaves.   330

"The day when I first walked alone
        Was thinned in grass and leaf,
And yet a goodly day o' the year:
The last bird's cry upon mine ear
Left my brain weak, it was so clear.

"The tears were sharp within mine eyes;
    I sat down, being glad,
And wept; but stayed the sudden flow
Anon, for footsteps that fell slow;
'Twas that youth passed me, bowing low.   340

"He passed me without speech; but when,
    At least an hour gone by,
Rethreading the same covert, he
Saw I was still beneath the tree,
He spoke and sat him down with me.

"Little we said; nor one heart heard
    Even what was said within;
And, faltering some farewell, I soon
Rose up; but then i' the autumn noon
My feeble brain whirled like a swoon.   350

"He made me sit. 'Cousin, I grieve
    Your sickness stays by you.'
'I would,' said I, 'that you did err
So grieving. I am wearier
Than death, of the sickening dying year.'

"He answered: 'If your weariness
    Accepts a remedy,
I hold one and can give it you.'
I gazed: 'What ministers thereto,
Be sure,' I said, 'that I will do.'   360

"He went on quickly: — 'Twas a cure
    He had not ever named
Unto our kin lest they should stint
Their favour, for some foolish hint
Of wizardry or magic in't:

"But that if he were let to come
    Within my bower that night,
(My women still attending me,
He said, while he remain'd there,) he
Could teach me the cure privily.   370

"I bade him come that night. He came;
    But little in his speech

Was cure or sickness spoken of,
Only a passionate fierce love
That clamoured upon God above.

"My women wondered, leaning close
 Aloof. At mine own heart
I think great wonder was not stirr'd.
I dared not listen, yet I heard
His tangled speech, word within word.   380

"He craved my pardon first, — all else
 Wild tumult. In the end
He remained silent at my feet
Fumbling the rushes. Strange quick heat
Made all the blood of my life meet.

"And lo! I loved him. I but said,
 If he would leave me then,
His hope some future might forecast.
His hot lips stung my hand: at last
My damsels led him forth in haste."   390

The bride took breath to pause; and turned
 Her gaze where Amelotte
Knelt, — the gold hair upon her back
Quite still in all its threads, — the track
Of her still shadow sharp and black.

That listening without sight had grown
 To stealthy dread; and now
That the one sound she had to mark
Left her alone too, she was stark
Afraid, as children in the dark.   400

Her fingers felt her temples beat;
 Then came that brain-sickness
Which thinks to scream, and murmureth;
And pent between her hands, the breath
Was damp against her face like death.

Her arms both fell at once; but when
 She gasped upon the light,
Her sense returned. She would have pray'd
To change whatever words still stay'd
Behind, but felt there was no aid.   410

So she rose up, and having gone
    Within the window's arch
Once more, she sat there, all intent
On torturing doubts, and once more bent
To hear, in mute bewilderment.

But Aloÿse still paused. Thereon
    Amelotte gathered voice
In somewise from the torpid fear
Coiled round her spirit. Low but clear
She said: "Speak, sister; for I hear."   **420**

But Aloÿse threw up her neck
    And called the name of God: —
"Judge, God, 'twixt her and me to-day!
She knows how hard this is to say,
Yet will not have one word away."

Her sister was quite silent. Then
    Afresh: — "Not she, dear Lord!
Thou be my judge, on Thee I call!"
She ceased, — her forehead smote the wall:
"Is there a God," she said, "at all?"   **430**

Amelotte shuddered at the soul,
    But did not speak. The pause
Was long this time. At length the bride
Pressed her hand hard against her side,
And trembling between shame and pride

Said by fierce effort: "From that night
    Often at nights we met:
That night, his passion could but rave:
The next, what grace his lips did crave
I knew not, but I know I gave."   **440**

Where Amelotte was sitting, all
    The light and warmth of day
Were so upon her without shade,
That the thing seemed by sunshine made
Most foul and wanton to be said.

She would have questioned more, and known
    The whole truth at its worst,
But held her silent, in mere shame

Of day. 'Twas only these words came: —
"Sister, thou hast not said his name."   450

"Sister," quoth Aloÿse, "thou know'st
    His name. I said that he
Was in a manner of our kin.
Waiting the title he might win,
They called him the Lord Urscelyn."

The bridegroom's name, to Amelotte
    Daily familiar, — heard
Thus in this dreadful history, —
Was dreadful to her; as might be
Thine own voice speaking unto thee.   460

The day's mid-hour was almost full;
    Upon the dial-plate
The angel's sword stood near at One.
An hour's remaining yet; the sun
Will not decrease till all be done.

Through the bride's lattice there crept in
    At whiles (from where the train
Of minstrels, till the marriage-call,
Loitered at windows of the wall,)
Stray lute-notes, sweet and musical.   470

They clung in the green growths and moss
    Against the outside stone;
Low like dirge-wail or requiem
They murmured, lost 'twixt leaf and stem:
There was no wind to carry them.

Amelotte gathered herself back
    Into the wide recess
That the sun flooded: it o'erspread
Like flame the hair upon her head
And fringed her face with burning red.   480

All things seemed shaken and at change:
    A silent place o' the hills
She knew, into her spirit came:
Within herself she said its name
And wondered was it still the same.

The bride (whom silence goaded) now
    Said strongly, — her despair
By stubborn will kept underneath: —
"Sister, 'twere well thou didst not breathe
That curse of thine. Give me my wreath."   490

"Sister," said Amelotte, "abide
    In peace. Be God thy judge,
As thou hast said — not I. For me,
I merely will thank God that he
Whom thou hast lovèd loveth thee."

Then Aloÿse lay back, and laughed
    With wan lips bitterly,
Saying, "Nay, thank thou God for this, —
That never any soul like his
Shall have its portion where love is."   500

Weary of wonder, Amelotte
    Sat silent: she would ask
No more, though all was unexplained:
She was too weak; the ache still pained
Her eyes, — her forehead's pulse remained.

The silence lengthened. Aloÿse
    Was fain to turn her face
Apart, to where the arras told
Two Testaments, the New and Old,
In shapes and meanings manifold.   510

One solace that was gained, she hid.
    Her sister, from whose curse
Her heart recoiled, had blessed instead:
Yet would not her pride have it said
How much the blessing comforted.

Only, on looking round again
    After some while, the face
Which from the arras turned away
Was more at peace and less at bay
With shame than it had been that day.   520

She spoke right on, as if no pause
    Had come between her speech:

"That year from warmth grew bleak and pass'd,"
She said; "the days from first to last
How slow, — woe's me! the nights how fast!

"From first to last it was not known:
    My nurse, and of my train
Some four or five, alone could tell
What terror kept inscrutable:
There was good need to guard it well.   530

"Not the guilt only made the shame,
    But he was without land
And born amiss. He had but come
To train his youth here at our home,
And, being man, depart therefrom.

"Of the whole time each single day
    Brought fear and great unrest:
It seemed that all would not avail
Some once, — that my close watch would fail,
And some sign, somehow, tell the tale.   540

"The noble maidens that I knew,
    My fellows, oftentimes
Midway in talk or sport, would look
A wonder which my fears mistook,
To see how I turned faint and shook.

"They had a game of cards, where each
    By painted arms might find
What knight she should be given to.
Ever with trembling hand I threw
Lest I should learn the thing I knew.   550

"And once it came. And Aure d'Honvaulx
    Held up the bended shield
And laughed: 'Gramercy for our share! —
If to our bridal we but fare
To smutch the blazon that we bear!'

"But proud Denise de Villenbois
    Kissed me, and gave her wench
The card, and said: 'If in these bowers
You women play at paramours,
You must not mix your game with ours.'   560

"And one upcast it from her hand:
    'Lo! see how high he'll soar!'
But then their laugh was bitterest;
For the wind veered at fate's behest
And blew it back into my breast.

"Oh! if I met him in the day
    Or heard his voice, — at meals
Or at the Mass or through the hall, —
A look turned towards me would appal
My heart by seeming to know all.   570

"Yet I grew curious of my shame,
    And sometimes in the church,
On hearing such a sin rebuked,
Have held my girdle-glass unhooked
To see how such a woman looked.

"But if at night he did not come,
    I lay all deadly cold
To think they might have smitten sore
And slain him, and as the night wore,
His corpse be lying at my door.   580

"And entering or going forth,
    Our proud shield o'er the gate
Seemed to arraign my shrinking eyes.
With tremors and unspoken lies
The year went past me in this wise.

"About the spring of the next year
    An ailing fell on me;
(I had been stronger till the spring;)
'Twas mine old sickness gathering,
I thought; but 'twas another thing.   590

"I had such yearnings as brought tears,
    And a wan dizziness:
Motion, like feeling, grew intense;
Sight was a haunting evidence
And sound a pang that snatched the sense.

"It now was hard on that great ill
    Which lost our wealth from us
And all our lands. Accursed be

The peevish fools of liberty
Who will not let themselves be free!   600

"The Prince was fled into the west:
    A price was on his blood,
But he was safe. To us his friends
He left that ruin which attends
The strife against God's secret ends.

"The league dropped all asunder, — lord,
    Gentle and serf. Our house
Was marked to fall. And a day came
When half the wealth that propped our name
Went from us in a wind of flame.   610

"Six hours I lay upon the wall
    And saw it burn. But when
It clogged the day in a black bed
Of louring vapour, I was led
Down to the postern, and we fled.

"But ere we fled, there was a voice
    Which I heard speak, and say
That many of our friends, to shun
Our fate, had left us and were gone,
And that Lord Urscelyn was one.   620

"That name, as was its wont, made sight
    And hearing whirl. I gave
No heed but only to the name:
I held my senses, dreading them,
And was at strife to look the same.

"We rode and rode. As the speed grew,
    The growth of some vague curse
Swarmed in my brain. It seemed to me
Numbed by the swiftness, but would be —
That still — clear knowledge certainly.   630

"Night lapsed. At dawn the sea was there
    And the sea-wind: afar
The ravening surge was hoarse and loud,
And underneath the dim dawn-cloud
Each stalking wave shook like a shroud.

"From my drawn litter I looked out
    Unto the swarthy sea,
And knew. That voice, which late had cross'd
Mine ears, seemed with the foam uptoss'd:
I knew that Urscelyn was lost.   640

"Then I spake all: I turned on one
    And on the other, and spake:
My curse laughed in me to behold
Their eyes: I sat up, stricken cold,
Mad of my voice till all was told.

"Oh! of my brothers, Hugues was mute,
    And Gilles was wild and loud,
And Raoul strained abroad his face,
As if his gnashing wrath could trace
Even there the prey that it must chase.   650

"And round me murmured all our train,
    Hoarse as the hoarse-tongued sea;
Till Hugues from silence louring woke,
And cried: 'What ails the foolish folk?
Know ye not frenzy's lightning-stroke?'

"But my stern father came to them
    And quelled them with his look,
Silent and deadly pale. Anon
I knew that we were hastening on,
My litter closed and the light gone.   660

"And I remember all that day
    The barren bitter wind
Without, and the sea's moaning there
That I first moaned with unaware,
And when I knew, shook down my hair.

"Few followed us or faced our flight:
    Once only I could hear,
Far in the front, loud scornful words,
And cries I knew of hostile lords,
And crash of spears and grind of swords.   670

"It was soon ended. On that day
    Before the light had changed

We reached our refuge; miles of rock
Bulwarked for war; whose strength might mock
Sky, sea, or man, to storm or shock.

"Listless and feebly conscious, I
    Lay far within the night
Awake. The many pains incurred
That day, — the whole, said, seen or heard, —
Stayed by in me as things deferred.   680

"Not long. At dawn I slept. In dreams
    All was passed through afresh
From end to end. As the morn heaved
Towards noon, I, waking sore aggrieved,
That I might die, cursed God, and lived.

"Many days went, and I saw none
    Except my women. They
Calmed their wan faces, loving me;
And when they wept, lest I should see,
Would chant a desolate melody.   690

"Panic unthreatened shook my blood
    Each sunset, all the slow
Subsiding of the turbid light.
I would rise, sister, as I might,
And bathe my forehead through the night

"To elude madness. The stark walls
    Made chill the mirk: and when
We oped our curtains, to resume
Sun-sickness after long sick gloom,
The withering sea-wind walked the room.   700

"Through the gaunt windows the great gales
    Bore in the tattered clumps
Of waif-weed and the tamarisk-boughs;
And sea-mews, 'mid the storm's carouse,
Were flung, wild-clamouring, in the house.

"My hounds I had not; and my hawk,
    Which they had saved for me,
Wanting the sun and rain to beat
His wings, soon lay with gathered feet;
And my flowers faded, lacking heat.   710

"Such still were griefs: for grief was still
    A separate sense, untouched
Of that despair which had become
My life. Great anguish could benumb
My soul, — my heart was quarrelsome.

"Time crept. Upon a day at length
    My kinsfolk sat with me:
That which they asked was bare and plain:
I answered: the whole bitter strain
Was again said, and heard again.   **720**

"Fierce Raoul snached his sword, and turned
    The point against my breast.
I bared it, smiling: 'To the heart
Strike home,' I said; 'another dart
Wreaks hourly there a deadlier smart.'

" 'Twas then my sire struck down the sword,
    And said with shaken lips:
'She from whom all of you receive
Your life, so smiled; and I forgive.'
Thus, for my mother's sake, I live.   **730**

"But I, a mother even as she,
    Turned shuddering to the wall:
For I said: 'Great God! and what would I do,
When to the sword, with the thing I knew,
I offered not one life but two!'

"Then I fell back from them, and lay
    Outwearied. My tired sense
Soon filmed and settled, and like stone
I slept; till something made me moan,
And I woke up at night alone.   **740**

"I woke at midnight, cold and dazed;
    Because I found myself
Seated upright, with bosom bare,
Upon my bed, combing my hair,
Ready to go, I knew not where.

"It dawned light day, — the last of those
    Long months of longing days.
That noon, the change was wrought on me

In somewise, — nought to hear or see, —
Only a trance and agony." 750

The bride's voice failed her, from no will
    To pause. The bridesmaid leaned,
And where the window-panes were white,
Looked for the day: she knew not quite
If there were either day or night.

It seemed to Aloÿse that the whole
    Day's weight lay back on her
Like lead. The hours that did remain
Beat their dry wings upon her brain
Once in mid-flight, and passed again. 760

There hung a cage of burnt perfumes
    In the recess: but these,
For some hours, weak against the sun,
Had simmered in white ash. From One
The second quarter was begun.

They had not heard the stroke. The air,
    Though altered with no wind,
Breathed now by pauses, so to say:
Each breath was time that went away, —
Each pause a minute of the day. 770

I' the almonry, the almoner,
    Hard by, had just dispensed
Church-dole and march-dole. High and wide
Now rose the shout of thanks, which cried
On God that He should bless the bride.

Its echo thrilled within their feet,
    And in the furthest rooms
Was heard, where maidens flushed and gay
Wove with stooped necks the wreaths alway
Fair for the virgin's marriage-day. 780

The mother leaned along, in thought
    After her child; till tears,
Bitter, not like a wedded girl's,
Fell down her breast along her curls,
And ran in the close work of pearls.

The speech ached at her heart. She said:
    "Sweet Mary, do thou plead
This hour with thy most blessed Son
To let these shameful words atone,
That I may die when I have done."   790

The thought ached at her soul. Yet now: —
    "Itself — that life" (she said,)
"Out of my weary life — when sense
Unclosed, was gone. What evil men's
Most evil hands had borne it thence

"I knew, and cursed them. Still in sleep
    I have my child; and pray
To know if it indeed appear
As in my dream's perpetual sphere,
That I — death reached — may seek it there.   800

"Sleeping, I wept; though until dark
    A fever dried mine eyes
Kept open; save when a tear might
Be forced from the mere ache of sight.
And I nursed hatred day and night.

"Aye, and I sought revenge by spells;
    And vainly many a time
Have laid my face in the lap
Of a wise woman, and heard clap
Her thunder, the fiend's juggling trap.   810

"At length I feared to curse them, lest
    From evil lips the curse
Should be a blessing; and would sit
Rocking myself and stifling it
With babbled jargon of no wit.

"But this was not at first: the days
    And weeks made frenzied months
Before this came. My curses, pil'd
Then with each hour unreconcil'd,
Still wait for those who took my child."   820

She stopped, grown fainter. "Amelotte,
    Surely," she said, "this sun

Sheds judgment-fire from the fierce south:
It does not let me breathe: the drouth
Is like sand spread within my mouth."

The bridesmaid rose. I' the outer glare
    Gleamed her pale cheeks, and eyes
Sore troubled; and aweary weigh'd
Her brows just lifted out of shade;
And the light jarred within her head.   830

'Mid flowers fair-heaped there stood a bowl
    With water. She therein
Through edying bubbles slid a cup,
And offered it, being risen up,
Close to her sister's mouth, to sup.

The freshness dwelt upon her sense,
    Yet did not the bride drink;
But she dipped in her hand anon
And cooled her temples; and all wan
With lids that held their ache, went on.   840

"Through those dark watches of my woe,
    Time, an ill plant, had waxed
Apace. That year was finished. Dumb
And blind, life's wheel with earth's had come
Whirled round: and we might seek our home.

"Our wealth was rendered back, with wealth
    Snatched from our foes. The house
Had more than its old strength and fame:
But still 'neath the fair outward claim
I rankled, — a fierce core of shame.   850

"It chilled me from their eyes and lips
    Upon a night of those
First days of triumph, as I gazed
Listless and sick, or scarcely raised
My face to mark the sports they praised.

"The endless changes of the dance
    Bewildered me: the tones
Of lute and cithern struggled tow'rds
Some sense; and still in the last chords
The music seemed to sing wild words.   860

"My shame possessed me in the light
    And pageant, till I swooned.
But from that hour I put my shame
From me, and cast it over them
By God's command and in God's name

"For my child's bitter sake. O thou
    Once felt against my heart
With longing of the eyes, — a pain
Since to my heart for ever, — then
Beheld not, and not felt again!"   **870**

She scarcely paused, continuing: —
    "That year drooped weak in March;
And April, finding the streams dry,
Choked, with no rain, in dust: the sky
Shall not be fainter this July.

"Men sickened; beasts lay without strength;
    The year died in the land.
But I, already desolate,
Said merely, sitting down to wait, —
'The seasons change and Time wears late.'   **880**

"For I had my hard secret told,
    In secret, to a priest;
With him I communed; and he said
The world's soul, for its sins, was sped,
And the sun's courses numberèd.

"The year slid like a corpse afloat:
    None trafficked, — who had bread
Did eat. That year our legions, come
Thinned from the place of war, at home
Found busier death, more burdensome.   **890**

"Tidings and rumours came with them,
    The first for months. The chiefs
Sat daily at our board, and in
Their speech were names of friend and kin:
One day they spoke of Urscelyn.

"The words were light, among the rest:
    Quick glance my brothers sent
To sift the speech; and I, struck through,

Sat sick and giddy in full view:
Yet did not gaze, so many knew.   900

"Because in the beginning, much
        Had caught abroad, through them
That heard my clamour on the coast:
But two were hanged; and then the most
Held silence wisdom, as thou know'st.

"That year the convent yielded thee
        Back to our home; and thou
Then knew'st not how I shuddered cold
To kiss thee, seeming to enfold
To my changed heart myself of old.   910

"Then there was showing thee the house,
        So many rooms and doors;
Thinking the while how thou would'st start
If once I flung the doors apart
Of one dull chamber in my heart.

"And yet I longed to open it;
        And often in that year
Of plague and want, when side by side
We've knelt to pray with them that died,
My prayer was, 'Show her what I hide!' "   920
[1848, 1859]   [1881]

THE HOUSE OF LIFE:

A SONNET-SEQUENCE

A Sonnet is a moment's monument, —
  Memorial from the Soul's eternity
  To one dead deathless hour. Look that it be,
Whether for lustral rite or dire portent,
Of its own arduous fulness reverent:
  Carve it in ivory or in ebony,
    As Day or Night may rule; and let Time see
Its flowering crest impearled and orient.

A Sonnet is a coin: its face reveals
  The soul, — its converse, to what Power 't is due: —   **10**
Whether for tribute to the august appeals
  Of Life, or dower in Love's high retinue,
It serve; or, 'mid the dark wharf's cavernous breath,
In Charon's palm it pay the toll to Death.
[1880]   [1881]

PART I

⇘ *Youth and Change* ⇙

Love brings everything unto Being

SONNET I

LOVE ENTHRONED

I MARKED all kindred Powers the heart finds fair: —
  Truth, with awed lips; and Hope, with eyes upcast;
  And Fame, whose loud wings fan the ashen Past
To signal-fires, Oblivion's flight to scare;
  And Youth, with still some single golden hair
  Unto his shoulder clinging, since the last
  Embrace wherein two sweet arms held him fast;
And Life, still wreathing flowers for Death to wear.

Love's throne was not with these; but far above
    All passionate wind of welcome and farewell   10
He sat in breathless bowers they dream not of;
    Though Truth foreknow Love's heart, and Hope foretell,
    And Fame be for Love's sake desirable,
And Youth be dear, and Life be sweet to Love.
[1871]   [1881]

SONNET II

BRIDAL BIRTH

As when desire, long darkling, dawns, and first
    The mother looks upon the newborn child,
    Even so my Lady stood at gaze and smiled
When her soul knew at length the Love it nurs'd.
Born with her life, creature of poignant thirst
    And exquisite hunger, at her heart Love lay
    Quickening in darkness, till a voice that day
Cried on him, and the bonds of birth were burst.

Now, shadowed by his wings, our faces yearn
    Together, as his full-grown feet now range   10
    The grove, and his warm hands our couch prepare:
Till to his song our bodiless souls in turn
    Be born his children, when Death's nuptial change
    Leaves us for light the halo of his hair.
[1869]   [1870]

SONNET III

LOVE'S TESTAMENT

O THOU who at Love's hour ecstatically
    Unto my heart dost ever more present,
    Clothed with his fire, thy heart his testament;
Whom I have neared and felt thy breath to be
The inmost incense of his sanctuary;
    Who without speech hast owned him, and, intent
    Upon his will, thy life with mine hast blent,
And murmured, "I am thine, thou 'rt one with me!"

O what from thee the grace, to me the prize,
 And what to Love the glory, — when the whole   10
  Of the deep stair thou tread'st to the dim shoal
And weary water of the place of sighs,
And there dost work deliverance, as thine eyes
 Draw up my prisoned spirit to thy soul!
[1869]   [1870]

SONNET IV

LOVESIGHT

WHEN do I see thee most, beloved one?
 When in the light the spirits of mine eyes
 Before thy face, their altar, solemnize
The worship of that Love through thee made known?
Or when in the dusk hours, (we two alone,)
 Close-kissed and eloquent of still replies
 Thy twilight-hidden glimmering visage lies,
And my soul only sees thy soul its own?

O love, my love! if I no more should see
Thyself, nor on the earth the shadow of thee,   10
 Nor image of thine eyes in any spring, —
How then should sound upon Life's darkening slope
The ground-whirl of the perished leaves of Hope,
 The wind of Death's imperishable wing?
[1869]   [1870]

SONNET V

HEART'S HOPE

BY what word's power, the key of paths untrod,
 Shall I the difficult deeps of Love explore,
 Till parted waves of Song yield up the shore
Even as that sea which Israel crossed dryshod?
For lo! in some poor rhythmic period,
 Lady, I fain would tell how evermore
 Thy soul I know not from thy body, nor
Thee from myself, neither our love from God.

Yea, in God's name, and Love's, and thine, would I
  Draw from one loving heart such evidence   10
As to all hearts all things shall signify;
  Tender as dawn's first hill-fire, and intense
    As instantaneous penetrating sense,
In Spring's birth-hour, of other Springs gone by.
[1871]   [1881]

SONNET VI

THE KISS

WHAT smouldering senses in death's sick delay
  Or seizure of malign vicissitude
  Can rob this body of honour, or denude
This soul of wedding-raiment worn to-day?
For lo! even now my lady's lips did play
  With these my lips such consonant interlude
  As laurelled Orpheus longed for when he wooed
The half-drawn hungering face with that last lay.

I was a child beneath her touch, — a man
  When breast to breast we clung, even I and she, —   10
  A spirit when her spirit looked through me, —
A god when all our life-breath met to fan
Our life-blood, till love's emulous ardors ran,
  Fire within fire, desire in deity.
[1869]   [1870]

SONNET VI*a*

NUPTIAL SLEEP

AT length their long kiss severed, with sweet smart:
  And as the last slow sudden drops are shed
  From sparkling eaves when all the storm has fled,
So singly flagged the pulses of each heart.
Their bosoms sundered, with the opening start
  Of married flowers to either side outspread
  From the knit stem; yet still their mouths, burnt red,
Fawned on each other where they lay apart.

Sleep sank them lower than the tide of dreams,
    And their dreams watched them sink, and slid away.   10
Slowly their souls swam up again, through gleams
    Of watered light and dull drowned waifs of day;
Till from some wonder of new woods and streams
    He woke, and wondered more: for there she lay.

[1869]   [1870]

SONNET VII

SUPREME SURRENDER

To all the spirits of Love that wander by
    Along his love-sown harvest-field of sleep
    My lady lies apparent; and the deep
Calls to the deep; and no man sees but I.
The bliss so long afar, at length so nigh,
    Rests there attained. Methinks proud Love must weep
    When Fate's control doth from his harvest reap
The sacred hour for which the years did sigh.

First touched, the hand now warm around my neck
    Taught memory long to mock desire: and lo!   10
    Across my breast the abandoned hair doth flow,
Where one shorn tress long stirred the longing ache:
And next the heart that trembled for its sake
    Lies the queen-heart in sovereign overthrow.

[1870]   [1870]

SONNET VIII

LOVE'S LOVERS

Some ladies love the jewels in Love's zone,
    And gold-tipped darts he hath for painless play
    In idle scornful hours he flings away;
And some that listen to his lute's soft tone
Do love to vaunt the silver praise their own;
    Some prize his blindfold sight; and there be they
    Who kissed his wings which brought him yesterday
And thank his wings to-day that he is flown.

My lady only loves the heart of Love:
   Therefore Love's heart, my lady, hath for thee   **10**
   His bower of unimagined flower and tree:
There kneels he now, and all-anhungered of
Thine eyes gray-lit in shadowing hair above,
   Seals with thy mouth his immortality.
[1869]   [1870]

SONNET IX

PASSION AND WORSHIP

ONE flame-winged brought a white-winged harp-player
   Even where my lady and I lay all alone;
   Saying: "Behold, this minstrel is unknown;
Bid him depart, for I am minstrel here:
Only my strains are to Love's dear ones dear."
   Then said I: "Through thine hautboy's rapturous tone
   Unto my lady still this harp makes moan,
And still she deems the cadence deep and clear."

Then said my lady: "Thou art Passion of Love,
   And this Love's Worship: both he plights to me.   **10**
   Thy mastering music walks the sunlit sea:
But where wan water trembles in the grove
And the wan moon is all the light thereof,
   This harp still makes my name its voluntary."
[1870]   [1870]

SONNET X

THE PORTRAIT

O LORD of all compassionate control,
   O Love! let this my lady's picture glow
   Under my hand to praise her name, and show
Even of her inner self the perfect whole:
That he who seeks her beauty's furthest goal,
   Beyond the light that the sweet glances throw
   And refluent wave of the sweet smile, may know
The very sky and sea-line of her soul.

heaven's bourne

Lo! it is done. Above the enthroning throat
   The mouth's mould testifies of voice and kiss,   10
     The shadowed eyes remember and foresee.
Her face is made her shrine. Let all men note
   That in all years (O Love, thy gift is this!)
     They that would look on her must come to me.
[1868]   [1870]

look to creator / immortalizing

SONNET XI

THE LOVE-LETTER

Warmed by her hand and shadowed by her hair
   As close she leaned and poured her heart through thee,
   Whereof the articulate throbs accompany
The smooth black stream that makes thy whiteness fair, —
Sweet fluttering sheet, even of her breath aware, —
   Oh let thy silent song disclose to me
   That soul wherewith her lips and eyes agree
Like married music in Love's answering air.

Fain had I watched her when, at some fond thought,
   Her bosom to the writing closelier press'd,   10
   And her breast's secrets peered into her breast;
When, through eyes raised an instant, her soul sought
My soul, and from the sudden confluence caught
   The words that made her love the loveliest.
[1870]   [1870]

SONNET XII

THE LOVERS' WALK

Sweet twining hedgeflowers wind-stirred in no wise
   On this June day; and hand that clings in hand: —
   Still glades; and meeting faces scarcely fann'd: —
An osier-odoured stream that draws the skies
Deep to its heart; and mirrored eyes in eyes: —
   Fresh hourly wonder o'er the Summer land
   Of light and cloud; and two souls softly spann'd
With one o'erarching heaven of smiles and sighs: —

Even such their path, whose bodies lean unto
   Each other's visible sweetness amorously, —   10
   Whose passionate hearts lean by Love's high decree
Together on his heart for ever true,
As the cloud-foaming firmamental blue
   Rests on the blue line of a foamless sea.
[1871]   [1881]

SONNET XIII

YOUTH'S ANTIPHONY

PRATTLE

"I LOVE you, sweet: how can you ever learn
   How much I love you?" "You I love even so,
   And so I learn it." "Sweet, you cannot know
How fair you are." "If fair enough to earn
Your love, so much is all my love's concern."
   "My love grows hourly, sweet." "Mine too doth grow,
   Yet love seemed full so many hours ago!"
Thus lovers speak, till kisses claim their turn.

Ah! happy they to whom such words as these
   In youth have served for speech the whole day long,   10
   Hour after hour, remote from the world's throng,
Work, contest, fame, all life's confederate pleas, —
What while Love breathed in sighs and silences
   Through two blent souls one rapturous undersong.
[1871]   [1881]

SONNET XIV

YOUTH'S SPRING-TRIBUTE

ON this sweet bank your head thrice sweet and dear
   I lay, and spread your hair on either side,
   And see the newborn woodflowers bashful-eyed
Look through the golden tresses here and there.
On these debateable borders of the year
   Spring's foot half falters; scarce she yet may know
   The leafless blackthorn-blossom from the snow;
And through her bowers the wind's way still is clear.

But April's sun strikes down the glades to-day;
   So shut your eyes upturned, and feel my kiss   10
Creep, as the Spring now thrills through every spray,
    Up your warm throat to your warm lips: for this
    Is even the hour of Love's sworn suitservice,
With whom cold hearts are counted castaway.
[1870]   [1881]

SONNET XV

THE BIRTH-BOND

HAVE you not noted, in some family
   Where two were born of a first marriage-bed,
   How still they own their gracious bond, though fed
And nursed on the forgotten breast and knee? —
How to their father's children they shall be
   In act and thought of one goodwill; but each
   Shall for the other have, in silence speech,
And in a word complete community?

Even so, when first I saw you, seemed it, love,
   That among souls allied to mine was yet   10
One nearer kindred than life hinted of.
   O born with me somewhere that men forget,
   And though in years of sight and sound unmet,
Known for my soul's birth-partner well enough!
[1854]   [1870]

SONNET XVI

A DAY OF LOVE

THOSE envied places which do know her well,
   And are so scornful of this lonely place,
   Even now for once are emptied of her grace:
Nowhere but here she is: and while Love's spell
From his predominant presence doth compel
   All alien hours, an outworn populace,
   The hours of Love fill full the echoing space
With sweet confederate music favourable.

Now many memories make solicitous
   The delicate love-lines of her mouth, till, lit   **10**
   With quivering fire, the words take wing from it;
As here between our kisses we sit thus
   Speaking of things remembered, and so sit
Speechless while things forgotten call to us.
[1870]   [1870]

SONNET XVII

BEAUTY'S PAGEANT

WHAT dawn-pulse at the heart of heaven, or last
   Incarnate flower of culminating day, —
   What marshalled marvels on the skirts of May,
Or song full-quired, sweet June's encomiast;
What glory of change by Nature's hand amass'd
   Can vie with all those moods of varying grace
   Which o'er one loveliest woman's form and face
Within this hour, within this room, have pass'd?

Love's very vesture and elect disguise
   Was each fine movement, — wonder new begot   **10**
   Of lily or swan or swan-stemmed galiot;
Joy to his sight who now the sadlier sighs,
Parted again; and sorrow yet for eyes
   Unborn, that read these words and saw her not.
[1871]   [1881]

SONNET XVIII

GENIUS IN BEAUTY

BEAUTY like hers is genius. Not the call
   Of Homer's or of Dante's heart sublime, —
   Not Michael's hand furrowing the zones of time, —
Is more with compassed mysteries musical;
Nay, not in Spring's or Summer's sweet footfall
   More gathered gifts exuberant Life bequeaths
   Than doth this sovereign face, whose love-spell breathes
Even from its shadowed contour on the wall.

As many men are poets in their youth,
　　But for one sweet-strung soul the wires prolong　　　　10
　　Even through all change the indomitable song;
So in likewise the envenomed years, whose tooth
Rends shallower grace with ruin void of ruth,
　　Upon this beauty's power shall wreak no wrong.
[1871]　　　　　　　　　　　　　　　[1881]

SONNET XIX

SILENT NOON

YOUR hands lie open in the long fresh grass, —
　　The finger-points look through like rosy blooms:
　　Your eyes smile peace. The pasture gleams and glooms
'Neath billowing skies that scatter and amass.
All round our nest, far as the eye can pass,
　　Are golden kingcup-fields with silver edge
　　Where the cow-parsley skirts the hawthorn-hedge.
'T is visible silence, still as the hour-glass.

Deep in the sun-searched growths the dragon-fly
Hangs like a blue thread loosened from the sky: —　　　　10
　　So this wing'd hour is dropt to us from above.
Oh! clasp we to our hearts, for deathless dower,
This close-companioned inarticulate hour
　　When twofold silence was the song of love.
[1871]　　　　　　　　　　　　　　　[1881]

SONNET XX

GRACIOUS MOONLIGHT

EVEN as the moon grows queenlier in mid-space
　　When the sky darkens, and her cloud-rapt car
　　Thrills with intenser radiance from afar, —
So lambent, lady, beams thy sovereign grace
When the drear soul desires thee. Of that face
　　What shall be said, — which, like a governing star,
　　Gathers and garners from all things that are
Their silent penetrative loveliness?

O'er water-daisies and wild waifs of Spring,
　There where the iris rears its gold-crowned sheaf　　　**10**
　With flowering rush and sceptred arrow-leaf,
So have I marked Queen Dian, in bright ring
Of cloud above and wave below, take wing
　And chase night's gloom, as thou the spirit's grief.
[1871]　　　　　　　　　　　　　　　　　[1881]

SONNET XXI

LOVE-SWEETNESS

SWEET dimness of her loosened hair's downfall
　About thy face; her sweet hands round thy head
　In gracious fostering union garlanded;
Her tremulous smiles; her glances' sweet recall
Of love; her murmuring sighs memorial;
　Her mouth's culled sweetness by thy kisses shed
　On cheeks and neck and eyelids, and so led
Back to her mouth which answers there for all: —

What sweeter than these things, except the thing
　In lacking which all these would lose their sweet: —　　　**10**
　The confident heart's still fervour: the swift beat
And soft subsidence of the spirit's wing,
Then when it feels, in cloud-girt wayfaring,
　The breath of kindred plumes against its feet?
[1870]　　　　　　　　　　　　　　　　　[1870]

SONNET XXII

HEART'S HAVEN

SOMETIMES she is a child within mine arms,
　Cowering beneath dark wings that love must chase, —
　With still tears showering and averted face,
Inexplicably filled with faint alarms:
And oft from mine own spirit's hurtling harms
　I crave the refuge of her deep embrace, —
　Against all ills the fortified strong place
And sweet reserve of sovereign counter-charms.

And Love, our light at night and shade at noon,
  Lulls us to rest with songs, and turns away   10
  All shafts of shelterless tumultuous day.
Like the moon's growth, his face gleams through his tune;
And as soft waters warble to the moon,
  Our answering spirits chime one roundelay.
[1871]   [1881]

SONNET XXIII

LOVE'S BAUBLES

I STOOD where Love in brimming armfuls bore
  Slight wanton flowers and foolish toys of fruit:
  And round him ladies thronged in warm pursuit,
Fingered and lipped and proffered the strange store.
And from one hand the petal and the core
  Savoured of sleep; and cluster and curled shoot
  Seemed from another hand like shame's salute, —
Gifts that I felt my cheek was blushing for.

At last Love bade my Lady give the same:
  And as I looked, the dew was light thereon;   10
  And as I took them, at her touch they shone
With inmost heaven-hue of the heart of flame.
  And then Love said: "Lo! when the hand is hers,
  Follies of love are love's true ministers."
[1870]   [1870]

SONNET XXIV

PRIDE OF YOUTH

EVEN as a child, of sorrow that we give
  The dead, but little in his heart can find,
  Since without need of thought to his clear mind
Their turn it is to die and his to live: —
Even so the winged New Love smiles to receive
  Along his eddying plumes the auroral wind,
  Nor, forward glorying, casts one look behind
Where night-rack shrouds the Old Love fugitive.

There is a change in every hour's recall,
   And the last cowslip in the fields we see   **10**
   On the same day with the first corn-poppy.
Alas for hourly change! Alas for all
The loves that from his hand proud Youth lets fall,
   Even as the beads of a told rosary!

[1880]   [*1881;* 1881]

SONNET XXV

WINGED HOURS

EACH hour until we meet is as a bird
   That wings from far his gradual way along
   The rustling covert of my soul, — his song
Still loudlier trilled through leaves more deeply stirr'd:
But at the hour of meeting, a clear word
   Is every note he sings, in Love's own tongue;
   Yet, Love, thou know'st the sweet strain suffers wrong,
Full oft through our contending joys unheard.

What of that hour at last, when for her sake
   No wing may fly to me nor song may flow;   **10**
   When, wandering round my life unleaved, I know
The bloodied feathers scattered in the brake,
   And think how she, far from me, with like eyes
   Sees through the untuneful bough the wingless skies?

[1869]   [*1869;* 1870]

SONNET XXVI

MID-RAPTURE

THOU lovely and beloved, thou my love;
   Whose kiss seems still the first; whose summoning eyes,
   Even now, as for our love-world's new sunrise,
Shed very dawn; whose voice, attuned above
All modulation of the deep-bowered dove,
   Is like a hand laid softly on the soul;
   Whose hand is like a sweet voice to control
Those worn tired brows it hath the keeping of: —

What word can answer to thy word, — what gaze
  To thine, which now absorbs within its sphere   10
  My worshipping face, till I am mirrored there
Light-circled in a heaven of deep-drawn rays?
  What clasp, what kiss mine inmost heart can prove,
  O lovely and beloved, O my love?
[1871]   [1881]

SONNET XXVII

HEART'S COMPASS

SOMETIMES thou seem'st not as thyself alone,
  But as the meaning of all things that are;
  A breathless wonder, shadowing forth afar
Some heavenly solstice hushed and halcyon;
  Whose unstirred lips are music's visible tone;
    Whose eyes the sun-gate of the soul unbar,
    Being of its furthest fires oracular; —
The evident heart of all life sown and mown.

Even such Love is; and is not thy name Love?
  Yea, by thy hand the Love-god rends apart   10
  All gathering clouds of Night's ambiguous art;
Flings them far down, and sets thine eyes above;
And simply, as some gage of flower or glove,
  Stakes with a smile the world against thy heart.
[1871]   [1881]

SONNET XXVIII

SOUL-LIGHT

WHAT other woman could be loved like you,
  Or how of you should love possess his fill?
  After the fulness of all rapture, still, —
As at the end of some deep avenue
A tender glamour of day, — there comes to view
  Far in your eyes a yet more hungering thrill, —
  Such fire as Love's soul-winnowing hands distil
Even from his inmost ark of light and dew.

And as the traveller triumphs with the sun,
　Glorying in heat's mid-height, yet startide brings　　　　**10**
　Wonder new-born, and still fresh transport springs
From limpid lambent hours of day begun; —
　Even so, through eyes and voice, your soul doth move
　My soul with changeful light of infinite love.
[1871]　　　　　　　　　　　　　　　　　　[1881]

SONNET XXIX

THE MOONSTAR

Lady, I thank thee for thy loveliness,
　Because my lady is more lovely still.
　Glorying I gaze, and yield with glad goodwill
To thee thy tribute; by whose sweet-spun dress
Of delicate life Love labors to assess
　My lady's absolute queendom; saying, "Lo!
　How high this beauty is, which yet doth show
But as that beauty's sovereign votaress."

Lady, I saw thee with her, side by side;
　And as, when night's fair fires their queen surround,　　**10**
An emulous star too near the moon will ride, —
　Even so thy rays within her luminous bound
　Were traced no more; and by the light so drown'd,
Lady, not thou but she was glorified.
[1871]　　　　　　　　　　　　　　　　　　[1881]

SONNET XXX

LAST FIRE

Love, through your spirit and mine what summer eve
　Now glows with glory of all things possess'd,
　Since this day's sun of rapture filled the west
And the light sweetened as the fire took leave?
Awhile now softlier let your bosom heave,
　As in Love's harbour, even that loving breast,
　All care takes refuge while we sink to rest,
And mutual dreams the bygone bliss retrieve.

Many the days that Winter keeps in store,
   Sunless throughout, or whose brief sun-glimpses   10
   Scarce shed the heaped snow through the naked trees.
This day at least was Summer's paramour,
Sun-coloured to the imperishable core
   With sweet well-being of love and full heart's ease.
[1871]   [1881]

SONNET XXXI

HER GIFTS

HIGH grace, the dower of queens; and therewithal
   Some wood-born wonder's sweet simplicity;
   A glance like water brimming with the sky
Or hyacinth-light where forest-shadows fall;
Such thrilling pallor of cheek as doth enthral
   The heart; a mouth whose passionate forms imply
   All music and all silence held thereby;
Deep golden locks, her sovereign coronal;
A round reared neck, meet column of Love's shrine
   To cling to when the heart takes sanctuary;   10
   Hands which for ever at Love's bidding be,
And soft-stirred feet still answering to his sign: —
   These are her gifts, as tongue may tell them o'er.
   Breathe low her name, my soul; for that means more.
[1871]   [1881]

SONNET XXXII

EQUAL TROTH

NOT by one measure mayst thou mete our love;
   For how should I be loved as I love thee? —
   I, graceless, joyless, lacking absolutely
All gifts that with thy queenship best behove; —
Thou, throned in every heart's elect alcove,
   And crowned with garlands culled from every tree,
   Which for no head but thine, by Love's decree,
All beauties and all mysteries interwove.

But here thine eyes and lips yield soft rebuke: —
    "Then only," (say'st thou) "could I love thee less,   10
    When thou couldst doubt my love's equality."
Peace, sweet! If not to sum but worth we look, —
    Thy heart's transcendence, not my heart's excess, —
    Then more a thousandfold thou lov'st than I.
[1871]   [1881]

SONNET XXXIII

VENUS VICTRIX

COULD Juno's self more sovereign presence wear
    Than thou, 'mid other ladies throned in grace? —
    Or Pallas, when thou bend'st with soul-stilled face
O'er poet's page gold-shadowed in thy hair?
Dost thou than Venus seem less heavenly fair
    When o'er the sea of love's tumultuous trance
    Hovers thy smile, and mingles with thy glance
That sweet voice like the last wave murmuring there?

Before such triune loveliness divine
    Awestruck I ask, which goddess here most claims   10
The prize that, howsoe'er adjudged, is thine?
    Then Love breathes low the sweetest of thy names;
And Venus Victrix to my heart doth bring
Herself, the Helen of her guerdoning.
[1871]   [1881]

SONNET XXXIV

THE DARK GLASS

NOT I myself know all my love for thee:
    How should I reach so far, who cannot weigh
    To-morrow's dower by gage of yesterday?
Shall birth and death, and all dark names that be
As doors and windows bared to some loud sea,
    Lash deaf mine ears and blind my face with spray;
    And shall my sense pierce love, — the last relay
And ultimate outpost of eternity?

Lo! what am I to Love, the lord of all? *love as person*
   One murmuring shell he gathers from the sand, —   **10**
   One little heart-flame sheltered in his hand. *him*
Yet through thine eyes he grants me clearest call   *reflect, penetrate*
And veriest touch of powers primordial
   That any hour-girt life may understand.
[1871]   [1881]

SONNET XXXV

THE LAMP'S SHRINE

SOMETIMES I fain would find in thee some fault,
   That I might love thee still in spite of it:
   Yet how should our Lord Love curtail one whit
Thy perfect praise whom most he would exalt?
Alas! he can but make my heart's low vault
   Even in men's sight unworthier, being lit
   By thee, who thereby show'st more exquisite
Like fiery chrysoprase in deep basalt.

Yet will I nowise shrink; but at Love's shrine
   Myself within the beams his brow doth dart   **10**
   Will set the flashing jewel of thy heart
In that dull chamber where it deigns to shine:
   For lo! in honour of thine excellencies
   My heart takes pride to show how poor it is.
[1871]   [1881]

SONNET XXXVI

LIFE-IN-LOVE

NOT in thy body is thy life at all,
   But in this lady's lips and hands and eyes;
   Through these she yields thee life that vivifies
What else were sorrow's servant and death's thrall.
Look on thyself without her, and recall
   The waste remembrance and forlorn surmise
   That lived but in a dead-drawn breath of sighs
O'er vanished hours and hours eventual.

Even so much life hath the poor tress of hair
   Which, stored apart, is all love hath to show   **10**
   For heart-beats and for fire-heats long ago;
Even so much life endures unknown, even where,
   'Mid change the changeless night environeth,
   Lies all that golden hair undimmed in death.
[1870]   [1870]

SONNET XXXVII

THE LOVE-MOON

"WHEN that dead face, bowered in the furthest years,
   Which once was all the life years held for thee,
   Can now scarce bid the tides of memory
Cast on thy soul a little spray of tears, —
How canst thou gaze into these eyes of hers
   Whom now thy heart delights in, and not see
   Within each orb Love's philtred euphrasy
Make them of buried troth remembrancers?"

"Nay, pitiful Love, nay, loving Pity! Well
   Thou knowest that in these twain I have confess'd   **10**
Two very voices of thy summoning bell.
   Nay, Master, shall not Death make manifest
In these the culminant changes which approve
The love-moon that must light my soul to Love?"
[1869]   [1870]

SONNET XXXVIII

THE MORROW'S MESSAGE

"THOU Ghost," I said, "and is thy name To-day? —
   Yesterday's son, with such an abject brow! —
   And can To-morrow be more pale than thou?"
While yet I spoke, the silence answered: "Yea,
Henceforth our issue is all grieved and gray,
   And each beforehand makes such poor avow
   As of old leaves beneath the budding bough
Or night-drift that the sundawn shreds away."

Then cried I: "Mother of many malisons,
   O Earth, receive me to thy dusty bed!"   10
  But therewithal the tremulous silence said: —
"Lo! Love yet bids thy lady greet thee once: —
Yea, twice, — whereby thy life is still the sun's;
   And thrice, — whereby the shadow of death is dead."
[1869]   [1870]

SONNET XXXIX

SLEEPLESS DREAMS

GIRT in dark growths, yet glimmering with one star,
   O night desirous as the nights of youth!
   Why should my heart within thy spell, forsooth,
Now beat, as the bride's finger-pulses are
Quickened within the girdling golden bar?
   What wings are these that fan my pillow smooth?
   And why does Sleep, waved back by Joy and Ruth,
Tread softly round and gaze at me from far?

Nay, night deep-leaved! And would Love feign in thee
   Some shadowy palpitating grove that bears   10
   Rest for man's eyes and music for his ears?
O lonely night! art thou not known to me,
A thicket hung with masks of mockery
   And watered with the wasteful warmth of tears?
[1869]   [*1869;* 1870]

SONNET XL

SEVERED SELVES

Two separate divided silences,
   Which, brought together, would find loving voice;
   Two glances which together would rejoice
In love, now lost like stars beyond dark trees;
Two hands apart whose touch alone gives ease;
   Two bosoms which, heart-shrined with mutual flame,
   Would, meeting in one clasp, be made the same;
Two souls, the shores wave-mocked of sundering seas: —

Such are we now. Ah! may our hope forecast
  Indeed one hour again, when on this stream   **10**
  Of darkened love once more the light shall gleam? —
An hour how slow to come, how quickly past, —
Which blooms and fades, and only leaves at last,
  Faint as shed flowers, the attenuated dream.
[1871]   [1881]

SONNET XLI

THROUGH DEATH TO LOVE

LIKE labor-laden moonclouds faint to flee
  From winds that sweep the winter-bitten wold, —
  Like multiform circumfluence manifold
Of night's flood-tide, — like terrors that agree
Of hoarse-tongued fire and inarticulate sea, —
  Even such, within some glass dimmed by our breath,
  Our hearts discern wild images of Death,
Shadows and shoals that edge eternity.

Howbeit athwart Death's imminent shade doth soar
  One Power, than flow of stream or flight of dove   **10**
  Sweeter to glide around, to brood above.
Tell me, my heart, — what angel-greeted door *(Passover) saved*
Or threshold of wing-winnowed threshing-floor
  Hath guest fire-fledged as thine, whose lord is Love?
[1871]   [1881]

[handwritten margin note: Angel of Love greater than Death?]

SONNET XLII

HOPE OVERTAKEN

I DEEMED thy garments, O my Hope, were grey,
  So far I viewed thee. Now the space between
  Is passed at length; and garmented in green
Even as in days of yore thou stand'st to-day.
Ah God! and but for lingering dull dismay,
  On all that road our footsteps erst had been
  Even thus commingled, and our shadows seen
Blent on the hedgerows and the water-way.

O Hope of mine whose eyes are living love,
  No eyes but hers, — O Love and Hope the same! —   10
    Lean close to me, for now the sinking sun
That warmed our feet scarce gilds our hair above.
  O hers thy voice and very hers thy name!
    Alas, cling round me, for the day is done!
[1871]   [1881]

SONNET XLIII

LOVE AND HOPE

BLESS love and hope. Full many a withered year
  Whirled past us, eddying to its chill doomsday;
  And clasped together where the blown leaves lay
We long have knelt and wept full many a tear.
Yet lo! one hour at last, the Spring's compeer,
  Flutes softly to us from some green byeway:
  Those years, those tears are dead, but only they: —
Bless love and hope, true soul; for we are here.

Cling heart to heart; nor of this hour demand
  Whether in very truth, when we are dead,   10
  Our hearts shall wake to know Love's golden head
Sole sunshine of the imperishable land;
  Or but discern, through night's unfeatured scope,
  Scorn-fired at length the illusive eyes of Hope.
[1871]   [1881]

SONNET XLIV

CLOUD AND WIND

LOVE, should I fear death most for you or me?
  Yet if you die, can I not follow you,
  Forcing the straits of change? Alas! but who
Shall wrest a bond from night's inveteracy,
Ere yet my hazardous soul put forth, to be
  Her warrant against all her haste might rue? —
  Ah! in your eyes so reached what dumb adieu,
What unsunned gyres of waste eternity?

And if I die the first, shall death be then
    A lampless watchtower whence I see you weep? —   10
    Or (woe is me!) a bed wherein my sleep
Ne'er notes (as death's dear cup at last you drain),
The hour when you too learn that all is vain
    And that Hope sows what Love shall never reap?
[1871]   [1881]

SONNET XLV

SECRET PARTING

BECAUSE our talk was of the cloud-control
    And moon-track of the journeying face of Fate,
    Her tremulous kisses faltered at love's gate
And her eyes dreamed against a distant goal:
But soon, remembering her how brief the whole
    Of joy, which its own hours annihilate,
    Her set gaze gathered, thirstier than of late,
And as she kissed, her mouth became her soul.

Thence in what ways we wandered, and how strove
    To build with fire-tried vows the piteous home   10
    Which memory haunts and whither sleep may roam, —
They only know for whom the roof of Love
Is the still-seated secret of the grove,
    Nor spire may rise nor bell be heard therefrom.
[1869]   [1870]

SONNET XLVI

PARTED LOVE

WHAT shall be said of this embattled day
    And armed occupation of this night
    By all thy foes beleaguered, — now when sight
Nor sound denotes the loved one far away?
Of these thy vanquished hours what shalt thou say, —
    As every sense to which she dealt delight
    Now labours lonely o'er the stark noon-height
To reach the sunset's desolate disarray?

Stand still, fond fettered wretch! while Memory's art
   Parades the Past before thy face, and lures   10
   Thy spirit to her passionate portraitures:
Till the tempestuous tide-gates flung apart
Flood with wild will the hollows of thy heart,
   And thy heart rends thee, and thy body endures.
[1869]   [1870]

SONNET XLVII

BROKEN MUSIC

THE mother will not turn, who thinks she hears
   Her nursling's speech first grow articulate;
   But breathless with averted eyes elate
She sits, with open lips and open ears,
That it may call her twice. 'Mid doubts and fears
   Thus oft my soul has hearkened; till the song,
   A central moan for days, at length found tongue,
And the sweet music welled and the sweet tears.

But now, whatever while the soul is fain
   To list that wonted murmur, as it were   10
The speech-bound sea-shell's low importunate strain, —
   No breath of song, thy voice alone is there,
O bitterly beloved! and all her gain
   Is but the pang of unpermitted prayer.
[1869]   [*1869;* 1870]

SONNET XLVIII

DEATH-IN-LOVE

THERE came an image in Life's retinue
   That had Love's wings and bore his gonfalon:
   Fair was the web, and nobly wrought thereon,
O soul-sequestered face, thy form and hue!
Bewildering sounds, such as Spring wakens to,
   Shook in its folds; and through my heart its power
   Sped trackless as the immemorable hour
When birth's dark portal groaned and all was new.

But a veiled woman followed, and she caught
   The banner round its staff, to furl and cling, —   **10**
   Then plucked a feather from the bearer's wing
And held it to his lips that stirred it not,
   And said to me, "Behold, there is no breath:
   I and this Love are one, and I am Death."
[1869]   [1870]

SONNETS XLIX, L, LI, LII

WILLOWWOOD

I

I SAT with Love upon a woodside well,
   Leaning across the water, I and he;
   Nor ever did he speak nor looked at me,
But touched his lute wherein was audible
The certain secret thing he had to tell:
   Only our mirrored eyes met silently
   In the low wave; and that sound came to be
The passionate voice I knew; and my tears fell.

And at their fall, his eyes beneath grew hers;
And with his foot and with his wing-feathers   **10**
   He swept the spring that watered my heart's drouth.
Then the dark ripples spread to waving hair,
And as I stooped, her own lips rising there
   Bubbled with brimming kisses at my mouth.
[1868]   [*1869;* 1870]

II

AND now Love sang: but his was such a song,
   So meshed with half-remembrance hard to free,
   As souls disused in death's sterility
May sing when the new birthday tarries long.
And I was made aware of a dumb throng
   That stood aloof, one form by every tree,
   All mournful forms, for each was I or she,
The shades of those our days that had no tongue.

They looked on us, and knew us and were known;
   While fast together, alive from the abyss,   10
   Clung the soul-wrung implacable close kiss;
And pity of self through all made broken moan
Which said, "For once, for once, for once alone!"
   And still Love sang, and what he sang was this: —
[1868]   [*1869;* 1870]

III

"O ʏᴇ, all ye that walk in Willowwood,
   That walk with hollow faces burning white;
What fathom-depth of soul-struck widowhood,
   What long, what longer hours, one lifelong night,
Ere ye again, who so in vain have wooed
   Your last hope lost, who so in vain invite
Your lips to that their unforgotten food,
   Ere ye, ere ye again shall see the light!

Alas! the bitter banks in Willowwood,
   With tear-spurge wan, with blood-wort burning red: 10
Alas! if ever such a pillow could
   Steep deep the soul in sleep till she were dead, —
Better all life forget her than this thing,
That Willowwood should hold her wandering!"
[1868]   [*1869;* 1870]

last hope lost

IV

So sang he: and as meeting rose and rose
   Together cling through the wind's wellaway
   Nor change at once, yet near the end of day
The leaves drop loosened where the heart-stain glows,—
So when the song died did the kiss unclose;
   And her face fell back drowned, and was as grey
   As its grey eyes; and if it ever may
Meet mine again I know not if Love knows.

Only I know that I leaned low and drank
A long draught from the water where she sank,   10
   Her breath and all her tears and all her soul:
And as I leaned, I know I felt Love's face
Pressed on my neck with moan of pity and grace,
   Till both our heads were in his aureole.
[1868]   [*1869;* 1870]

(Halo consecrating Love in death

SONNET LIII

WITHOUT HER

WHAT of her glass without her? The blank grey
  There where the pool is blind of the moon's face.
  Her dress without her? The tossed empty space
Of cloud-rack whence the moon has passed away.
Her paths without her? Day's appointed sway
  Usurped by desolate night. Her pillowed place
  Without her? Tears, ah me! for love's good grace,
And cold forgetfulness of night or day.

What of the heart without her? Nay, poor heart,
  Of thee what word remains ere speech be still?   10
  A wayfarer by barren ways and chill,
Steep ways and weary, without her thou art,
Where the long cloud, the long wood's counterpart,
  Sheds doubled darkness up the labouring hill.
[1871]   [1881]

SONNET LIV

LOVE'S FATALITY

SWEET Love, — but oh! most dread Desire of Love
  Life-thwarted. Linked in gyves I saw them stand,
  Love shackled with Vain-longing, hand to hand:
And one was eyed as the blue vault above:
But hope tempestuous like a fire-cloud hove
  I' the other's gaze, even as in his whose wand
  Vainly all night with spell-wrought power has spann'd
The unyielding caves of some deep treasure-trove.

Also his lips, two writhen flakes of flame,
  Made moan: "Alas O Love, thus leashed with me!   10
  Wing-footed thou, wing-shouldered, once born free:
And I, thy cowering self, in chains grown tame, —
Bound to thy body and soul, named with thy name, —
  Life's iron heart, even Love's Fatality."
[1871]   [1881]

SONNET LV

STILLBORN LOVE

THE hour which might have been yet might not be,
    Which man's and woman's heart conceived and bore
    Yet whereof life was barren, — on what shore
Bides it the breaking of Time's weary sea?
Bondchild of all consummate joys set free,
    It somewhere sighs and serves, and mute before
    The house of Love, hears through the echoing door
His hours elect in choral consonancy.

But lo! what wedded souls now hand in hand
Together tread at last the immortal strand   10
    With eyes where burning memory lights love home?
Lo! how the little outcast hour has turned
And leaped to them and in their faces yearned: —
    "I am your child: O parents, ye have come!"
[1869]   [1870]

SONNETS LVI, LVII, LVIII

TRUE WOMAN

i. *Herself*

To be a sweetness more desired than Spring;
    A bodily beauty more acceptable
    Than the wild rose-tree's arch that crowns the fell;
To be an essence more environing
Than wine's drained juice; a music ravishing
    More than the passionate pulse of Philomel; —
    To be all this 'neath one soft bosom's swell
That is the flower of life: — how strange a thing!

How strange a thing to be what Man can know
    But as a sacred secret! Heaven's own screen   10
Hides her soul's purest depth and loveliest glow;
    Closely withheld, as all things most unseen, —
    The wave-bowered pearl, — the heart-shaped seal of green
That flecks the snowdrop underneath the snow.
[1881]   [1881]

ii. *Her Love*

SHE loves him; for her infinite soul is Love,
  And he her lodestar. Passion in her is
  A glass facing his fire, where the bright bliss
Is mirrored, and the heat returned. Yet move
That glass, a stranger's amorous flame to prove,
  And it shall turn, by instant contraries,
  Ice to the moon; while her pure fire to his
For whom it burns, clings close i' the heart's alcove.

Lo! they are one. With wifely breast to breast
  And circling arms, she welcomes all command   10
  Of love, — her soul to answering ardours fann'd:
Yet as morn springs or twilight sinks to rest,
Ah! who shall say she deems not loveliest
  The hour of sisterly sweet hand-in-hand?
[1881]   [1881]

iii. *Her Heaven*

IF to grow old in Heaven is to grow young,
  (As the Seer saw and said,) then blest were he
  With youth for evermore, whose heaven should be
True Woman, she whom these weak notes have sung.
Here and hereafter, — choir-strains of her tongue, —
  Sky-spaces of her eyes, — sweet signs that flee
  About her soul's immediate sanctuary, —
Were Paradise all uttermost worlds among.

The sunrise blooms and withers on the hill
  Like any hillflower; and the noblest troth   10
  Dies here to dust. Yet shall Heaven's promise clothe
Even yet those lovers who have cherished still
  This test for love: — in every kiss sealed fast
  To feel the first kiss and forebode the last.
[1881]   [1881]

SONNET LIX

LOVE'S LAST GIFT

LOVE to his singer held a glistening leaf,
  And said: "The rose-tree and the apple-tree

Have fruits to vaunt or flowers to lure the bee;
And golden shafts are in the feathered sheaf
Of the great harvest-marshal, the year's chief,
 Victorious Summer; aye, and 'neath warm sea
 Strange secret grasses lurk inviolably
Between the filtering channels of sunk reef.

All are my blooms; and all sweet blooms of love
 To thee I gave while Spring and Summer sang;   10
 But Autumn stops to listen, with some pang
From those worse things the wind is moaning of.
 Only this laurel dreads no winter days:
 Take my last gift; thy heart hath sung my praise."
[1871]   [1881]

Not love but now art

PART II

⋙ *Change and Fate* ⋘

SONNET LX

TRANSFIGURED LIFE

As growth of form or momentary glance
 In a child's features will recall to mind
 The father's with the mother's face combin'd —
Sweet interchange that memories still enhance:
And yet, as childhood's years and youth's advance,
 The gradual mouldings leave one stamp behind,
 Till in the blended likeness now we find
A separate man's or woman's countenance: —

So in the Song, the singer's Joy and Pain,
 Its very parents, evermore expand   10
To bid the passion's fullgrown birth remain,
 By Art's transfiguring essence subtly spann'd;
 And from that song-cloud shaped as a man's hand
There comes the sound as of abundant rain.
[1873]   [1881]

SONNET LXI

THE SONG-THROE

By thine own tears thy song must tears beget,
    O Singer! Magic mirror thou hast none
    Except thy manifest heart; and save thine own
Anguish or ardour, else no amulet.
Cisterned in Pride, verse is the feathery jet
    Of soulless air-flung fountains; nay, more dry
    Than the Dead Sea for throats that thirst and sigh,
That song o'er which no singer's lids grew wet.

The Song-god — He the Sun-god — is no slave
    Of thine: thy Hunter he, who for thy soul   10
    Fledges his shaft: to no august control
Of thy skilled hand his quivered store he gave:
    But if thy lips' loud cry leap to his smart,
    The inspir'd recoil shall pierce thy brother's heart.
[1880]   [1881]

SONNET LXII

THE SOUL'S SPHERE

Some prisoned moon in steep cloud-fastnesses, —
    Throned queen and thralled; some dying sun whose pyre
    Blazed with momentous memorable fire; —
Who hath not yearned and fed his heart with these?
Who, sleepless, hath not anguished to appease
    Tragical shadow's realm of sound and sight
    Conjectured in the lamentable night? . . .
Lo! the soul's sphere of infinite images!

What sense shall count them? Whether it forecast
    The rose-winged hours that flutter in the van   10
    Of Love's unquestioning unrevealèd span, —
Visions of golden futures: or that last
Wild pageant of the accumulated past
    That clangs and flashes for a drowning man.
[1873]   [1881]

SONNET LXIII

INCLUSIVENESS

THE changing guests, each in a different mood,
    Sit at the roadside table and arise:
    And every life among them in likewise
Is a soul's board set daily with new food.
What man has bent o'er his son's sleep, to brood
    How that face shall watch his when cold it lies? —
    Or thought, as his own mother kissed his eyes,
Of what her kiss was when his father wooed?

May not this ancient room thou sit'st in dwell
    In separate living souls for joy or pain?   10
    Nay, all its corners may be painted plain
Where Heaven shows pictures of some life spent well;
    And may be stamped, a memory all in vain,
Upon the sight of lidless eyes in Hell.
[1869]   [*1869;* 1870]

SONNET LXIV

ARDOUR AND MEMORY

THE cuckoo-throb, the heartbeat of the Spring;
    The rosebud's blush that leaves it as it grows
    Into the full-eyed fair unblushing rose;
The summer clouds that visit every wing
With fires of sunrise and of sunsetting;
    The furtive flickering streams to light re-born
    'Mid airs new-fledged and valorous lusts of morn,
While all the daughters of the daybreak sing: —

These ardour loves, and memory: and when flown
    All joys, and through dark forest-boughs in flight   10
    The wind swoops onward brandishing the light,
Even yet the rose-tree's verdure left alone
Will flush all ruddy though the rose be gone;
    With ditties and with dirges infinite.
[1879]   [1881]

SONNET LXV

KNOWN IN VAIN

As two whose love, first foolish, widening scope,
  Knows suddenly, to music high and soft,
  The Holy of holies; who because they scoff'd
Are now amazed with shame, nor dare to cope
With the whole truth aloud, lest heaven should ope;
  Yet, at their meetings, laugh not as they laugh'd
  In speech; nor speak, at length; but sitting oft
Together, within hopeless sight of hope
For hours are silent: — So it happeneth
  When Work and Will awake too late, to gaze   10
After their life sailed by, and hold their breath.
  Ah! who shall dare to search through what sad maze
  Thenceforth their incommunicable ways
Follow the desultory feet of Death?
[1853]   [*1869;* 1870]

SONNET LXVI

THE HEART OF THE NIGHT

FROM child to youth; from youth to arduous man;
  From lethargy to fever of the heart;
  From faithful life to dream-dowered days apart;
From trust to doubt; from doubt to brink of ban; —
Thus much of change in one swift cycle ran
  Till now. Alas, the soul! — how soon must she
  Accept her primal immortality, —
The flesh resume its dust whence it began?

O Lord of work and peace! O Lord of life!
  O Lord, the awful Lord of will! though late,   10
  Even yet renew this soul with duteous breath:
That when the peace is garnered in from strife,
  The work retrieved, the will regenerate,
  This soul may see thy face, O Lord of death!
[1873]   [1881]

SONNET LXVII

THE LANDMARK

Was *that* the landmark? What, — the foolish well
  Whose wave, low down, I did not stoop to drink,
  But sat and flung the pebbles from its brink
In sport to send its imaged skies pell-mell,
(And mine own image, had I noted well!) —
  Was that my point of turning? — I had thought
  The stations of my course should rise unsought,
As altar-stone or ensigned citadel.

But lo! the path is missed, I must go back,
  And thirst to drink when next I reach the spring   10
Which once I stained, which since may have grown black.
  Yet though no light be left nor bird now sing
  As here I turn, I'll thank God, hastening,
That the same goal is still on the same track.
[1854]   [*1869;* 1870]

SONNET LXVIII

A DARK DAY

The gloom that breathes upon me with these airs
  Is like the drops which strike the traveller's brow
  Who knows not, darkling, if they bring him now
Fresh storm, or be old rain the covert bears.
Ah! bodes this hour some harvest of new tares, *field*
  Or hath but memory of the day whose plough
  Sowed hunger once, — the night at length when thou,
O prayer found vain, didst fall from out my prayers?

How prickly were the growths which yet how smooth,
  Along the hedgerows of this journey shed,   10
Lie by Time's grace till night and sleep may soothe!
  Even as the thistledown from pathsides dead
Gleaned by a girl in autumns of her youth,
  Which one new year makes soft her marriage-bed.
[1855]   [1870]

SONNET LXIX

AUTUMN IDLENESS

THIS sunlight shames November where he grieves
   In dead red leaves, and will not let him shun
   The day, though bough with bough be over-run.
But with a blessing every glade receives
High salutation; while from hillock-eaves
   The deer gaze calling, dappled white and dun,
   As if, being foresters of old, the sun
Had marked them with the shade of forest-leaves.

Here dawn to-day unveiled her magic glass;
   Here noon now gives the thirst and takes the dew;   10
Till eve bring rest when other good things pass.
   And here the lost hours the lost hours renew
While I still lead my shadow o'er the grass,
   Nor know, for longing, that which I should do.
  [1850]   [1870]

SONNET LXX

THE HILL SUMMIT

THIS feast-day of the sun, his altar there
   In the broad west has blazed for vesper-song;
   And I have loitered in the vale too long
And gaze now a belated worshipper.
Yet may I not forget that I was 'ware,
   So journeying, of his face at intervals
   Transfigured where the fringed horizon falls, —
A fiery bush with coruscating hair.

And now that I have climbed and won this height,
   I must tread downward through the sloping shade   10
And travel the bewildered tracks till night.
   Yet for this hour I still may here be stayed
   And see the gold air and the silver fade
And the last bird fly into the last light.
  [1853]   [1870]

SONNETS LXXI, LXXII, LXXIII

THE CHOICE

I

EAT thou and drink; to-morrow thou shalt die.
　Surely the earth, that's wise being very old,
　Needs not our help. Then loose me, love, and hold
Thy sultry hair up from my face; that I
May pour for thee this golden wine, brim-high,
　Till round the glass thy fingers glow like gold.
　We'll drown all hours: thy song, while hours are toll'd,
Shall leap, as fountains veil the changing sky.

Now kiss, and think that there are really those,
　My own high-bosomed beauty, who increase　　　　　　10
　　Vain gold, vain lore, and yet might choose our way!
　　Through many years they toil; then on a day
　They die not, — for their life was death, — but cease;
And round their narrow lips the mould falls close.
[1847–48]　　　　　　　　　　　　　　　　[1870]

II

WATCH thou and fear; to-morrow thou shalt die.
　Or art thou sure thou shalt have time for death?
　Is not the day which God's word promiseth
To come man knows not when? In yonder sky,
Now while we speak, the sun speeds forth: can I
　Or thou assure him of his goal? God's breath
　Even at this moment haply quickeneth
The air to a flame; till spirits, always nigh
Though screened and hid, shall walk the daylight here.
　And dost thou prate of all that man shall do?　　　　　10
　　Canst thou, who hast but plagues, presume to be
　　Glad in his gladness that comes after thee?
　Will *his* strength slay *thy* worm in Hell? Go to:
Cover thy countenance, and watch, and fear.
[1847–48]　　　　　　　　　　　　　　　　[1870]

III　　　*develop himself, growth*

THINK thou and act; to-morrow thou shalt die.
　Outstretched in the sun's warmth upon the shore,

Thou say'st: "Man's measured path is all gone o'er:
Up all his years, steeply, with strain and sigh,
Man clomb until he touched the truth; and I,
  Even I, am he whom it was destined for."
  How should this be? Art thou then so much more
Than they who sowed, that thou shouldst reap thereby?

Nay, come up hither. From this wave-washed mound
  Unto the furthest flood-brim look with me;   10
Then reach on with thy thought till it be drown'd.
  Miles and miles distant though the last line be,
And though thy soul sail leagues and leagues beyond, —
  Still, leagues beyond those leagues, there is more sea.
[1847–48]   [1870]

SONNETS LXXIV, LXXV, LXXVI

OLD AND NEW ART

I. *St. Luke the Painter*

GIVE honour unto Luke Evangelist;
  For he it was (the aged legends say)
  Who first taught Art to fold her hands and **pray**.
Scarcely at once she dared to rend the mist
Of devious symbols: but soon having wist
  How sky-breadth and field-silence and this day
  Are symbols also in some deeper way,
She looked through these to God and was God's priest.

And if, past noon, her toil began to irk,
  And she sought talismans, and turned in vain   10
    To soulless self-reflections of man's skill, —
    Yet now, in this the twilight, she might still
  Kneel in the latter grass to pray again,
Ere the night cometh and she may not work.
[1849]   [1870]

II. *Not as These*

"I AM not as these are," the poet saith
  In youth's pride, and the painter, among men
  At bay, where never pencil comes nor pen,
And shut about with his own frozen breath.

To others, for whom only rhyme wins faith
  As poets, — only paint as painters, — then
  He turns in the cold silence; and again
Shrinking, "I am not as these are," he saith.

And say that this is so, what follows it?
  For were thine eyes set backwards in thine head,   **10**
    Such words were well; but they see on, and far.
Unto the lights of the great Past, new-lit
  Fair for the Future's track, look thou instead, —
    Say thou instead, "I am not as *these* are."
[1848]   [1881]

III. *The Husbandmen*

THOUGH God, as one that is an householder,
  Called these to labour in his vineyard first,
  Before the husk of darkness was well burst
Bidding them grope their way out and bestir,
(Who, questioned of their wages, answered, "Sir,
  Unto each man a penny:") though the worst
  Burthen of heat was theirs and the dry thirst:
Though God hath since found none such as these were
To do their work like them: — Because of this
  Stand not ye idle in the market-place.   **10**
    Which of ye knoweth *he* is not that last
Who may be first by faith and will? — yea, his
  The hand which after the appointed days
    And hours shall give a Future to their Past?
[1848]   [1881]

SONNET LXXVII

SOUL'S BEAUTY

UNDER the arch of Life, where love and death,
  Terror and mystery, guard her shrine, I saw
  Beauty enthroned; and though her gaze struck awe,
I drew it in as simply as my breath.
Hers are the eyes which, over and beneath,
  The sky and sea bend on thee, — which can draw,
  By sea or sky or woman, to one law,
The allotted bondman of her palm and wreath.

This is that Lady Beauty, in whose praise
   Thy voice and hand shake still, — long known to thee   **10**
      By flying hair and fluttering hem, — the beat
      Following her daily of thy heart and feet,
   How passionately and irretrievably,
In what fond flight, how many ways and days!
[1866]   [*1868;* 1870]

SONNET LXXVIII

BODY'S BEAUTY

OF Adam's first wife, Lilith, it is told
   (The witch he loved before the gift of Eve,)
   That, ere the snake's, her sweet tongue could deceive,
And her enchanted hair was the first gold.
And still she sits, young while the earth is old,
   And, subtly of herself contemplative,
   Draws men to watch the bright web she can weave,
Till heart and body and life are in its hold.

The rose and poppy are her flowers; for where
   Is he not found, O Lilith, whom shed scent   **10**
And soft-shed kisses and soft sleep shall snare?
   Lo! as that youth's eyes burned at thine, so went
   Thy spell through him, and left his straight neck bent
And round his heart one strangling golden hair.
[1867]   [*1868;* 1870]

SONNET LXXIX

THE MONOCHORD

Is it this sky's vast vault or ocean's sound
   That is Life's self and draws my life from me,
   And by instinct ineffable decree
Holds my breath quailing on the bitter bound?
Nay, is it Life or Death, thus thunder-crown'd,
   That 'mid the tide of all emergency
   Now notes my separate wave, and to what sea
Its difficult eddies labour in the ground?

Oh! what is this that knows the road I came,
The flame turned cloud, the cloud returned to flame,   10
  The lifted shifted steeps and all the way? —
That draws round me at last this wind-warm space,
And in regenerate rapture turns my face
  Upon the devious coverts of dismay?
[1870]   [1870]

SONNET LXXX

FROM DAWN TO NOON

As the child knows not if his mother's face
  Be fair; nor of his elders yet can deem
  What each most is; but as of hill or stream
At dawn, all glimmering life surrounds his place:
Who yet, tow'rd noon of his half-weary race,
  Pausing awhile beneath the high sun-beam
  And gazing steadily back, — as through a dream,
In things long past new features now can trace: —

Even so the thought that is at length fullgrown
  Turns back to note the sun-smit paths, all grey   10
And marvellous once, where first it walked alone;
  And haply doubts, amid the unblenching day,
  Which most or least impelled its onward way, —
Those unknown things or these things overknown.
[1873]   [1881]

SONNET LXXXI

MEMORIAL THRESHOLDS

WHAT place so strange, — though unrevealèd snow
  With unimaginable fires arise
  At the earth's end, — what passion of surprise
Like frost-bound fire-girt scenes of long ago?
Lo! this is none but I this hour; and lo!
  This is the very place which to mine eyes
  Those mortal hours in vain immortalize,
'Mid hurrying crowds, with what alone I know.

City, of thine a single simple door,
 By some new Power reduplicate, must be   10
 Even yet my life-porch in eternity,
Even with one presence filled, as once of yore:
Or mocking winds whirl round a chaff-strown floor
 Thee and thy years and these my words and me.
[1873]   [1881]

SONNET LXXXII

HOARDED JOY

I SAID: "Nay, pluck not, — let the first fruit be:
 Even as thou sayest, it is sweet and red,
 But let it ripen still. The tree's bent head
Sees in the stream its own fecundity
And bides the day of fulness. Shall not we
 At the sun's hour that day possess the shade,
 And claim our fruit before its ripeness fade,
And eat it from the branch and praise the tree?"

I say: "Alas! our fruit hath wooed the sun
 Too long, — 'tis fallen and floats adown the stream.   10
Lo, the last clusters! Pluck them every one,
 And let us sup with summer; ere the gleam
Of autumn set the year's pent sorrow free,
And the woods wail like echoes from the sea."
[1870]   [1870]

SONNET LXXXIII

BARREN SPRING

ONCE more the changed year's turning wheel returns:
 And as a girl sails balanced in the wind,
 And now before and now again behind
Stoops as it swoops, with cheek that laughs and burns, —
So Spring comes merry towards me here, but earns
 No answering smile from me, whose life is twin'd
 With the dead boughs that winter still must bind,
And whom to-day the Spring no more concerns.

Behold, this crocus is a withering flame;
  This snowdrop, snow; this apple-blossom's part   10
  To breed the fruit that breeds the serpent's art.
Nay, for these Spring-flowers, turn thy face from them,
Now stay till on the year's last lily-stem
  The white cup shrivels round the golden heart.
[1870]   [1870]

SONNET LXXXIV

FAREWELL TO THE GLEN

Sweet stream-fed glen, why say "farewell" to thee
  Who far'st so well and find'st for ever smooth
  The brow of Time where man may read no ruth?
Nay, do thou rather say "farewell" to me,
Who now fare forth in bitterer fantasy
  Than erst was mine where other shade might soothe
  By other streams, what while in fragrant youth
The bliss of being sad made melancholy.

And yet, farewell! For better shalt thou fare
  When children bathe sweet faces in thy flow   10
And happy lovers blend sweet shadows there
  In hours to come, than when an hour ago
Thine echoes had but one man's sighs to bear
  And thy trees whispered what he feared to know.
[1869]   [1870]

SONNET LXXXV

VAIN VIRTUES

What is the sorriest thing that enters Hell?
  None of the sins, — but this and that fair deed
  Which a soul's sin at length could supersede.
These yet are virgins, whom death's timely knell
Might once have sainted; whom the fiends compel
  Together now, in snake-bound shuddering sheaves
  Of anguish, while the pit's pollution leaves
Their refuse maidenhood abominable.

Night sucks them down, the tribute of the pit,
  Whose names, half entered in the book of Life,   10
    Were God's desire at noon. And as their hair
And eyes sink last, the Torturer deigns no whit
  To gaze, but, yearning, waits his destined wife,
    The Sin still blithe on earth that sent them there.
[1869]   [1870]

SONNET LXXXVI

LOST DAYS

THE lost days of my life until to-day,
  What were they, could I see them on the street
  Lie as they fell? Would they be ears of wheat
Sown once for food but trodden into clay?
Or golden coins squandered and still to pay?
  Or drops of blood dabbling the guilty feet?
  Or such spilt water as in dreams must cheat
The undying throats of Hell, athirst alway?

I do not see them here; but after death
  God knows I know the faces I shall see,   10
Each one a murdered self, with low last breath.
  "I am thyself, — what hast thou done to me?"
"And I — and I — thyself," (lo! each one saith,)
  "And thou thyself to all eternity!"
[1862]   [1863; *1869*; 1870]

SONNET LXXXVII

DEATH'S SONGSTERS

WHEN first that horse, within whose populous womb
  The birth was death, o'ershadowed Troy with fate,
  Her elders, dubious of its Grecian freight,
Brought Helen there to sing the songs of home;
She whispered, "Friends, I am alone; come, come!"
  Then, crouched within, Ulysses waxed afraid,
  And on his comrades' quivering mouths he laid
His hands, and held them till the voice was dumb.

The same was he who, lashed to his own mast,
   There where the sea-flowers screen the charnel-caves,   10
Beside the sirens' singing island pass'd,
   Till sweetness failed along the inveterate waves. . . .
Say, soul, — are songs of Death no heaven to thee,
Nor shames her lip the cheek of Victory?
[1870]   [1870]

SONNET LXXXVIII

HERO'S LAMP*

THAT lamp thou fill'st in Eros' name to-night,
   O Hero, shall the Sestian augurs take
   To-morrow, and for drowned Leander's sake
To Anteros its fireless lip shall plight.
Aye, waft the unspoken vow: yet dawn's first light
   On ebbing storm and life twice ebb'd must break;
   While 'neath no sunrise, by the Avernian Lake,
Lo where Love walks, Death's pallid neophyte.

That lamp within Anteros' shadowy shrine
   Shall stand unlit (for so the gods decree)   10
   Till some one man the happy issue see
Of a life's love, and bid its flame to shine:
Which still may rest unfir'd; for, theirs or thine,
   O brother, what brought love to them or thee?
[1875]   [1881]

SONNET LXXXIX

THE TREES OF THE GARDEN

YE who have passed Death's haggard hills; and ye
   Whom trees that knew your sires shall cease to know
   And still stand silent: — is it all a show, —
A wisp that laughs upon the wall? — decree
Of some inexorable supremacy
   Which ever, as man strains his blind surmise

* After the deaths of Leander and of Hero, the signal-lamp was dedi-
cated to Anteros, with the edict that no man should light it unless his love
had proved fortunate. [ROSSETTI]

From depth to ominous depth, looks past his eyes,
Sphinx-faced with unabashèd augury?

Nay, rather question the Earth's self. Invoke
  The storm-felled forest-trees moss-grown to-day   **10**
  Whose roots are hillocks where the children play;
Or ask the silver sapling 'neath what yoke
  Those stars, his spray-crown's clustering gems, shall wage
  Their journey still when his boughs shrink with age.
[1875]   [1881]

SONNET XC

"RETRO ME, SATHANA!"

GET thee behind me. Even as, heavy-curled,
  Stooping against the wind, a charioteer
  Is snatched from out his chariot by the hair,
So shall Time be; and as the void car, hurled
Abroad by reinless steeds, even so the world:
  Yea, even as chariot-dust upon the air,
  It shall be sought and not found anywhere.
Get thee behind me, Satan. Oft unfurled,
Thy perilous wings can beat and break like lath
  Much mightiness of men to win thee praise.   **10**
  Leave these weak feet to tread in narrow ways.
Thou still, upon the broad vine-sheltered path,
Mayst wait the turning of the phials of wrath
  For certain years, for certain months and days.
[1847]   [1870]

SONNET XCI

LOST ON BOTH SIDES

As when two men have loved a woman well,
  Each hating each, through Love's and Death's deceit;
  Since not for either this stark marriage-sheet
And the long pauses of this wedding-bell;
Yet o'er her grave the night and day dispel
  At last their feud forlorn, with cold and heat;
  Nor other than dear friends to death may fleet
The two lives left that most of her can tell: —

So separate hopes, which in a soul had wooed
   The one same Peace, strove with each other long,   10
     And Peace before their faces perished since:
So through that soul, in restless brotherhood,
   They roam together now, and wind among
     Its bye-streets, knocking at the dusty inns.
[1854]   [*1869;* 1870]

SONNETS XCII, XCIII

THE SUN'S SHAME

I

BEHOLDING youth and hope in mockery caught
   From life; and mocking pulses that remain
   When the soul's death of bodily death is fain;
Honour unknown, and honour known unsought;
And penury's sedulous self-torturing thought
   On gold, whose master therewith buys his bane;
   And longed-for woman longing all in vain
For lonely man with love's desire distraught;
And wealth, and strength, and power, and pleasantness,
   Given unto bodies of whose souls men say,   10
   None poor and weak, slavish and foul, as they: —
Beholding these things, I behold no less
   The blushing morn and blushing eve confess
   The shame that loads the intolerable day.
[1869]   [1870]

II

As some true chief of men, bowed down with stress
   Of life's disastrous eld, on blossoming youth
   May gaze, and murmur with self-pity and ruth, —
"Might I thy fruitless treasure but possess,
Such blessing of mine all coming years should bless;" —
   Then sends one sigh forth to the unknown goal,
   And bitterly feels breathe against his soul
The hour swift-winged of nearer nothingness: —

Even so the World's gray Soul to the green World
   Perchance one hour must cry: "Woe's me, for whom   10
   Inveteracy of ill portends the doom, —

Whose heart's old fire in shadow of shame is furl'd:
  While thou even as of yore art journeying,
  All soulless now, yet merry with the Spring!"
[1873]   [1881]

SONNET XCIV

MICHELANGELO'S KISS

GREAT Michelangelo, with age grown bleak
  And uttermost labours, having once o'ersaid
  All grievous memories on his long life shed,
This worst regret to one true heart could speak: —
That when, with sorrowing love and reverence meek,
  He stooped o'er sweet Colonna's dying bed,
  His Muse and dominant Lady, spirit-wed, —
Her hand he kissed, but not her brow or cheek.

O Buonarruoti, — good at Art's fire-wheels
  To urge her chariot! — even thus the Soul,   10
  Touching at length some sorely-chastened goal,
Earns oftenest but a little: her appeals
  Were deep and mute, — lowly her claim. Let be:
  What holds for her Death's garner? And for thee?
[1881]   [1881]

SONNET XCV

THE VASE OF LIFE

AROUND the vase of Life at your slow pace
  He has not crept, but turned it with his hands,
  And all its sides already understands.
There, girt, one breathes alert for some great race;
Whose road runs far by sands and fruitful space;
  Who laughs, yet through the jolly throng has pass'd;
  Who weeps, nor stays for weeping; who at last,
A youth, stands somewhere crowned, with silent face.

And he has filled this vase with wine for blood,
  With blood for tears, with spice for burning vow,   10
  With watered flowers for buried love most fit;

And would have cast it shattered to the flood,
    Yet in Fate's name has kept it whole; which now
      Stands empty till his ashes fall in it.
[1869]   [*1869;* 1870]

SONNET XCVI

LIFE THE BELOVED

As thy friend's face, with shadow of soul o'erspread,
    Somewhile unto thy sight perchance hath been
      Ghastly and strange, yet never so is seen
In thought, but to all fortunate favour wed;
As thy love's death-bound features never dead
    To memory's glass return, but contravene
      Frail fugitive days, and alway keep, I ween,
Than all new life a livelier lovelihead: —

So Life herself, thy spirit's friend and love,
    Even still as Spring's authentic harbinger   10
      Glows with fresh hours for hope to glorify;
Though pale she lay when in the winter grove
    Her funeral flowers were snow-flakes shed on her
      And the red wings of frost-fire rent the sky.
[1873]   [1881]

SONNET XCVII

A SUPERSCRIPTION

Look in my face; my name is Might-have-been;
    I am also called No-more, Too-late, Farewell;
      Unto thine ear I hold the dead-sea shell
Cast up thy Life's foam-fretted feet between;
Unto thine eyes the glass where that is seen
    Which had Life's form and Love's, but by my spell
      Is now a shaken shadow intolerable,
Of ultimate things unuttered the frail screen.

Mark me, how still I am! But should there dart
    One moment through thy soul the soft surprise   10
      Of that winged Peace which lulls the breath of sighs, —

Then shalt thou see me smile, and turn apart
Thy visage to mine ambush at thy heart
  Sleepless with cold commemorative eyes.
[1869]   [*1869;* 1870]

SONNET XCVIII

HE AND I

WHENCE came his feet into my field, and why?
  How is it that he sees it all so drear?
  How do I see his being, and how hear
The name his bitter silence knows it by?
This was the little fold of separate sky
  Whose pasturing clouds in the soul's atmosphere
  Drew living light from one continual year:
How should he find it lifeless? He, or I?

Lo! this new Self now wanders round my field,
  With plaints for every flower, and for each tree   10
  A moan, the sighing wind's auxiliary:
And o'er sweet waters of my life, that yield
Unto his lips no draught but tears unseal'd,
  Even in my place he weeps. Even I, not he.
[1870]   [1870]

SONNETS XCIX, C

NEWBORN DEATH

I

TO-DAY Death seems to me an infant child
  Which her worn mother Life upon my knee
  Has set to grow my friend and play with me;
If haply so my heart might be beguil'd
To find no terrors in a face so mild, —
  If haply so my weary heart might be
  Unto the newborn milky eyes of thee,
O Death, before resentment reconcil'd.

How long, O Death? And shall thy feet depart
  Still a young child's with mine, or wilt thou stand   10
Fullgrown the helpful daughter of my heart,

What time with thee indeed I reach the strand
Of the pale wave which knows thee what thou art,
   And drink it in the hollow of thy hand?
[1868–69]   [*1869;* 1870]

II

AND thou, O Life, the lady of all bliss,
   With whom, when our first heart beat full and fast,
   I wandered till the haunts of men were pass'd,
And in fair places found all bowers amiss
Till only woods and waves might hear our kiss,
   While to the winds all thought of Death we cast: —
   Ah, Life! and must I have from thee at last
No smile to greet me and no babe but this?

Lo! Love, the child once ours; and Song, whose hair
   Blew like a flame and blossomed like a wreath;   **10**
And Art, whose eyes were worlds by God found fair;
   These o'er the book of Nature mixed their breath
With neck-twined arms, as oft we watched them there:
   And did these die that thou mightst bear me Death?
[1868–69]   [*1869;* 1870]

SONNET CI

THE ONE HOPE

WHEN vain desire at last and vain regret
   Go hand in hand to death, and all is vain,
   What shall assuage the unforgotten pain
And teach the unforgetful to forget?
Shall Peace be still a sunk stream long unmet, —
   Or may the soul at once in a green plain
   Stoop through the spray of some sweet life-fountain
And cull the dew-drenched flowering amulet?

Ah! when the wan soul in that golden air
   Between the scriptured petals softly blown   **10**
   Peers breathless for the gift of grace unknown, —
Ah! let none other alien spell soe'er
But only the one Hope's one name be there, —
   Not less nor more, but even that word alone.
[?1870]   [1870]

Christina Georgina Rossetti

no hero

allegory of Temptation

GOBLIN MARKET

MORNING and evening
Maids heard the goblins cry:
"Come buy our orchard fruits,
Come buy, come buy:
Apples and quinces,
Lemons and oranges,
Plump unpecked cherries,
Melons and raspberries,
Bloom-down-cheeked peaches,
Swart-headed mulberries,   10
Wild free-born cranberries,
Crab-apples, dewberries,
Pine-apples, blackberries,
Apricots, strawberries; —
All ripe together
In summer weather, —
Morns that pass by,
Fair eves that fly;
Come buy, come buy:
Our grapes fresh from the vine,   20
Pomegranates full and fine,
Dates and sharp bullaces,
Rare pears and greengages,
Damsons and bilberries,

Taste them and try:
Currants and gooseberries,
Bright-fire-like barberries,
Figs to fill your mouth,
Citrons from the South,
Sweet to tongue and sound to eye;   30
Come buy, come buy."

Evening by evening
Among the brookside rushes,
Laura bowed her head to hear,
Lizzie veiled her blushes:
Crouching close together
In the cooling weather,
With clasping arms and cautioning lips,
With tingling cheeks and fingertips.
"Lie close," Laura said,   40
Pricking up her golden head:
"We must not look at goblin men,
We must not buy their fruits:
Who knows upon what soil they fed
Their hungry thirsty roots?"
"Come buy," call the goblins
Hobbling down the glen.
"Oh," cried Lizzie, "Laura, Laura,
You should not peep at goblin men."
Lizzie covered up her eyes,   50
Covered close lest they should look;
Laura reared her glossy head,
And whispered like the restless brook:
"Look, Lizzie, look, Lizzie,
Down the glen tramp little men.
One hauls a basket,
One bears a plate,
One lugs a golden dish
Of many pounds' weight.
How fair the vine must grow   60
Whose grapes are so luscious;
How warm the wind must blow
Through those fruit bushes."
"No," said Lizzie: "No, no, no;
Their offers should not charm us,
Their evil gifts would harm us."
She thrust a dimpled finger

In each ear, shut eyes and ran:
Curious Laura chose to linger
Wondering at each merchant man.   70
One had a cat's face,
One whisked a tail,
One tramped at a rat's pace,
One crawled like a snail,
One like a wombat prowled obtuse and furry,
One like a ratel tumbled hurry skurry.
She heard a voice like voice of doves
Cooing all together:
They sounded kind and full of loves
In the pleasant weather.   80

Laura stretched her gleaming neck
Like a rush-imbedded swan,
Like a lily from the beck,
Like a moonlit poplar branch,
Like a vessel at the launch
When its last restraint is gone.

Backwards up the mossy glen
Turned and trooped the goblin men,
With their shrill repeated cry,
"Come buy, come buy."   90
When they reached where Laura was
They stood stock still upon the moss,
Leering at each other,
Brother with queer brother;
Signalling each other,
Brother with sly brother.
One set his basket down,
One reared his plate;
One began to weave a crown
Of tendrils, leaves, and rough nuts brown   100
(Men sell not such in any town);
One heaved the golden weight
Of dish and fruit to offer her:
"Come buy, come buy," was still their cry.
Laura stared but did not stir,
Longed but had no money.
The whisk-tailed merchant bade her taste
In tones as smooth as honey,
The cat-faced purr'd,

The rat-paced spoke a word   110
Of welcome, and the snail-paced even was heard;
One parrot-voiced and jolly
Cried "Pretty Goblin" still for "Pretty Polly";
One whistled like a bird.

But sweet-tooth Laura spoke in haste:
"Good Folk, I have no coin;
To take were to purloin:
I have no copper in my purse,
I have no silver either,
And all my gold is on the furze   120
That shakes in windy weather
Above the rusty heather."
"You have much gold upon your head,"
They answered all together:
"Buy from us with a golden curl."
She clipped a precious golden lock,
She dropped a tear more rare than pearl,
Then sucked their fruit globes fair or red.
Sweeter than honey from the rock,
Stronger than man-rejoicing wine,   130
Clearer than water flowed that juice;
She never tasted such before,
How should it cloy with length of use? *mother-like*
She sucked and sucked and sucked the more
Fruits which that unknown orchard bore;
She sucked until her lips were sore;
Then flung the emptied rinds away
But gathered up one kernel stone,
And knew not was it night or day
As she turned home alone.   140

Lizzie met her at the gate
Full of wise upbraidings:
"Dear, you should not stay so late,
Twilight is not good for maidens;
Should not loiter in the glen
In the haunts of goblin men.
Do you not remember Jeanie,
How she met them in the moonlight,
Took their gifts both choice and many,
Ate their fruits and wore their flowers   150
Plucked from bowers

Where summer ripens at all hours?
But ever in the noonlight
She pined and pined away;
Sought them by night and day,
Found them no more, but dwindled and grew grey;
Then fell with the first snow,
While to this day no grass will grow
Where she lies low: — Innocence   sterility -
I planted daisies there a year ago   life-denying   160
That never blow.
You should not loiter so."
"Nay, hush," said Laura:
"Nay, hush, my sister:
I ate and ate my fill,
Yet my mouth waters still:
To-morrow night I will
Buy more;" and kissed her.
"Have done with sorrow;
I'll bring you plums to-morrow   170
Fresh on their mother twigs,
Cherries worth getting;
You cannot think what figs
My teeth have met in,
What melons icy-cold
Piled on a dish of gold
Too huge for me to hold,
What peaches with a velvet nap,
Pellucid grapes without one seed:
Odorous indeed must be the mead   180
Whereon they grow, and pure the wave they drink
With lilies at the brink,
And sugar-sweet their sap."

Golden head by golden head,
Like two pigeons in one nest
Folded in each other's wings,
They lay down in their curtained bed: lower-like
Like two blossoms on one stem,   innocence
Like two flakes of new-fall'n snow,
Like two wands of ivory   190
Tipped with gold for awful kings.
Moon and stars gazed in at them,
Wind sang to them lullaby,
Lumbering owls forebore to fly,

Not a bat flapped to and fro
Round their nest:
Cheek to cheek and breast to breast
Locked together in one nest.

Early in the morning
When the first cock crowed his warning,   200
Neat like bees, as sweet and busy,
Laura rose with Lizzie:
Fetched in honey, milked the cows,
Aired and set to rights the house,
Kneaded cakes of whitest wheat,
Cakes for dainty mouths to eat,
Next churned butter, whipped up cream,
Fed their poultry, sat and sewed;
Talked as modest maidens should:
Lizzie with an open heart,   210
Laura in an absent dream,
One content, one sick in part;
One warbling for the mere bright day's delight,
One longing for the night.

At length slow evening came:
They went with pitchers to the reedy brook;
Lizzie most placid in her look,
Laura most like a leaping flame.
They drew the gurgling water from its deep.
Lizzie plucked purple and rich golden flags,   220
Then turning homeward said: "The sunset flushes
Those furthest loftiest crags;
Come, Laura, not another maiden lags.
No wilful squirrel wags,
The beasts and birds are fast asleep."
But Laura loitered still among the rushes,
And said the bank was steep.

And said the hour was early still,
The dew not fall'n, the wind not chill;
Listening ever, but not catching   230
The customary cry,
"Come buy, come buy,"
With its iterated jingle
Of sugar-baited words:
Not for all her watching

Once discerning even one goblin
Racing, whisking, tumbling, hobbling —
Let alone the herds
That used to tramp along the glen,
In groups or single,   240
Of brisk fruit-merchant men.

Till Lizzie urged, "O Laura, come;
I hear the fruit-call, but I dare not look:
You should not loiter longer at this brook:
Come with me home.
The stars rise, the moon bends her arc,
Each glow-worm winks her spark,
Let us get home before the night grows dark:
For clouds may gather
Though this is summer weather,   250
Put out the lights and drench us through;
Then if we lost our way what should we do?"

Laura turned cold as stone
To find her sister heard that cry alone,
That goblin cry,
"Come buy our fruits, come buy."
Must she then buy no more such dainty fruit?
Must she no more such succous pasture find,
Gone deaf and blind?
Her tree of life drooped from the root: 260
She said not one word in her heart's sore ache:
But peering thro' the dimness, nought discerning,
Trudged home, her pitcher dripping all the way;
So crept to bed, and lay
Silent till Lizzie slept;
Then sat up in a passionate yearning,
And gnashed her teeth for baulked desire, and wept
As if her heart would break.

Day after day, night after night,
Laura kept watch in vain   270
In sullen silence of exceeding pain.
She never caught again the goblin cry,
"Come buy, come buy;" —
She never spied the goblin men
Hawking their fruits along the glen:
But when the noon waxed bright

Her hair grew thin and grey;
She dwindled, as the fair full moon doth turn
To swift decay and burn
Her fire away.   280

One day remembering her kernel-stone
She set it by a wall that faced the south;
Dewed it with tears, hoped for a root,
Watched for a waxing shoot,
But there came none.
It never saw the sun,
It never felt the trickling moisture run:
While with sunk eyes and faded mouth
She dreamed of melons, as a traveller sees
False waves in desert drouth   290
With shade of leaf-crowned trees,
And burns the thirstier in the sandful breeze.

She no more swept the house,
Tended the fowls or cows,
Fetched honey, kneaded cakes of wheat,
Brought water from the brook:
But sat down listless in the chimney-nook
And would not eat.

Tender Lizzie could not bear
To watch her sister's cankerous care,   300
Yet not to share.
She night and morning
Caught the goblins' cry:
"Come buy our orchard fruits,
Come buy, come buy:" —
Beside the brook, along the glen,
She heard the tramp of goblin men,
The voice and stir
Poor Laura could not hear;
Longed to buy fruit to comfort her,   310
But feared to pay too dear.
She thought of Jeanie in her grave,
Who should have been a bride;
But who for joys brides hope to have
Fell sick and died
In her gay prime,
In earliest winter time,

With the first glazing rime,
With the first snow-fall of crisp winter time.

Till Laura dwindling   320
Seemed knocking at Death's door.
Then Lizzie weighed no more
Better and worse;
But put a silver penny in her purse,
Kissed Laura, crossed the heath with clumps of furze
At twilight, halted by the brook:
And for the first time in her life
Began to listen and look.

Laughed every goblin
When they spied her peeping: 330
Came towards her hobbling,
Flying, running, leaping,
Puffing and blowing,
Chuckling, clapping, crowing,
Clucking and gobbling,
Mopping and mowing,
Full of airs and graces,
Pulling wry faces,
Demure grimaces
Cat-like and rat-like,   340
Ratel- and wombat-like,
Snail-paced in a hurry,
Parrot-voiced and whistler,
Helter skelter, hurry skurry,
Chattering like magpies,
Fluttering like pigeons,
Gliding like fishes, —
Hugged her and kissed her:
Squeezed and caressed her:
Stretched up their dishes,   350
Panniers, and plates:
"Look at our apples
Russet and dun,
Bob at our cherries,
Bite at our peaches,
Citrons and dates,
Grapes for the asking,
Pears red with basking
Out in the sun,

Plums on their twigs;   360
Pluck them and suck them, —
Pomegranates, figs."

"Good folk," said Lizzie,
Mindful of Jeanie:
"Give me much and many:"
Held out her apron,
Tossed them her penny.
"Nay, take a seat with us,
Honour and eat with us,"
They answered grinning: 370
"Our feast is but beginning.
Night yet is early,
Warm and dew-pearly,
Wakeful and starry:
Such fruits as these
No man can carry;
Half their bloom would fly,
Half their dew would dry,
Half their flavour would pass by.
Sit down and feast with us,   380
Be welcome guest with us,
Cheer you and rest with us." —
"Thank you," said Lizzie: "But one waits
At home alone for me:
So without further parleying,
If you will not sell me any
Of your fruits though much and many,
Give me back my silver penny
I tossed you for a fee." —
They began to scratch their pates,   390
No longer wagging, purring,
But visibly demurring,
Grunting and snarling.
One called her proud,
Cross-grained, uncivil;
Their tones waxed loud,
Their looks were evil.
Lashing their tails
They trod and hustled her,
Elbowed and jostled her,   400
Clawed with their nails,
Barking, mewing, hissing, mocking,

Tore her gown and soiled her stocking,
Twitched her hair out by the roots,
Stamped upon her tender feet,
Held her hands and squeezed their fruits
Against her mouth to make her eat.

White and golden Lizzie stood,
Like a lily in a flood, —
Like a rock of blue-veined stone   410
Lashed by tides obstreperously, —
Like a beacon left alone
In a hoary roaring sea,
Sending up a golden fire, —
Like a fruit-crowned orange-tree
White with blossoms honey-sweet
Sore beset by wasp and bee, —
Like a royal virgin town
Topped with gilded dome and spire
Close beleaguered by a fleet   420
Mad to tug her standard down.

One may lead a horse to water,
Twenty cannot make him drink.
Though the goblins cuffed and caught her,
Coaxed and fought her,
Bullied and besought her,
Scratched her, pinched her black as ink,
Kicked and knocked her,
Mauled and mocked her,
Lizzie uttered not a word;   430
Would not open lip from lip
Lest they should cram a mouthful in:
But laughed in heart to feel the drip
Of juice that syruped all her face,
And lodged in dimples of her chin,
And streaked her neck which quaked like curd.
At last the evil people,
Worn out by her resistance,
Flung back her penny, kicked their fruit
Along whichever road they took,   440
Not leaving root or stone or shoot;
Some writhed into the ground,
Some dived into the brook
With ring and ripple,

Some scudded on the gale without a sound,
Some vanished in the distance.

In a smart, ache, tingle,
Lizzie went her way;
Knew not was it night or day;
Sprang up the bank, tore thro' the furze,   450
Threaded copse and dingle,
And heard her penny jingle
Bouncing in her purse, —
Its bounce was music to her ear.
She ran and ran
As if she feared some goblin man
Dogged her with gibe or curse
Or something worse:
But not one goblin skurried after,
Nor was she pricked by fear;   460
The kind heart made her windy-paced
That urged her home quite out of breath with haste
And inward laughter.

She cried, "Laura," up the garden,
"Did you miss me?
Come and kiss me.
Never mind my bruises,
Hug me, kiss me, suck my juices
Squeezed from goblin fruits for you,
Goblin pulp and goblin dew.   470
Eat me, drink me, love me;
Laura, make much of me;
For your sake I have braved the glen
And had to do with goblin merchant men."

Laura started from her chair,
Flung her arms up in the air,
Clutched her hair:
"Lizzie, Lizzie, have you tasted
For my sake the fruit forbidden?
Must your light like mine be hidden,   480
Your young life like mine be wasted,
Undone in mine undoing,
And ruined in my ruin,
Thirsty, cankered, goblin-ridden?" —
She clung about her sister,

Kissed and kissed and kissed her:
Tears once again
Refreshed her shrunken eyes,
Dropping like rain
After long sultry drouth;   490
Shaking with aguish fear, and pain,
She kissed and kissed her with a hungry mouth.

Her lips began to scorch,
That juice was wormwood to her tongue,
She loathed the feast:
Writhing as one possessed she leaped and sung,
Rent all her robe, and wrung
Her hands in lamentable haste,
And beat her breast.
Her locks streamed like the torch   500
Borne by a racer at full speed,
Or like the mane of horses in their flight,
Or like an eagle when she stems the light
Straight toward the sun,
Or like a caged thing freed,
Or like a flying flag when armies run.

Swift fire spread through her veins, knocked at her heart,
Met the fire smouldering there
And overbore its lesser flame;
She gorged on bitterness without a name: 510
Ah fool, to choose such part
Of soul-consuming care!
Sense failed in the mortal strife:
Like the watch-tower of a town
Which an earthquake shatters down,
Like a lightning-stricken mast,
Like a wind-uprooted tree
Spun about,
Like a foam-topped waterspout
Cast down headlong in the sea,   520
She fell at last;
Pleasure past and anguish past,
Is it death or is it life?

Life out of death.
That night long Lizzie watched by her,
Counted her pulse's flagging stir,

Felt for her breath,
Held water to her lips, and cooled her face
With tears and fanning leaves.
But when the first birds chirped about their eaves   530
And early reapers plodded to the place
Of golden sheaves,
And dew-wet grass
Bowed in the morning winds so brisk to pass,
And new buds with new day
Opened of cup-like lilies on the stream,
Laura awoke as from a dream,
Laughed in the innocent old way,
Hugged Lizzie but not twice or thrice;
Her gleaming locks showed not one thread of grey,   540
Her breath was sweet as May,
And light danced in her eyes.

Days, weeks, months, years
Afterwards, when both were wives
With children of their own;
Their mother-hearts beset with fears,
Their lives bound up in tender lives;
Laura would call the little ones
And tell them of her early prime,
Those pleasant days long gone   550
Of not-returning time:
Would talk about the haunted glen,
The wicked quaint fruit-merchant men,
Their fruits like honey to the throat
But poison in the blood
(Men sell not such in any town):
Would tell them how her sister stood
In deadly peril to do her good,
And win the fiery antidote:
Then joining hands to little hands   560
Would bid them cling together, —
"For there is no friend like a sister
In calm or stormy weather;
To cheer one on the tedious way,
To fetch one if one goes astray,
To lift one if one totters down,
To strengthen whilst one stands."
27 April 1859.   [1862]

MONNA INNOMINATA

A Sonnet of Sonnets

Beatrice, immortalized by "altissimo poeta . . . cotanto amante"; Laura, celebrated by a great though an inferior bard, — have alike paid the exceptional penalty of exceptional honour, and have come down to us resplendent with charms, but (at least, to my apprehension) scant of attractiveness.

These heroines of world-wide fame were preceded by a bevy of unnamed ladies, "donne innominate," sung by a school of less conspicuous poets; and in that land and that period which gave simultaneous birth to Catholics, to Albigenses, and to Troubadours, one can imagine many a lady as sharing her lover's poetic aptitude, while the barrier between them might be one held sacred by both, yet not such as to render mutual love incompatible with mutual honour.

Had such a lady spoken for herself, the portrait left us might have appeared more tender, if less dignified, than any drawn even by a devoted friend. Or had the Great Poetess of our own day and nation only been unhappy instead of happy, her circumstances would have invited her to bequeath to us, in lieu of the "Portuguese Sonnets," an inimitable "donna innominata" drawn not from fancy but from feeling, and worthy to occupy a niche beside Beatrice and Laura.

Frustrated like those poets

Unhappy female lovers point of view.

1

Lo dì che han detto a' dolci amici addio.
DANTE.
Amor, con quanto sforzo oggi mi vinci!
PETRARCA.

COME back to me, who wait and watch for you: —
    Or come not yet, for it is over then,
    And long it is before you come again,
So far between my pleasures are and few.
While, when you come not, what I do I do
    Thinking "Now when he comes," my sweetest "when":
    For one man is my world of all the men
This wide world holds; O love, my world is you.
Howbeit, to meet you grows almost a pang
    Because the pang of parting comes so soon;   **10**
My hope hangs waning, waxing, like a moon
    Between the heavenly days on which we meet:
Ah me, but where are now the songs I sang
    When life was sweet because you called them sweet?

2

Era già l'ora che volge il desio.
DANTE.
Riccorro al tempo ch' io vi vidi prima.
PETRARCA.

I wish I could remember that first day,
　First hour, first moment of your meeting me,
　If bright or dim the season, it might be
Summer or Winter for aught I can say;
So unrecorded did it slip away,
　So blind was I to see and to foresee,
　So dull to mark the budding of my tree
That would not blossom yet for many a May.
If only I could recollect it, such
　A day of days! I let it come and go　　　　　　　　10
　As traceless as a thaw of bygone snow;
It seemed to mean so little, meant so much;
If only now I could recall that touch,
　First touch of hand in hand — Did one but know!

3

O ombre vane, fuor che ne l'aspetto!
DANTE.
Immaginata guida la conduce.
PETRARCA.

I dream of you, to wake: would that I might
　Dream of you and not wake but slumber on;
　Nor find with dreams the dear companion gone,
As, Summer ended, Summer birds take flight.
In happy dreams I hold you full in sight,
　I blush again who waking look so wan;
　Brighter than sunniest day that ever shone,
In happy dreams your smile makes day of night.
Thus only in a dream we are at one,
　Thus only in a dream we give and take　　　　　　　10
　The faith that maketh rich who take or give;
If thus to sleep is sweeter than to wake,
　To die were surely sweeter than to live,
Though there be nothing new beneath the sun.

4

Poca favilla gran fiamma seconda.
DANTE.
Ogni altra cosa, ogni pensier va fore,
E sol ivi con voi rimansi amore.
PETRARCA.

I loved you first: but afterwards your love,
  Outsoaring mine, sang such a loftier song
As drowned the friendly cooings of my dove.
  Which owes the other most? My love was long,
    And yours one moment seemed to wax more strong;
I loved and guessed at you, you construed me
And loved me for what might or might not be —
  Nay, weights and measures do us both a wrong.
For verily love knows not "mine" or "thine";
    With separate "I" and "thou" free love has done,
    For one is both and both are one in love: 10
Rich love knows nought of "thine that is not mine;"
    Both have the strength and both the length thereof,
  Both of us, of the love which makes us one.

5

Amor che a nullo amato amar perdona.
DANTE.
Amor m'addusse in sì gioiosa spene.
PETRARCA.

O my heart's heart, and you who are to me
  More than myself myself, God be with you,
  Keep you in strong obedience leal and true
To Him whose noble service setteth free;
Give you all good we see or can foresee,
  Make your joys many and your sorrows few,
  Bless you in what you bear and what you do,
Yea, perfect you as He would have you be.
So much for you; but what for me, dear friend?
  To love you without stint and all I can, 10
To-day, to-morrow, world without an end;
To love you much and yet to love you more,
  As Jordan at his flood sweeps either shore;
  Since woman is the helpmeet made for man.

6

Or puoi la quantitate
Comprender de l'amor che a te mi scalda.
DANTE.
Non vo' che da tal nodo amor mi scioglia.
PETRARCA.

Trust me, I have not earned your dear rebuke, —
 I love, as you would have me, God the most;
 Would lose not Him, but you, must one be lost,
Nor with Lot's wife cast back a faithless look,
Unready to forego what I forsook;
 This say I, having counted up the cost,
 This, though I be the feeblest of God's host,
The sorriest sheep Christ shepherds with His crook.
Yet while I love my God the most, I deem
 That I can never love you overmuch;
  I love Him more, so let me love you too;
 Yea, as I apprehend it, love is such
I cannot love you if I love not Him,
 I cannot love Him if I love not you.

7

Qui primavera sempre ed ogni frutto.
DANTE.
Ragionando con meco ed io con lui.
PETRARCA.

"Love me, for I love you" — and answer me,
 "Love me, for I love you": so shall we stand
 As happy equals in the flowering land
Of love, that knows not a dividing sea.
Love builds the house on rock and not on sand,
 Love laughs what while the winds rave desperately;
And who hath found love's citadel unmanned?
 And who hath held in bonds love's liberty? —
My heart's a coward though my words are brave —
 We meet so seldom, yet we surely part
 So often; there's a problem for your art!
 Still I find comfort in his Book who saith,
Though jealousy be cruel as the grave,
 And death be strong, yet love is strong as death.

8

Come dicesse a Dio, D'altro non calme.
DANTE.
Spero trovar pietà non che perdono.
PETRARCA.

"I, if I perish, perish" — Esther spake:
 And bride of life or death she made her fair
 In all the lustre of her perfumed hair
And smiles that kindle longing but to slake.
She put on pomp of loveliness, to take
 Her husband through his eyes at unaware;
 She spread abroad her beauty for a snare,
Harmless as doves and subtle as a snake.
She trapped him with one mesh of silken hair,
 She vanquished him by wisdom of her wit,   10
  And built her people's house that it should stand: —
  If I might take my life so in my hand,
And for my love to Love put up my prayer,
 And for love's sake by Love be granted it!

9

O dignitosa coscienza e netta!
DANTE.
Spirto più acceso di virtuti ardenti.
PETRARCA.

Thinking of you, and all that was, and all
 That might have been and now can never be,
 I feel your honoured excellence, and see
Myself unworthy of the happier call:
For woe is me who walk so apt to fall,
 So apt to shrink afraid, so apt to flee,
 Apt to lie down and die (ah woe is me!)
Faithless and hopeless turning to the wall.
And yet not hopeless quite nor faithless quite,
Because not loveless; love may toil all night,   10
But take at morning; wrestle till the break
 Of day, but then wield power with God and man: —
 So take I heart of grace as best I can,
Ready to spend and be spent for your sake.

10

Con miglior corso e con migliore stella.
DANTE.
La vita fugge e non s'arresta un' ora.
PETRARCA.

Time flies, hope flags, life plies a wearied wing;
Death following hard on life gains ground apace;
Faith runs with each and rears an eager face,
Outruns the rest, makes light of everything,
Spurns earth, and still finds breath to pray and sing;
While love ahead of all uplifts his praise,
Still asks for grace and still gives thanks for grace,
Content with all day brings and night will bring.
Life wanes; and when love folds his wings above
Tired hope, and less we feel his conscious pulse,
Let us go fall asleep, dear friend, in peace:
A little while, and age and sorrow cease;
A little while, and life reborn annuls
Loss and decay and death, and all is love.

11

Vien dietro a me e lascia dir le genti.
DANTE.
Contando i casi della vita nostra.
PETRARCA.

Many in aftertimes will say of you
"He loved her" — while of me what will they say?
Not that I loved you more than just in play,
For fashion's sake as idle women do.
Even let them prate; who know not what we knew
Of love and parting in exceeding pain,
Of parting hopeless here to meet again,
Hopeless on earth, and heaven is out of view.
But by my heart of love laid bare to you,
My love that you can make not void nor vain,
Love that foregoes you but to claim anew
Beyond this passage of the gate of death,
I charge you at the Judgment make it plain
My love of you was life and not a breath.

12

Amor che ne la mente mi ragiona.
DANTE.
Amor vien nel bel viso di costei.
PETRARCA.

If there be any one can take my place
    And make you happy whom I grieve to grieve,
    Think not that I can grudge it, but believe
I do commend you to that nobler grace,
That readier wit than mine, that sweeter face;
    Yea, since your riches make me rich, conceive
    I too am crowned, while bridal crowns I weave,
And thread the bridal dance with jocund pace.
For if I did not love you, it might be
    That I should grudge you some one dear delight;   10
        But since the heart is yours that was mine own,
    Your pleasure is my pleasure, right my right,
    Your honourable freedom makes me free,
        And you companioned I am not alone.

13

E drizzeremo gli occhi al Primo Amore.
DANTE.
Ma trovo peso non da le mie braccia.
PETRARCA.

If I could trust mine own self with your fate,
    Shall I not rather trust it in God's hand?
    Without Whose Will one lily doth not stand,
Nor sparrow fall at his appointed date;
    Who numbereth the innumerable sand,
    Who weighs the wind and water with a weight,
    To Whom the world is neither small nor great,
        Whose knowledge foreknew every plan we planned.
Searching my heart for all that touches you,
    I find there only love and love's goodwill   10
Helpless to help and impotent to do,
Of understanding dull, of sight most dim;
And therefore I commend you back to Him
    Whose love your love's capacity can fill.

14

E la Sua Volontade è nostra pace.
DANTE.
Sol con questi pensier, con altre chiome.
PETRARCA.

Youth gone, and beauty gone if ever there
   Dwelt beauty in so poor a face as this;
   Youth gone and beauty, what remains of bliss?
I will not bind fresh roses in my hair,
To shame a cheek at best but little fair, —
   Leave youth his roses, who can bear a thorn, —
I will not seek for blossoms anywhere,
   Except such common flowers as blow with corn.
Youth gone and beauty gone, what doth remain?
   The longing of a heart pent up forlorn,   10
   A silent heart whose silence loves and longs;
   The silence of a heart which sang its songs
While youth and beauty made a summer morn,
Silence of love that cannot sing again.

[1881]

ADVENT

EARTH grown old, yet still so green,
   Deep beneath her crust of cold
Nurses fire unfelt, unseen:
   Earth grown old.

We who live are quickly told:
Millions more lie hid between
   Inner swathings of her fold.

When will fire break up her screen?
   When will life burst thro' her mould?
Earth, earth, earth, thy cold is keen,   10
   Earth grown old.

[1885]

PARADISE

ONCE in a dream I saw the flowers
    That bud and bloom in Paradise;
    More fair they are than waking eyes
Have seen in all this world of ours.
And faint the perfume-bearing rose,
    And faint the lily on its stem,
And faint the perfect violet,
    Compared with them.

I heard the songs of Paradise:
    Each bird sat singing in his place;   10
    A tender song so full of grace
It soared like incense to the skies.
Each bird sat singing to his mate
    Soft cooing notes among the trees:
The nightingale herself were cold
    To such as these.

I saw the fourfold River flow,
    And deep it was, with golden sand;
    It flowed between a mossy land
With murmured music grave and low.   20
It hath refreshment for all thirst,
    For fainting spirits strength and rest;
Earth holds not such a draught as this
    From east to west.

The Tree of Life stood budding there,
    Abundant with its twelvefold fruits;
    Eternal sap sustains its roots,
Its shadowing branches fill the air,
Its leaves are healing for the world,
    Its fruit the hungry world can feed,   30
Sweeter than honey to the taste
    And balm indeed.

I saw the Gate called Beautiful;
    And looked, but scarce could look within;
    I saw the golden streets begin,
And outskirts of the glassy pool.

Oh harps, oh crowns of plenteous stars,
 Oh green palm branches many-leaved —
Eye hath not seen, nor ear hath heard,
  Nor heart conceived.   **40**

I hope to see these things again,
 But not as once in dreams by night;
 To see them with my very sight,
And touch and handle and attain:
To have all heaven beneath my feet
 For narrow way that once they trod;
To have my part with all the saints,
  And with my God.
28 February 1854.   [1875]

OLD AND NEW YEAR DITTIES

1

NEW Year met me somewhat sad:
 Old Year leaves me tired,
Stripped of favourite things I had,
 Baulked of much desired:
Yet farther on my road to-day,
God willing, farther on my way.
New Year coming on apace,
 What have you to give me?
Bring you scathe or bring you grace,
Face me with an honest face,   **10**
 You shall not deceive me:
Be it good or ill, be it what you will,
It needs shall help me on my road,
My rugged way to heaven, please God.
13 December 1856.

2

Watch with me, men, women, and children dear,
You whom I love, for whom I hope and fear,
Watch with me this last vigil of the year.
Some hug their business, some their pleasure scheme:
Some seize the vacant hour to sleep or dream;
Heart locked in heart some kneel and watch apart.

Watch with me, blessed spirits, who delight
All through the holy night to walk in white,
Or take your ease after the longdrawn fight.
I know not if they watch with me: I know   10
They count this eve of resurrection slow,
And cry "How long?" with urgent utterance strong.

Watch with me, Jesus, in my loneliness:
Though others say me nay, yet say Thou yes;
Though others pass me by, stop Thou to bless.
Yea, Thou dost stop with me this vigil night;
To-night of pain, to-morrow of delight:
I, Love, am Thine; Thou, Lord my God, art mine.
31 December 1858.

3

Passing away, saith the World, passing away:
Chances, beauty, and youth, sapped day by day:
Thy life never continueth in one stay.
Is the eye waxen dim, is the dark hair changing to grey
That hath won neither laurel nor bay?
I shall clothe myself in Spring and bud in May:
Thou, root-stricken, shalt not rebuild thy decay
On my bosom for aye.
Then I answered: Yea.

Passing away, saith my Soul, passing away: 10
With its burden of fear and hope, of labour and play,
Hearken what the past doth witness and say:
Rust in thy gold, a moth is in thine array,
A canker is in thy bud, thy leaf must decay.
At midnight, at cockcrow, at morning, one certain day
Lo the Bridegroom shall come and shall not delay;
Watch thou and pray.
Then I answered: Yea.

Passing away, saith my God, passing away:
Winter passeth after the long delay: 20
New grapes on the vine, new figs on the tender spray,
Turtle calleth turtle in Heaven's May.
Though I tarry, wait for Me, trust Me, watch and pray:
Arise, come away, night is past and lo it is day,
My love, My sister, My spouse, thou shalt hear Me say.
Then I answered: Yea.
31 December 1860.   [1862]

THE LOWEST PLACE

GIVE me the lowest place; not that I dare
  Ask for that lowest place, but Thou hast died
That I might live and share
  Thy glory by Thy side.

Give me the lowest place: or if for me
  That lowest place too high, make one more low
Where I may sit and see
  My God and love Thee so.

25 July 1863.   [1866]

BITTER FOR SWEET

SUMMER is gone with all its roses,
  Its sun and perfumes and sweet flowers,
  Its warm air and refreshing showers:
    And even Autumn closes.

Yea, Autumn's chilly self is going,
  And Winter comes which is yet colder;
  Each day the hoar-frost waxes bolder,
    And the last buds cease blowing.

December 1848.   [1862]

SONG

WHEN I am dead, my dearest,
  Sing no sad songs for me;
Plant thou no roses at my head,
  Nor shady cypress tree:
Be the green grass above me
  With showers and dewdrops wet:
And if thou wilt, remember,
  And if thou wilt, forget.

I shall not see the shadows,
  I shall not feel the rain;

10

I shall not hear the nightingale
  Sing on as if in pain:
And dreaming through the twilight
  That doth not rise nor set,
Haply I may remember,
  And haply may forget.

12 December 1848.   [1862]

SONG

OH roses for the flush of youth,
  And laurel for the perfect prime;
But pluck an ivy branch for me
  Grown old before my time.
Oh violets for the grave of youth,
  And bay for those dead in their prime;
Give me the withered leaves I chose
  Before in the old time.

6 February 1849.   [*1850;* 1862]

REST

O EARTH, lie heavily upon her eyes;
  Seal her sweet eyes weary of watching, Earth;
  Lie close around her; leave no room for mirth
With its harsh laughter, nor for sound of sighs.
She hath no questions, she hath no replies,
  Hushed in and curtained with a blessed dearth
  Of all that irked her from the hour of birth;
With stillness that is almost Paradise.
Darkness more clear than noonday holdeth her,
  Silence more musical than any song;
Even her very heart has ceased to stir:
Until the morning of Eternity
Her rest shall not begin nor end, but be;
  And when she wakes she will not think it long.

15 May 1849.   [1862]

12

REMEMBER

REMEMBER me when I am gone away,
   Gone far away into the silent land;
   When you can no more hold me by the hand,
Nor I half turn to go yet turning stay.
Remember me when no more day by day
   You tell me of our future that you plann'd:
   Only remember me; you understand
It will be late to counsel then or pray.
Yet if you should forget me for a while
   And afterwards remember, do not grieve: **10**
   For if the darkness and corruption leave
   A vestige of the thoughts that once I had,
Better by far you should forget and smile
   Than that you should remember and be sad.
25 July 1849.   [1862]

ECHO

COME to me in the silence of the night;
   Come in the speaking silence of a dream;
Come with soft rounded cheeks and eyes as bright
   As sunlight on a stream;
      Come back in tears,
O memory, hope, love of finished years.

O dream how sweet, too sweet, too bitter sweet,
   Whose wakening should have been in Paradise,
Where souls brimfull of love abide and meet;
   Where thirsting longing eyes   **10**
      Watch the slow door
That opening, letting in, lets out no more.

Yet come to me in dreams, that I may live
   My very life again though cold in death:
Come back to me in dreams, that I may give
   Pulse for pulse, breath for breath:
      Speak low, lean low,
As long ago, my love, how long ago.
18 December 1854.   [1862]

A BIRTHDAY

My heart is like a singing bird
    Whose nest is in a watered shoot:
My heart is like an apple-tree
    Whose boughs are bent with thickset fruit;
My heart is like a rainbow shell
    That paddles in a halcyon sea;
My heart is gladder than all these
    Because my love is come to me.

Raise me a dais of silk and down;
    Hang it with vair and purple dyes;   10
Carve it in doves and pomegranates,
    And peacocks with a hundred eyes;
Work it in gold and silver grapes,
    In leaves and silver fleurs-de-lys;
Because the birthday of my life
    Is come, my love is come to me.
18 November 1857.   [1862]

UP-HILL

Does the road wind up-hill all the way?
    Yes, to the very end.
Will the day's journey take the whole long day?
    From morn to night, my friend.

But is there for the night a resting-place?
    A roof for when the slow dark hours begin.
May not the darkness hide it from my face?
    You cannot miss that inn.

Shall I meet other wayfarers at night?
    Those who have gone before.   10
Then must I knock, or call when just in sight?
    They will not keep you standing at that door.

Shall I find comfort, travel-sore and weak?
    Of labour you shall find the sum.

Will there be beds for me and all who seek?
    Yea, beds for all who come.
29 June 1858.   [1862]

AMOR MUNDI

"OH where are you going with your love-locks flowing,
    On the west wind blowing along this valley track?"
"The downhill path is easy, come with me an it please ye,
    We shall escape the uphill by never turning back."
So they two went together in glowing August weather,
    The honey-breathing heather lay to their left and right;
And dear she was to doat on, her swift feet seemed to float on
    The air like soft twin pigeons too sportive to alight.

"Oh what is that in heaven where grey cloud-flakes are seven,
    Where blackest clouds hang riven just at the rainy skirt?"   10
"Oh that's a meteor sent us, a message dumb, portentous,
    An undeciphered solemn signal of help or hurt."

"Oh what is that glides quickly where velvet flowers grow thickly,
    Their scent comes rich and sickly?" "A scaled and hooded worm."
"Oh what's that in the hollow, so pale I quake to follow?"
    "Oh that's a thin dead body which waits the eternal term."

"Turn again, O my sweetest, — turn again, false and fleetest:
    This beaten way thou beatest, I fear, is hell's own track."
"Nay, too steep for hill mounting; nay, too late for cost counting:
    This downhill path is easy, but there's no turning back."   20
21 February 1865.   [1875]

DE PROFUNDIS

Oh why is heaven built so far,
    Oh why is earth set so remote?
I cannot reach the nearest star
    That hangs afloat.

I would not care to reach the moon,
    One round monotonous of change;
Yet even she repeats her tune
    Beyond my range.

I never watch the scattered fire
  Of stars, or sun's far-trailing train,
But all my heart is one desire,
  And all in vain: 10

For I am bound with fleshly bands,
  Joy, beauty, lie beyond my scope;
I strain my heart, I stretch my hands,
  And catch at hope.

[1881]

ASH WEDNESDAY

My God, my God, have mercy on my sin,
For it is great; and if I should begin
To tell this all, the day would be too small
  To tell it in.

My God, thou wilt have mercy on my sin
For Thy love's sake: yea, if I should begin
To tell this all, the day would be too small
  To tell it in.

[1885, 1893]

SLEEPING AT LAST

Sleeping at last, the trouble and tumult over,
  Sleeping at last, the struggle and horror past,
Cold and white, out of sight of friend and of lover,
  Sleeping at last.

No more a tired heart downcast or overcast,
No more pangs that wring or shifting fears that hover,
  Sleeping at last in a dreamless sleep locked fast.

Fast asleep. Singing birds in their leafy cover
  Cannot wake her, nor shake her the gusty blast.
Under the purple thyme and the purple clover   10
  Sleeping at last.

[1896]

PLATE 1. Three drawings by D. G. Rossetti

a. Elizabeth Siddal

b. Jane Morris

c. Fanny Cornforth

PLATE 2. D. G. Rossetti, *The Girlhood of Mary Virgin*

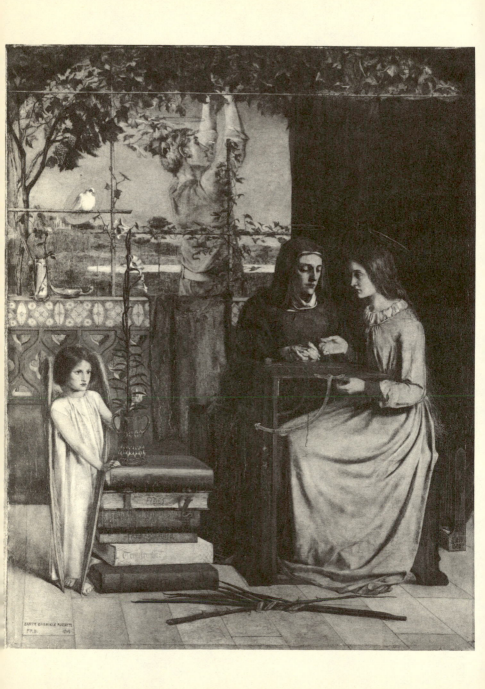

PLATE 3. D. G. Rossetti, *Ecce Ancilla Domini*

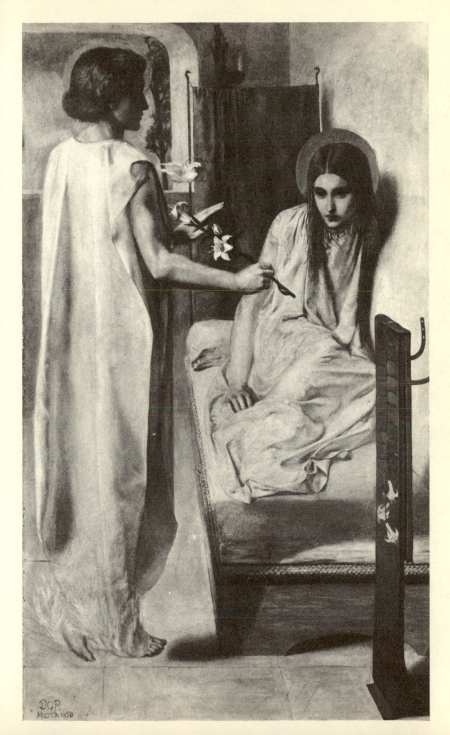

PLATE 4. D. G. Rossetti, *The Wedding of St. George*

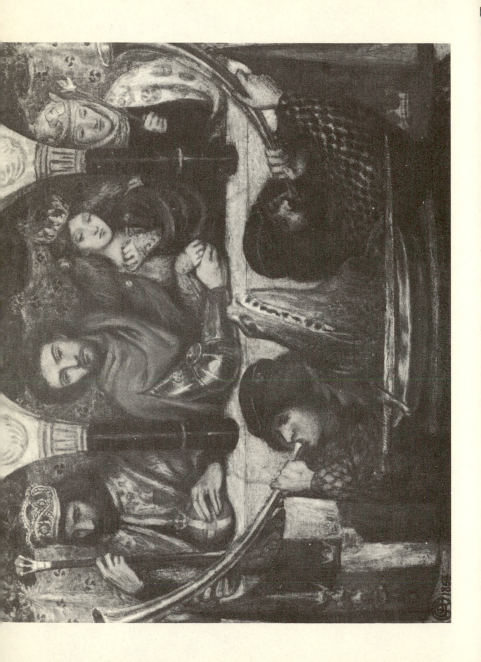

PLATE 5. D. G. Rossetti, *The Blessed Damozel*

THE BLESSED DAMOZEL

PLATE 6. D. G. Rossetti, *La Pia de' Tolomei*

PLATE 7. D. G. Rossetti, *The Sermon on the Mount*

PLATE 8. W. H. Hunt, *The Hireling Shepherd*

PLATE 9. W. H. Hunt, *May Morning on Magdalen Tower*

PLATE 10. J. E. Millais, *Christ in the House of his Parents*

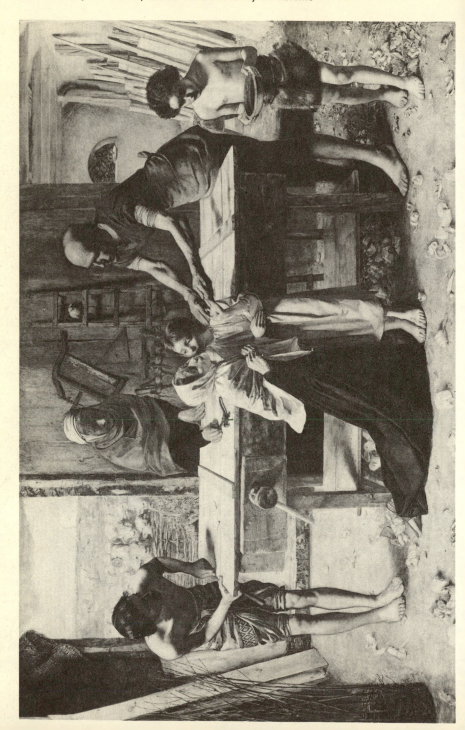

PLATE 11. J. E. Millais, *Ophelia*

PLATE 12. Ford Madox Brown, *An English Autumn Afternoon*

PLATE 13. John Ruskin, *Study of Trees*

PLATE 14. Edward Burne-Jones, *The Chess Players*

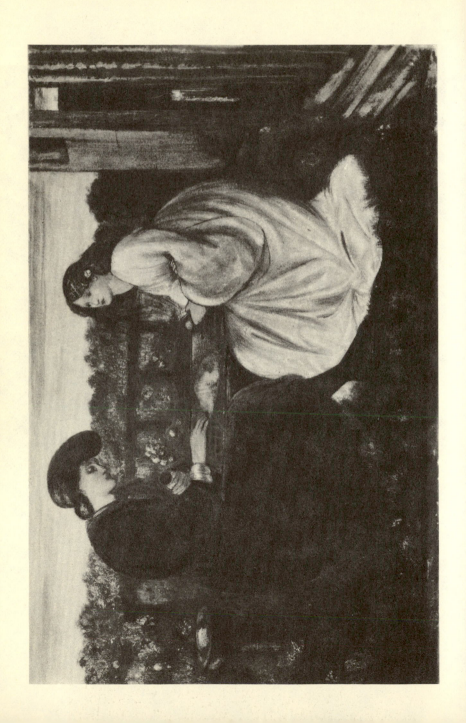

PLATE 15. Edward Burne-Jones, *The Building of the Brazen Tower*

PLATE 16. A page from the Kelmscott Press *Chaucer*

Incipit secunda pars

fER fRO THILKE PALAYS HONUR-
ABLE
Theras this markys shoop his mariage,
Ther stood a throop, of site delitable,
In which that povre folk of that village
Hadden hir beestes and hir herbergage,
And of hire labour tooke hir sustenance,
After that the erthe yaf hem habundance.

MONGES thise povre folk ther
dwelte a man
Which that was holden povrest of
hem alle;
But hye God som tyme senden kan
His grace into a litel oxes stalle:
Janicula men of that throop hym calle.
A doghter hadde he, fair ynogh to sighte,
And Grisildis this yonge mayden highte.

But for to speke of vertuous beautee,
Thanne was she oon the faireste under sonne;
for povreliche yfostred up was she,
No likerous lust was thurgh hire herte yronne;
Wel ofter of the welle than of the tonne
She drank, and for she wolde vertu plese,
She knew wel labour, but noon ydel ese.

But thogh this mayde tendre were of age,
Yet in the brest of hire virginitee
Ther was enclosed rype and sad corage,
And in greet reverence and charitee
Hir olde povre fader fostred shee;
A fewe sheep, spynnynge, on feeld she kepte,
She wolde noght been ydel til she slepte.

And whan she homward cam, she wolde brynge
Wortes, or other herbes, tymes ofte,

William Morris

THE DEFENCE OF GUENEVERE

But, knowing now that they would have her speak,
She threw her wet hair backward from her brow,
Her hand close to her mouth touching her cheek,

As though she had had there a shameful blow,
And feeling it shameful to feel aught but shame
All through her heart, yet felt her cheek burned so,

She must a little touch it; like one lame
She walked away from Gauwaine, with her head
Still lifted up; and on her cheek of flame

The tears dried quick; she stopped at last and said: 10
"O knights and lords, it seems but little skill
To talk of well-known things past now and dead.

"God wot I ought to say, I have done ill,
And pray you all forgiveness heartily!
Because you must be right, such great lords — still

"Listen, suppose your time were come to die,
And you were quite alone and very weak;
Yea, laid a dying while very mightily

161

"The wind was ruffling up the narrow streak
Of river through your broad lands running well: 20
Suppose a hush should come, then some one speak:

" 'One of these cloths is heaven, and one is hell,
Now choose one cloth for ever; which they be,
I will not tell you, you must somehow tell

" 'Of your own strength and mightiness; here, see!'
Yea, yea, my lord, and you to ope your eyes,
At foot of your familiar bed to see

"A great God's angel standing, with such dyes,
Not known on earth, on his great wings, and hands
Held out two ways, light from the inner skies   30

"Showing him well, and making his commands
Seem to be God's commands, moreover, too,
Holding within his hands the cloths on wands;

"And one of these strange choosing cloths was blue,
Wavy and long, and one cut short and red;
No man could tell the better of the two.

"After a shivering half-hour you said:
'God help! heaven's colour, the blue;' and he said, 'hell.'
Perhaps you then would roll upon your bed,

"And cry to all good men that loved you well,   40
'Ah Christ! if only I had known, known, known;'
Launcelot went away, then I could tell,

"Like wisest man how all things would be, moan,
And roll and hurt myself, and long to die,
And yet fear much to die for what was sown.

"Nevertheless you, O Sir Gauwaine, lie,
Whatever may have happened through these years,
God knows I speak truth, saying that you lie."

Her voice was low at first, being full of tears,
But as it cleared, it grew full loud and shrill,   50
Growing a windy shriek in all men's ears,

A ringing in their startled brains, until
She said that Gauwaine lied, then her voice sunk,
And her great eyes began again to fill,

Though still she stood right up, and never shrunk,
But spoke on bravely, glorious lady fair!
Whatever tears her full lips may have drunk,

She stood, and seemed to think, and wrung her hair,
Spoke out at last with no more trace of shame,
With passionate twisting of her body there: 60

"It chanced upon a day that Launcelot came
To dwell at Arthur's court: at Christmas-time
This happened; when the heralds sung his name,

" 'Son of King Ban of Benwick,' seemed to chime
Along with all the bells that rang that day,
O'er the white roofs, with little change of rhyme.

"Christmas and whitened winter passed away,
And over me the April sunshine came,
Made very awful with black hail-clouds, yea

"And in the Summer I grew white with flame,   70
And bowed my head down — Autumn, and the sick
Sure knowledge things would never be the same,

"However often Spring might be most thick
Of blossoms and buds, smote on me, and I grew
Careless of most things, let the clock tick, tick,

"To my unhappy pulse, that beat right through
My eager body; while I laughed out loud,
And let my lips curl up at false or true,

"Seemed cold and shallow without any cloud.
Behold my judges, then the cloths were brought;   80
While I was dizzied thus, old thoughts would crowd,

"Belonging to the time ere I was bought
By Arthur's great name and his little love;
Must I give up for ever then, I thought,

"That which I deemed would ever round me move
Glorifying all things; for a little word, "yes"
Scarce ever meant at all, must I now prove

"Stone-cold for ever? Pray you, does the Lord
Will that all folks should be quite happy and good?
I love God now a little, if this cord 90

"Were broken, once and for all what striving could
Make me love anything in earth or heaven?
So day by day it grew, as if one should

"Slip slowly down some path worn smooth and even,
Down to a cool sea on a summer day;
Yet still in slipping was there some small leaven *lightens mass*

"Of stretched hands catching small stones by the way,
Until one surely reached the sea at last,
And felt strange new joy as the worn head lay

"Back, with the hair like sea-weed; yea all past 100
Sweat of the forehead, dryness of the lips,
Washed utterly out by the dear waves o'ercast,

"In the lone sea, far off from any ships!
Do I not know now of a day in Spring?
No minute of that wild day ever slips

"From out my memory; I hear thrushes sing,
And wheresoever I may be, straightway
Thoughts of it all come up with most fresh sting:

"I was half mad with beauty on that day,
And went without my ladies all alone, 110
In a quiet garden walled round every way;

"I was right joyful of that wall of stone, *castle*
That shut the flowers and trees up with the sky,
And trebled all the beauty: to the bone,

"Yea right through to my heart, grown very shy
With weary thoughts, it pierced, and made me glad;
Exceedingly glad, and I knew verily,

"A little thing just then had made me mad;
I dared not think, as I was wont to do,
Sometimes, upon my beauty; if I had   120

"Held out my long hand up against the blue,
And, looking on the tenderly darken'd fingers,
Thought that by rights one ought to see quite through,

"There, see you, where the soft still light yet lingers,
Round by the edges; what should I have done,
If this had joined with yellow spotted singers,

"And startling green drawn upward by the sun?
But shouting, loosed out, see now! all my hair,
And trancedly stood watching the west wind run

"With faintest half-heard breathing sound — why there   130
I lose my head e'en now in doing this;
But shortly listen — In that garden fair

"Came Launcelot walking; this is true, the kiss
Wherewith we kissed in meeting that spring day,
I scarce dare talk of the remember'd bliss,

*Intense
Experience*

"When both our mouths went wandering in one way,
And aching sorely, met among the leaves;
Our hands being left behind strained far away.

"Never within a yard of my bright sleeves
Had Launcelot come before — and now, so nigh!   140
After that day why is it Guenevere grieves?

"Nevertheless you, O Sir Gauwaine, lie,
Whatever happened on through all those years,
God knows I speak truth, saying that you lie.

"Being such a lady could I weep these tears
If this were true? A great queen such as I
Having sinn'd this way, straight her conscience sears;

"And afterwards she liveth hatefully,
Slaying and poisoning, certes never weeps, —
Gauwaine, be friends now, speak me lovingly.   150

"Do I not see how God's dear pity creeps
All through your frame, and trembles in your mouth?
Remember in what grave your mother sleeps,

"Buried in some place far down in the south,
Men are forgetting as I speak to you;
By her head sever'd in that awful drouth

"Of pity that drew Agravaine's fell blow,
I pray your pity! let me not scream out
For ever after, when the shrill winds blow

"Through half your castle-locks! let me not shout   160
For ever after in the winter night
When you ride out alone! in battle-rout

"Let not my rusting tears make your sword light!
Ah! God of mercy, how he turns away!
So, ever must I dress me to the fight;

"So — let God's justice work! Gauwaine, I say,
See me hew down your proofs: yea, all men know
Even as you said how Mellyagraunce one day,

"One bitter day in *la Fausse Garde,* for so
All good knights held it after, saw —   170
Yea, sirs, by cursed unknightly outrage; though

"You, Gauwaine, held his word without a flaw,
This Mellyagraunce saw blood upon my bed —
Whose blood then pray you? is there any law

"To make a queen say why some spots of red
Lie on her coverlet? or will you say:
'Your hands are white, lady, as when you wed,

" 'Where did you bleed?' and must I stammer out: 'Nay,
I blush indeed, fair lord, only to rend
My sleeve up to my shoulder, where there lay   180

" 'A knife-point last night:' so must I defend
The honour of the lady Guenevere?
Not so, fair lords, even if the world should end

"This very day, and you were judges here
Instead of God. Did you see Mellyagraunce
When Launcelot stood by him? what white fear

"Curdled his blood, and how his teeth did dance,
His side sink in? as my knight cried and said:
'Slayer of unarm'd men, here is a chance!

" 'Setter of traps, I pray you guard your head,   190
By God I am so glad to fight with you,
Stripper of ladies, that my hand feels lead

" 'For driving weight; hurrah now! draw and do,
For all my wounds are moving in my breast,
And I am getting mad with waiting so.'

"He struck his hands together o'er the beast
Who fell down flat and grovell'd at his feet,
And groan'd at being slain so young — 'at least.'

"My knight said: 'Rise you, sir, who are so fleet
At catching ladies, half-arm'd will I fight,
My left side all uncovered!' then I weet,   200

"Up sprang Sir Mellyagraunce with great delight
Upon his knave's face; not until just then
Did I quite hate him, as I saw my knight

"Along the lists look to my stake and pen
With such a joyous smile, it made me sigh
From agony beneath my waist-chain, when

"The fight began, and to me they drew nigh;
Ever Sir Launcelot kept him on the right,
And traversed warily, and ever high   210

"And fast leapt caitiff's sword, until my knight
Sudden threw up his sword to his left hand,
Caught it, and swung it; that was all the fight,

"Except a spout of blood on the hot land;
For it was hottest summer; and I know
I wonder'd how the fire, while I should stand,

at stake

"And burn, against the heat, would quiver so,
Yards above my head; thus these matters went;
Which things were only warnings of the woe

"That fell on me. Yet Mellyagraunce was shent,   220
For Mellyagraunce had fought against the Lord;
Therefore, my lords, take heed lest you be blent

"With all this wickedness; say no rash word
Against me, being so beautiful; my eyes,
Wept all away to grey, may bring some sword

"To drown you in your blood; see my breast rise,
Like waves of purple sea, as here I stand;
And how my arms are moved in wonderful wise,

"Yea also at my full heart's strong command,
See through my long throat how the words go up   230
In ripples to my mouth; how in my hand

"The shadow lies like wine within a cup
Of marvellously colour'd gold; yea now
This little wind is rising, look you up,

removal?

"And wonder how the light is falling so
Within my moving tresses: will you dare,
When you have looked a little on my brow,

aesthetics vs. morality

"To say this thing is vile? or will you care
For any plausible lies of cunning woof,
When you can see my face with no lie there   240

"For ever? am I not a gracious proof —
'But in your chamber Launcelot was found' —   *charge*
Is there a good knight then would stand aloof,

defence of Launcelot

"When a queen says with gentle queenly sound:
'O true as steel, come now and talk with me,
I love to see your step upon the ground

" 'Unwavering, also well I love to see
That gracious smile light up your face, and hear
Your wonderful words, that all mean verily

" 'The thing they seem to mean: good friend, so dear   250
To me in everything, come here to-night,
Or else the hours will pass most dull and drear;

*Come up & see
me sometime*

" 'If you come not, I fear this time I might
Get thinking over much of times gone by,
When I was young, and green hope was in sight:

" 'For no man cares now to know why I sigh;
And no man comes to sing me pleasant songs,
Nor any brings me the sweet flowers that lie

" 'So thick in the gardens; therefore one so longs
To see you, Launcelot; that we may be   260
Like children once again, free from all wrongs

" 'Just for one night.' Did he not come to me?
What thing could keep true Launcelot away
If I said 'Come?' there was one less than three

"In my quiet room that night, and we were gay;
Till sudden I rose up, weak, pale, and sick,
Because a bawling broke our dream up, yea

"I looked at Launcelot's face and could not speak,
For he looked helpless too, for a little while;
Then I remember how I tried to shriek,   270

"And could not, but fell down; from tile to tile
The stones they threw up rattled o'er my head
And made me dizzier; till within a while

end of flashback

"My maids were all about me, and my head
On Launcelot's breast was being soothed away
From its white chattering, until Launcelot said —

that's enough!

"By God! I will not tell you more to-day,
Judge any way you will — what matters it?
You know quite well the story of that fray,

"How Launcelot still'd their bawling, the mad fit   280
That caught up Gauwaine — all, all, verily,
But just that which would save me; these things flit.

"Nevertheless you, O Sir Gauwaine, lie,
Whatever may have happen'd these long years,
God knows I speak truth, saying that you lie!

"All I have said is truth, by Christ's dear tears."
She would not speak another word, but stood
Turn'd sideways; listening, like a man who hears

His brother's trumpet sounding through the wood
Of his foes' lances. She lean'd eagerly,   290
And gave a slight spring sometimes, as she could

At last hear something really; joyfully
Her cheek grew crimson, as the headlong speed
Of the roan charger drew all men to see,
The knight who came was Launcelot at good need.

[1858]

KING ARTHUR'S TOMB

Hot August noon — already on that day
  Since sunrise through the Wiltshire downs, most sad
Of mouth and eye, he had gone leagues of way;
  Ay and by night, till whether good or bad

He was, he knew not, though he knew perchance
  That he was Launcelot, the bravest knight
Of all who since the world was, have borne lance,
  Or swung their swords in wrong cause or in right.

Nay, he knew nothing now, except that where
  The Glastonbury gilded towers shine,   10
A lady dwelt, whose name was Guenevere;
  This he knew also; that some fingers twine,

Not only in a man's hair, even his heart,
  (Making him good or bad I mean,) but in his life,
Skies, earth, men's looks and deeds, all that has part,
  Not being ourselves, in that half-sleep, half-strife,

(Strange sleep, strange strife,) that men call living; so
 Was Launcelot most glad when the moon rose,
Because it brought new memories of her — "Lo,
 Between the trees a large moon, the wind lows   20

"Not loud, but as a cow begins to low,
 Wishing for strength to make the herdsman hear:
The ripe corn gathereth dew; yea, long ago,
 In the old garden life, my Guenevere

"Loved to sit still among the flowers, till night
 Had quite come on, hair loosen'd, for she said,
Smiling like heaven, that its fairness might
 Draw up the wind sooner to cool her head.

"Now while I ride how quick the moon gets small,
 As it did then — I tell myself a tale   30
That will not last beyond the whitewashed wall,
 Thoughts of some joust must help me through the vale,

"Keep this till after — How Sir Gareth ran
 A good course that day under my Queen's eyes,
And how she sway'd laughing at Dinadan —
 No — back again, the other thoughts will rise,

"And yet I think so fast 'twill end right soon —
 Verily then I think, that Guenevere,
Made sad by dew and wind, and tree-barred moon,
 Did love me more than ever, was more dear   40

"To me than ever, she would let me lie
 And kiss her feet, or, if I sat behind,
Would drop her hand and arm most tenderly,
 And touch my mouth. And she would let me wind

"Her hair around my neck, so that it fell
 Upon my red robe, strange in the twilight
With many unnamed colours, till the bell
 Of her mouth on my cheek sent a delight

"Through all my ways of being; like the stroke
 Wherewith God threw all men upon the face   50
When he took Enoch, and when Enoch woke
 With a changed body in the happy place.

"Once, I remember, as I sat beside,
　　She turn'd a little and laid back her head,
And slept upon my breast; I almost died
　　In those night-watches with my love and dread.

"There lily-like she bow'd her head and slept,
　　And I breathed low and did not dare to move,
But sat and quiver'd inwardly, thoughts crept,
　　And frighten'd me with pulses of my Love.　　　　　**60**

"The stars shone out above the doubtful green
　　Of her bodice, in the green sky overhead;
Pale in the green sky were the stars I ween,
　　Because the moon shone like a star she shed

"When she dwelt up in heaven a while ago,
　　And ruled all things but God: the night went on,
The wind grew cold, and the white moon grew low,
　　One hand had fallen down, and now lay on

"My cold stiff palm; there were no colours then
　　For near an hour, and I fell asleep　　　　　　　**70**
In spite of all my striving, even when
　　I held her whose name-letters make me leap.

"I did not sleep long, feeling that in sleep
　　I did some loved one wrong, so that the sun
Had only just arisen from the deep
　　Still land of colours, when before me one

"Stood whom I knew, but scarcely dared to touch,
　　She seemed to have changed so in the night;
Moreover she held scarlet lilies, such
　　As Maiden Margaret bears upon the light　　　　**80**

"Of the great church walls, natheless did I walk
　　Through the fresh wet woods and the wheat that morn,
Touching her hair and hand and mouth, and talk
　　Of love we held, nigh hid among the corn.

"Back to the palace, ere the sun grew high,
　　We went, and in a cool green room all day
I gazed upon the arras giddily,
　　Where the wind set the silken kings a-sway.

"I could not hold her hand, or see her face;
 For which may God forgive me! but I think,   90
Howsoever, that she was not in that place."
 These memories Launcelot was quick to drink;

And when these fell, some paces past the wall,
 There rose yet others, but they wearied more,
And tasted not so sweet; they did not fall
 So soon, but vaguely wrenched his strained heart sore

In shadowy slipping from his grasp; these gone,
 A longing followed; if he might but touch
That Guenevere at once! Still night, the lone
 Grey horse's head before him vex'd him much,   100

In steady nodding over the grey road —
 Still night, and night, and night, and emptied heart
Of any stories; what a dismal load
 Time grew at last, yea, when the night did part,

And let the sun flame over all, still there
 The horse's grey ears turn'd this way and that,
And still he watch'd them twitching in the glare
 Of the morning sun, behind them still he sat,

Quite wearied out with all the wretched night,
 Until about the dustiest of the day,   110
On the last down's brow he drew his rein in sight
 Of the Glastonbury roofs that choke the way.

And he was now quite giddy as before,
 When she slept by him, tired out and her hair
Was mingled with the rushes on the floor,
 And he, being tired too, was scarce aware

Of her presence; yet as he sat and gazed,
 A shiver ran throughout him, and his breath
Came slower, he seem'd suddenly amazed,
 As though he had not heard of Arthur's death. 120

This for a moment only, presently
 He rode on giddy still, until he reach'd
A place of apple-trees, by the thorn-tree
 Wherefrom St. Joseph in the days past preached.

Dazed there he laid his head upon a tomb,
　　Not knowing it was Arthur's, at which sight
One of her maidens told her, "He is come,"
　　And she went forth to meet him; yet a blight

Had settled on her, all her robes were black,
　　With a long white veil only; she went slow,　　　130
As one walks to be slain, her eyes did lack
　　Half her old glory, yea, alas! the glow

Had left her face and hands; this was because
　　As she lay last night on her purple bed,
Wishing for morning, grudging every pause
　　Of the palace clocks, until that Launcelot's head

Should lie on her breast, with all her golden hair
　　Each side — when suddenly the thing grew drear,
In morning twilight, when the grey downs bare
　　Grew into lumps of sin to Guenevere.　　　140

At first she said no word, but lay quite still,
　　Only her mouth was open, and her eyes
Gazed wretchedly about from hill to hill;
　　As though she asked, not with so much surprise

As tired disgust, what made them stand up there
　　So cold and grey. After, a spasm took
Her face, and all her frame, she caught her hair,
　　All her hair, in both hands, terribly she shook,

And rose till she was sitting in the bed,
　　Set her teeth hard, and shut her eyes and seem'd　　　150
As though she would have torn it from her head,
　　Natheless she dropp'd it, lay down, as she deem'd

It matter'd not whatever she might do —
　　O Lord Christ! pity on her ghastly face!
Those dismal hours while the cloudless blue
　　Drew the sun higher — He did give her grace;

Because at last she rose up from her bed,
　　And put her raiment on, and knelt before
The blessed rood, and with her dry lips said,
　　Muttering the words against the marble floor:　　　160

"Unless you pardon, what shall I do, Lord,
　But go to hell? and there see day by day
Foul deed on deed, hear foulest word on word,
　For ever and ever, such as on the way

"To Camelot I heard once from a churl,
　That curled me up upon my jennet's neck
With bitter shame; how then, Lord, should I curl
　For ages and for ages? dost thou reck

[handwritten: rustic fellow]
[handwritten: abuse from peasants]

"That I am beautiful, Lord, even as you
　And your dear Mother? why did I forget
You were so beautiful, and good, and true,
　That you loved me so, Guenevere? O yet

[handwritten: 176]
[handwritten: christmas sermon]

"If even I go to hell, I cannot choose
　But love you, Christ, yea, though I cannot keep
From loving Launcelot; O Christ! must I lose
　My own heart's love? see, though I cannot weep,

"Yet am I very sorry for my sin;
　Moreover, Christ, I cannot bear that hell,
I am most fain to love you, and to win
　A place in heaven some time — I cannot tell —　　　　180

"Speak to me, Christ! I kiss, kiss, kiss your feet;
　Ah! now I weep!" — The maid said, "By the tomb
He waiteth for you, lady," coming fleet,
　Not knowing what woe filled up all the room.

So Guenevere rose and went to meet him there;
　He did not hear her coming, as he lay
On Arthur's head, till some of her long hair
　Brush'd on the new-cut stone — "Well done! to pray

"For Arthur, my dear lord, the greatest king
　That ever lived." "Guenevere! Guenevere!　　　　190
Do you not know me, are you gone mad? fling
　Your arms and hair about me, lest I fear

"You are not Guenevere, but some other thing."
　"Pray you forgive me, fair lord Launcelot!
I am not mad, but I am sick; they cling,
　God's curses, unto such as I am; not

"Ever again shall we twine arms and lips."
  "Yea, she is mad: thy heavy law, O Lord,
Is very tight about her now, and grips
  Her poor heart, so that no right word   200

"Can reach her mouth; so, Lord, forgive her now,
  That she not knowing what she does, being mad,
Kills me in this way — Guenevere, bend low
  And kiss me once! for God's love kiss me! sad

"Though your face is, you look much kinder now;
  Yea once, once for the last time kiss me, lest I die."
"Christ! my hot lips are very near his brow,
    Help me to save his soul! — Yea, verily,

"Across my husband's head, fair Launcelot!
  Fair serpent mark'd with V upon the head!   210
This thing we did while yet he was alive,
  Why not, O twisting knight, now he is dead?

"Yea, shake! shake now and shiver! if you can
  Remember anything for agony,
Pray you remember how when the wind ran
  One cool spring evening through fair aspen-tree,

"And elm and oak about the palace there,
  The king came back from battle, and I stood
To meet him, with my ladies, on the stair,
  My face made beautiful with my young blood!"   220

"Will she lie now, Lord God?" "Remember too,
  Wrung heart, how first before the knights there came
A royal bier, hung round with green and blue,
  About it shone great tapers with sick flame.

"And thereupon Lucius, the Emperor,
  Lay royal-robed, but stone-cold now and dead,
Not able to hold sword or sceptre more,
  But not quite grim; because his cloven head

"Bore no marks now of Launcelot's bitter sword,
  Being by embalmers deftly solder'd up;   230
So still it seem'd the face of a great lord,
  Being mended as a craftsman mends a cup.

"Also the heralds sung rejoicingly
    To their long trumpets; 'Fallen under shield,
Here lieth Lucius, King of Italy,
    Slain by Lord Launcelot in open field.'

"Thereat the people shouted 'Launcelot!'
    And through the spears I saw you drawing nigh,
You and Lord Arthur — nay, I saw you not,
    But rather Arthur, God would not let die,   240

"I hoped, these many years; he should grow great,
    And in his great arms still encircle me,
Kissing my face, half blinded with the heat
    Of king's love for the queen I used to be.

"Launcelot, Launcelot, why did he take your hand,
    When he had kissed me in his kingly way?
Saying, 'This is the knight whom all the land
    Calls Arthur's banner, sword, and shield to-day;

" 'Cherish him, love.' Why did your long lips cleave
    In such strange way unto my fingers then?   250
So eagerly glad to kiss, so loath to leave
    When you rose up? Why among helmed men

"Could I always tell you by your long strong arms,
    And sway like an angel's in your saddle there?
Why sicken'd I so often with alarms
    Over the tilt-yard? Why were you more fair

"Than aspens in the autumn at their best?
    Why did you fill all lands with your great fame,
So that Breuse even, as he rode, fear'd lest
    At turning of the way your shield should flame?   260

"Was it nought then, my agony and strife?
    When as day passed by day, year after year,
I found I could not live a righteous life?
    Didst ever think queens held their truth for dear?

"O, but your lips say, 'Yea, but she was cold
    Sometimes, always uncertain as the spring;
When I was sad she would be overbold,
    Longing for kisses;' when war-bells did ring,

"The back-toll'd bells of noisy Camelot —"
   "Now, Lord God, listen! listen, Guenevere,   270
Though I am weak just now, I think there's not
   A man who dares to say: 'You hated her,

" 'And left her moaning while you fought your fill
   In the daisied meadows;' lo you her thin hand,
That on the carven stone can not keep still,
   Because she loves me against God's command,

"Has often been quite wet with tear on tear,
   Tears Launcelot keeps somewhere, surely not
In his own heart, perhaps in Heaven, where
   He will not be these ages." — "Launcelot!   280

"Loud lips, wrung heart! I say, when the bells rang,
   The noisy back-toll'd bells of Camelot,
There were two spots on earth, the thrushes sang
   In the lonely gardens where my love was not,

"Where I was almost weeping; I dared not
   Weep quite in those days, lest one maid should say,
In tittering whispers: 'Where is Launcelot
   To wipe with some kerchief those tears away?'

"Another answer sharply with brows knit,
   And warning hand up, scarcely lower though: 290
"You speak too loud, see you, she heareth it,
   This tigress fair has claws, as I well know,

" 'As Launcelot knows too, the poor knight! well-a-day!
   Why met he not with Iseult from the West,
Or better still, Iseult of Brittany,
   Perchance indeed quite ladyless were best.'

"Alas, my maids, you loved not overmuch
   Queen Guenevere, uncertain as sunshine
In March; forgive me! for my sin being such,
   About my whole life, all my deeds did twine,   300

"Made me quite wicked; as I found out then,
   I think; in the lonely palace where each morn
We went, my maids and I, to say prayers when
   They sang mass in the chapel on the lawn.

"And every morn I scarce could pray at all,
　For Launcelot's red-golden hair would play,
Instead of sunlight, on the painted wall,
　Mingled with dreams of what the priest did say;

"Grim curses out of Peter and of Paul;
　Judging of strange sins in Leviticus;　　　　　　　　　310
Another sort of writing on the wall,
　Scored deep across the painted heads of us.

"Christ sitting with the woman at the well,
　And Mary Magdalen repenting there,
Her dimmed eyes scorch'd and red at sight of hell
　So hardly 'scaped, no gold light on her hair.

"And if the priest said anything that seemed
　To touch upon the sin they said we did, —
(This in their teeth) they look'd as if they deem'd
　That I was spying what thoughts might be hid　　　320

"Under green-cover'd bosoms, heaving quick
　Beneath quick thoughts; while they grew red with shame,
And gazed down at their feet — while I felt sick,
　And almost shriek'd if one should call my name.

"The thrushes sang in the lone garden there —
　But where you were the birds were scared I trow —
Clanging of arms about pavilions fair,
　Mixed with the knights' laughs; there, as I well know,

"Rode Launcelot, the king of all the band,
　And scowling Gauwaine, like the night in day,　　　330
And handsome Gareth, with his great white hand
　Curl'd round the helm-crest, ere he join'd the fray;

"And merry Dinadan with sharp dark face,
　All true knights loved to see; and in the fight
Great Tristram, and though helmed you could trace
　In all his bearing the frank noble knight;

"And by him Palomydes; helmet off,
　He fought, his face brush'd by his hair,
Red heavy swinging hair; he fear'd a scoff
　So overmuch, though what true knight would dare　　　340

"To mock that face, fretted with useless care,
    And bitter useless striving after love?
O Palomydes, with much honour bear
    Beast Glatysaunt upon your shield, above

"Your helm that hides the swinging of your hair,
    And think of Iseult, as your sword drives through
Much mail and plate — O God, let me be there
    A little time, as I was long ago!

"Because stout Gareth lets his spear fall low,
    Gauwaine and Launcelot and Dinadan   350
Are helm'd and waiting; let the trumpets go!
    Bend over, ladies, to see all you can!

"Clench teeth, dames, yea, clasp hands, for Gareth's spear
    Throws Kay from out his saddle, like a stone
From a castle-window when the foe draws near —
    'Iseult!' — Sir Dinadan rolleth overthrown.

" 'Iseult' — again — the pieces of each spear
    Fly fathoms up, and both the great steeds reel;
'Tristram for Iseult!' 'Iseult!' and 'Guenevere,'
    The ladies' names bite verily like steel.   360

"They bite — bite me, Lord God! — I shall go mad,
    Or else die kissing him, he is so pale;
He thinks me mad already, O bad! bad!
    Let me lie down a little while and wail."

"No longer so, rise up, I pray you, love,
    And slay me really, then we shall be heal'd,
Perchance, in the aftertime by God above."
    "Banner of Arthur — with black-bended shield

"Sinister-wise across the fair gold ground!
    Here let me tell you what a knight you are,   370
O sword and shield of Arthur! you are found
    A crooked sword, I think, that leaves a scar

"On the bearer's arm, so be he thinks it straight,
    Twisted Malay's crease beautiful blue-grey,
Poison'd with sweet fruit; as he found too late,
    My husband Arthur, on some bitter day!

"O sickle cutting hemlock the day long!
   That the husbandman across his shoulder hangs,
And, going homeward about evensong,
   Dies the next morning, struck through by the fangs!   380

"Banner and sword and shield, you dare not pray to die,
   Lest you meet Arthur in the other world,
And knowing who you are, he pass you by,
   Taking short turns that he may watch you curl'd

"Body and face and limbs in agony,
   Lest he weep presently and go away,
Saying, ' I loved him once,' with a sad sigh —
   Now I have slain him, Lord, let me go too, I pray.

                                     LAUNCELOT *falls.*

"Alas, alas! I know not what to do,
   If I run fast it is perchance that I   390
May fall and stun myself, much better so,
   Never, never again! not even when I die."

          LAUNCELOT, *on awaking*
"I stretch'd my hands towards her and fell down,
   How long I lay in swoon I cannot tell:
My head and hands were bleeding from the stone,
   When I rose up, also I heard a bell."

                                [1858]

SIR GALAHAD: A CHRISTMAS MYSTERY

IT is the longest night in all the year,
    Near on the day when the Lord Christ was born;
Six hours ago I came and sat down here,
    And ponder'd sadly, wearied and forlorn.

The winter wind that pass'd the chapel-door,
    Sang out a moody tune, that went right well
With mine own thoughts: I look'd down on the floor,
    Between my feet, until I heard a bell

Sound a long way off through the forest deep,
    And toll on steadily; a drowsiness   10
Came on me, so that I fell half asleep,
    As I sat there not moving: less and less

I saw the melted snow that hung in beads
    Upon my steel-shoes; less and less I saw
Between the tiles the bunches of small weeds:
    Heartless and stupid, with no touch of awe

Upon me, half-shut eyes upon the ground,
    I thought; O Galahad! the days go by,
Stop and cast up now that which you have found,
    So sorely you have wrought and painfully.   20

Night after night your horse treads down alone
    The sere damp fern, night after night you sit
Holding the bridle like a man of stone,
    Dismal, unfriended, what thing comes of it.

And what if Palomydes also ride,
    And over many a mountain and bare heath
Follow the questing beast with none beside?
    Is he not able still to hold his breath

With thoughts of Iseult? doth he not grow pale
    With weary striving, to seem best of all   30
To her, "as she is best," he saith? to fail
    Is nothing to him, he can never fall.

For unto such a man love-sorrow is
　So dear a thing unto his constant heart,
That even if he never win one kiss,
　Or touch from Iseult, it will never part.

And he will never know her to be worse
　Than in his happiest dreams he thinks she is:
Good knight, and faithful, you have 'scaped the curse
　In wonderful-wise; you have great store of bliss.　　　40

Yea, what if Father Launcelot ride out,
　Can he not think of Guenevere's arms, round,
Warm and lithe, about his neck, and shout
　Till all the place grows joyful with the sound?

And when he lists can often see her face,
　And think, "Next month I kiss you, or next week,
And still you think of me:" therefore the place
　Grows very pleasant, whatsoever he seek.

But me, who ride alone, some carle shall find
　Dead in my arms in the half-melted snow,　　　50
When all unkindly with the shifting wind,
　The thaw comes on at Candlemas: I know

Indeed that they will say: "This Galahad
　If he had lived had been a right good knight;
Ah! poor chaste body!" but they will be glad,
　Not most alone, but all, when in their sight

That very evening in their scarlet sleeves
　The gay-dress'd minstrels sing; no maid will talk
Of sitting on my tomb, until the leaves,
　Grown big upon the bushes of the walk,　　　60

East of the Palace-pleasaunce, make it hard
　To see the minster therefrom: well-a-day!
Before the trees by autumn were well bared,
　I saw a damozel with gentle play,

Within that very walk say last farewell
　To her dear knight, just riding out to find
(Why should I choke to say it?) the Sangreal,
　And their last kisses sunk into my mind,

Yea, for she stood lean'd forward on his breast,
    Rather, scarce stood; the back of one dear hand,   70
That it might well be kiss'd, she held and press'd
    Against his lips; long time they stood there, fann'd

By gentle gusts of quiet frosty wind, *other's moment.*
    Till Mador de la porte a-going by,
And my own horsehoofs roused them; they untwined,
    And parted like a dream. In this way I,

With sleepy face bent to the chapel floor,
    Kept musing half asleep, till suddenly
A sharp bell rang from close beside the door,
    And I leapt up when something pass'd me by,   80

Shrill ringing going with it, still half blind
    I stagger'd after, a great sense of awe
At every step kept gathering on my mind,
    Thereat I have no marvel, for I saw

One sitting on the altar as a throne,
    Whose face no man could say he did not know,
And though the bell still rang, he sat alone,
    With raiment half blood-red, half white as snow.

Right so I fell upon the floor and knelt,
    Not as one kneels in church when mass is said,   90
But in a heap, quite nerveless, for I felt
    The first time what a thing was perfect dread.

But mightily the gentle voice came down:
    "Rise up, and look and listen, Galahad,
Good knight of God, for you will see no frown
    Upon my face; I come to make you glad.

"For that you say that you are all alone,
    I will be with you always, and fear not
You are uncared for, though no maiden moan
    Above your empty tomb; for Launcelot,   100

"He in good time shall be my servant too,
    Meantime, take note whose sword first made him knight,
And who has loved him alway, yea, and who
    Still trusts him alway, though in all men's sight,

"He is just what you know, O Galahad,
  This love is happy even as you say,
But would you for a little time be glad,
  To make ME sorry long day after day?

"Her warm arms round his neck half-throttle ME,
  The hot love-tears burn deep like spots of lead,   110
Yea, and the years pass quick: right dismally
  Will Launcelot at one time hang his head; *sooner or later*

"Yea, old and shrivell'd he shall win my love.
  Poor Palomydes fretting out his soul!
Not always is he able, son, to move
  His love, and do it honour: needs must roll

"The proudest destrier sometimes in the dust,
  And then 'tis weary work; he strives beside
Seem better than he is, so that his trust
  Is always on what chances may betide;   120

"And so he wears away, my servant, too,
  When all these things are gone, and wretchedly
He sits and longs to moan for Iseult, who
  Is no care now to Palomydes: see,

"O good son Galahad, upon this day,
  Now even, all these things are on your side,
But these you fight not for; look up, I say,
  And see how I can love you, for no pride

"Closes your eyes, no vain lust keeps them down.
  See now you have ME always; following   130
That holy vision, Galahad, go on,
  Until at last you come to Me to sing

"In Heaven always, and to walk around
  The garden where I am." He ceased, my face
And wretched body fell upon the ground;
  And when I look'd again, the holy place

Was empty; but right so the bell again
  Came to the chapel-door, there entered
Two angels first, in white, without a stain,
  And scarlet wings, then after them, a bed   140

Four ladies bore, and set it down beneath
  The very altar-step, and while for fear
I scarcely dared to move or draw my breath,
  Those holy ladies gently came a-near,

And quite unarm'd me, saying: "Galahad,
  Rest here awhile and sleep, and take no thought
Of any other thing than being glad;
  Hither the Sangreal will be shortly brought,

"Yet must you sleep the while it stayeth here."
  Right so they went away, and I, being weary,   150
Slept long and dream'd of Heaven: the bell comes near,
I doubt it grows to morning. Miserere!

Enter Two Angels in white, with scarlet wings; also Four Ladies
    in gowns of red and green; also an Angel, bearing in his
    hands a surcoat of white, with a red cross.

AN ANGEL

O servant of the high God, Galahad!
  Rise and be arm'd, the Sangreal is gone forth
Through the great forest, and you must be had
  Unto the sea that lieth on the north:

There shall you find the wondrous ship wherein
  The spindles of King Solomon are laid,
And the sword that no man draweth without sin,
  But if he be most pure: and there is stay'd,   160

Hard by, Sir Launcelot, whom you will meet
  In some short space upon that ship: first, though,
Will come here presently that lady sweet,
  Sister of Percival, whom you well know,

And with her Bors and Percival: stand now,
  These ladies will to arm you.

FIRST LADY *putting on the hauberk.*
Galahad,
  That I may stand so close beneath your brow,
    I, Margaret of Antioch, am glad.

SECOND LADY *girding him with the sword.*

That I may stand and touch you with my hand,
 O Galahad, I, Cecily, am glad.   170

THIRD LADY *buckling on the spurs.*

That I may kneel while up above you stand,
 And gaze at me, O holy Galahad,

I, Lucy, am most glad.

FOURTH LADY *putting on the basnet.*

    O gentle knight,
 That you bow down to us in reverence,
We are most glad, I, Katherine, with delight
 Must needs fall trembling.

ANGEL *putting on the crossed surcoat.*

    Galahad, we go hence,
For here, amid the straying of the snow,
 Come Percival's sister, Bors, and Percival.
    The Four Ladies carry out the bed,
    and all go but Galahad.

GALAHAD

How still and quiet everything seems now:
 They come, too, for I hear the horsehoofs fall.   180

Enter Sir Bors, Sir Percival *and* his Sister.

Fair friends and gentle lady, God you save!
 A many marvels have been here to-night;
Tell me what news of Launcelot you have,
 And has God's body ever been in sight?

SIR BORS

Why, as for seeing that same holy thing,
 As we were riding slowly side by side,
An hour ago, we heard a sweet voice sing,
 And through the bare twigs saw a great light glide,

With many-colour'd raiment, but far off,
 And so pass'd quickly — from the court nought good;   190
Poor merry Dinadan, that with jape and scoff
 Kept us all merry, in a little wood

Was found all hack'd and dead: Sir Lionel
  And Gauwaine have come back from the great quest,
Just merely shamed; and Lauvaine, who loved well
  Your father Launcelot, at the king's behest

Went out to seek him, but was almost slain,
  Perhaps is dead now; everywhere
The knights come foil'd from the great quest, in vain;
  In vain they struggle for the vision fair.   200

                                        [1858]

THE CHAPEL IN LYONESS

SIR OZANA LE CURE HARDY. SIR GALAHAD.
  SIR BORS DE GANYS.

SIR OZANA

ALL day long and every day,
From Christmas-Eve to Whit-Sunday,
Within that Chapel-aisle I lay,
  And no man came a-near.

Naked to the waist was I,
And deep within my breast did lie,
Though no man any blood could spy,
  The truncheon of a spear.

No meat did ever pass my lips
Those days — (Alas! the sunlight slips   10
From off the gilded parclose, dips,
  And night comes on a-pace.)

My arms lay back behind my head;
Over my raised-up knees was spread
A samite cloth of white and red;
  A rose lay on my face.

Many a time I tried to shout;
But as in dream of battle-rout,
My frozen speech would not well out;
  I could not even weep.   20

With inward sigh I see the sun
Fade off the pillars one by one,
My heart faints when the day is done,
    Because I cannot sleep.

Sometimes strange thoughts pass through my head;
Not like a tomb is this my bed,
Yet oft I think that I am dead;
    That round my tomb is writ:

"Ozana of the hardy heart,
    Knight of the Table Round,   30
Pray for his soul, lords of your part;
    A true knight he was found."
Ah! me, I cannot fathom it.

                                          He sleeps.

SIR GALAHAD

All day long and every day,
Till his madness pass'd away,
I watch'd Ozana as he lay
    Within the gilded screen.

All my singing moved him not;
As I sung my heart grew hot,
With the thought of Launcelot   40
    Far away, I ween.

So I went a little space
From out the chapel, bathed my face
In the stream that runs apace
    By the churchyard wall.

There I pluck'd a faint wild rose,
Hard by where the linden grows,
Sighing over silver rows
    Of the lilies tall.

I laid the flower across his mouth;   50
The sparkling drops seem'd good for drouth;
He smiled, turn'd round towards the south,
    Held up a golden tress.

The light smote on it from the west:
He drew the covering from his breast,
Against his heart that hair he prest;
    Death him soon will bless.

SIR BORS

I enter'd by the western door;
    I saw a knight's helm lying there:
I raised my eyes from off the floor,   60
    And caught the gleaming of his hair.

I stept full softly up to him;
    I laid my chin upon his head;
I felt him smile; my eyes did swim,
    I was so glad he was not dead.

I heard Ozana murmur low,
    "There comes no sleep nor any love."
But Galahad stoop'd and kiss'd his brow:
    He shiver'd; I saw his pale lips move.

SIR OZANA

There comes no sleep nor any love;   70
    Ah me! I shiver with delight.
I am so weak I cannot move;
    God move me to thee, dear, to-night!
Christ help! I have but little wit:
My life went wrong; I see it writ:

"Ozana of the hardy heart,
    Knight of the Table Round,
Pray for his soul, lords, on your part;
    A good knight he was found."
Now I begin to fathom it.   79 *He dies.*

SIR BORS

Galahad sits dreamily;
What strange things may his eyes see,
Great blue eyes fix'd full on me?
On his soul, Lord, have mercy.

SIR GALAHAD

Ozana, shall I pray for thee?
    Her cheek is laid to thine;

No long time hence, also I see
Thy wasted fingers twine

Within the tresses of her hair
That shineth gloriously,
Thinly outspread in the clear air
Against the jasper sea.
[*1856; 1858*]

90

*reunion of
lovers in
heaven*

*correspondant redemptions are in discovering
what they lack*

SIR PETER HARPDON'S END

In an English castle in Poictou.

SIR PETER HARPDON, *a Gascon knight in the English
service, and* JOHN CURZON, *his lieutenant.*

JOHN CURZON

OF those three prisoners, that before you came
We took down at St. John's hard by the mill,
Two are good masons; we have tools enough,
And you have skill to set them working.

SIR PETER

So —
What are their names?

JOHN CURZON

Why, Jacques Aquadent,
And Peter Plombiere, but —

SIR PETER

What colour'd hair
Has Peter now? has Jacques got bow legs?

JOHN CURZON

Why, sir, you jest — what matters Jacques' hair,
Or Peter's legs to us?

SIR PETER

O! John, John, John!
Throw all your mason's tools down the deep well,

10

Hang Peter up and Jacques; they're no good,
We shall not build, man.

JOHN CURZON going

Shall I call the guard

To hang them, sir? and yet, sir, for the tools,
We'd better keep them still; sir, fare you well.

Muttering as he goes.

What have I done that he should jape at me?
And why not build? the walls are weak enough,
And we've two masons and a heap of tools.

Goes, still muttering.

SIR PETER

To think a man should have a lump like that
For his lieutenant! I must call him back,
Or else, as surely as St. George is dead,   20
He'll hang our friends the masons — here, John! John!

JOHN CURZON

At your good service, sir.

SIR PETER

Come now, and talk

This weighty matter out; there, we've no stone
To mend our walls with, — neither brick nor stone.

JOHN CURZON

There is a quarry, sir, some ten miles off.

SIR PETER

We are not strong enough to send ten men
Ten miles to fetch us stone enough to build.
In three hours' time they would be taken or slain,
The cursed Frenchmen ride abroad so thick.

JOHN CURZON

But we can send some villaynes to get stone.   30

SIR PETER

Alas! John, that we cannot bring them back,
They would go off to Clisson or Sanxere,
And tell them we were weak in walls and men,
Then down go we; for, look you, times are changed,

And now no longer does the country shake
At sound of English names; our captains fade
From off our muster-rolls. At Lusac bridge
I daresay you may even yet see the hole
That Chandos beat in dying; far in Spain
Pembroke is prisoner; Phelton prisoner here;   **40**
Manny lies buried in the Charterhouse;
Oliver Clisson turn'd these years agone;
The Captal died in prison; and, over all,
Edward the prince lies underneath the ground;
Edward the king is dead; at Westminster
The carvers smooth the curls of his long beard.
Everything goes to rack — eh! and we too.
Now, Curzon, listen; if they come, these French,
Whom have I got to lean on here, but you?
A man can die but once, will you die then,   **50**
Your brave sword in your hand, thoughts in your heart
Of all the deeds we have done here in France —
And yet may do? So God will have your soul,
Whoever has your body.

JOHN CURZON

Why, sir, I

Will fight till the last moment, until then
Will do whate'er you tell me. Now I see
We must e'en leave the walls; well, well, perhaps
They're stronger than I think for; pity though,
For some few tons of stone, if Guesclin comes!

SIR PETER

Farewell, John, pray you watch the Gascons well,   **60**
I doubt them.

JOHN CURZON

Truly, sir, I will watch well.   *Goes.*

SIR PETER

Farewell, good lump! and yet, when all is said,
'Tis a good lump. Why then, if Guesclin comes;
Some dozen stones from his petrariae,
And, under shelter of his crossbows, just
An hour's steady work with pickaxes,
Then a great noise — some dozen swords and glaives
A-playing on my basnet all at once,

And little more cross purposes on earth
For me.
    Now this is hard: a month ago,   **70**
And a few minutes' talk had set things right
'Twixt me and Alice — if she had a doubt,
As (may Heaven bless her!) I scarce think she had,
'Twas but their hammer, hammer in her ears,
Of "how Sir Peter fail'd at Lusac bridge:"
And "how he was grown moody of late days;"
And "how Sir Lambert," (think now!) "his dear friend,
His sweet dear cousin, could not but confess
That Peter's talk tended towards the French,
Which he" (for instance Lambert) "was glad of,   **80**
Being" (Lambert, you see) "on the French side."
          Well,
If I could but have seen her on that day,
Then, when they sent me off!
        I like to think,
Although it hurts me, makes my head twist, what,
If I had seen her, what I should have said,
What she, my darling, would have said and done.
As thus perchance:
       To find her sitting there,
In the window-seat, not looking well at all,
Crying perhaps, and I say quietly:
"Alice!" she looks up, chokes a sob, looks grave,   **90**
Changes from pale to red, but ere she speaks,
Straightway I kneel down there on both my knees,
And say: "O lady, have I sinn'd, your knight?
That still you ever let me walk alone
In the rose garden, that you sing no songs
When I am by, that ever in the dance
You quietly walk away when I come near?
Now that I have you, will you go, think you?"

  Ere she could answer I would speak again,
Still kneeling there:
       "What! they have frighted you,   **100**
By hanging burs, and clumsily carven puppets,
Round my good name; but afterwards, my love,
I will say what this means; this moment, see!
Do I kneel here, and can you doubt me? Yea,"
(For she would put her hands upon my face),
"Yea, that is best, yea feel, love, am I changed?"

And she would say: "Good knight, come, kiss my lips!"
And afterwards as I sat there would say:
"Please a poor silly girl by telling me
What all those things they talk of really were,   110
For it is true you did not help Chandos,
And true, poor love! you could not come to me
When I was in such peril."
                        I should say:
"I am like Balen, all things turn to blame.
I did not come to you? At Bergerath
The Constable had held us close shut up;
If from the barriers I had made three steps,
I should have been but slain; at Lusac, too,
We struggled in a marish half the day,
And came too late at last: you know, my love,   120
How heavy men and horses are all arm'd.
All that Sir Lambert said was pure, unmix'd,
Quite groundless lies; as you can think, sweet love."

She, holding tight my hand as we sat there,
Started a little at Sir Lambert's name,
But otherwise she listen'd scarce at all
To what I said. Then with moist, weeping eyes,
And quivering lips, that scarcely let her speak,
She said: "I love you."
                        Other words were few,
The remnant of that hour; her hand smooth'd down   130
My foolish head; she kiss'd me all about
My face, and through the tangles of my beard
Her little fingers crept.
                        O God! my Alice,
Not this good way: my lord but sent and said
That Lambert's sayings were taken at their worth,
Therefore that day I was to start, and keep
This hold against the French; and I am here, —
                                        Looks out of the window.

A sprawling lonely gard with rotten walls,
And no one to bring aid if Guesclin comes,
Or any other.
                        There's a pennon now!   140
At last.
                But not the Constable's: whose arms,
I wonder, does it bear? Three golden rings
On a red ground; my cousin's by the rood!

Well, I should like to kill him, certainly,
But to be kill'd by him —

A trumpet sounds

                    That's for a herald;
I doubt this does not mean assaulting yet.

          Enter JOHN CURZON

What says the herald of our cousin, sir?

            JOHN CURZON

So please you, sir, concerning your estate,
He has good will to talk with you.

            SIR PETER

                    Outside,
I'll talk with him, close by the gate St Ives.   150
Is he unarm'd?

            JOHN CURZON

          Yea, sir, in a long gown.

            SIR PETER

Then bid them bring me hither my furr'd gown
With the long sleeves, and under it I'll wear,
By Lambert's leave, a secret coat of mail;
And will you lend me, John, your little axe?
I mean the one with Paul wrought on the blade,
And I will carry it inside my sleeve,
Good to be ready always — you, John, go
And bid them set up many suits of arms,
Bows, archgays, lances, in the base-court, and   160
Yourself, from the south postern setting out,
With twenty men, be ready to break through
Their unguarded rear when I cry out 'St. George!'

            JOHN CURZON

How, sir! will you attack him unawares,
And slay him unarm'd?

            SIR PETER

          Trust me, John, I know
The reason why he comes here with sleeved gown,
Fit to hide axes up. So, let us go.

They go.

Outside the castle by the great gate; Sir Lambert *and* Sir Peter *seated;*
guards attending each, the rest of Sir Lambert's *men drawn up*
about a furlong off.

SIR PETER

And if I choose to take the losing side
Still, does it hurt you?

SIR LAMBERT

O! no hurt to me;
I see you sneering, "Why take trouble then,   170
Seeing you love me not?" Look you, our house
(Which, taken altogether, I love much)
Had better be upon the right side now,
If, once for all, it wishes to bear rule
As such a house should: cousin, you're too wise
To feed your hope up fat, that this fair France
Will ever draw two ways again; this side
The French, wrong-headed, all a-jar
With envious longings; and the other side
The order'd English, orderly led on   180
By those two Edwards through all wrong and right,
And muddling right and wrong to a thick broth
With that long stick, their strength. This is all changed,
The true French win, on either side you have
Cool-headed men, good at a tilting match,
And good at setting battles in array,
And good at squeezing taxes at due time;
Therefore by nature we French being here
Upon our own big land —   SIR PETER *laughs aloud.*
        Well, Peter! well!
What makes you laugh?

SIR PETER

Hearing you sweat to prove   190
All this I know so well; but you have read
The siege of Troy?

SIR LAMBERT

O! yea, I know it well.

SIR PETER

There! they were wrong, as wrong as men could be;
For, as I think, they found it such delight

To see fair Helen going through their town: *exagerated*
Yea, any little common thing she did
(As stooping to pick a flower) seem'd so strange,
So new in its great beauty, that they said:
"Here we will keep her living in this town,
Till all burns up together." And so, fought,   200
In a mad whirl of knowing they were wrong;
Yea, they fought well, and ever, like a man
That hangs legs off the ground by both his hands,
Over some great height, did they struggle sore,
Quite sure to slip at last; wherefore, take note
How almost all men, reading that sad siege,
Hold for the Trojans; as I did at least,
Thought Hector the best knight a long way.
                                                    Now
Why should I not do this thing that I think,
For even when I come to count the gains,   210
I have them my side: men will talk, you know,
(We talk of Hector, dead so long agone,)
When I am dead, of how this Peter clung
To what he thought the right; of how he died,
Perchance, at last, doing some desperate deed
Few men would care do now, and this is gain
To me, as ease and money is to you.
Moreover, too, I like the straining game
Of striving well to hold up things that fall;
So one becomes great. See you! in good times   220
All men live well together, and you, too,
Live dull and happy — happy? not so quick,
Suppose sharp thoughts begin to burn you up.
Why then, but just to fight as I do now,
A halter round my neck, would be great bliss.
O! I am well off.

                                                    Aside.

                Talk, and talk, and talk,
I know this man has come to murder me,
And yet I talk still.

                    SIR LAMBERT
                If your side were right,
You might be, though you lost; but if I said:
"You are a traitor, being, as you are,   230
Born Frenchman." What are Edwards unto you,
Or Richards?

SIR PETER

Nay, hold there, my Lambert, hold!
For fear your zeal should bring you to some harm,
Don't call me traitor.

SIR LAMBERT

Furthermore, my knight,
Men call you slippery on your losing side;
When at Bordeaux I was ambassador,
I heard them say so, and could scarce say "Nay."
He takes hold of something in his sleeve, and rises.

SIR PETER *rising.*

They lied — and you lie, not for the first time.
What have you got there, fumbling up your sleeve,
A stolen purse?

SIR LAMBERT

Nay, liar in your teeth!   240
Dead liar too; St. Dennis and St. Lambert!
Strikes at Sir Peter *with a dagger.*

SIR PETER *striking him flatlings with his axe.*

How thief! thief! thief! so there, fair thief, so there,
St. George Guienne! glaives for the castellan!
You French, you are but dead, unless you lay
Your spears upon the earth. St. George Guienne!

Well done, John Curzon, how he has them now.

In the Castle.

JOHN CURZON

What shall we do with all these prisoners, sir?

SIR PETER

Why, put them all to ransom, those that can
Pay anything, but not too light though, John,
Seeing we have them on the hip: for those   250
That have no money, that being certified,
Why, turn them out of doors before they spy;
But bring Sir Lambert guarded unto me.

JOHN CURZON

I will, fair sir.   *He goes.*

SIR PETER
                    I do not wish to kill him,
Although I think I ought; he shall go mark'd,
By all the saints, though!

                    Enter Lambert *guarded.*
                    Now, Sir Lambert, now!
What sort of death do you expect to get,
Being taken this way?

SIR LAMBERT
                    Cousin! cousin! think!
I am your own blood; may God pardon me!
I am not fit to die; if you knew all,   260
All I have done since I was young and good,
O! you would give me yet another chance,
As God would, that I might wash all clear out,
By serving you and Him. Let me go now!
And I will pay you down more golden crowns
Of ransom than the king would!

SIR PETER
                    Well, stand back,
And do not touch me! No, you shall not die,
Nor yet pay ransom. You, John Curzon, cause
Some carpenters to build a scaffold, high,
Outside the gate; when it is built, sound out   270
To all good folks, "Come, see a traitor punish'd!"
Take me my knight, and set him up thereon,
And let the hangman shave his head quite clean,
And cut his ears off close up to the head;
And cause the minstrels all the while to play
Soft music and good singing; for this day
Is my high day of triumph; is it not,
Sir Lambert?

SIR LAMBERT
                    Ah! on your own blood,
Own name, you heap this foul disgrace? you dare,
With hands and fame thus sullied, to go back   280
And take the Lady Alice —

SIR PETER
Say her name
Again, and you are dead, slain here by me.
Why should I talk with you, I'm master here,
And do not want your schooling; is it not
My mercy that you are not dangling dead
There in the gateway with a broken neck?

SIR LAMBERT
Such mercy! why not kill me then outright?
To die is nothing; but to live that all
May point their fingers! yea, I'd rather die.

JOHN CURZON
Why, will it make you any uglier man   290
To lose your ears? they're much too big for you,
You ugly Judas!

SIR PETER
Hold, John!   *To* Lambert.
          That's your choice,
To die, mind! Then you shall die — Lambert mine,
I thank you now for choosing this so well,
It saves me much perplexity and doubt;
Perchance an ill deed too, for half I count
This sparing traitors is an ill deed.
                    Well,
Lambert, die bravely, and we're almost friends.

SIR LAMBERT *grovelling.*
O God! this is a fiend and not a man;
Will some one save me from him? help, help, help!   300
I will not die.

SIR PETER
          Why, what is this I see?
A man who is a knight, and bandied words
So well just now with me, is lying down,
Gone mad for fear like this! So, so, you thought
You knew the worst, and might say what you pleased.
I should have guess'd this from a man like you.
Eh! righteous Job would give up skin for skin,
Yea, all a man can have for simple life,
And we talk fine, yea, even a hound like this,

Who needs must know that when he dies, deep hell   310
Will hold him fast for ever — so fine we talk,
"Would rather die" — all that. Now sir, get up!
And choose again: shall it be head sans ears,
Or trunk sans head?
                    John Curzon, pull him up!
What, life then? go and build the scaffold, John.

Lambert, I hope that never on this earth
We meet again; that you'll turn out a monk,
And mend the life I give you, so, farewell,
I'm sorry you're a rascal. John, despatch.

                In the French camp before the Castle.
            Sir Peter *prisoner*, Guesclin, Clisson, Sir Lambert.

                       SIR PETER
So now is come the ending of my life;   320
If I could clear this sickening lump away
That sticks in my dry throat, and say a word,
Guesclin might listen.

                       GUESCLIN
                    Tell me, fair sir knight,
If you have been clean liver before God,
And then you need not fear much; as for me,
I cannot say I hate you, yet my oath,
And cousin Lambert's ears here clench the thing.

                       SIR PETER
I knew you could not hate me, therefore I
Am bold to pray for life; 'twill harm your cause
To hang knights of good name, harm here in France   330
I have small doubt, at any rate hereafter
Men will remember you another way
Than I should care to be remember'd. Ah!
Although hot leads runs through me for my blood,
All this falls cold as though I said: "Sweet lords,
Give back my falcon!"
                    See how young I am;
Do you care altogether more for France,
Say rather one French faction, than for all
The state of Christendom? a gallant knight,
As (yea, by God!) I have been, is more worth   340

Than many castles; will you bring this death,
For a mere act of justice, on my head?

Think how it ends all, death! all other things
Can somehow be retrieved, yea, send me forth
Naked and maimed, rather than slay me here;
Then somehow will I get me other clothes,
And somehow will I get me some poor horse,
And, somehow clad in poor old rusty arms,
Will ride and smite among the serried glaives,
Fear not death so; for I can tilt right well,   350
Let me not say "I could"; I know all tricks,
That sway the sharp sword cunningly; ah you,
You, my Lord Clisson, in the other days
Have seen me learning these, yea, call to mind,
How in the trodden corn by Chartrès town,
When you were nearly swooning from the back
Of your black horse, those three blades slid at once
From off my sword's edge; pray for me, my lord!

CLISSON

Nay, this is pitiful, to see him die.
My Lord the Constable, I pray you note   360
That you are losing some few thousand crowns
By slaying this man; also think: his lands
Along the Garonne river lie for leagues,
And are right rich, a many mills he has,
Three abbeys of grey monks do hold of him,
Though wishing well for Clement, as we do;
I know the next heir, his old uncle, well,
Who does not care two deniers for the knight
As things go now, but slay him, and then see
How he will bristle up like any perch,   370
With curves of spears. What! do not doubt, my lord,
You'll get the money, this man saved my life,
And I will buy him for two thousand crowns;
Well, five then — eh! what! "No" again? well then,
Ten thousand crowns?

GUESCLIN

                    My sweet lord, much I grieve
I cannot please you; yea, good sooth, I grieve
This knight must die, as verily he must;
For I have sworn it, so men take him out,
Use him not roughly.

SIR LAMBERT *coming forward.*
                           Music, do you know,
Music will suit you well, I think, because   380
You look so mild, like Laurence being grill'd;
Or perhaps music soft and slow, because
This is high day of triumph unto me,
Is it not, Peter?
                  You are frighten'd, though,
Eh! you are pale, because this hurts you much,
Whose life was pleasant to you, not like mine,
You ruin'd wretch! Men mock me in the streets,
Only in whispers loud, because I am
Friend of the Constable; will this please you,
Unhappy Peter? once a-going home,   390
Without my servants, and a little drunk,
At midnight through the lone dim lamp-lit streets,
A whore came up and spat into my eyes,
(Rather to blind me than to make me see,)
But she was very drunk, and tottering back,
Even in the middle of her laughter, fell
And cut her head against the pointed stones,
While I lean'd on my staff, and look'd at her,
And cried, being drunk.
                         Girls would not spit at you.
You are so handsome, I think verily   400
Most ladies would be glad to kiss your eyes,
And yet you will be hung like a cur dog
Five minutes hence, and grow black in the face,
And curl your toes up. Therefore I am glad.

Guess why I stand and talk this nonsense now,
With Guesclin getting ready to play chess,
And Clisson doing something with his sword,
I can't see what, talking to Guesclin though,
I don't know what about, perhaps of you.
But, cousin Peter, while I stroke your beard,   410
Let me say this, I'd like to tell you now
That your life hung upon a game of chess,
That if, say, my squire Robert here should beat,
Why you should live, but hang if I beat him;
Then guess, clever Peter, what I should do then:
Well, give it up? why, Peter, I should let
My squire Robert beat me, then you would think
That you were safe, you know; Eh? not at all,
But I should keep you three days in some hold,

Giving you salt to eat, which would be kind,   420
Considering the tax there is on salt;
And afterwards should let you go, perhaps?
No, I should not, but I should hang you, sir,
With a red rope in lieu of mere grey rope.

But I forgot, you have not told me yet
If you can guess why I talk nonsense thus,
Instead of drinking wine while you are hang'd?
You are not quick at guessing, give it up.
This is the reason; here I hold your hand,
And watch you growing paler, see you writhe   430
And this, my Peter, is a joy so dear,
I cannot by all striving tell you how
I love it, nor I think, good man, would you
Quite understand my great delight therein;
You, when you had me underneath you once,
Spat as it were, and said: "Go take him out,"
(That they might do that thing to me whereat,
E'en now this long time off I could well shriek,)
And then you tried forget I ever lived,
And sunk your hating into other things;   440
While I — St. Denis! though, I think you'll faint,
Your lips are grey so; yes, you will, unless
You let it out and weep like a hurt child;
Hurrah! you do now. Do not go just yet,
For I am Alice, am right like her now,
Will you not kiss me on the lips, my love? —

                              CLISSON

You filthy beast, stand back and let him go,
Or by God's eyes I'll choke you.

                                        Kneeling to Sir Peter.
                    Fair sir knight,

I kneel upon my knees and pray to you
That you would pardon me for this your death;   450
God knows how much I wish you still alive,
Also how heartily I strove to save
Your life at this time; yea, He knows quite well,
(I swear it, so forgive me!) how I would,
If it were possible, give up my life
Upon this grass for yours; fair knight, although,
He knowing all things knows this thing too, well,
Yet when you see His face some short time hence,
Tell Him I tried to save you.

SIR PETER

O! my lord,

I cannot say this is as good as life,   460
But yet it makes me feel far happier now,
And if at all, after a thousand years,
I see God's face, I will speak loud and bold,
And tell Him you were kind, and like Himself;
Sir, may God bless you!

Did you note how I

Fell weeping just now? pray you, do not think
That Lambert's taunts did this, I hardly heard
The base things that he said, being deep in thought
Of all things that have happen'd since I was
A little child; and so at last I thought   470
Of my true lady: truly, sir, it seem'd
No longer gone than yesterday, that this
Was the sole reason God let me be born
Twenty-five years ago, that I might love
Her, my sweet lady, and be loved by her;
This seem'd so yesterday, to-day death comes,
And is so bitter strong, I cannot see
Why I was born.

But as a last request,

I pray you, O kind Clisson, send some man,
Some good man, mind you, to say how I died,   480
And take my last love to her: fare-you-well,
And may God keep you; I must go now, lest
I grow too sick with thinking on these things;
Likewise my feet are wearied of the earth,
From whence I shall be lifted up right soon.

As he goes.

Ah me! shamed too, I wept at fear of death;
And yet not so, I only wept because
There was no beautiful lady to kiss me
Before I died, and sweetly wish good speed
From her dear lips. O for some lady, though   490
I saw her ne'er before; Alice, my love,
I do not ask for; Clisson was right kind,
If he had been a woman, I should die
Without this sickness: but I am all wrong,
So wrong and hopelessly afraid to die.
There, I will go.

My God! how sick I am,

If only she could come and kiss me now.

The Hotel de la Barde, Bordeaux.

The LADY ALICE DE LA BARDE *looking out of a window
into the street.*

No news yet! surely, still he holds his own:
That garde stands well; I mind me passing it
Some months ago; God grant the walls are strong!   500
I heard some knights say something yestereve,
I tried hard to forget: words far apart
Struck on my heart; something like this; one said:
"What eh! a Gascon with an English name,
Harpdon?" then nought, but afterwards: "Poictou."
As one who answers to a question ask'd;
Then carelessly regretful came: "No, no."
Whereto in answer loud and eagerly,
One said: "Impossible! Christ, what foul play!"
And went off angrily; and while thenceforth   510
I hurried gaspingly afraid, I heard:
"Guesclin," "Five thousand men-at-arms;" "Clisson."
My heart misgives me it is all in vain
I send these succours; and in good time there!
Their trumpet sounds, ah! here they are; good knights,
God up in Heaven keep you.
      If they come
And find him prisoner —for I can't believe
Guesclin will slay him, even though they storm —
(The last horse turns the corner.)
       God in Heaven!
What have I got to thinking of at last!   520
That thief I will not name is with Guesclin,
Who loves him for his lands. My love! my love!
O, if I lose you after all the past,
What shall I do?
     I cannot bear the noise
And light street out there, with this thought alive,
Like any curling snake within my brain;
Let me just hide my head within these soft
Deep cushions, there to try and think it out.
        Lying in the window-seat.

I cannot hear much noise now, and I think
That I shall go to sleep: it all sounds dim   530
And faint, and I shall soon forget most things;
Yea, almost that I am alive and here;
It goes slow, comes slow, like a big mill-wheel

On some broad stream, with long green weeds a-sway,
And soft and slow it rises and it falls,
Still going onward.
        Lying so, one kiss,
And I should be in Avalon asleep,
Among the poppies, and the yellow flowers;
And they should brush my cheek, my hair being spread
Far out among the stems; soft mice and small   **540**
Eating and creeping all about my feet,
Red shod and tired; and the flies should come
Creeping o'er my broad eyelids unafraid;
And there should be a noise of water going,
Clear blue, fresh water breaking on the slates,
Likewise the flies should creep — God's eyes! God help!
A trumpet? I will run fast, leap adown
The slippery sea-stairs, where the crabs fight.
                        Ah!
I was half dreaming, but the trumpet's true;
He stops here at our house. The Clisson arms?   **550**
Ah, now for news. But I must hold my heart,
And be quite gentle till he is gone out;
And afterwards, — but he is still alive,
He must be still alive.

        Enter a Squire *of* Clisson's.

                Good day, fair sir,
I give you welcome, knowing whence you come.

             SQUIRE

My Lady Alice de la Barde, I come
From Oliver Clisson, knight and mighty lord,
Bringing you tidings: I make bold to hope
You will not count me villain, even if
They wring your heart; nor hold me still in hate.   **560**
For I am but a mouthpiece after all,
A mouthpiece, too, of one who wishes well
To you and your's.

             ALICE

              Can you talk faster, sir,
Get over all this quicker? fix your eyes
On mine, I pray you, and whate'er you see,
Still go on talking fast, unless I fall,
Or bid you stop.

SQUIRE

I pray your pardon then,
And looking in your eyes, fair lady, say
I am unhappy that your knight is dead.
Take heart, and listen! let me tell you all.   570
We were five thousand goodly men-at-arms,
And scant five hundred had he in that hold:
His rotten sand-stone walls were wet with rain,
And fell in lumps wherever a stone hit;
Yet for three days about the barrier there
The deadly glaives were gather'd, laid across,
And push'd and pull'd; the fourth our engines came;
But still amid the crash of falling walls,
And roar of lombards, rattle of hard bolts,
The steady bow-strings flash'd, and still stream'd out   580
St. George's banner, and the seven swords,
And still they cried: "St. George Guienne," until
Their walls were flat as Jericho's of old,
And our rush came, and cut them from the keep.

ALICE

Stop, sir, and tell me if you slew him then,
And where he died, if you can really mean
That Peter Harpdon, the good knight, is dead?

SQUIRE

Fair lady, in the base-court —

ALICE

What base-court?
What do you talk of? Nay, go on; go on;
'Twas only something gone within my head: 590
Do you not know, one turns one's head round quick,
And something cracks there with sore pain? go on,
And still look at my eyes.

SQUIRE

Almost alone,
There in the base-court fought he with his sword,
Using his left hand much, more than the wont
Of most knights now-a-days; our men gave back,
For wheresoever he hit a downright blow,
Some one fell bleeding, for no plate could hold
Against the sway of body and great arm;

Till he grew tired, and some man (no! not I,   600
I swear not I, fair lady, as I live!)
Thrust at him with a glaive between the knees,
And threw him; down he fell, sword undermost;
Many fell on him, crying out their cries,
Tore his sword from him, tore his helm off, and —

ALICE

Yea, slew him: I am much too young to live,
Fair God, so let me die.
                    You have done well,
Done all your message gently; pray you go,
Our knights will make you cheer; moreover, take
This bag of franks for your expenses.   *The* Squire *kneels.*
                              But   610
You do not go; still looking at my face,
You kneel! what, squire, do you mock me then?
You need not tell me who has set you on,
But tell me only, 'tis a made-up tale.
You are some lover may-be, or his friend;
Sir, if you loved me once, or your friend loved,
Think, is it not enough that I kneel down
And kiss your feet? your jest will be right good
If you give in now, carry it too far,
And 'twill be cruel: not yet? but you weep   620
Almost, as though you loved me; love me then,
And go to Heaven by telling all your sport,
And I will kiss you then with all my heart,
Upon the mouth; O! what can I do then
To move you?

SQUIRE

                    Lady fair, forgive me still!
You know I am so sorry, but my tale
Is not yet finish'd:
                    So they bound his hands,
And brought him tall and pale to Guesclin's tent,
Who, seeing him, leant his head upon his hand,
And ponder'd somewhile, afterwards, looking up —   630
Fair dame, what shall I say?

ALICE

                    Yea, I know now,
Good squire, you may go now with my thanks.

SQUIRE

Yet, lady, for your own sake I say this,
Yea, for my own sake, too, and Clisson's sake:
When Guesclin told him he must be hanged soon,
Within a while he lifted up his head
And spoke for his own life; not crouching, though,
As abjectly afraid to die, nor yet
Sullenly brave as many a thief will die;
Nor yet as one that plays at japes with God: 640
Few words he spoke; not so much what he said
Moved us, I think, as, saying it, there played
Strange tenderness from that big soldier there
About his pleading; eagerness to live
Because folk loved him, and he loved them back,
And many gallant plans unfinish'd now
For ever. Clisson's heart, which may God bless!
Was moved to pray for him, but all in vain;
Wherefore I bring this message:
                              That he waits,
Still loving you, within the little church   650
Whose windows, with the one eye of the light
Over the altar, every night behold
The great dim broken walls he strove to keep!

There my Lord Clisson did his burial well.
Now, lady, I will go; God give you rest!

ALICE

Thank Clisson from me, squire, and farewell!
And now to keep myself from going mad.
Christ! I have been a many times to church,
And, ever since my mother taught me prayers,
Have used them daily, but to-day I wish   660
To pray another way; come face to face,
O Christ, that I may clasp your knees and pray
I know not what; at any rate come now
From one of many places where you are,
Either in Heaven amid thick angel wings,
Or sitting on the altar strange with gems,
Or high up in the dustiness of the apse;
Let us go, You and I, a long way off,
To the little damp, dark, Poitevin church;
While you sit on the coffin in the dark,   670
Will I lie down, my face on the bare stone

Between your feet, and chatter anything
I have heard long ago, what matters it
So I may keep you there, your solemn face
And long hair even-flowing on each side,
Until you love me well enough to speak,
And give me comfort; yea, till o'er your chin,
And cloven red beard the great tears roll down
In pity for my misery, and I die,
Kissed over by you.

     Eh Guesclin! if I were   680
Like Countess Mountfort now, that kiss'd the knight,
Across the salt sea come to fight for her;
Ah! just to go about with many knights,
Wherever you went, and somehow on one day,
In a thick wood to catch you off your guard,
Let you find, you and your some fifty friends,
Nothing but arrows wheresoe'er you turn'd,
Yea, and red crosses, great spears over them;
And so, between a lane of my true men,
To walk up pale and stern and tall, and with   690
My arms on my surcoat, and his therewith,
And then to make you kneel, O knight Guesclin;
And then — alas! alas! when all is said,
What could I do but let you go again,
Being pitiful woman? I get no revenge,
Whatever happens; and I get no comfort,
I am but weak, and cannot move my feet,
But as men bid me.

      Strange I do not die.
Suppose this had not happen'd after all?
I will lean out again and watch for news.   700

I wonder how long I can still feel thus,
As though I watch'd for news, feel as I did
Just half-an-hour ago, before this news.
How all the street is humming, some men sing,
And some men talk; some look up at the house,
Then lay their heads together and look grave:
Their laughter pains me sorely in the heart,
Their thoughtful talking makes my head turn round;
Yea, some men sing, what is it then they sing?
Eh? Launcelot, and love and fate and death;   710
They ought to sing of him who was as wight
As Launcelot or Wade, and yet avail'd

Just nothing, but to fail and fail and fail,
And so at last to die and leave me here,
Alone and wretched; yea, perhaps they will,
When many years are past, make songs of us;
God help me, though, truly I never thought
That I should make a story in this way,
A story that his eyes can never see.

ONE SINGS FROM OUTSIDE.

Therefore be it believed   720
Whatsoever he grieved,
Whan his horse was relieved,
 This Launcelot,

Beat down on his knee,
Right valiant was he
God's body to see,
 Though he saw it not.

Right valiant to move,
But for his sad love
The high God above   730
 Stinted his praise.

Yet so he was glad
That his son, Lord Galahad,
That high joyaunce had
 All his life-days.

Sing we therefore then
Launcelot's praise again,
For he wan crownès ten,
 If he wan not twelve.

To his death from his birth   740
He was muckle of worth,
Lay him in the cold earth,
 A long grave ye may delve.

Omnes homines benedicite!
This last fitte ye may see,
All men pray for me,
Who made this history
Cunning and fairly.

[1858]

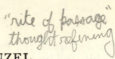
"rite of passage"
thoughts refining

RAPUNZEL

THE PRINCE *being in the wood near the tower,*
in the evening.

I COULD not even think
   What made me weep that day,
When out of the council-hall
   The courtiers pass'd away, —

THE WITCH

   Rapunzel, Rapunzel,
   Let down your hair!

RAPUNZEL

Is it not true that every day
She climbeth up the same strange way,
Her scarlet cloak spread broad and gay,
   Over my golden hair?   10

THE PRINCE

And left me there alone,
   To think on what they said:
"Thou art a king's own son,
   'Tis fit that thou should'st wed."

THE WITCH

   Rapunzel, Rapunzel,
   Let down your hair!

RAPUNZEL

When I undo the knotted mass,
Fathoms below the shadows pass
Over my hair along the grass.
   O my golden hair!   20

THE PRINCE

I put my armour on,
   Thinking on what they said:
"Thou art a king's own son,
   'Tis fit that thou should'st wed."

THE WITCH

   Rapunzel, Rapunzel,
   Let down your hair!

RAPUNZEL

See on the marble parapet
I lean my brow, strive to forget
That fathoms below my hair grows wet
    With the dew, my golden hair.   30

THE PRINCE

I rode throughout the town,
  Men did not bow the head,
Though I was the king's own son;
  "He rides to dream," they said.

THE WITCH

Rapunzel, Rapunzel,
  Wind up your hair!

RAPUNZEL

See, on the marble parapet,
The faint red stains with tears are wet;
The long years pass, no help comes yet
    To free my golden hair.   40

THE PRINCE

For leagues and leagues I rode,
  Till hot my armour grew,
Till underneath the leaves *yeah...*
  I felt the evening dew.

THE WITCH

Rapunzel, Rapunzel,
  Weep through your hair!

RAPUNZEL

And yet — but I am growing old,
For want of love my heart is cold,
Years pass, the while I loose and fold
    The fathoms of my hair.   50

blind

THE PRINCE *in the morning.*   *2nd*

    religion

I have heard tales of men, who in the night
  Saw paths of stars let down to earth from heaven,
Who follow'd them until they reach'd the light
  Wherein they dwell, whose sins are all forgiven;

But who went backward when they saw the gate
  Of diamond, nor dared to enter in;
All their life long they were content to wait,
  Purging them patiently of every sin.

couldn't really "see"
why he wanted Rapunzel
till he was blind.

I must have had a dream of some such thing,
  And now am just awaking from that dream;   60
For even in grey dawn those strange words ring
  Through heart and brain, and still I see that gleam.

another dream

For in my dream at sunset-time I lay
  Beneath these beeches, mail and helmet off,
Right full of joy that I had come away
  From court; for I was patient of the scoff

That met me always there from day to day,
  From any knave or coward of them all:
I was content to live that wretched way;
  For truly till I left the council-hall,   70

And rode forth arm'd beneath the burning sun,
  My gleams of happiness were faint and few,
But then I saw my real life had begun,
  And that I should be strong quite well I knew.

For I was riding out to look for love,
  Therefore the birds within the thickets sung,
Even in hot noontide, as I pass'd, above
  The elms o'ersway'd with longing towards me hung.

Now some few fathoms from the place where I
  Lay in the beech-wood, was a tower fair,   80
The marble corners faint against the sky;
  And dreamily I wonder'd what lived there:

Because it seem'd a dwelling for a queen,
  No belfry for the swinging of great bells;
No bolt or stone had ever crush'd the green
  Shafts, amber and rose walls; no soot that tells

Of the Norse torches burning up the roofs,
  On the flower-carven marble could I see;
But rather on all sides I saw the proofs
  Of a great loneliness that sicken'd me;   90

Making me feel a doubt that was not fear,
　　Whether my whole life long had been a dream,
And I should wake up soon in some place, where
　　The piled-up arms of the fighting angels gleam;

Not born as yet, but going to be born,
　　No naked baby as I was at first,
But an armèd knight, whom fire, hate and scorn
　　Could turn from nothing: my heart almost burst

Beneath the beeches, as I lay a-dreaming,
　　I tried so hard to read this riddle through,　　　　　100
To catch some golden cord that I saw gleaming
　　Like gossamer against the autumn blue.

But while I ponder'd these things, from the wood
　　There came a black-hair'd woman, tall and bold,
Who strode straight up to where the tower stood,
　　And cried out shrilly words, whereon behold —

　　　　　THE WITCH, *from the tower.*
　　　　　Rapunzel, Rapunzel,
　　　　　Let down your hair!

　　　　　THE PRINCE

Ah Christ! it was no dream then, but there stood
　　(She comes again) a maiden passing fair,　　　　　110
Against the roof, with face turn'd to the wood,
　　Bearing within her arms waves of her yellow hair.

I read my riddle when I saw her stand,
　　Poor love! her face quite pale against her hair,
Praying to all the leagues of empty land
　　To save her from the woe she suffer'd there.

To think! they trod upon her golden hair　　　*defile, pervert*
　　In the witches' sabbaths; it was a delight
For these foul things, while she, with thin feet bare,
　　Stood on the roof upon the winter night,　　　　　120

To plait her dear hair into many plaits,
　　And then, while God's eye look'd upon the thing,
In the very likenesses of Devil's bats, (WITCH)
　　Upon the ends of her long hair to swing.

And now she stood above the parapet,
  And, spreading out her arms, let her hair flow,
Beneath that veil her smooth white forehead set
  Upon the marble, more I do not know;

Because before my eyes a film of gold
  Floated, as now it floats. O unknown love,   130
Would that I could thy yellow stair behold,
  If still thou standest with lead roof above!

> THE WITCH, *as she passes.*
> Is there any who will dare
> To climb up the yellow stair,
> Glorious Rapunzel's golden hair?

THE PRINCE

If it would please God make you sing again,
  I think that I might very sweetly die,
My soul somehow reach heaven in joyous pain,
  My heavy body on the beech-nuts lie.

Now I remember what a most strange year,   140
  Most strange and awful, in the beechen wood
I have pass'd now; I still have a faint fear
  It is a kind of dream not understood.

I have seen no one in this wood except
  The witch and her; have heard no human tones,
But when the witches' revelry has crept
  Between the very jointing of my bones.

Ah! I know now; I could not go away,
  But needs must stop to hear her sing that song
She always sings at dawning of the day.   150
  I am not happy here, for I am strong,

And every morning do I whet my sword,
  Yet Rapunzel still weeps within the tower,
And still God ties me down to the green sward,
  Because I cannot see the gold stair floating lower.

RAPUNZEL *sings from the tower.*
  My mother taught me prayers
  To say when I had need;

I have so many cares,
That I can take no heed
Of many words in them;   160
But I remember this:
Christ, bring me to thy bliss.
Mary, maid withouten wem,
Keep me! I am alone, I wis,
Yet besides I have made this
By myself: *Give me a kiss,*
Dear God, dwelling up in heaven!
Also: *Send me a true knight,*
Lord Christ, with a steel sword, bright,
Broad, and trenchant; yea, and seven   170
Spans from hilt to point, O Lord!
And let the handle of his sword
Be gold on silver, Lord in heaven!
Such a sword as I see gleam
Sometimes, when they let me dream.

    Yea, besides, I have made this:
Lord, give Mary a dear kiss,
And let gold Michael, who looked down,
When I was there, on Rouen town
From the spire, bring me that kiss   180
On a lily! Lord, do this!

    These prayers on the dreadful nights,
When the witches plait my hair,
And the fearfullest of sights
On the earth and in the air,
Will not let me close my eyes,
I murmur often, mix'd with sighs,
That my weak heart will not hold
At some things that I behold.
Nay, not sighs, but quiet groans,   190
That swell out the little bones
Of my bosom; till a trance
God sends in middle of that dance,
And I behold the countenance
Of Michael, and can feel no more
The bitter east wind biting sore
My naked feet; can see no more
The crayfish on the leaden floor,
That mock with feeler and grim claw.

Yea, often in that happy trance,   200
Beside the blessed countenance
Of golden Michael, on the spire
Glowing all crimson in the fire
Of sunset, I behold a face,
Which sometime, if God give me grace,
May kiss me in this very place.

Evening in the tower.

RAPUNZEL

It grows half way between the dark and light;
  Love, we have been six hours here alone,
I fear that she will come before the night,
  And if she finds us thus we are undone.   210

THE PRINCE

Nay, draw a little nearer, that your breath
  May touch my lips, let my cheek feel your arm;
Now tell me, did you ever see a death,
  Or ever see a man take mortal harm?

RAPUNZEL

Once came two knights and fought with swords below,
  And while they fought I scarce could look at all,
My head swam so, after a moaning low
  Drew my eyes down; I saw against the wall

One knight lean dead, bleeding from head and breast,
  Yet seem'd it like a line of poppies red   220
In the golden twilight, as he took his rest,
  In the dusky time he scarcely seemèd dead.

But the other, on his face six paces off,
  Lay moaning, and the old familiar name
He mutter'd through the grass, seem'd like a scoff
  Of some lost soul remembering his past fame.

His helm all dinted lay beside him there,
  The visor-bars were twisted towards the face,
The crest, which was a lady very fair,
  Wrought wonderfully, was shifted from its place.   230

The shower'd mail-rings on the speedwell lay,
   Perhaps my eyes were dazzled with the light
That blazed in the west, yet surely on that day
   Some crimson thing had changed the grass from bright

Pure green I love so. But the knight who died
   Lay there for days after the other went;
Until one day I heard a voice that cried:
   "Fair knight, I see Sir Robert we were sent

"To carry dead or living to the king."
   So the knights came and bore him straight away   240
On their lance truncheons, such a batter'd thing,
   His mother had not known him on that day,

But for his helm-crest, a gold lady fair
   Wrought wonderfully.

THE PRINCE

             Ah, they were brothers then,
And often rode together, doubtless where
   The swords were thickest, and were loyal men,

Until they fell in these same evil dreams.

RAPUNZEL

   Yea, love; but shall we not depart from hence?
The white moon groweth golden fast, and gleams
   Between the aspen stems; I fear — and yet a sense   250

Of fluttering victory comes over me,
   That will not let me fear aright; my heart —
Feel how it beats, love, strives to get to thee,
   I breathe so fast that my lips needs must part;

Your breath swims round my mouth, but let us go.

THE PRINCE

   I, Sebald, also, pluck from off the staff
The crimson banner, let it lie below,
   Above it in the wind let grasses laugh.

Now let us go, love, down the winding stair,
   With fingers intertwined: ay, feel my sword!   260

I wrought it long ago, with golden hair
   Flowing about the hilts, because a word,

Sung by a minstrel old, had set me dreaming
   Of a sweet bow'd-down face with yellow hair,
Betwixt green leaves I used to see it gleaming,
   A half smile on the lips, though lines of care

Had sunk the cheeks, and made the great eyes hollow;
   What other work in all the world had I,
But through all turns of fate that face to follow?
   But wars and business kept me there to die.   270

O child, I should have slain my brother, too,
   My brother, Love, lain moaning in the grass,
Had I not ridden out to look for you,
   When I had watch'd the gilded courtiers pass

From the golden hall. But it is strange your name
   Is not the same the minstrel sung of yore;
You call'd it Rapunzel, 'tis not the name.
   See, love, the stems shine through the open door

Morning, in the woods.

RAPUNZEL

O Love! me and my unknown name you have well won;
   The witch's name was Rapunzel; eh! not so sweet?   280
No! — but is this real grass, love, that I tread upon?
   What call they these blue flowers that lean across my feet?

THE PRINCE

Dip down your dear face in the dewy grass, O love!
   And ever let the sweet slim harebells tenderly hung,
Kiss both your parted lips; and I will hang above,
   And try to sing that song the dreamy harper sung.

He sings.[1]
   'Twixt the sunlight and the shade
   Float up memories of my maid:
      God, remember Guendolen!

[1] This song, entitled "Hands," was first published in *The Oxford and Cambridge Magazine* (1856).

Gold or gems she did not wear,   290
But her yellow rippled hair,
    Like a veil, hid Guendolen!

'Twixt the sunlight and the shade,
My rough hands so strangely made,
    Folded Golden Guendolen;

Hands used to grip the sword-hilt hard,
Framed her face, while on the sward
    Tears fell down from Guendolen.

Guendolen now speaks no word,
Hands fold round about the sword.   300
    Now no more of Guendolen.

Only 'twixt the light and shade
Floating memories of my maid
    Make me pray for Guendolen.

GUENDOLEN

I kiss thee, new-found name; but I will never go:
    Your hands need never grip the hammer'd sword again,
But all my golden hair shall ever round you flow,
    Between the light and shade from Golden Guendolen.

Afterwards in the Palace.

KING SEBALD

I took my armour off,
    Put on king's robes of gold,   310
Over her kirtle green
    The gold fell fold on fold.

THE WITCH, *out of hell.*

Guendolen! Guendolen!
One lock of hair!

GUENDOLEN

I am so glad, for every day
He kisses me much the same way
As in the tower; under the sway
    Of all my golden hair.

KING SEBALD

We rode throughout the town,
  A gold crown on my head,
Through all the gold-hung streets,
  "Praise God!" the people said.   320

THE WITCH

Guendolen! Guendolen!
Lend me your hair!

GUENDOLEN

Verily, I seem like one
Who, when day is almost done,
Through a thick wood meets the sun
  That blazes in her hair.

KING SEBALD

Yea, at the palace gates,
  "Praise God!" the great knights said,   330
"For Sebald the high king,
  And the lady's golden head."

THE WITCH

Woe is me! Guendolen
Sweeps back her hair.

GUENDOLEN

Nothing wretched now, no screams;
I was unhappy once in dreams,
And even now a harsh voice seems
  To hang about my hair.

THE WITCH

WOE! THAT ANY MAN COULD DARE
TO CLIMB UP THE YELLOW STAIR,   340
GLORIOUS GUENDOLEN'S GOLDEN HAIR.
                              [1858]

CONCERNING GEFFRAY TESTE NOIRE

AND if you meet the Canon of Chimay,
   As going to Ortaise you well may do,
Greet him from John of Castel Neuf, and say,
   All that I tell you, for all this is true.

This Geffray Teste Noire was a Gascon thief,
   Who, under shadow of the English name,
Pilled all such towns and countries as were lief
   To King Charles and St. Denis; thought it blame

If anything escaped him; so my lord
   The Duke of Berry sent Sir John Bonne Lance,   10
And other knights, good players with the sword,
   To check this thief, and give the land a chance.

Therefore we set our bastides round the tower
   That Geffray held, the strong thief! like a king,
High perch'd upon the rock of Ventadour,
   Hopelessly strong by Christ! it was mid spring,

When first I joined the little army there
   With ten good spears; Auvergne is hot, each day
We sweated armed before the barrier;
   Good feats of arms were done there often — eh?   20

Your brother was slain there? I mind me now,
   A right good man-at-arms, God pardon him!
I think 'twas Geffray smote him on the brow
   With some spiked axe, and while he totter'd, dim

About the eyes, the spear of Alleyne Roux
   Slipped through his camaille and his throat; well, well!
Alleyne is paid now; your name Alleyne too?
   Mary! how strange — but this tale I would tell —

For spite of all our bastides, damned Blackhead
   Would ride abroad whene'er he chose to ride,
We could not stop him; many a burgher bled   30
   Dear gold all round his girdle; far and wide

The villaynes dwelt in utter misery
  'Twixt us and thief Sir Geffray; hauled this way
By Sir Bonne Lance at one time, he gone by,
  Down comes this Teste Noire on another day,

And therefore they dig up the stone, grind corn,
  Hew wood, draw water, yea, they lived, in short,
As I said just now, utterly forlorn,
  Till this our knave and Blackhead was out-fought.   **40**

So Bonne Lance fretted, thinking of some trap
  Day after day, till on a time he said:
"John of Newcastle, if we have good hap,
  We catch our thief in two days." "How?" I said.

"Why, Sir, to-day he rideth out again,
  Hoping to take well certain sumpter mules
From Carcassonne, going with little train,
  Because, forsooth, he thinketh us mere fools;

"But if we set an ambush in some wood,
  He is but dead: so, Sir, take thirty spears   **50**
To Verville forest, if it seem you good."
  Then felt I like the horse in Job, who hears

The dancing trumpet sound, and we went forth;
  And my red lion on the spear-head flapped,
As faster than the cool wind we rode north,
  Towards the wood of Verville; thus it happed.

We rode a soft space on that day, while spies
  Got news about Sir Geffray; the red wine
Under the road-side bush was clear; the flies,
  The dragon-flies I mind me most, did shine   **60**

In brighter arms than ever I put on;
  So — "Geffray," said our spies, "would pass that way
Next day at sundown;" then he must be won;
  And so we enter'd Verville wood next day,

In the afternoon; through it the highway runs,
  'Twixt copses of green hazel, very thick,
And underneath, with glimmering of suns,
  The primroses are happy; the dews lick

The soft green moss. "Put cloths about your arms,
  Lest they should glitter; surely they will go   70
In a long thin line, watchful for alarms,
  With all their carriages of booty, so —

"Lay down my pennon in the grass — Lord God!
  What have we lying here? will they be cold,   *past, find*
I wonder, being so bare, above the sod,   *rusty skeleton*
  Instead of under? This was a knight too, fold

"Lying on fold of ancient rusted mail;
  No plate at all, gold rowels to the spurs,   *wheel on spurs*
And see the quiet gleam of turquoise pale
  Along the ceinture; but the long time blurs   80

gold gleam dies   *worst*
"Even the tinder of his coat to nought,
  Except these scraps of leather; see how white
The skull is, loose within the coif! He fought
  A good fight, maybe, ere he was slain quite.

"No armour on the legs too; strange in faith —
  A little skeleton for a knight, though — ah!
This one is bigger, truly without scathe   *gone a good fight*
  His enemies escaped not — ribs driven out far, —

                            companion
"That must have reach'd the heart, I doubt — how now,
  What say you, Aldovrand — a woman? why?"   90
Aldo: "Under the coif a gold wreath on the brow,
  Yea, see the hair not gone to powder, lie,

"Golden, no doubt, once — yea, and very small   *turned on by*
  This for a knight; but for a dame, my lord,   *skeleton*
These loose-hung bones seem shapely still, and tall, —
  Didst ever see a woman's bones, my lord?"

Often, God help me! I remember when   *back*
  I was a simple boy, fifteen years old,
The Jacquerie froze up the blood of men
  With their fell deeds, not fit now to be told: 100

God help again! we enter'd Beauvais town,
  Slaying them fast, whereto I help'd, mere boy
As I was then; we gentles cut them down,
  These burners and defilers, with great joy.

Reason for that, too: in the great church there
  These fiends had lit a fire, that soon went out,
The church at Beauvais being so great and fair —
  My father, who was by me, gave a shout

Between a beast's howl and a woman's scream,
  Then, panting, chuckled to me:, "John, look! look!   110
Count the dames' skeletons!" from some bad dream
  Like a man just waked, my father shook;

And I, being faint with smelling the burnt bones,
  And very hot with fighting down the street,
And sick of such a life, fell down, with groans
  My head went weakly nodding to my feet.

— An arrow had gone through her tender throat,
  And her right wrist was broken; then I saw
The reason why she had on that war-coat,
  Their story came out clear without a flaw;   120

For when he knew that they were being waylaid,
  He threw it over her, yea, hood and all;
Whereby he was much hack'd, while they were stay'd
  By those their murderers; many an one did fall

Beneath his arm, no doubt, so that he clear'd
  Their circle, bore his death-wound out of it;
But as they rode, some archer least afear'd
  Drew a strong bow, and thereby she was hit.

Still as he rode he knew not she was dead,
  Thought her but fainted from her broken wrist,   130
He bound with his great leathern belt — she bled?
  Who knows! he bled too, neither was there miss'd

The beating of her heart, his heart beat well
  For both of them, till here, within this wood,
He died scarce sorry; easy this to tell;
  After these years the flowers forget their blood. —

How could it be? never before that day,
  However much a soldier I might be,
Could I look on a skeleton and say
  I care not for it, shudder not — now see,   140

Over those bones I sat and pored for hours,
  And thought, and dream'd, and still I scarce could see
The small white bones that lay upon the flowers,
  But evermore I saw the lady; she

With her dear gentle walking leading in,
  By a chain of silver twined about her wrists,
Her loving knight, mounted and arm'd to win
Great honour for her, fighting in the lists.

O most pale face, that brings such joy and sorrow
  Into men's hearts — yea, too, so piercing sharp   150
That joy is, that it marcheth nigh to sorrow
  For ever — like an overwinded harp. —

Your face must hurt me always; pray you now,
  Doth it not hurt you too? seemeth some pain
To hold you always, pain to hold your brow
  So smooth, unwrinkled ever; yea again,

Your long eyes where the lids seem like to drop,
  Would you not, lady, were they shut fast, feel
Far merrier? there so high they will not stop,
  They are most sly to glide forth and to steal   160

Into my heart, I kiss their soft lids there,
  And in green gardens scarce can stop my lips
From wandering on your face, but that your hair
  Falls down and tangles me, back my face slips.

Or say your mouth — I saw you drink red wine
  Once at a feast; how slowly it sank in,
As though you fear'd that some wild fate might twine
  Within that cup, and slay you for a sin.

And when you talk your lips do arch and move
  In such wise that a language new I know   170
Besides their sound; they quiver, too, with love
  When you are standing silent; know this, too,

I saw you kissing once, like a curved sword
  That bites with all its edge, did your lips lie,
Curled gently, slowly, long time could afford
  For caught-up breathings; like a dying sigh

They gather'd up their lines and went away,
  And still kept twitching with a sort of smile,
As likely to be weeping presently, —
  Your hands too — how I watch'd them all the while!   180

"Cry out St. Peter now," quoth Aldovrand;
  I cried, "St Peter!" broke out from the wood
With all my spears; we met them hand to hand,
  And shortly slew them; natheless, by the rood,

We caught not Blackhead then, or any day;
  Months after that he died at last in bed,
From a wound pick'd up at a barrier-fray;
  That same year's end a steel bolt in the head,

And much bad living kill'd Teste Noire at last;
  John Froissart knoweth he is dead by now,   190
No doubt, but knoweth not this tale just past;
  Perchance then you can tell him what I show.

In my new castle, down beside the Eure,
  There is a little chapel of squared stone,
Painted inside and out; in green nook pure
  There did I lay them, every wearied bone;

And over it they lay, with stone-white hands
  Clasped fast together, hair made bright with gold;
This Jaques Picard, known through many lands,
  Wrought cunningly; he's dead now — I am old.   200

                                                    [1858]

A GOOD KNIGHT IN PRISON

        SIR GUY *being in the court of a Pagan castle.*
  THIS castle where I dwell, it stands
  A long way off from Christian lands,
  A long way off my lady's hands,
  A long way off the aspen trees,
  And murmur of the lime-tree bees.

    But down the Valley of the Rose
  My lady often hawking goes,
  Heavy of cheer; oft turns behind,

Leaning towards the western wind,
Because it bringeth to her mind   10
Sad whisperings of happy times,
The face of him who sings these rhymes.

    King Guilbert rides beside her there,
Bends low and calls her very fair,
And strives, by pulling down his hair,
To hide from my dear lady's ken
The grisly gash I gave him, when
I cut him down at Camelot;
However he strives, he hides it not,
That tourney will not be forgot,   20
Besides, it is King Guilbert's lot,
Whatever he says she answers not.

    Now tell me, you that are in love,
From the king's son to the wood-dove,
Which is the better, he or I?

    For this king means that I should die
In this lone Pagan castle, where
The flowers droop in the bad air
On the September evening.

    Look, now I take mine ease and sing,   30
Counting as but a little thing
The foolish spite of a bad king.

    For these vile things that hem me in,
These Pagan beasts who live in sin,
The sickly flowers pale and wan,
The grim blue-bearded castellan,
The stanchions half worn-out with rust,
Whereto their banner vile they trust —
Why, all these things I hold them just
Like dragons in a missal-book,   40
Wherein, whenever we may look,
We see no horror, yea, delight
We have, the colours are so bright;
Likewise we note the specks of white,
And the great plates of burnish'd gold.

    Just so this Pagan castle old,
And everything I can see there,

Sick-pining in the marshland air,
I note; I will go over now,
Like one who paints with knitted brow,   50
The flowers and all things one by one,
From the snail on the wall to the setting sun.

  Four great walls, and a little one
That leads down to the barbican,
Which walls with many spears they man,
When news comes to the castellan
Of Launcelot being in the land.

  And as I sit here, close at hand
Four spikes of sad sick sunflowers stand,
The castellan with a long wand   60
Cuts down their leaves as he goes by,
Ponderingly, with screw'd-up eye,
And fingers twisted in his beard —
Nay, was it a knight's shout I heard?
I have a hope makes me afeard:
It cannot be, but if some dream
Just for a minute made me deem
I saw among the flowers there
My lady's face with long red hair,
Pale, ivory-colour'd dear face come,   70
As I was wont to see her some
Fading September afternoon,
And kiss me, saying nothing, soon
To leave me by myself again;
Could I get this by longing: vain!

  The castellan is gone: I see
On one broad yellow flower a bee
Drunk with much honey —

                              Christ! again,
Some distant knight's voice brings me pain,
I thought I had forgot to feel,   80
I never heard the blissful steel
These ten years past; year after year,
Through all my hopeless sojourn here,
No Christian pennon has been near;
Laus Deo! the dragging wind draws on
Over the marshes, battle won,
Knights' shouts, and axes hammering,

Yea, quicker now the dint and ring
Of flying hoofs; ah! castellan,
When they come back, count man for man,   90
Say whom you miss.

THE PAGANS from the battlements.

Mahound to aid!
Why flee ye so like men dismay'd?

THE PAGANS from without.

Nay, haste! for here is Launcelot,
Who follows quick upon us, hot
And shouting with his men-at-arms.

SIR GUY

Also the Pagans raise alarms,
And ring the bells for fear; at last
My prison walls will be well past.

SIR LAUNCELOT from outside.

Ho! in the name of the Trinity,
Let down the drawbridge quick to me,   100
And open doors, that I may see
Guy the good knight.

THE PAGANS from the battlements.

Nay, Launcelot,
With mere big words ye win us not.

SIR LAUNCELOT

Bid Miles bring up la perriere,
And archers clear the vile walls there,
Bring back the notches to the ear,
Shoot well together! God to aid!
These miscreants will be well paid.

Hurrah! all goes together; Miles
Is good to win my lady's smiles   110
For his good shooting — Launcelot!
On knights a-pace! this game is hot!

SIR GUY sayeth afterwards.

I said, I go to meet her now,
And saying so, I felt a blow
From some clench'd hand across my brow,

And fell down on the sunflowers
Just as a hammering smote my ears,
After which this I felt in sooth;
My bare hands throttling without ruth
The hairy-throated castellan;   120
Then a grim fight with those that ran
To slay me, while I shouted: "God
For the Lady Mary!" deep I trod
That evening in my own red blood;
Nevertheless so stiff I stood,
That when the knights burst the old wood
Of the castle-doors, I was not dead.

I kiss the Lady Mary's head,
Her lips and her hair golden red,
Because to-day we have been wed.   130

[1858]

OLD LOVE

"You must be very old, Sir Giles,"
  I said; he said: "Yea, very old:"
Whereat the mournfullest of smiles
  Creased his dry skin with many a fold.

"They hammer'd out my basnet point
  Into a round salade," he said,
"The basnet being quite out of joint,
  Natheless the salade rasps my head."

He gazed at the great fire awhile:
  "And you are getting old, Sir John;   10
(He said this with that cunning smile
  That was most sad) "we both wear on,

"Knights come to court and look at me,
  With eyebrows up, except my lord
And my dear lady, none I see
  That know the ways of my old sword."

(My lady! at that word no pang
  Stopp'd all my blood). "But tell me, John,

Is it quite true that Pagans hang
  So thick about the east, that on   20

"The eastern sea no Venice flag
  Can fly unpaid for?" "True," I said,
"And in such way the miscreants drag
  Christ's cross upon the ground, I dread

"That Constantine must fall this year."
  Within my heart: "These things are small;
This is not small, that things outwear
  I thought were made for ever, yea, all,

"All things go soon or late," I said.
  I saw the duke in court next day;   30
Just as before, his grand great head
  Above his gold robes dreaming lay,

Only his face was paler; there
  I saw his duchess sit by him;
And she — she was changed more; her hair
  Before my eyes that used to swim,

And make me dizzy with great bliss
  Once, when I used to watch her sit —
Her hair is bright still, yet it is
  As though some dust were thrown on it.   40

Her eyes are shallower, as though
  Some grey glass were behind; her brow
And cheeks the straining bones show through,
  Are not so good for kissing now.

Her lips are drier now she is
  A great duke's wife these many years;
They will not shudder with a kiss
  As once they did, being moist with tears.

Also her hands have lost that way
  Of clinging that they used to have;   50
They look'd quite easy, as they lay
  Upon the silken cushions brave

With broidery of the apples green
  My Lord Duke bears upon his shield.

Her face, alas! that I have seen
Look fresher than an April field,

This is all gone now; gone also
Her tender walking; when she walks
She is most queenly I well know,
And she is fair still — as the stalks   60

Of faded summer-lilies are,
So is she grown now unto me
This spring-time, when the flowers star
The meadows, birds sing wonderfully.

I warrant once she used to cling
About his neck, and kiss'd him so,
And then his coming step would ring
Joy-bells for her, — some time ago.

Ah! sometimes like an idle dream
That hinders true life overmuch,
Sometimes like a lost heaven, these seem —
This love is not so hard to smutch. *soil, smudge*

[1858]

THE GILLIFLOWER OF GOLD

A GOLDEN gilliflower to-day
I wore upon my helm alway,
And won the prize of this tourney.
    Hah! hah! la belle jaune giroflée.

However well Sir Giles might sit,
His sun was weak to wither it,
Lord Miles's blood was dew on it:
    Hah! hah! la belle jaune giroflée.

Although my spear in splinters flew,
From John's steel-coat, my eye was true;   10
I wheel'd about, and cried for you,
    Hah! hah! la belle jaune giroflée.

Yea, do not doubt my heart was good,
Though my sword flew like rotten wood,

To shout, although I scarcely stood:
    Hah! hah! la belle jaune giroflée.

My hand was steady too, to take
My axe from round my neck, and break
John's steel-coat up for my love's sake.
    Hah! hah! la belle jaune giroflée.   **20**

When I stood in my tent again,
Arming afresh, I felt a pain
Take hold of me, I was so fain —
    Hah! hah! la belle jaune giroflée.

To hear: "*Honneur aux fils des preux!*"
Right in my ears again, and shew
The gilliflower blossom'd new.
    Hah! hah! la belle jaune giroflée.

The Sieur Guillaume against me came,
His tabard bore three points of flame   **30**
From a red heart: with little blame —
    Hah! hah! la belle jaune giroflée.

Our tough spears crackled up like straw;
He was the first to turn and draw
His sword, that had nor speck nor flaw, —
    Hah! hah! la belle jaune giroflée.

But I felt weaker than a maid,
And my brain, dizzied and afraid,
Within my helm a fierce tune play'd, —
    Hah! hah! la belle jaune giroflée.   **40**

Until I thought of your dear head,
Bow'd to the gilliflower bed,
The yellow flowers stain'd with red; —
    Hah! hah! la belle jaune giroflée.

Crash! how the swords met: "*giroflée!*"
The fierce tune in my helm would play,
"*La belle! la belle! jaune giroflée!*"
    Hah! hah! la belle jaune giroflée.

Once more the great swords met again:
"*La belle! la belle!*" but who fell then?   **50**

Le Sieur Guillaume, who struck down ten;
 Hah! hah! la belle jaune giroflée.

And as with mazed and unarm'd face,
Toward my own crown and the Queen's place,
They led me at a gentle pace —
 Hah! hah! la belle jaune giroflée.

I almost saw your quiet head
Bow'd o'er the gilliflower bed,
The yellow flowers stain'd with red —
 Hah! hah! la belle jaune giroflée.   **60**

        [1858]

SHAMEFUL DEATH

THERE were four of us about that bed;
 The mass-priest knelt at the side,
I and his mother stood at the head,
 Over his feet lay the bride;
We were quite sure that he was dead,
 Though his eyes were open wide.

He did not die in the night,
 He did not die in the day,
But in the morning twilight
 His spirit pass'd away,   **10**
When neither sun nor moon was bright,
 And the trees were merely grey.

He was not slain with the sword,
 Knight's axe, or the knightly spear,
Yet spoke he never a word
 After he came in here;
I cut away the cord
 From the neck of my brother dear.

He did not strike one blow,
 For the recreants came behind,
In a place where the hornbeams grow,
 A path right hard to find,
For the hornbeam boughs swing so,
 That the twilight makes it blind.

They lighted a great torch then,
   When his arms were pinion'd fast,
Sir John the knight of the Fen,
   Sir Guy of the Dolorous Blast,
With knights threescore and ten,
   Hung brave Lord Hugh at last.   30

I am threescore and ten,
   And my hair is all turn'd grey,
But I met Sir John of the Fen
   Long ago on a summer day,
And am glad to think of the moment when
   I took his life away.

I am threescore and ten,
   And my strength is mostly pass'd,
But long ago I and my men,
   When the sky was overcast,   40
And the smoke roll'd over the reeds of the fen,
   Slew Guy of the Dolorous Blast.

And now, knights all of you,
I pray you pray for Sir Hugh,
A good knight and a true,
And for Alice, his wife, pray too.

                       [1858]

THE EVE OF CRECY

GOLD on her head, and gold on her feet,
And gold where the hems of her kirtle meet,
And a golden girdle round my sweet; —
   Ah! qu'elle est belle La Marguerite.

Margaret's maids are fair to see,
Freshly dress'd and pleasantly;
Margaret's hair falls down to her knee; —
   Ah! qu'elle est belle La Marguerite.

If I were rich I would kiss her feet,
I would kiss the place where the gold hems meet,   10
And the golden girdle round my sweet —
   Ah! qu'elle est belle La Marguerite.

Ah me! I have never touch'd her hand;
When the arriere-ban goes through the land,
Six basnets under my pennon stand; —
 Ah! qu'elle est belle La Marguerite.

And many an one grins under his hood:
"Sir Lambert de Bois, with all his men good,
Has neither food nor firewood." —
 Ah! qu'elle est belle La Marguerite.   20

If I were rich I would kiss her feet,
And the golden girdle of my sweet,
And thereabouts where the gold hems meet;
 Ah! qu'elle est belle La Marguerite.

Yet even now it is good to think,
While my few poor varlets grumble and drink
In my desolate hall, where the fires sink, —
 Ah! qu'elle est belle La Marguerite.

Of Margaret sitting glorious there,
In glory of gold and glory of hair,   30
And glory of glorious face most fair; —
 Ah! qu'elle est belle La Marguerite.

Likewise to-night I make good cheer,
Because this battle draweth near:
For what have I to lose or fear? —
 Ah! qu'elle est belle La Marguerite.

For, look you, my horse is good to prance
A right fair measure in this war-dance,
Before the eyes of Philip of France; —
 Ah! qu'elle est belle La Marguerite.   40

And sometime it may hap, perdie,
While my new towers stand up three and three,
And my hall gets painted fair to see —
 Ah! qu'elle est belle La Marguerite.

That folks may say: 'Times change, by the rood,
For Lambert, banneret of the wood,
Has heaps of food and firewood; —
 Ah! qu'elle est belle La Marguerite.

"And wonderful eyes, too, under the hood
Of a damsel of right noble blood."   50
St. Ives, for Lambert of the Wood! —
    Ah! qu'elle est belle La Marguerite.

[1858]

fought to find who was at fault

THE JUDGMENT OF GOD

"Swerve to the left, son Roger," he said,
    "When you catch his eyes through the helmet-slit,
Swerve to the left, then out at his head,
    And the Lord God give you joy of it!"

The blue owls on my father's hood   *family tree diminished*
    Were a little dimm'd as I turn'd away;
This giving up of blood for blood
    Will finish here somehow to-day.

not crowd favorite

So — when I walk'd out from the tent,
    Their howling almost blinded me;   10
Yet for all that I was not bent
    By any shame. Hard by, the sea

Made a noise like the aspens where
    We did that wrong, but now the place
Is very pleasant, and the air
    Blows cool on any passer's face.

And all the wrong is gather'd now
    Into the circle of these lists —
Yea, howl out, butchers! tell me how
    His hands were cut off at the wrists;   20

And how Lord Roger bore his face   *dignity*
    A league above his spear-point, high
Above the owls, to that strong place
    Among the waters — yea, yea, cry:

"What a brave champion we have got!   *challenge*
    Sir Oliver, the flower of all
The Hainault knights." The day being hot,
    He sat beneath a broad white pall,

White linen over all his steel;
  What a good knight he look'd! his sword   **30**
Laid thwart his knees; he liked to feel
  Its steadfast edge clear as his word.

And he look'd solemn; how his love
  Smiled whitely on him, sick with fear!
How all the ladies up above
  Twisted their pretty hands! so near

inspiration

The fighting was — Ellayne! Ellayne!
  They cannot love like you can, who
Would burn your hands off, if that pain
  Could win a kiss — am I not true   **40**

To you for ever? therefore I
  Do not fear death or anything;
If I should limp home wounded, why,
  While I lay sick you would but sing,

And soothe me into quiet sleep. *coward, deserter*
  If they spat on the recreant knight,
Threw stones at him, and cursed him deep,
  Why then — what then; your hand would light

So gently on his drawn-up face,
  And you would kiss him, and in soft   **50**
Cool scented clothes would lap him, pace
  The quiet room and weep oft, — oft

Would turn and smile, and brush his cheek
  With your sweet chin and mouth; and in
The order'd garden you would seek
  The biggest roses — any sin.

Ellayne says: And these say: "No more now my knight,
  Or God's knight any longer" — you, *Ellayne*
Being than they so much more white,
  So much more pure and good and true,   **60**

for acceptance is more desirable

Will cling to me for ever — there,
  Is not that wrong turn'd right at last
Through all these years, and I wash'd clean?
  Say, yea, Ellayne; the time is past,

Since on that Christmas-day last year
  Up to your feet the fire crept,
And the smoke through the brown leaves sere
  Blinded your dear eyes that you wept;

Was it not I that caught you then,
  And kiss'd you on the saddle-bow?
Did not the blue owl mark the men
  Whose spears stood like the corn a-row? 70

This Oliver is a right good knight,
  And must needs beat me, as I fear,
Unless I catch him in the fight,
  My father's crafty way — John, here!

Bring up the men from the south gate,
  To help me if I fall or win,
For even if I beat, their hate
  Will grow to more than this mere grin. 80

[1858]

THE LITTLE TOWER

Up and away through the drifting rain!
Let us ride to the Little Tower again,

Up and away from the council board!
Do on the hauberk, gird on the sword.

The king is blind with gnashing his teeth,
Change gilded scabbard to leather sheath:

Though our arms are wet with the slanting rain,
This is joy to ride to my love again:

I laugh in his face when he bids me yield;
Who knows one field from the other field, 10

For the grey rain driveth all astray? —
"Which way through the floods, good carle, I pray?"

"The left side yet! the left side yet!
Till your hand strikes on the bridge parapet."

"Yea so: the causeway holdeth good
Under the water?" "Hard as wood,

"Right away to the uplands; speed, good knight."
Seven hours yet before the light.

Shake the wet off on the upland road;
My tabard has grown a heavy load.   20

What matter? up and down hill after hill;
Dead grey night for five hours still.

The hill-road droppeth lower again,
Lower, down to the poplar plain.

No furlong farther for us to-night,
The Little Tower draweth in sight;

They are ringing the bells, and the torches glare,
Therefore the roofs of wet slate stare.

There she stands, and her yellow hair slantingly
Drifts the same way that the rain goes by.   30

Who will be faithful to us to-day,
With little but hard glaive-strokes for pay?

The grim king fumes at the council-board:
"Three more days, and then the sword;

"Three more days, and my sword through his head;
And above his white brows, pale and dead,

"A paper crown on the top of the spire;
And for her the stake and the witches' fire."

Therefore though it be long ere day,
Take axe and pick and spade, I pray.   40

Break the dams down all over the plain:
God send us three more days such rain!

Block all the upland roads with trees;
The Little Tower with no great ease

Is won, I warrant; bid them bring
Much sheep and oxen, everything

The spits are wont to turn with; wine
And wheaten bread, that we may dine

In plenty each day of the siege;
Good friends, ye know me no hard liege;⁣   50

My lady is right fair, see ye!
Pray God to keep you frank and free.

Love Isabeau, keep goodly cheer;
The Little Tower will stand well here

Many a year when we are dead,
And over it our green and red,
Barred with the Lady's golden head;
From mere old age when we are dead.

[1858]

THE SAILING OF THE SWORD

Across the empty garden-beds,
 When the Sword went out to sea,
I scarcely saw my sisters' heads
 Bowed each beside a tree.
I could not see the castle leads,
 When the Sword went out to sea.

Alicia wore a scarlet gown,
 When the Sword went out to sea,
But Ursula's was russet brown:
 For the mist we could not see   10
The scarlet roofs of the good town,
 When the Sword went out to sea.

Green holly in Alicia's hand,
 When the Sword went out to sea;
With sere oak-leaves did Ursula stand;
 O! yet alas for me!

I did but bear a peel'd white wand,
  When the Sword went out to sea.

O, russet brown and scarlet bright,
  When the Sword went out to sea,
My sisters wore; I wore but white:
  Red, brown, and white, are three;
Three damozels; each had a knight,
  When the Sword went out to sea.

Sir Robert shouted loud, and said:
  When the Sword went out to sea,
"Alicia, while I see thy head,
  What shall I bring for thee?"
"O, my sweet lord, a ruby red:"
  The Sword went out to sea.

Sir Miles said, while the sails hung down:
  When the Sword went out to sea,
"Oh, Ursula! while I see the town,
  What shall I bring for thee?"
"Dear knight, bring back a falcon brown:"
  The Sword went out to sea.

But my Roland, no word he said
  When the Sword went out to sea,
But only turn'd away his head;
  A quick shriek came from me:
"Come back, dear lord, to your white maid."
  The Sword went out to sea.

The hot sun bit the garden-beds
  When the Sword came back from sea;
Beneath an apple-tree our heads
  Stretched out toward the sea;
Grey gleam'd the thirsty castle-leads,
  When the Sword came back from sea.

Lord Robert brought a ruby red,
  When the Sword came back from sea;
He kissed Alicia on the head:
  "I am come back to thee;
'Tis time, sweet love, that we were wed,
  Now the Sword is back from sea!"

20

30

40

50

Sir Miles he bore a falcon brown,
  When the Sword came back from sea;
His arms went round tall Ursula's gown:
  "What joy, O love, but thee?
Let us be wed in the good town,
  Now the Sword is back from sea!"   50

My heart grew sick, no more afraid,
  When the Sword came back from sea;
Upon the deck a tall white maid
  Sat on Lord Roland's knee;
His chin was press'd upon her head,
  When the Sword came back from sea!
                                    [1858]

SPELL-BOUND

How weary is it none can tell,
  How dismally the days go by!
I hear the tinkling of the bell,
  I see the cross against the sky.

The year wears round to autumn-tide,
  Yet comes no reaper to the corn;
The golden land is like a bride
  When first she knows herself forlorn —

She sits and weeps with all her hair
  Laid downward over tender hands;   10
For stainèd silk she hath no care,
  No care for broken ivory wands;

The silver cups beside her stand;
  The golden stars on the blue roof
Yet glitter, though against her hand
  His cold sword presses, for a proof

He is not dead, but gone away.
  How many hours did she wait
For me, I wonder? Till the day
  Had faded wholly, and the gate   20

Clanged to behind returning knights?
 I wonder did she raise her head
And go away, fleeing the lights;
 And lay the samite on her bed,

The wedding samite strewn with pearls:
 Then sit with hands laid on her knees,
Shuddering at half-heard sound of girls
 That chatter outside in the breeze?

I wonder did her poor heart throb
 At distant tramp of coming knight?   **30**
How often did the choking sob
 Raise up her head and lips? The light,

Did it come on her unawares,
 And drag her sternly down before
People who loved her not? in prayers
 Did she say one name and no more?

And once — all songs they ever sung,
 All tales they ever told to me,
This only burden through them rung:
 O golden love that waitest me,   **40**

The days pass on, pass on a-pace,
 Sometimes I have a little rest
In fairest dreams, when on thy face
 My lips lie, or thy hands are prest

About my forehead, and thy lips
 Draw near and nearer to mine own;
But when the vision from me slips,
 In colourless dawn I lie and moan,

And wander forth with fever'd blood,
 That makes me start at little things,   **50**
The blackbird screaming from the wood,
 The sudden whirr of pheasants' wings.

O dearest, scarcely seen by me —
 But when that wild time had gone by,
And in these arms I folded thee,
 Who ever thought those days could die?

Yet now I wait, and you wait too,
    For what perchance may never come;
You think I have forgotten you,
    That I grew tired and went home.   60

But what if some day as I stood
    Against the wall with strainèd hands,
And turn'd my face toward the wood,
    Away from all the golden lands;

And saw you come with tired feet,
    And pale face thin and wan with care,
And stainèd raiment no more neat,
    The white dust lying on your hair: —

Then I should say, I could not come;
    This land was my wide prison, dear;   70
I could not choose but go; at home
    There is a wizard whom I fear:

He bound me round with silken chains
    I could not break; he set me here
Above the golden-waving plains,
    Where never reaper cometh near.

And you have brought me my good sword,
    Wherewith in happy days of old
I won you well from knight and lord;
    My heart upswells and I grow bold.   80

But I shall die unless you stand,
    — Half lying now, you are so weak, —
Within my arms, unless your hand
    Pass to and fro across my cheek.

             [1858]

THE WIND

Ah! no, no, it is nothing, surely nothing at all,
Only the wild-going wind round by the garden-wall,
For the dawn just now is breaking, the wind beginning to fall.

> *Wind, wind! thou art sad, art thou kind?*
> *Wind, wind, unhappy! thou art blind,*
> *Yet still thou wanderest the lily-seed to find.*

So I will sit, and think and think of the days gone by,
Never moving my chair for fear the dogs should cry,
Making no noise at all while the flambeau burns awry.
For my chair is heavy and carved, and with sweeping green behind 10
It is hung, and the dragons thereon grin out in the gusts of the wind;
On its folds an orange lies, with a deep gash cut in the rind.

> *Wind, wind! thou art sad, art thou kind?*
> *Wind, wind, unhappy! thou art blind,*
> *Yet still thou wanderest the lily-seed to find.*

If I move my chair it will scream, and the orange will roll out far,
And the faint yellow juice ooze out like blood from a wizard's jar;
And the dogs will howl for those who went last month to the war.

> *Wind, wind! thou art sad, art thou kind?*
> *Wind, wind, unhappy! thou art blind,*   20
> *Yet still thou wanderest the lily-seed to find.*

So I will sit and think of love that is over and past,
O! so long ago — yes, I will be quiet at last;
Whether I like it or not, a grim half-slumber is cast
Over my worn old brains, that touches the roots of my heart,
And above my half-shut eyes the blue roof 'gins to part,
And show the blue spring sky, till I am ready to start
From out of the green-hung chair; but something keeps me still,
And I fall in a dream that I walk'd with her on the side of a hill,
Dotted — for was it not spring? — with tufts of the daffodil.   30

> *Wind, wind! thou art sad, art thou kind?*
> *Wind, wind, unhappy! thou art blind,*
> *Yet still thou wanderest the lily-seed to find.*

And Margaret as she walk'd held a painted book in her hand;
Her finger kept the place; I caught her, we both did stand
Face to face, on the top of the highest hill in the land.

> *Wind, wind! thou art sad, art thou kind?*
> *Wind, wind, unhappy! thou art blind,*
> *Yet still thou wanderest the lily-seed to find.*

I held to her long bare arms, but she shudder'd away from me   40
While the flush went out of her face as her head fell back on a tree,
And a spasm caught her mouth, fearful for me to see;

And still I held to her arms till her shoulder touch'd my mail,
Weeping she totter'd forward, so glad that I should prevail,
And her hair went over my robe, like a gold flag over a sail.

> *Wind, wind! thou art sad, art thou kind?*
> *Wind, wind, unhappy! thou art blind,*
> *Yet still thou wanderest the lily-seed to find.*

I kiss'd her hard by the ear, and she kiss'd me on the brow,
And then lay down on the grass, where the mark on the moss is now, 50
And spread her arms out wide while I went down below.

> *Wind, wind! thou art sad, art thou kind?*
> *Wind, wind, unhappy! thou art blind,*
> *Yet still thou wanderest the lily-seed to find.*

And then I walk'd for a space to and fro on the side of the hill,
Till I gather'd and held in my arms great sheaves of the daffodil,
And when I came again my Margaret lay there still.

I piled them high and high above her heaving breast,
How they were caught and held in her loose ungirded vest!
But one beneath her arm died, happy so to be prest!   60

> *Wind, wind! thou art sad, art thou kind?*
> *Wind, wind, unhappy! thou art blind,*
> *Yet still thou wanderest the lily-seed to find.*

Again I turn'd my back and went away for an hour;
She said no word when I came again, so, flower by flower,
I counted the daffodils over, and cast them languidly lower.

> *Wind, wind! thou art sad, art thou kind?*
> *Wind, wind, unhappy! thou art blind,*
> *Yet still thou wanderest the lily-seed to find.*

My dry hands shook and shook as the green gown show'd again,   **70**
Clear'd from the yellow flowers, and I grew hollow with pain,
And on to us both there fell from the sun-shower drops of rain.

> *Wind, wind! thou art sad, art thou kind?*
> *Wind, wind, unhappy! thou art blind,*
> *Yet still thou wanderest the lily-seed to find.*

Alas! alas! there was blood on the very quiet breast,
Blood lay in the many folds of the loose ungirded vest,
Blood lay upon her arm where the flower had been prest.

I shriek'd and leapt from my chair, and the orange roll'd out far,
The faint yellow juice oozed out like blood from a wizard's jar;   **80**
And then in march'd the ghosts of those that had gone to the war.

I knew them by the arms that I was used to paint
Upon their long thin shields; but the colours were all grown faint,
And faint upon their banner was Olaf, king and saint.

> *Wind, wind! thou art sad, art thou kind?*
> *Wind, wind, unhappy! thou art blind,*
> *Yet still thou wanderest the lily-seed to find.*

> [1858]

causeless

THE BLUE CLOSET

THE DAMOZELS

Lady Alice, Lady Louise,
Between the wash of the tumbling seas
We are ready to sing, if so ye please;
So lay your long hands on the keys;
  Sing: *"Laudate pueri."*

And ever the great bell overhead
Boom'd in the wind a knell for the dead,
Though no one toll'd it, a knell for the dead.

LADY LOUISE

Sister, let the measure swell
Not too loud; for you sing not well   10
If you drown the faint boom of the bell;
     He is weary, so am I.

And ever the chevron overhead
Flapp'd on the banner of the dead;
(Was he asleep, or was he dead?)

waiting for arthur

LADY ALICE

Alice the Queen, and Louise the Queen,
Two damozels wearing purple and green,
Four lone ladies dwelling here
From day to day and year to year;
And there is none to let us go;   20
To break the locks of the doors below,
Or shovel away the heaped-up snow;
And when we die no man will know
That we are dead; but they give us leave,
Once every year on Christmas-eve,
To sing in the Closet Blue one song;
And we should be so long, so long,
If we dared, in singing; for dream on dream,
They float on in a happy stream;
Float from the gold strings, float from the keys,   30
Float from the open'd lips of Louise;
But, alas! the sea-salt oozes through
The chinks of the tiles of the Closet Blue;
And ever the great bell overhead
Booms in the wind a knell for the dead,
The wind plays on it a knell for the dead.

     They sing all together.
How long ago was it, how long ago,
He came to this tower with hands full of snow?

"Kneel down, O love Louise, kneel down!" he said,
And sprinkled the dusty snow over my head.   40

baptism

He watch'd the snow melting, it ran through my hair,
Ran over my shoulders, white shoulders and bare.

"I cannot weep for thee, poor love Louise,
For my tears are all hidden deep under the seas;

"In a gold and blue casket she keeps all my tears,
But my eyes are no longer blue, as in old years;

"Yea, they grow grey with time, grow small and dry,
I am so feeble now, would I might die."

   And in truth the great bell overhead
   Left off his pealing for the dead,   50
   Perchance, because the wind was dead.

Will he come back again, or is he dead?
O! is he sleeping, my scarf round his head?

Or did they strangle him as he lay there,
With the long scarlet scarf I used to wear?

Only I pray thee, Lord, let him come here!
Both his soul and his body to me are most dear.

Dear Lord, that loves me, I wait to receive
Either body or spirit this wild Christmas-eve.

Through the floor shot up a lily red,   60
With a patch of earth from the land of the dead,
For he was strong in the land of the dead.

   What matter that his cheeks were pale,
      His kind kiss'd lips all grey?
   "O, love Louise, have you waited long?"
      "O, my lord Arthur, yea."

   What if his hair that brush'd her cheek
      Was stiff with frozen rime?
   His eyes were grown quite blue again,
      As in the happy time.   70

   "O, love Louise, this is the key
      Of the happy golden land!
   O, sisters, cross the bridge with me,
      My eyes are full of sand.
   What matter that I cannot see,
      If ye take me by the hand?"

And ever the great bell overhead,
And the tumbling seas mourn'd for the dead;
For their song ceased, and they were dead.   79

               [1858]

THE TUNE OF SEVEN TOWERS

No one goes there now:
  For what is left to fetch away
From the desolate battlements all arow,
    And the lead roof heavy and grey?
      "Therefore," said fair Yoland of the flowers,
      "This is the tune of Seven Towers."

No one walks there now;
  Except in the white moonlight
The white ghosts walk in a row;
    If one could see it, an awful sight, —   10
      "Listen!" said fair Yoland of the flowers,
      "This is the tune of Seven Towers."

But none can see them now,
  Though they sit by the side of the moat,
Feet half in the water, there in a row,
    Long hair in the wind afloat.
      "Therefore," said fair Yoland of the flowers,
      "This is the tune of Seven Towers."

If any will go to it now,
  He must go to it all alone,
Its gates will not open to any row   20
    Of glittering spears — will *you* go alone?
      "Listen!" said fair Yoland of the flowers,
      "This is the tune of Seven Towers."

By my love go there now,
  To fetch me my coif away,
My coif and my kirtle, with pearls arow,
    Oliver, go to-day!
      "Therefore," said fair Yoland of the flowers,
      "This is the tune of Seven Towers."   30

I am unhappy now,
  I cannot tell you why;
If you go, the priests and I in a row
    Will pray that you may not die.
      "Listen!" said fair Yoland of the flowers,
      "This is the tune of Seven Towers."

If you will go for me now,
  I will kiss your mouth at last;
    [*She sayeth inwardly.*]
  (*The graves stand grey in a row.*)
    Oliver, hold me fast!   40
      "*Therefore,*" *said fair Yoland of the flowers,*
      "*This is the tune of Seven Towers.*"

                                [1858]

GOLDEN WINGS

Midways of a wallèd garden,
  In the happy poplar land,
  Did an ancient castle stand,
With an old knight for a warden.

Many scarlet bricks there were
  In its walls, and old grey stone;
  Over which red apples shone
At the right time of the year.

On the bricks the green moss grew,
  Yellow lichen on the stone,   10
  Over which red apples shone;
Little war that castle knew.

Deep green water fill'd the moat,
  Each side had a red-brick lip,
  Green and mossy with the drip
Of dew and rain; there was a boat

Of carven wood, with hangings green
  About the stern; it was great bliss
  For lovers to sit there and kiss
In the hot summer noons, not seen.   20

Across the moat the fresh west wind
  In very little ripples went;
  The way the heavy aspens bent
Towards it, was a thing to mind.

The painted drawbridge over it
    Went up and down with gilded chains.
    'Twas pleasant in the summer rains
Within the bridge-house there to sit.

There were five swans that ne'er did eat
    The water-weeds, for ladies came   30
    Each day, and young knights did the same,
And gave them cakes and bread for meat.

They had a house of painted wood,
    A red roof gold-spiked over it,
    Wherein upon their eggs to sit
Week after week; no drop of blood,

Drawn from men's bodies by sword-blows,
    Came over there, or any tear;
    Most certainly from year to year
'Twas pleasant as a Provence rose.   40

The banners seem'd quite full of ease,
    That over the turret-roofs hung down;
    The battlements could get no frown
From the flower-moulded cornices.

Who walked in that garden there?
    Miles and Giles and Isabeau,
    Tall Jehane du Castel beau,
Alice of the golden hair,

Big Sir Gervaise, the good knight,
    Fair Ellayne le Violet,   50
    Mary, Constance fille de fay,
Many dames with footfall light.

Whosoever wander'd there,
    Whether it be dame or knight,
    Half of scarlet, half of white
Their raiment was; of roses fair

Each wore a garland on the head,
    At Ladies' Gard the way was so:
    Fair Jehane du Castel beau
Wore her wreath till it was dead.   60

Little joy she had of it,
  Of the raiment white and red,
  Or the garland on her head,
She had none with whom to sit

In the carven boat at noon;
  None the more did Jehane weep,
  She would only stand and keep
Saying: "He will be here soon."

Many times in the long day
  Miles and Giles and Gervaise passed,   70
  Holding each some white hand fast,
Every time they heard her say:

"Summer cometh to an end,
  Undern cometh after noon;
  Golden wings will be here soon,
What if I some token send?"

Wherefore that night within the hall,
  With open mouth and open eyes,
  Like some one listening with surprise,
She sat before the sight of all.   80

Stoop'd down a little she sat there,
  With neck stretch'd out and chin thrown up,
  One hand around a golden cup;
And strangely with her fingers fair

She beat some tune upon the gold;
  The minstrels in the gallery
  Sung: "Arthur, who will never die,
In Avallon he groweth old."

And when the song was ended, she
  Rose and caught up her gown and ran;   90
  None stopp'd her eager face and wan
Of all that pleasant company.

Right so within her own chamber
  Upon her bed she sat; and drew
  Her breath in quick gasps; till she knew
That no man follow'd after her.

She took the garland from her head,
  Loosed all her hair, and let it lie
  Upon the coverlit; thereby
She laid the gown of white and red;   100

And she took off her scarlet shoon,
  And bared her feet; still more and more
  Her sweet face redden'd; evermore
She murmur'd: "He will be here soon;

"Truly he cannot fail to know
  My tender body waits him here;
  And if he knows, I have no fear
For poor Jehane du Castel beau."

She took a sword within her hand,
  Whose hilts were silver, and she sung   110
  Somehow like this, wild words that rung
A long way over the moonlit land:

      Gold wings across the sea!
      Grey light from tree to tree,
      Gold hair beside my knee,
      I pray thee come to me,
      Gold wings!

            The water slips,
      The red-bill'd moorhen dips.
      Sweet kisses on red lips;
      Alas! the red rust grips,   120
      And the blood-red dagger rips,
      Yet, O knight, come to me!

      Are not my blue eyes sweet?
      The west wind from the wheat
      Blows cold across my feet;
      Is it not time to meet
      Gold wings across the sea?

      White swans on the green moat.
      Small feathers left afloat
      By the blue-painted boat;   130
      Swift running of the stoat;
      Sweet gurgling note by note
      Of sweet music.

O gold wings,
Listen how gold hair sings,
And the Ladies' Castle rings,
Gold wings across the sea.

I sit on a purple bed,
Outside, the wall is red,
Thereby the apple hangs,
And the wasp, caught by the fangs,   140

Dies in the autumn night,
And the bat flits till light,
And the love-crazèd knight

Kisses the long wet grass:
The weary days pass, —
Gold wings across the sea!

Gold wings across the sea!
Moonlight from tree to tree,
Sweet hair laid on my knee,
O, sweet knight, come to me!   150

Gold wings, the short night slips,
The white swan's long neck drips,
I pray thee, kiss my lips,
Gold wings, the short night slips,

No answer through the moonlit night;
No answer in the cold grey dawn;
No answer when the shaven lawn
Grew green, and all the roses bright.

Her tired feet look'd cold and thin,
Her lips were twitch'd and wretched tears,   160
Some, as she lay, roll'd past her ears,
Some fell from off her quivering chin.

Her long throat, stretched to its full length,
Rose up and fell right brokenly;
As though the unhappy heart was nigh
Striving to break with all its strength.

And when she slipp'd from off the bed,
Her cramp'd feet would not hold her; she

Sank down and crept on hand and knee,
On the window-sill she laid her head.   170

There, with crookèd arm upon the sill,
   She look'd out, muttering dismally:
   "There is no sail upon the sea,
No pennon on the empty hill.

"I cannot stay here all alone,
   Or meet their happy faces here,
   And wretchedly I have no fear;
A little while, and I am gone."

Therewith she rose upon her feet,
   And totter'd; cold and misery   180
   Still made the deep sobs come, till she
At last stretch'd out her fingers sweet,

And caught the great sword in her hand;
   And, stealing down the silent stair,
   Barefooted in the morning air,
And only in her smock, did stand

Upright upon the green lawn grass;
   And hope grew in her as she said:
   "I have thrown off the white and red,
And pray God it may come to pass   190

"I meet him; if ten years go by
   Before I meet him; if, indeed,
   Meanwhile both soul and body bleed,
Yet there is end of misery,

"And I have hope. He could not come,
   But I can go to him and show
   These new things I have got to know,
And make him speak, who has been dumb."

O Jehane! the red morning sun
   Changed her white feet to glowing gold,   200
   Upon her smock, on crease and fold,
Changed that to gold which had been dun.

O Miles and Giles and Isabeau,
   Fair Ellayne le Violet,

Mary, Constance fille de fay!
Where is Jehane du Castel beau?

O big Gervaise, ride apace!
  Down to the hard yellow sand,
  Where the water meets the land.
This is Jehane by her face;   210

Why has she a broken sword?
  Mary! she is slain outright;
  Verily a piteous sight;
Take her up without a word!

Giles and Miles and Gervaise there,
  Ladies Gard must meet the war;
  Whatsoever knights these are,
Man the walls withouten fear!

Axes to the apple-trees,
  Axes to the aspens tall!   220
  Barriers without the wall
May be lightly made of these.

O poor shivering Isabeau;
  Poor Ellayne le Violet,
  Bent with fear! we miss to-day
Brave Jehane du Castel beau.

O poor Mary, weeping so!
  Wretched Constance fille de fay!
  Verily we miss to-day
Fair Jehane du Castel beau.   230

The apples now grow green and sour
  Upon the mouldering castle-wall,
  Before they ripen there they fall:
There are no banners on the tower.

The draggled swans most eagerly eat
  The green weeds trailing in the moat;
  Inside the rotting leaky boat
You see a slain man's stiffen'd feet.

                        [1858]

THE HAYSTACK IN THE FLOODS

HAD she come all the way for this,
To part at last without a kiss? *foreshadow*
Yea, had she borne the dirt and rain
That her own eyes might see him slain
Beside the haystack in the floods?

Along the dripping leafless woods, *(early winter)*
The stirrup touching either shoe,
She rode astride as troopers do;
With kirtle kilted to her knee,
To which the mud splash'd wretchedly;   10
And the wet dripp'd from every tree
Upon her head and heavy hair,
And on her eyelids broad and fair;
The tears and rain ran down her face.
By fits and starts they rode apace,
And very often was his place
Far off from her; he had to ride
Ahead, to see what might betide
When the roads cross'd; and sometimes, when
There rose a murmuring from his men,   20
Had to turn back with promises;
Wow! Ah me! she had but little ease;
And often for pure doubt and dread
She sobb'd, made giddy in the head
By the swift riding; while, for cold,
Her slender fingers scarce could hold
The wet reins; yea, and scarcely, too,
She felt the foot within her shoe
Against the stirrup: all for this,
To part at last without a kiss   30
Beside the haystack in the floods.

For when they near'd that old soak'd hay, *ambush*
They saw across the only way   *behind*
That Judas, Godmar, and the three   *haystack*
Red running lions dismally
Grinn'd from his pennon, under which
In one straight line along the ditch,
They counted thirty heads.
                    So then,

While Robert turn'd round to his men,
She saw at once the wretched end,   40
And, stooping down, tried hard to rend
Her coif the wrong way from her head,
And hid her eyes; while Robert said:
"Nay, love, 'tis scarcely two to one,
At Poictiers where we made them run
So fast — why, sweet my love, good cheer.
The Gascon frontier is so near,
Nought after this."

             But, "O," she said,
"My God! my God! I have to tread
The long way back without you; then   50
The court at Paris; those six men;
The gratings of the Chatelet;
The swift Seine on some rainy day
Like this, and people standing by,
And laughing, while my weak hands try
To recollect how strong men swim.
All this, or else a life with him,
For which I should be damned at last.
Would God that this next hour were past!"

He answer'd not, but cried his cry,   60
"St. George for Marny!" cheerily;
And laid his hand upon her rein.
Alas! no man of all his train
Gave back that cheery cry again;
And, while for rage his thumb beat fast
Upon his sword-hilts, some one cast
About his neck a kerchief long,
And bound him.

            Then they went along
To Godmar; who said: "Now, Jehane,
Your lover's life is on the wane   70
So fast, that, if this very hour
You yield not as my paramour,
He will not see the rain leave off —
Nay, keep your tongue from gibe and scoff,
Sir Robert, or I slay you now."

She laid her hand upon her brow,
Then gazed upon the palm, as though

She thought her forehead bled, and — "No!"
She said, and turn'd her head away,
As there were nothing else to say,   80
And everything were settled: red   *anger & passion*
Grew Godmar's face from chin to head:
"Jehane, on yonder hill there stands
My castle, guarding well my lands:
What hinders me from taking you,   *why can't I just*
And doing that I list to do   *take you anyway*
To your fair wilful body, while
Your knight lies dead?"

                                        A wicked smile
Wrinkled her face, her lips grew thin,
A long way out she thrust her chin: 90
"You know that I should strangle you
While you were sleeping; or bite through
Your throat, by God's help — ah!" she said,
"Lord Jesus, pity your poor maid!
For in such wise they hem me in,
I cannot choose but sin and sin,
Whatever happens: yet I think
They could not make me eat or drink,
And so should I just reach my rest."
"Nay, if you do not my behest,   100
O Jehane! though I love you well,"   *look what I know*
Said Godmar, "would I fail to tell
All that I know?" "Foul lies," she said.
"Eh? lies my Jehane? by God's head,
At Paris folks would deem them true!
Do you know, Jehane, they cry for you:
'Jehane the brown! Jehane the brown!
Give us Jehane to burn or drown!' —
Eh — gag me Robert! — sweet my friend,
This were indeed a piteous end   110
For those long fingers, and long feet,
And long neck, and smooth shoulders sweet;
An end that few men would forget
That saw it — So, an hour yet: *60 minutes*   *Like choice*
Consider, Jehane, which to take   *to choose*   *of Lambert*
Of life or death!"

                            So, scarce awake,
Dismounting, did she leave that place,
And totter some yards: with her face
Turn'd upward to the sky she lay,
Her head on a wet heap of hay,   120

And fell asleep: and while she slept,
And did not dream, the minutes crept
Round to the twelve again; but she,
Being waked at last, sigh'd quietly,
And strangely childlike came, and said:
"I will not." Straightway Godmar's head,
As though it hung on strong wires, turn'd
Most sharply round, and his face burn'd.

For Robert — both his eyes were dry,
He could not weep, but gloomily   130
He seem'd to watch the rain; yea, too,
His lips were firm; he tried once more
To touch her lips; she reach'd out, sore
And vain desire so tortured them,
The poor grey lips, and now the hem
Of his sleeve brush'd them.
                            With a start
Up Godmar rose, thrust them apart;
From Robert's throat he loosed the bands
Of silk and mail; with empty hands
Held out, she stood and gazed, and saw   140
The long bright blade without a flaw
Glide out from Godmar's sheath, his hand
In Robert's hair; she saw him bend
Back Robert's head; she saw him send
The thin steel down; the blow told well,
Right backward the knight Robert fell,
And moan'd as dogs do, being half dead,
Unwitting, as I deem: so then
Godmar turn'd grinning to his men,
Who ran, some five or six, and beat   150
His head to pieces at their feet.

Then Godmar turn'd again and said:
"So, Jehane, the first fitte is read!
Take note, my lady, that your way
Lies backward to the Chatelet!"
She shook her head and gazed awhile
At her cold hands with a rueful smile,
As though this thing had made her mad.

This was the parting that they had
Beside the haystack in the floods.   160
                            [1858]

TWO RED ROSES ACROSS THE MOON

THERE was a lady lived in a hall,
Large of her eyes, and slim and tall;
And ever she sung from noon to noon,
Two red roses across the moon.

There was a knight came riding by
In early spring, when the roads were dry;
And he heard that lady sing at the noon,
Two red roses across the moon.

Yet none the more he stopp'd at all,
But he rode a-gallop past the hall;　　　　　　10
And left that lady singing at noon,
Two red roses across the moon.

Because, forsooth, the battle was set,
And the scarlet and blue had got to be met,
He rode on the spur till the next warm noon: —
Two red roses across the moon.

But the battle was scatter'd from hill to hill,
From the windmill to the watermill;
And he said to himself, as it near'd the noon,
Two red roses across the moon.　　　　　　20

You scarce could see for the scarlet and blue
A golden helm or a golden shoe;
So he cried, as the fight grew thick at the noon,
Two red roses across the moon!

Verily then the gold bore through
The huddled spears of the scarlet and blue;
And they cried, as they cut them down at the noon,
Two red roses across the moon!

I trow he stopp'd when he rode again
By the hall, though draggled sore with the rain;　　30
And his lips were pinch'd to kiss at the noon
Two red roses across the moon.

Under the may she stoop'd to the crown,
All was gold, there was nothing of brown;
And the horns blew up in the hall at noon,
Two red roses across the moon.

[1858]

WELLAND RIVER

FAIR Ellayne she walk'd by Welland river,
    Across the lily lee:
O, gentle Sir Robert, ye are not kind
    To stay so long at sea.

Over the marshland none can see
    Your scarlet pennon fair;
O, leave the Easterlings alone,
    Because of my golden hair.

The day when over Stamford bridge
    That dear pennon I see   10
Go up toward the goodly street,
    'Twill be a fair day for me.

O, let the bonny pennon bide
    At Stamford, the good town,
And let the Easterlings go free,
    And their ships go up and down.

For every day that passes by
    I wax both pale and green,
From gold to gold of my girdle
    There is an inch between.   20

I sew'd it up with scarlet silk
    Last night upon my knee,
And my heart grew sad and sore to think
    Thy face I'd never see.

I sew'd it up with scarlet silk,
    As I lay upon my bed:
Sorrow! the man I'll never see
    That had my maidenhead.

But as Ellayne sat on her window-seat
    And comb'd her yellow hair,   30
She saw come over Stamford bridge
    The scarlet pennon fair.

As Ellayne lay and sicken'd sore,
    The gold shoes on her feet,
She saw Sir Robert and his men
    Ride up the Stamford street.

He had a coat of fine red gold,
    And a bascinet of steel;
Take note his goodly Collayne sword
    Smote the spur upon his heel.   40

And by his side, on a grey jennet,
    There rode a fair lady,
For every ruby Ellayne wore,
    I count she carried three.

Say, was not Ellayne's gold hair fine,
    That fell to her middle free?
But that lady's hair down in the street,
    Fell lower than her knee.

Fair Ellayne's face, from sorrow and grief,
    Was waxen pale and green: 50
That lady's face was goodly red,
    She had but little tene.

But as he pass'd by her window
    He grew a little wroth:
O, why does yon pale face look at me,
    From out the golden cloth?

It is some burd, the fair dame said,
    That aye rode him beside,
Has come to see your bonny face
    This merry summer-tide.   60

But Ellayne let a lily-flower
    Light on his cap of steel:
O, I have gotten two hounds, fair knight,
    The one has served me well,

But the other, just an hour agone,
  Has come from over sea,
And all his fell is sleek and fine,
  But little he knows of me.

Now, which shall I let go, fair knight,
  And which shall bide with me?   70
O, lady, have no doubt to keep
  The one that best loveth thee.

O, Robert, see how sick I am!
  Ye do not so by me.
Lie still, fair love! have ye gotten harm
  While I was on the sea?

Of one gift, Robert, that ye gave,
  I sicken to the death,
I pray you nurse-tend me, my knight,
  Whiles that I have my breath.   80

Six fathoms from the Stamford bridge
  He left that dame to stand,
And whiles she wept, and whiles she cursed
  That she ever had taken land,

He has kiss'd sweet Ellayne on the mouth,
  And fair she fell asleep,
And long and long days after that
  Sir Robert's house she did keep.

                                        [1858]

RIDING TOGETHER

For many, many days together
  The wind blew steady from the East;
For many days hot grew the weather,
  About the time of our Lady's Feast.

For many days we rode together,
  Yet met we neither friend nor foe;
Hotter and clearer grew the weather,
  Steadily did the East wind blow.

We saw the trees in the hot, bright weather,
    Clear-cut, with shadows very black,   10
As freely we rode on together
    With helms unlaced and bridles slack.

And often as we rode together,
    We, looking down the green bank'd stream,
Saw flowers in the sunny weather,
    And saw the bubble-making bream. Sunfish

And in the night lay down together,
    And hung above our heads the rood,
Or watch'd night-long in the dewy weather,
    The while the moon did watch the wood.   20

Our spears stood bright and thick together,
    Straight out the banners stream'd behind,
As we gallop'd on in the sunny weather,
    With faces turn'd towards the wind.

Down sank our threescore spears together,
    As thick we saw the pagans ride;
His eager face in the clear fresh weather,
    Shone out that last time by my side.

Up the sweep of the bridge we dash'd together,
    It rock'd to the crash of the meeting spears,   30
Down rain'd the buds of the dear spring weather,
    The elm-tree flowers fell like tears.

There, as we roll'd and writhed together,
    I threw my arms above my head,
For close by my side, in the lovely weather,
    I saw him reel and fall back dead.

I and the slayer met together,
    He wanted the death-stroke there in his place,
With thoughts of death, in the lovely weather,
    Gapingly mazed at my madden'd face.   40

Madly I fought as we fought together;
    In vain: the little Christian band
The pagans drown'd, as in stormy weather
    The river drowns low-lying land.

They bound my blood-stain'd hands together,
They bound his corpse to nod by my side:
Then on we rode, in the bright March weather,
With clash of cymbals did we ride.

We ride no more, no more together;
My prison-bars are thick and strong,   50
I take no heed of any weather,
The sweet Saints grant I live not long.

[*1856; 1858*]

FATHER JOHN'S WAR-SONG

THE REAPERS

So many reapers, Father John,
So many reapers and no little son,
To meet you when the day is done,
With little stiff legs to waddle and run?
Pray you beg, borrow or steal one son.
Hurrah for the corn-sheaves of Father John!

FATHER JOHN

O maiden Mary, be wary, be wary!
And go not down to the river,
Lest the kingfisher, your evil wisher,
Lure you down to the river,   10
Lest your white feet grow muddy,
Your red hair too ruddy
With the river-mud so red;
But when you are wed
Go down to the river;
O maiden Mary, be very wary,
And dwell among the corn!
See, this dame Alice, maiden Mary,
Her hair is thin and white,
But she is a housewife good and wary,   20
And a great steel key hangs bright
From her gown, as red as the flowers in corn;
She is good and old like the autumn corn.

MAIDEN MARY

This is knight Roland, Father John,
Stark in his arms from a field half-won;
Ask him if he has seen your son:
Roland, lay your sword on the corn,
The piled-up sheaves of the golden corn.

KNIGHT ROLAND

Why does she kiss me, Father John?
She is my true love truly won;   30
Under my helm is room for one,
But the molten lead-streams trickle and run
From my roof-tree, burning under the sun;
No corn to burn, we had eaten the corn,
There was no waste of the golden corn.

FATHER JOHN

Ho, you reapers, away from the corn,
To march with the banner of Father John!

THE REAPERS

We will win a house for Roland his son,
And for maiden Mary with hair like corn,
As red as the reddest of golden corn.   40

OMNES

Father John, you have got a son,
Seven feet high when his helm is on!
Pennon of Roland, banner of John,
Star of Mary, march well on.

[1858]

SIR GILES' WAR-SONG

Ho! is there any will ride with me,
Sir Giles, le bon des barrières?

The clink of arms is good to hear,
The flap of pennons fair to see;
  Ho! is there any will ride with me,
    Sir Giles, le bon des barrières?

The leopards and lilies are fair to see,
"St. George Guienne" right good to hear:
   Ho! is there any will ride with me,
    Sir Giles, le bon des barrières?   10

I stood by the barrier,
My coat being blazon'd fair to see;
   Ho! is there any will ride with me,
    Sir Giles, le bon des barrières?

Clisson put out his head to see,
And lifted his basnet up to hear;
   I pull'd him through the bars to ME,
    Sir Giles, le bon des barrières.

                [1858]

NEAR AVALON

A SHIP with shields before the sun,
Six maidens round the mast,
A red-gold crown on every one,
A green gown on the last.

The fluttering green banners there
Are wrought with ladies' heads most fair,
And a portraiture of Guenevere
The middle of each sail doth bear.

A ship with sails before the wind,
And round the helm six knights,   10
Their heaumes are on, whereby, half blind,
They pass by many sights.

The tatter'd scarlet banners there,
Right soon will leave the spear-heads bare,
Those six knights sorrowfully bear
In all their heaumes some yellow hair.

                [1858]

PRAISE OF MY LADY

My lady seems of ivory
Forehead, straight nose, and cheeks that be
Hollow'd a little mournfully.
    Beata mea Domina!

Her forehead, overshadow'd much
By bows of hair, has a wave such
As God was good to make for me.
    Beata mea Domina!

Not greatly long my lady's hair,
Nor yet with yellow colour fair,   10
But thick and crispèd wonderfully:
    Beata mea Domina!

Heavy to make the pale face sad,
And dark, but dead as though it had
Been forged by God most wonderfully
    — *Beata mea Domina!* —

Of some strange metal, thread by thread,
To stand out from my lady's head,
Not moving much to tangle me.
    Beata mea Domina!   20

Beneath her brows the lids fall slow,
The lashes a clear shadow throw
Where I would wish my lips to be.
    Beata mea Domina!

Her great eyes, standing far apart,
Draw up some memory from her heart,
And gaze out very mournfully;
    — *Beata mea Domina!* —

So beautiful and kind they are,
But most times looking out afar,   30
Waiting for something, not for me.
    Beata mea Domina!

I wonder if the lashes long
Are those that do her bright eyes wrong,
For always half tears seem to be
    — *Beata mea Domina!* —

Lurking below the underlid,
Darkening the place where they lie hid —
If they should rise and flow for me!
    Beata mea Domina!   40

Her full lips being made to kiss,
Curl'd up and pensive each one is;
This makes me faint to stand and see.
    Beata mea Domina!

Her lips are not contented now,
Because the hours pass so slow
Towards a sweet time: (pray for me,)
    — *Beata mea Domina!* —

Nay, hold thy peace! for who can tell?
But this at least I know full well,   50
Her lips are parted longingly,
    — *Beata mea Domina!* —

So passionate and swift to move,
To pluck at any flying love,
That I grow faint to stand and see.
    Beata mea Domina!

Yea! there beneath them is her chin,
So fine and round, it were a sin
To feel no weaker when I see
    — *Beata mea Domina!* —   60

God's dealings; for with so much care
And troublous, faint lines wrought in there,
He finishes her face for me.
    Beata mea Domina!

Of her long neck what shall I say?
What things about her body's sway,
Like a knight's pennon or slim tree
    — *Beata mea Domina!* —

Set gently waving in the wind;
Or her long hands that I may find   70
On some day sweet to move o'er me?
      Beata mea Domina!

God pity me though, if I miss'd
The telling, how along her wrist
The veins creep, dying languidly
      — *Beata mea Domina!* —

Inside her tender palm and thin.
Now give me pardon, dear, wherein
My voice is weak and vexes thee.
      Beata mea Domina!   80

All men that see her any time,
I charge you straightly in this rhyme,
What, and wherever you may be,
      — *Beata mea Domina!* —

To kneel before her; as for me,
I choke and grow quite faint to see
My lady moving graciously.
      Beata mea Domina!
          [1858]

SUMMER DAWN

PRAY but one prayer for me twixt thy closed lips,
    Think but one thought of me up in the stars.
The summer night waneth, the morning light slips,
    Faint and grey 'twixt the leaves of the aspen, betwixt the cloud-bars,
That are patiently waiting there for the dawn:
    Patient and colourless, though Heaven's gold
Waits to float through them along with the sun.
Far out in the meadows, above the young corn,
    The heavy elms wait, and restless and cold
The uneasy wind rises; the roses are dun;   10
Through the long twilight they pray for the dawn.
Round the lone house in the midst of the corn.
    Speak but one word to me over the corn,
    Over the tender, bow'd locks of the corn.

                                            [*1856;* 1858]

IN PRISON

WEARILY, drearily,
Half the day long,
Flap the great banners
High over the stone;
Strangely and eerily
Sounds the wind's song,
Bending the banner-poles.

While, all alone,
Watching the loophole's spark,
Lie I, with life all dark,   10
Feet tether'd, hands fetter'd
Fast to the stone,
The grim walls, square letter'd
With prison'd men's groan.

Still strain the banner-poles
Through the wind's song,
Westward the banner rolls
Over my wrong.
                    [*1856;* 1858]

From

THE EARTHLY PARADISE

APOLOGY

OF Heaven or Hell I have no power to sing,
I cannot ease the burden of your fears,
Or make quick-coming death a little thing,
Or bring again the pleasure of past years,
Nor for my words shall ye forget your tears,
Or hope again for aught that I can say,
The idle singer of an empty day.

But rather, when aweary of your mirth,
From full hearts still unsatisfied ye sigh,
And, feeling kindly unto all the earth,   10
Grudge every minute as it passes by,
Made the more mindful that the sweet days die —
Remember me a little then I pray,
The idle singer of an empty day.

The heavy trouble, the bewildering care
That weighs us down who live and earn our bread,
These idle verses have no power to bear;
So let me sing of names rememberèd,
Because they, living not, can ne'er be dead,
Or long time take their memory quite away   20
From us poor singers of an empty day.

Dreamer of dreams, born out of my due time,
Why should I strive to set the crooked straight?
Let it suffice me that my murmuring rhyme
Beats with light wing against the ivory gate,
Telling a tale not too importunate
To those who in the sleepy region stay,
Lulled by the singer of an empty day.

Folk say, a wizard to a northern king
At Christmas-tide such wondrous things did show,   30
That through one window men beheld the spring,
And through another saw the summer glow,
And through a third the fruited vines a-row,

While still, unheard, but in its wonted way,
Piped the drear wind of that December day.

So with this Earthly Paradise it is,
If ye will read aright, and pardon me,
Who strive to build a shadowy isle of bliss
Midmost the beating of the steely sea,
Where tossed about all hearts of men must be;   40
Whose ravening monsters mighty men shall slay,
Not the poor singer of an empty day.

[1868]

The Argument

Certain gentlemen and mariners of Norway, having considered all that
they had heard of the earthly paradise, set sail to find it, and so after many
troubles and the lapse of many years came old men to some western land,
of which they had never before heard: there they died, when they had dwelt
there certain years, much honoured of the strange people.

Forget six counties overhung with smoke,
Forget the snorting steam and piston stroke,
Forget the spreading of the hideous town;
Think rather of the pack-horse on the down,
And dream of London, small and white and clean,
The clear Thames bordered by its gardens green;
Think, that below bridge the green lapping waves
Smite some few keels that bear Levantine staves,
Cut from the yew wood on the burnt-up hill,
And pointed jars that Greek hands toiled to fill,   10
And treasured scanty spice from some far sea,
Florence gold cloth, and Ypres napery,
And cloth of Bruges, and hogsheads of Guienne;
While nigh the thronged wharf Geoffrey Chaucer's pen
Moves over bills of lading — mid such times
Shall dwell the hollow puppets of my rhymes.

A nameless city in a distant sea,
White as the changing walls of faerie,
Thronged with much people clad in ancient guise,
I now am fain to set before your eyes;   20
There, leave the clear green water and the quays,
And pass betwixt its marble palaces,
Until ye come unto the chiefest square;
A bubbling conduit is set midmost there,
And round about it now the maidens throng

With jest and laughter, and sweet broken song,
Making but light of labour new begun
While in their vessels gleams the morning sun.
On one side of the square a temple stands,
Wherein the gods worshipped in ancient lands   30
Still have their altars; a great market-place
Upon two other sides fills all the space,
And thence the busy hum of men comes forth;
But on the cold side looking toward the north
A pillared council-house may you behold,
Within whose porch are images of gold,
Gods of the nations who dwelt anciently
About the borders of the Grecian sea.

    Pass now between them, push the brazen door,
And standing on the polished marble floor   40
Leave all the noises of the square behind;
Most calm that reverent chamber shall ye find,
Silent at first, but for the noise you made
When on the brazen door your hand you laid
To shut it after you — but now behold
The city rulers on their thrones of gold,
Clad in most fair attire, and in their hands
Long carven silver-banded ebony wands;
Then from the dais drop your eyes and see
Soldiers and peasants standing reverently   50
Before those elders, round a little band
Who bear such arms as guard the English land,
But battered, rent and rusted sore, and they,
The men themselves, are shrivelled, bent and grey;
And as they lean with pain upon their spears
Their brows seem furrowed deep with more than years;
For sorrow dulls their heavy sunken eyes;
Bent are they less with time than miseries.

    Pondering on them the city grey-beards gaze
Through kindly eyes, midst thoughts of other days,   60
And pity for poor souls, and vague regret
For all the things that might have happened yet,
Until, their wonder gathering to a head,
The wisest man, who long that land has led,
Breaks the deep silence, unto whom again
A wanderer answers. Slowly as in pain,
And with a hollow voice as from a tomb
At first he tells the story of his doom,

But as it grows, and once more hopes and fears,
Both measureless, are ringing round his ears,   70
His eyes grow bright, his seeming days decrease,
For grief once told brings somewhat back of peace.

[1868]

L'Envoi

HERE are we for the last time face to face,
Thou and I, Book, before I bid thee speed
Upon thy perilous journey to that place
For which I have done on thee pilgrim's weed,
Striving to get thee all things for thy need —
— I love thee, whatso time or men may say
Of the poor singer of an empty day.

Good reason why I love thee, e'en if thou
Be mocked or clean forgot as time wears on;
For ever as thy fashioning did grow,   10
Kind word and praise because of thee I won
From those without whom were my world all gone,
My hope fallen dead, my singing cast away,
And I set soothly in an empty day.

I love thee; yet this last time must it be
That thou must hold thy peace and I must speak,
Lest if thou babble I begin to see
Thy gear too thin, thy limbs and heart too weak,
To find the land thou goest forth to seek —
— Though what harm if thou die upon the way,   20
Thou idle singer of an empty day?

But though this land desired thou never reach,
Yet folk who know it mayst thou meet or death;
Therefore a word unto thee would I teach
To answer these, who, noting thy weak breath,
Thy wandering eyes, thy heart of little faith,
May make thy fond desire a sport and play,
Mocking the singer of an empty day.

That land's name, say'st thou? and the road thereto?
Nay, Book, thou mockest, saying thou know'st it not;   30
Surely no book of verse I ever knew
But ever was the heart within him hot
To gain the Land of Matters Unforgot —

— There, now we both laugh — as the whole world may,
At us poor singers of an empty day.

Nay, let it pass, and hearken! Hast thou heard
That therein I believe I have a friend,
Of whom for love I may not be afeard?
It is to him indeed I bid thee wend;
Yea, he perchance may meet thee ere thou end,   40
Dying so far off from the hedge of bay,
Thou idle singer of an empty day!

Well, think of him, I bid thee, on the road,
And if it hap that midst of thy defeat,
Fainting beneath thy follies' heavy load,
My Master, GEOFFREY CHAUCER, thou do meet,
Then shalt thou win a space of rest full sweet;
Then be thou bold, and speak the words I say,
The idle singer of an empty day!

"O Master, O thou great of heart and tongue,   50
Thou well mayst ask me why I wander here,
In raiment rent of stories oft besung!
But of thy gentleness draw thou anear,
And then the heart of one who held thee dear
Mayst thou behold! So near as that I lay
Unto the singer of an empty day.

"For this he ever said, who sent me forth
To seek a place amid thy company;
That howsoever little was my worth,
Yet was he worth e'en just so much as I;   60
He said that rhyme hath little skill to lie;
Nor feigned to cast his worser part away
In idle singing for an empty day.

"I have beheld him tremble oft enough
At things he could not choose but trust to me,
Although he knew the world was wise and rough:
And never did he fail to let me see
His love, — his folly and faithlessness, maybe;
And still in turn I gave him voice to pray
Such prayers as cling about an empty day.   70

"Thou, keen-eyed, reading me, mayst read him through,
For surely little is there left behind;

No power great deeds unnameable to do;
No knowledge for which words he may not find,
No love of things as vague as autumn wind —
— Earth of the earth lies hidden by my clay,
The idle singer of an empty day!

"Children we twain are, saith he, late made wise
In love, but in all else most childish still,
And seeking still the pleasure of our eyes, 80
And what our ears with sweetest sounds may fill;
Not fearing Love, lest these things he should kill;
Howe'er his pain by pleasure doth he lay,
Making a strange tale of an empty day.

"Death have we hated, knowing not what it meant;
Life have we loved, through green leaf and through sere,
Though still the less we knew of its intent:
The Earth and Heaven through countless year on year,
Slow changing, were to us but curtains fair,
Hung round about a little room, where play 90
Weeping and laughter of man's empty day.

"O Master, if thine heart could love us yet,
Spite of things left undone, and wrongly done,
Some place in loving hearts then should we get,
For thou, sweet-souled, didst never stand alone,
But knew'st the joy and woe of many an one —
— By lovers dead, who live through thee, we pray,
Help us thou singers of an empty day!"

Fearest thou, Book, what answer thou mayst gain
Lest he should scorn thee, and thereof thou die? 100
Nay, it shall not be. — Thou mayst toil in vain,
And never draw the House of Fame anigh;
Yet he and his shall know whereof we cry,
Shall call it not ill done to strive to lay
The ghosts that crowd about life's empty day.

Then let the others go! and if indeed
In some old garden thou and I have wrought,
And made fresh flowers spring up from hoarded seed,
And fragrance of old days and deeds have brought
Back to folk weary; and all was not for nought. 110
— No little part it was for me to play —
The idle singer of an empty day.

[1870]

FRENCH NOEL

Masters, in this Hall,
  Hear ye news to-day
Brought from over sea,
  And ever I you pray.

Nowell! Nowell! Nowell! Nowell sing we clear
Holpen are all folk on earth, Born is God's Son so dear:
Nowell! Nowell! Nowell! Nowell sing we loud!
God to-day hath poor folk rais'd, And cast down the proud.

Going over the hills,
  Through the milk-white snow,   10
Heard I ewes bleat
  While the wind did blow.
      Nowell! etc.

Shepherds many an one
  Sat among the sheep,
No man spake more word
  Than they had been asleep.
      Nowell! etc.

Quoth I "Fellows mine,
  Why this guise sit ye?
Making but dull cheer,
  Shepherds though ye be?   20
      Nowell! etc.

"Shepherds should of right
  Leap and dance and sing;
Thus to see ye sit
  Is a right strange thing."
      Nowell! etc.

Quoth these fellows then,
  "To Bethlem town we go,
To see a mighty Lord
  Lie in a manger low."
      Nowell! etc.

"How name ye this Lord,
  Shepherds?" then said I.   **30**
"Very *God*," they said,
"Come from Heaven high."
      Nowell! etc.

Then to Bethlem town
  We went two and two
And in a sorry place
  Heard the oxen low.
      Nowell! etc.

Therein did we see
  A sweet and goodly May
And a fair old man;
  Upon the straw She lay.   **40**
      Nowell! etc.

And a little Child
  On Her arm had She;
"Wot ye Who this is?"
  Said the hinds to me.
      Nowell! etc.

Ox and ass Him know,
  Kneeling on their knee:
Wondrous joy had I
  This little Babe to see.
      Nowell! etc.

This is Christ the Lord
  Masters, be ye glad!   **50**
Christmas is come in,
  And no folk should be sad.
      Nowell! etc.

          [1860, 1885]

THUNDER IN THE GARDEN

When the boughs of the garden hang heavy with rain
And the blackbird reneweth his song,
And the thunder departing yet rolleth again,
I remember the ending of wrong.

When the day that was dusk while his death was aloof
Is ending wide-gleaming and strange
For the clearness of all things beneath the world's roof,
I call back the wild chance and the change.

For once we twain sat through the hot afternoon
While the rain held aloof for a while,   10
Till she, the soft-clad, for the glory of June
Changed all with the change of her smile.

For her smile was of longing, no longer of glee,
And her fingers, entwined with mine own,
With caresses unquiet sought kindness of me
For the gift that I never had known.

Then down rushed the rain, and the voice of the thunder
Smote dumb all the sound of the street,
And I to myself was grown nought but a wonder,
As she leaned down my kisses to meet.   20

That she craved for my lips that had craved her so often,
And the hand that had trembled to touch,
That the tears filled her eyes I had hoped not to soften
In this world was a marvel too much.

It was dusk 'mid the thunder, dusk e'en as the night,
When first brake out our love like the storm,
But no night-hour was it, and back came the light
While our hands with each other were warm.

And her smile killed with kisses, came back as at first
As she rose up and led me along,   30
And out to the garden, where nought was athirst.
And the blackbird renewing his song.

Earth's fragrance went with her, as in the wet grass
Her feet little hidden were set;
She bent down her head, 'neath the roses to pass,
And her arm with the lily was wet.

In the garden we wandered while day waned apace
And the thunder was dying aloof;
Till the moon o'er the minster-wall lifted his face,
And grey gleamed out the lead of the roof.   40

Then we turned from the blossoms, and cold were they grown
In the trees the wind westering moved;
Till over the threshold back fluttered her gown,
And in the dark house was I loved.

                                                    [1891]

LOVE'S GLEANING-TIDE

Draw not away thy hands, my love,
With wind alone the branches move,
And though the leaves be scant above
        The Autumn shall not shame us.

Say: Let the world wax cold and drear,
What is the worst of all the year
But life, and what can hurt us, dear,
        Or death, and who shall blame us?

Ah, when the summer comes again
How shall we say, we sowed in vain?   10
The root was joy, the stem was pain,
        The ear a nameless blending.

The root is dead and gone, my love,
The stem's a rod our truth to prove;
The ear is stored for nought to move
        Till heaven and earth have ending.
[1872]   [*1874;* 1891]

SPRING'S BEDFELLOW

SPRING went about the woods to-day,
The soft-foot winter-thief,
And found where idle sorrow lay
'Twixt flower and faded leaf.

She looked on him, and found him fair
For all she had been told;
She knelt adown beside him there,
And sang of days of old.

His open eyes beheld her nought,
Yet 'gan his lips to move;   10
But life and deeds were in her thought,
And he would sing of love.

So sang they till their eyes did meet,
And faded fear and shame;
More bold he grew, and she more sweet,
Until they sang the same.

Until, say they who know the thing,
Their very lips did kiss,
And sorrow laid abed with Spring
Begat an earthly bliss.   20
[1873]   [1891]

A GARDEN BY THE SEA

I KNOW a little garden-close,
Set thick with lily and red rose,
Where I would wander if I might
From dewy dawn to dewy night,
And have one with me wandering.

And though within it no birds sing,
And though no pillared house is there,
And though the apple-boughs are bare
Of fruit and blossom, would to God

Her feet upon the green grass trod,   10
And I beheld them as before.

There comes a murmur from the shore,
And in the place two fair streams are,
Drawn from the purple hills afar,
Drawn down unto the restless sea:
Dark hills whose heath-bloom feeds no bee,
Dark shore no ship has ever seen,
Tormented by the billows green
Whose murmur comes unceasingly
Unto the place for which I cry.   20

For which I cry both day and night,
For which I let slip all delight,
Whereby I grow both deaf and blind,
Careless to win, unskilled to find,
And quick to lose what all men seek.
Yet tottering as I am and weak,
Still have I left a little breath
To seek within the jaws of death
An entrance to that happy place,
To seek the unforgotten face,   30
Once seen, once kissed, once reft from me
Anigh the murmuring of the sea.

                              [1867, 1891]

FOR THE BED AT KELMSCOTT

THE wind's on the wold
And the night is a-cold,
And Thames runs chill
'Twixt mead and hill;
But kind and dear
Is the old house here,
And my heart is warm
Midst winter's harm.

"Bed" talking

Rest, then, and rest,
And think of the best
'Twixt summer and spring,   10
When all birds sing

In the town of the tree,
And ye lie in me
And scarce dare move,
Lest the earth and its love
Should fade away
Ere the full of the day.
I am old and have seen
Many things that have been —
Both grief and peace
And wane and increase.
No tale I tell
Of ill or well,
But this I say:
Night treadeth on day,
And for worst or best
Right good is rest.

20

[1893, 1899]

George Meredith

LOVE IN THE VALLEY

UNDER yonder beech-tree single on the green-sward,
  Couched with her arms behind her golden head,
Knees and tresses folded to slip and ripple idly,
  Lies my young love sleeping in the shade.
Had I the heart to slide an arm beneath her,
  Press her parting lips as her waist I gather slow,
Waking in amazement she could not but embrace me:
  Then would she hold me and never let me go?

    .   .   .   .   .   .

Shy as the squirrel and wayward as the swallow,
  Swift as the swallow along the river's light   10
Circleting the surface to meet his mirrored winglets,
  Fleeter she seems in her stay than in her flight.
Shy as the squirrel that leaps among the pine-tops,
  Wayward as the swallow overhead at set of sun,
She whom I love is hard to catch and conquer,
  Hard, but O the glory of the winning were she won!

When her mother tends her before the laughing mirror,
  Tying up her laces, looping up her hair,
Often she thinks, were this wild thing wedded,
  More love should I have, and much less care.   20

292

When her mother tends her before the lighted mirror,
    Loosening her laces, combing down her curls,
Often she thinks, were this wild thing wedded,
    I should miss but one for many boys and girls.

      ·   ·   ·   ·   ·

Heartless she is as the shadow in the meadows
    Flying to the hills on a blue and breezy noon.
No, she is athirst and drinking up her wonder:
    Earth to her is young as the slip of the new moon.
Deals she an unkindness, 'tis but her rapid measure,
    Even as in a dance; and her smile can heal no less: 30
Like the swinging May-cloud that pelts the flowers with
      hailstones
    Off a sunny border, she was made to bruise and bless.

Lovely are the curves of the white owl sweeping
    Wavy in the dusk lit by one large star.
Lone on the fir-branch, his rattle-note unvaried,
    Brooding o'er the gloom, spins the brown eve-jar.
Darker grows the valley, more and more forgetting:
    So were it with me if forgetting could be willed.
Tell the grassy hollow that holds the bubbling well-spring,
    Tell it to forget the source that keeps it filled.   40

      ·   ·   ·   ·   ·

Stepping down the hill with her fair companions,
    Arm in arm, all against the raying West,
Boldly she sings, to the merry tune she marches,
    Brave in her shape, and sweeter unpossessed.
Sweeter, for she is what my heart first awaking
    Whispered the world was; morning light is she.
Love that so desires would fain keep her changeless;
    Fain would fling the net, and fain have her free.

Happy happy time, when the white star hovers
    Low over dim fields fresh with bloomy dew,   50
Near the face of dawn, that draws athwart the darkness,
    Threading it with colour, like yewberries the yew.
Thicker crowd the shades as the grave East deepens
    Glowing, and with crimson a long cloud swells.
Maiden still the morn is; and strange she is, and secret;
    Strange her eyes; her cheeks are cold as cold sea-shells.

      ·   ·   ·   ·   ·

Sunrays, leaning on our southern hills and lighting
    Wild cloud-mountains that drag the hills along,
Oft ends the day of your shifting brilliant laughter
    Chill as a dull face frowning on a song.   60
Ay, but shows the South-West a ripple-feathered bosom
    Blown to silver while the clouds are shaken and ascend
Scaling the mid-heavens as they stream, there comes a sunset
    Rich, deep like love in beauty without end.

When at dawn she sighs, and like an infant to the window
    Turns grave eyes craving light, released from dreams,
Beautiful she looks, like a white water-lily
    Bursting out of bud in havens of the streams.
When from bed she rises clothed from neck to ankle
    In her long nightgown sweet as boughs of May,   70
Beautiful she looks, like a tall garden lily
    Pure from the night, and splendid for the day.

·   ·   ·   ·   ·   ·

Mother of the dews, dark eye-lashed twilight,
    Low-lidded twilight, o'er the valley's brim,
Rounding on thy breast sings the dew-delighted skylark,
    Clear as though the dewdrops had their voice in him.
Hidden where the rose-flush drinks the rayless planet,
    Fountain-full he pours the spraying fountain-showers.
Let me hear her laughter, I would have her ever
    Cool as dew in twilight, the lark above the flowers.   80

All the girls are out with their baskets for the primrose;
    Up lanes, woods through, they troop in joyful bands.
My sweet leads: she knows not why, but now she loiters,
    Eyes the bent anemones, and hangs her hands.
Such a look will tell that the violets are peeping,
    Coming the rose: and unaware a cry
Springs in her bosom for odours and for colour,
    Covert and the nightingale; she knows not why.

·   ·   ·   ·   ·   ·

Kerchiefed head and chin she darts between her tulips,
    Streaming like a willow grey in arrowy rain: 90
Some bend beaten cheek to gravel, and their angel
    She will be; she lifts them, and on she speeds again.
Black the driving raincloud breasts the iron gateway:
    She is forth to cheer a neighbour lacking mirth.

So when sky and grass met rolling dumb for thunder
Saw I once a white dove, sole light of earth.

. . . .

Prim little scholars are the flowers of her garden,
Trained to stand in rows, and asking if they please.
I might love them well but for loving more the wild ones:
O my wild ones! they tell me more than these.   100
You, my wild one, you tell of honied field-rose,
Violet, blushing eglantine in life; and even as they,
They by the wayside are earnest of your goodness,
You are of life's, on the banks that line the way.

looking
for complementary
existence

. . . .

Peering at her chamber the white crowns the red rose,
Jasmine winds the porch with stars two and three.
Parted is the window; she sleeps; the starry jasmine
Breathes a falling breath that carries thoughts of me,
Sweeter unpossessed, have I said of her my sweetest?   109
Not while she sleeps: while she sleeps the jasmine breathes,
Luring her to love; she sleeps; the starry jasmine
Bears me to her pillow under white rose-wreaths.

Yellow with birdfoot-trefoil are the grass-glades;
Yellow with cinquefoil of the dew-grey leaf;
Yellow with stonecrop; the moss-mounds are yellow;
Blue-necked the wheat sways, yellowing to the sheaf.
Green-yellow bursts from the copse the laughing yaffle;
Sharp as a sickle is the edge of shade and shine:
Earth in her heart laughs looking at the heavens,
Thinking of the harvest: I look and think of mine.   120

. . . .

This I may know: her dressing and undressing
Such a change of light shows as when the skies in sport
Shift from cloud to moonlight; or edging over thunder
Slips a ray of sun; or sweeping into port
White sails furl; or on the ocean borders
White sails lean along the waves leaping green.
Visions of her shower before me, but from eyesight
Guarded she would be like the sun were she seen.

. . . .

Front door and back of the mossed old farmhouse
    Open with the morn, and in a breezy link   130
Freshly sparkles garden to stripe-shadowed orchard,
    Green across a rill where on sand the minnows wink.
Busy in the grass the early sun of summer
    Swarms, and the blackbird's mellow fluting notes
Call my darling up with round and roguish challenge:
    Quaintest, richest carol of all the singing throats!

        ·   ·   ·   ·   ·   ·

Cool was the woodside; cool as her white dairy
    Keeping sweet the cream pan; and there the boys from school,
Cricketing below, rushed brown and red with sunshine;
    O the dark translucence of the deep-eyed cool!   140
Spying from the farm, herself she fetched a pitcher
    Full of milk, and tilted for each in turn the beak.
Then a little fellow, mouth up and on tiptoe,
    Said, "I will kiss you"; she laughed and leaned her cheek.

        ·   ·   ·   ·   ·   ·

Doves of the fir-wood walling high our red roof
    Through the long noon coo, crooning through the coo.
Loose droop the leaves, and down the sleepy roadway
    Sometimes pipes a chaffinch; loose droops the blue.
Cows flap a slow tail knee-deep in the river,
    Breathless, given up to sun and gnat and fly.   150
Nowhere is she seen; and if I see her nowhere,
    Lightning may come, straight rains and tiger sky.

O the golden sheaf, the rustling treasure-armful!
    O the nutbrown tresses nodding interlaced!
O the treasure-tresses one another over
    Nodding! O the girdle slack about the waist!
Slain are the poppies that shot their random scarlet
    Quick amid the wheatears: wound about the waist,
Gathered, see the brides of Earth one blush of ripeness!
    O the nutbrown tresses nodding interlaced!   160

        ·   ·   ·   ·   ·   ·

Large and smoky red the sun's cold disk drops,
    Clipped by naked hills, on violet shaded snow:
Eastward large and still lights up a bower of moonrise,
    Whence at her leisure steps the moon aglow.

Nightlong on black print-branches our beech-tree
  Gazes in this whiteness; nightlong could I.
Here may life on death or death on life be painted.
  Let me clasp her soul to know she cannot die!

. . . . . .

Gossips count her faults: they scour a narrow chamber
  Where there is no window, read not heaven or her.   170
"When she was a tiny," one aged woman quavers,
  Plucks at my heart and leads me by the ear.
Faults she had once as she learnt to run and tumbled:
  Faults of feature some see, beauty not complete.
Yet, good gossips, beauty that makes holy
  Earth and air, may have faults from head to feet.

. . . . . .

Hither she comes; she comes to me; she lingers,
  Deepens her brown eyebrows, while in new surprise
High rise the lashes in wonder of a stranger;
  Yet am I the light and living of her eyes.   180
Something friends have told her fills her heart to brimming,
  Nets her in her blushes, and wounds her, and tames. —
Sure of her haven, O like a dove alighting,
  Arms up, she dropped: our souls were in our names.

. . . . . .

Soon will she lie like a white frost sunrise.
  Yellow oats and brown wheat, barley pale as rye,
Long since your sheaves have yielded to the thresher,
  Felt the girdle loosened, seen the tresses fly.
Soon will she lie like a blood-red sunset.
  Swift with the to-morrow, green-winged Spring!   190
Sing from the South-West, bring her back the truants,
  Nightingale and swallow, song and dipping wing.

. . . . . .

Soft new beech-leaves, up to beamy April
  Spreading bough on bough a primrose mountain, you,
Lucid in the moon, raise lilies to the skyfields,
  Youngest green transfused in silver shining through:
Fairer than the lily, than the wild white cherry:
  Fair as in image my seraph love appears

Borne to me by dreams when dawn is at my eyelids:
Fair as in the flesh she swims to me on tears.   **200**

.   .   .   .   .   .

Could I find a place to be alone with heaven,
    I would speak my heart out: heaven is my need.
Every woodland tree is flushing like the dogwood,
    Flashing like the whitebeam, swaying like the reed.
Flushing like the dogwood crimson in October;
    Streaming like the flag-reed South-West blown;
Flashing as in gusts the sudden-lighted whitebeam:
    All seem to know what is for heaven alone.

[1851, *1878*]

MODERN LOVE

THE PROMISE IN DISTURBANCE

How low when angels fall their black descent,
Our primal thunder tells: known is the pain
Of music, that nigh throning wisdom went,
And one false note cast wailful to the insane.
Now seems the language heard of Love as rain
To make a mire where fruitfulness was meant.
The golden harp gives out a jangled strain,
Too like revolt from heaven's Omnipotent.
But listen in the thought; so may there come
Conception of a newly-added chord,   10
Commanding space beyond where ear has home.
In labour of the trouble at its fount,
Leads Life to an intelligible Lord
The rebel discords up the sacred mount.

[1892]

I

By this he knew she wept with waking eyes:
That, at his hand's light quiver by her head,
The strange low sobs that shook their common bed,
Were called into her with a sharp surprise,
And strangled mute, like little gaping snakes,
Dreadfully venomous to him. She lay
Stone-still, and the long darkness flowed away
With muffled pulses. Then, as midnight makes
Her giant heart of Memory and Tears
Drink the pale drug of silence, and so beat   10
Sleep's heavy measure, they from head to feet
Were moveless, looking through their dead black years,
By vain regret scrawled over the blank wall.
Like sculptured effigies they might be seen
Upon their marriage-tomb, the sword between;
Each wishing for the sword that severs all.

II

It ended, and the morrow brought the task.
Her eyes were guilty gates, that let him in

By shutting all too zealous for their sin:
Each sucked a secret, and each wore a mask.
But, oh, the bitter taste her beauty had!
He sickened as at breath of poison-flowers:
A languid humour stole among the hours,
And if their smiles encountered, he went mad,
And raged deep inward, till the light was brown
Before his vision, and the world, forgot,   10
Looked wicked as some old dull murder-spot.
A star with lurid beams, she seemed to crown
The pit of infamy: and then again
He fainted on his vengefulness, and strove
To ape the magnanimity of love,
And smote himself, a shuddering heap of pain.

III

This was the woman; what now of the man?
But pass him. If he comes beneath a heel,
He shall be crushed until he cannot feel,
Or, being callous, haply till he can.
But he is nothing: — nothing? Only mark
The rich light striking out from her on him!
Ha! what a sense it is when her eyes swim
Across the man she singles, leaving dark
All else! Lord God, who mad'st the thing so fair,
See that I am drawn to her even now!   10
It cannot be such harm on her cool brow
To put a kiss? Yet if I meet him there!
But she is mine! Ah, no! I know too well
I claim a star whose light is overcast:
I claim a phantom-woman in the Past.
The hour has struck, though I heard not the bell!

IV

All other joys of life he strove to warm,
And magnify, and catch them to his lip:
But they had suffered shipwreck with the ship,
And gazed upon him sallow from the storm.
Or if Delusion came, 't was but to show
The coming minute mock the one that went.
Cold as a mountain in its star-pitched tent,
Stood high Philosophy, less friend than foe:
Whom self-caged Passion, from its prison-bars,

Is always watching with a wondering hate. 10
Not till the fire is dying in the grate,
Look we for any kinship with the stars.
Oh, wisdom never comes when it is gold,
And the great price we pay for it full worth:
We have it only when we are half earth.
Little avails that coinage to the old!

V

A message from her set his brain aflame.
A world of household matters filled her mind,
Wherein he saw hypocrisy designed:
She treated him as something that is tame,
And but at other provocation bites.
Familiar was her shoulder in the glass,
Through that dark rain: yet it may come to pass
That a changed eye finds such familiar sights
More keenly tempting than new loveliness.
The "What has been" a moment seemed his own: 10
The splendours, mysteries, dearer because known,
Nor less divine: Love's inmost sacredness
Called to him, "Come!" — In his restraining start,
Eyes nurtured to be looked at scarce could see
A wave of the great waves of Destiny
Convulsed at a checked impulse of the heart.

VI

It chanced his lips did meet her forehead cool.
She had no blush, but slanted down her eye.
Shamed nature, then, confesses love can die:
And most she punishes the tender fool
Who will believe what honours her the most!
Dead! is it dead? She has a pulse, and flow
Of tears, the price of blood-drops, as I know,
For whom the midnight sobs around Love's ghost,
Since then I heard her, and so will sob on.
The love is here; it has but changed its aim. 10
O bitter barren woman! what's the name?
The name, the name, the new name thou hast won?
Behold me striking the world's coward stroke!
That will I not do, though the sting is dire.
— Beneath the surface this, while by the fire
They sat, she laughing at a quiet joke.

VII

She issues radiant from her dressing-room,
Like one prepared to scale an upper sphere:
— By stirring up a lower, much I fear!
How deftly that oiled barber lays his bloom!
That long-shanked dapper Cupid with frisked curls
Can make known women torturingly fair;
The gold-eyed serpent dwelling in rich hair,
Awakes beneath his magic whisks and twirls.
His art can take the eyes from out my head,
Until I see with eyes of other men;   10
While deeper knowledge crouches in its den,
And sends a spark up: — is it true we are wed?
Yea! filthiness of body is most vile,
But faithlessness of heart I do hold worse.
The former, it were not so great a curse
To read on the steel-mirror of her smile.

VIII

Yet it was plain she struggled, and that salt
Of righteous feeling made her pitiful.
Poor twisting worm, so queenly beautiful!
Where came the cleft between us? whose the fault?
My tears are on thee, that have rarely dropped
As balm for any bitter wound of mine:
My breast will open for thee at a sign!
But, no: we are two reed-pipes, coarsely stopped:
The God once filled them with his mellow breath;
And they were music till he flung them down,   10
Used! used! Hear now the discord-loving clown
Puff his gross spirit in them, worse than death!
I do not know myself without thee more:
In this unholy battle I grow base:
If the same soul be under the same face,
Speak, and a taste of that old time restore!

IX

He felt the wild beast in him betweenwhiles
So masterfully rude, that he would grieve
To see the helpless delicate thing receive
His guardianship through certain dark defiles.
Had he not teeth to rend, and hunger too?
But still he spared her. Once: "Have you no fear?"
He said: 'twas dusk; she in his grasp; none near.

She laughed: "No, surely; am I not with you?"
And uttering that soft starry "you," she leaned
Her gentle body near him, looking up;   10
And from her eyes, as from a poison-cup,
He drank until the flittering eyelids screened.
Devilish malignant witch! and oh, young beam
Of heaven's circle-glory! Here thy shape
To squeeze like an intoxicating grape —
I might, and yet thou goest safe, supreme.

X

But where began the change; and what's my crime?
The wretch condemned, who has not been arraigned,
Chafes at his sentence. Shall I, unsustained,
Drag on Love's nerveless body thro' all time?
I must have slept, since now I wake. Prepare,
You lovers, to know Love a thing of moods:
Not like hard life, of laws. In Love's deep woods, *that he could*
I dreamt of loyal Life: — the offence is there!   *keep it.*
Love's jealous woods about the sun are curled;
At least, the sun far brighter there did beam. —   10
My crime is, that the puppet of a dream,
I plotted to be worthy of the world.
Oh, had I with my darling helped to mince
The facts of life, you still had seen me go
With hindward feather and with forward toe,
Her much-adored delightful Fairy Prince!

XI

Out in the yellow meadows, where the bee
Hums by us with the honey of the Spring,
And showers of sweet notes from the larks on wing,
Are dropping like a noon-dew, wander we.
Or is it now? or was it then? for now,
As then, the larks from running rings pour showers:
The golden foot of May is on the flowers,
And friendly shadows dance upon her brow.
What's this, when Nature swears there is no change
To challenge eyesight? Now, as then, the grace   10
Of heaven seems holding earth in its embrace.
Nor eyes, nor heart, has she to feel it strange?
Look, woman, in the West. There wilt thou see
An amber cradle near the sun's decline:
Within it, featured even in death divine,
Is lying a dead infant, slain by thee.

XII

Not solely that the Future she destroys,
And the fair life which in the distance lies
For all men, beckoning out from dim rich skies:
Nor that the passing hour's supporting joys
Have lost the keen-edged flavour, which begat
Distinction in old times, and still should breed
Sweet Memory, and Hope, — earth's modest seed,
And heaven's high-prompting: not that the world is flat
Since that soft-luring creature I embraced
Among the children of Illusion went: 10
Methinks with all this loss I were content,
If the mad Past, on which my foot is based,
Were firm, or might be blotted: but the whole
Of life is mixed: the mocking Past will stay:
And if I drink oblivion of a day,
So shorten I the stature of my soul.

XIII

"I play for Seasons; not Eternities!"
Says Nature, laughing on her way. "So must
All those whose stake is nothing more than dust!"
And lo, she wins, and of her harmonies
She is full sure! Upon her dying rose
She drops a look of fondness, and goes by,
Scarce any retrospection in her eye;
For she the laws of growth most deeply knows,
Whose hands bear, here, a seed-bag — there, an urn.
Pledged she herself to aught, 'twould mark her end!   10
This lesson of our only visible friend
Can we not teach our foolish hearts to learn?
Yes! yes! — but oh, our human rose is fair
Surpassingly! Lose calmly Love's great bliss,
When the renewed for ever of a kiss
Whirls life within the shower of loosened hair!

XIV

What soul would bargain for a cure that brings
Contempt the nobler agony to kill?
Rather let me bear on the bitter ill,
And strike this rusty bosom with new stings!
It seems there is another veering fit,
Since on a gold-haired lady's eyeballs pure
I looked with little prospect of a cure,

The while her mouth's red bow loosed shafts of wit.
Just heaven! can it be true that jealousy
Has decked the woman thus? and does her head   10
Swim somewhat for possessions forfeited?
Madam, you teach me many things that be.
I open an old book, and there I find,
That "Women still may love whom they deceive."
Such love I prize not, madam: by your leave,
The game you play at is not to my mind.

xv

I think she sleeps; it must be sleep, when low
Hangs that abandoned arm toward the floor;
The face turned with it. Now make fast the door.
Sleep on: it is your husband, not your foe.
The Poet's black stage-lion of wronged love
Frights not our modern dames: — well if he did!
Now will I pour new light upon that lid,
Full-sloping like the breasts beneath. "Sweet dove,
Your sleep is pure. Nay, pardon: I disturb.
I do not? good!" Her waking infant-stare   10
Grows woman to the burden my hands bear:
Her own handwriting to me when no curb
Was left on Passion's tongue. She trembles through;
A woman's tremble — the whole instrument: —
I show another letter lately sent.
The words are very like: the name is new.

xvi

In our old shipwrecked days there was an hour,
When in the firelight steadily aglow,
Joined slackly, we beheld the red chasm grow
Among the clicking coals. Our library-bower
That eve was left to us: and hushed we sat
As lovers to whom Time is whispering.
From sudden-opened doors we heard them sing:
The nodding elders mixed good wine with chat.
Well knew we that Life's greatest treasure lay
With us, and of it was our talk. "Ah, yes!   10
Love dies!" I said: I never thought it less.
She yearned to me that sentence to unsay.
Then when the fire domed blackening, I found
Her cheek was salt against my kiss, and swift
Up the sharp scale of sobs her breast did lift: —
Now am I haunted by that taste! that sound!

XVII

At dinner, she is hostess, I am host.
Went the feast ever cheerfuller? She keeps
The Topic over intellectual deeps
In buoyancy afloat. They see no ghost.
With sparkling surface-eyes we ply the ball:
It is in truth a most contagious game:
HIDING THE SKELETON, shall be its name.
Such play as this the devils might appal!
But here's the greater wonder; in that we,
Enamoured of an acting nought can tire,   10
Each other, like true hypocrites, admire;
Warm-lighted looks, Love's ephemerioe,
Shoot gaily o'er the dishes and the wine.
We waken envy of our happy lot.
Fast, sweet, and golden, shows the marriage-knot.
Dear guests, you now have seen Love's corpse-light shine.

XVIII

Here Jack and Tom are paired with Moll and Meg.
Curved open to the river-reach is seen
A country merry-making on the green.
Fair space for signal shakings of the leg.
That little screwy fiddler from his booth,
Whence flows one nut-brown stream, commands the joints
Of all who caper here at various points.
I have known rustic revels in my youth:
The May-fly pleasures of a mind at ease.
An early goddess was a country lass: 10
A charmed Amphion-oak she tripped the grass.
What life was that I lived? The life of these?
Heaven keep them happy! Nature they seem near.
They must, I think, be wiser than I am;
They have the secret of the bull and lamb.
'Tis true that when we trace its source, 'tis beer.

XIX

No state is enviable. To the luck alone
Of some few favoured men I would put claim.
I bleed, but her who wounds I will not blame.
Have I not felt her heart as 'twere my own
Beat thro' me? could I hurt her? heaven and hell!
But I could hurt her cruelly! Can I let
My Love's old time-piece to another set,

Swear it can't stop, and must for ever swell?
Sure, that's one way Love drifts into the mart
Where goat-legged buyers throng. I see not plain: —   10
My meaning is, it must not be again.
Great God! the maddest gambler throws his heart.
If any state be enviable on earth,
'Tis yon born idiot's, who, as days go by,
Still rubs his hands before him, like a fly,
In a queer sort of meditative mirth.

XX

I am not of those miserable males
Who sniff at vice, and daring not to snap,
Do therefore hope for heaven. I take the hap
Of all my deeds. The wind that fills my sails
Propels; but I am helmsman. Am I wrecked,
I know the devil has sufficient weight
To bear: I lay it not on him, or fate.
Besides, he's damned. That man I do suspect
A coward, who would burden the poor deuce
With what ensues from his own slipperiness.   10
I have just found a wanton-scented tress
In an old desk, dusty for lack of use.
Of days and nights it is demonstrative,
That, like some aged star, gleam luridly
If for those times I must ask charity.
Have I not any charity to give?

XXI

We three are on the cedar-shadowed lawn;
My friend being third. He who at love once laughed
Is in the weak rib by a fatal shaft
Struck through, and tells his passion's bashful dawn
And radiant culmination, glorious crown,
When "this" she said: went "thus": most wondrous she.
Our eyes grow white, encountering: that we are three,
Forgetful; then together we look down.
But he demands our blessing; is convinced
That words of wedded lovers must bring good.   10
We question; if we dare! or if we should!
And pat him, with light laugh. We have not winced.
Next, she has fallen. Fainting points the sign
To happy things in wedlock. When she wakes,
She looks the star that thro' the cedar shakes:
Her lost moist hand clings mortally to mine.

XXII

What may the woman labour to confess?
There is about her mouth a nervous twitch.
'Tis something to be told, or hidden: — which?
I get a glimpse of hell in this mild guess.
She has desires of touch, as if to feel
That all the household things are things she knew.
She stops before the glass. What sight in view?
A face that seems the latest to reveal!
For she turns from it hastily, and tossed
Irresolute, steals shadow-like to where   10
I stand; and wavering pale before me there,
Her tears fall still as oak-leaves after frost.
She will not speak. I will not ask. We are
League-sundered by the silent gulf between.
You burly lovers on the village green,
Yours is a lower, and a happier star!

XXIII

'Tis Christmas weather, and a country house
Receives us: rooms are full: we can but get
An attic-crib. Such lovers will not fret
At that, it is half-said. The great carouse
Knocks hard upon the midnight's hollow door,
But when I knock at hers, I see the pit.
Why did I come here in that dullard fit?
I enter, and lie couched upon the floor.
Passing, I caught the coverlet's quick beat: —
Come, Shame, burn to my soul! and Pride, and Pain —   10
Foul demons that have tortured me, enchain!
Out in the freezing darkness the lambs bleat.
The small bird stiffens in the low starlight.
I know not how, but shuddering as I slept,
I dreamed a banished angel to me crept:
My feet were nourished on her breasts all night.

XXIV

The misery is greater, as I live!
To know her flesh so pure, so keen her sense,
That she does penance now for no offence,
Save against Love. The less can I forgive!
The less can I forgive, though I adore
That cruel lovely pallor which surrounds
Her footsteps; and the low vibrating sounds

That come on me, as from a magic shore.
Low are they, but most subtle to find out
The shrinking soul. Madam, 'tis understood   10
When women play upon their womanhood,
It means, a Season gone. And yet I doubt
But I am duped. That nun-like look waylays
My fancy. Oh! I do but wait a sign!
Pluck out the eyes of pride! thy mouth to mine!
Never! though I die thirsting. Go thy ways!

XXV

You like not that French novel? Tell me why.
You think it quite unnatural. Let us see.
The actors are, it seems, the usual three:
Husband, and wife and lover. She — but fie!
In England we'll not hear of it. Edmond
The lover, her devout chagrin doth share;
Blanc-mange and absinthe are his penitent fare,
Till his pale aspect makes her over-fond:
So, to preclude fresh sin, he tries rosbif.
Meantime the husband is no more abused: 10
Auguste forgives her ere the tear is used.
Then hangeth all on one tremendous IF: —
If she will choose between them. She does choose;
And takes her husband, like a proper wife.
Unnatural? My dear, these things are life:
And life, some think, is worthy of the Muse.

XXVI

Love ere he bleeds, an eagle in high skies,
Has earth beneath his wings: from reddened eve
He views the rosy down. In vain they weave
The fatal web below while far he flies.
But when the arrow strikes him, there's a change.
He moves but in the track of his spent pain,
Whose red drops are the links of a harsh chain,
Binding him to the ground, with narrow range.
A subtle serpent then has Love become.
I had the eagle in my bosom erst: 10
Henceforward with the serpent I am cursed.
I can interpret where the mouth is dumb.
Speak, and I see the side-lie of a truth.
Perchance my heart may pardon you this deed:
But be no coward: — you that made Love bleed,
You must bear all the venom of his tooth!

XXVII

Distraction is the panacea, Sir!
I hear my oracle of Medicine say.
Doctor! that same specific yesterday
I tried, and the result will not deter
A second trial. Is the devil's line
Of golden hair, or raven black, composed?
And does a cheek, like any sea-shell rosed,
Or clear as widowed sky, seem most divine?
No matter, so I taste forgetfulness.
And if the devil snare me, body and mind,   10
Here gratefully I score: — he seemëd kind,
When not a soul would comfort my distress!
O sweet new world, in which I rise new made!
O Lady, once I gave love: now I take!
Lady, I must be flattered. Shouldst thou wake
The passion of a demon, be not afraid.

XXVIII

I must be flattered. The imperious
Desire speaks out. Lady, I am content
To play with you the game of Sentiment,
And with you enter on paths perilous;
But if across your beauty I throw light,
To make it threefold, it must be all mine.
First secret; then avowed. For I must shine
Envied, — I, lessened in my proper sight!
Be watchful of your beauty, Lady dear!
How much hangs on that lamp you cannot tell.   10
Most earnestly I pray you, tend it well:
And men shall see me as a burning sphere;
And men shall mark you eyeing me, and groan
To be the God of such a grand sunflower!
I feel the promptings of Satanic power,
While you do homage unto me alone.

XXIX

Am I failing? For no longer can I cast
A glory round about this head of gold.
Glory she wears, but springing from the mould;
Not like the consecration of the Past!
Is my soul beggared? Something more than earth
I cry for still: I cannot be at peace
In having Love upon a mortal lease.

I cannot take the woman at her worth!
Where is the ancient wealth wherewith I clothed
Our human nakedness, and could endow
With spiritual splendour a white brow
That else had grinned at me the fact I loathed?
A kiss is but a kiss now! and no wave
Of a great flood that whirls me to the sea.
But, as you will! we'll sit contentedly,
And eat our pot of honey on the grave.

10

XXX

What are we first? First, animals; and next
Intelligences at a leap, on whom
Pale lies the distant shadow of the tomb,
And all that draweth on the tomb for text.
Into which state comes Love, the crowning sun:
Beneath whose light the shadow loses form.
We are the lords of life, and life is warm.
Intelligence and instinct now are one.
But nature says: "My children most they seem
When they least know me: therefore I decree
That they shall suffer." Swift doth young Love flee,
And we stand wakened, shivering from our dream.
Then if we study Nature we are wise.
Thus do the few who live but with the day:
The scientific animals are they. —
Lady, this is my sonnet to your eyes.

10

XXXI

This golden head has wit in it. I live
Again, and a far higher life, near her.
Some women like a young philosopher;
Perchance because he is diminutive.
For woman's manly god must not exceed
Proportions of the natural nursing size.
Great poets and great sages draw no prize
With women: but the little lap-dog breed,
Who can be hugged, or on a mantel-piece
Perched up for adoration, these obtain
Her homage. And of this we men are vain?
Of this! 'Tis ordered for the world's increase!
Small flattery! Yet she has that rare gift
To beauty, Common Sense. I am approved.
It is not half so nice as being loved,
And yet I do prefer it. What's my drift?

10

XXXII

Full faith I have she holds that rarest gift
To beauty, Common Sense. To see her lie
With her fair visage an inverted sky
Bloom-covered, while the underlids uplift,
Would almost wreck the faith; but when her mouth
(Can it kiss sweetly? sweetly!) would address
The inner me that thirsts for her no less,
And has so long been languishing in drouth,
I feel that I am matched; that I am man!
One restless corner of my heart or head,   10
That holds a dying something never dead,
Still frets, though Nature giveth all she can.
It means, that woman is not, I opine,
Her sex's antidote. Who seeks the asp
For serpents' bites? 'Twould calm me could I clasp
Shrieking Bacchantes with their souls of wine!

XXXIII

"In Paris, at the Louvre, there have I seen
The sumptuously-feathered angel pierce
Prone Lucifer, descending. Looked he fierce,
Showing the fight a fair one? Too serene!
The young Pharsalians did not disarray
Less willingly their locks of floating silk:
That suckling mouth of his, upon the milk
Of heaven might still be feasting through the fray.
Oh, Raphael! when men the Fiend do fight,
They conquer not upon such easy terms.   10
Half serpent in the struggle grow these worms.
And does he grow half human, all is right."
This to my Lady in a distant spot,
Upon the theme: *While mind is mastering clay,
Gross clay invades it.* If the spy you play,
My wife, read this! Strange love-talk, is it not?

XXXIV

Madam would speak with me. So, now it comes:
The Deluge or else Fire! She's well; she thanks
My husbandship. Our chain on silence clanks.
Time leers between, above his twiddling thumbs.
Am I quite well? Most excellent in health!
The journals, too, I diligently peruse.
Vesuvius is expected to give news:

Niagara is no noisier. By stealth
Our eyes dart scrutinizing snakes. She's glad
I'm happy, says her quivering under-lip.   10
"And are not you?" "How can I be?" "Take ship!
For happiness is somewhere to be had."
"Nowhere for me!" Her voice is barely heard.
I am not melted, and make no pretence.
With commonplace I freeze her, tongue and sense.
Niagara or Vesuvius is deferred.

XXXV

It is no vulgar nature I have wived.
Secretive, sensitive, she takes a wound
Deep to her soul, as if the sense had swooned,
And not a thought of vengeance had survived.
No confidences has she: but relief
Must come to one whose suffering is acute.
O have a care of natures that are mute!
They punish you in acts: their steps are brief.
What is she doing? What does she demand
From Providence or me? She is not one   10
Long to endure this torpidly, and shun
The drugs that crowd about a woman's hand.
At Forfeits during snow we played, and I
Must kiss her. "Well performed!" I said: then she:
" 'Tis hardly worth the money, you agree?"
Save her? What for? To act this wedded lie!

XXXVI

My Lady unto Madam makes her bow.
The charm of women is, that even while
You're probed by them for tears, you yet may smile,
Nay, laugh outright, as I have done just now.
The interview was gracious: they anoint
(To me aside) each other with fine praise:
Discriminating compliments they raise,
That hit with wondrous aim on the weak point:
My Lady's nose of Nature might complain.
It is not fashioned aptly to express   10
Her character of large-browed steadfastness.
But Madam says: Thereof she may be vain!
Now, Madam's faulty feature is a glazed
And inaccessible eye, that has soft fires,
Wide gates, at love-time, only. This admires
My Lady. At the two I stand amazed.

XXXVII

Along the garden terrace, under which
A purple valley (lighted at its edge
By smoky torch-flame on the long cloud-ledge
Whereunder dropped the chariot) glimmers rich,
A quiet company we pace, and wait
The dinner-bell in prae-digestive calm.
So sweet up violet banks the Southern balm
Breathes round, we care not if the bell be late:
Though here and there grey seniors question Time
In irritable coughings. With slow foot   10
The low rosed moon, the face of Music mute,
Begins among her silent bars to climb.
As in and out, in silvery dusk, we thread,
I hear the laugh of Madam, and discern
My Lady's heel before me at each turn.
Our tragedy, is it alive or dead?

XXXVIII

Give to imagination some pure light
In human form to fix it, or you shame
The devils with that hideous human game: —
Imagination urging appetite!
Thus fallen have earth's greatest Gogmagogs,
Who dazzle us, whom we can not revere:
Imagination is the charioteer
That, in default of better, drives the hogs.
So, therefore, my dear Lady, let me love!
My soul is arrowy to the light in you.   10
You know me that I never can renew
The bond that woman broke: what would you have?
'Tis Love, or Vileness! not a choice between,
Save petrifaction! What does Pity here?
She killed a thing, and now it's dead, 'tis dear.
Oh, when you counsel me, think what you mean!

XXXIX

She yields: my Lady in her noblest mood
Has yielded: she, my golden-crownèd rose!
The bride of every sense! more sweet than those
Who breathe the violet breath of maidenhood.
O visage of still music in the sky!
Soft moon! I feel thy song, my fairest friend!
True harmony within can apprehend

Dumb harmony without. And hark! 'tis nigh!
Belief has struck the note of sound: a gleam
Of living silver shows me where she shook   10
Her long white fingers down the shadowy brook,
That sings her song, half waking, half in dream.
What two come here to mar this heavenly tune?
A man is one: the woman bears my name,
And honour. Their hands touch! Am I still tame?
God, what a dancing spectre seems the moon!

XL

I bade my Lady think what she might mean.
Know I my meaning, I? Can I love one,
And yet be jealous of another? None
Commits such folly. Terrible Love, I ween,
Has might, even dead, half sighing to upheave
The lightless seas of selfishness amain:
Seas that in a man's heart have no rain
To fall and still them. Peace can I achieve,
By turning to this fountain-source of woe,
This woman, who's to Love as fire to wood?   10
She breathed the violet breath of maidenhood
Against my kisses once! but I say, No!
The thing is mocked at! Helplessly afloat,
I know not what I do, whereto I strive,
The dread that my old love may be alive
Has seized my nursling new love by the throat.

XLI

How many a thing which we cast to the ground,
When others pick it up becomes a gem!
We grasp at all the wealth it is to them;
And by reflected light its worth is found.
Yet for us still 'tis nothing! and that zeal
Of false appreciation quickly fades.
This truth is little known to human shades,
How rare from their own instinct 'tis to feel!
They waste the soul with spurious desire,
That is not the ripe flame upon the bough.   10
We two have taken up a lifeless vow
To rob a living passion: dust for fire!
Madam is grave, and eyes the clock that tells
Approaching midnight. We have struck despair
Into two hearts. O, look we like a pair
Who for fresh nuptials joyfully yield all else?

XLII

I am to follow her. There is much grace
In woman when thus bent on martyrdom.
They think that dignity of soul may come,
Perchance, with dignity of body. Base!
But I was taken by that air of cold
And statuesque sedateness, when she said
"I'm going"; lit a taper, bowed her head,
And went, as with the stride of Pallas bold.
Fleshly indifference horrible! The hands
Of Time now signal: O, she's safe from me!   10
Within those secret walls what do I see?
Where first she set the taper down she stands:
Not Pallas: Hebe shamed! Thoughts black as death,
Like a stirred pool in sunshine break. Her wrists
I catch: she faltering, as she half resists,
"You love . . . ? love . . . ? love . . . ?" all on an indrawn
    breath.

XLIII

Mark where the pressing wind shoots javelin-like
Its skeleton shadow on the broad-backed wave!
Here is a fitting spot to dig Love's grave;
Here where the ponderous breakers plunge and strike,
And dart their hissing tongues high up the sand:
In hearing of the ocean, and in sight
Of those ribbed wind-streaks running into white.
If I the death of Love had deeply planned,
I never could have made it half so sure,
As by the unblest kisses which upbraid   10
The full-waked sense; or failing that, degrade!
'Tis morning: but no morning can restore
What we have forfeited. I see no sin:
The wrong is mixed. In tragic life, God wot,
No villain need be! Passions spin the plot:
We are betrayed by what is false within.

XLIV

They say, that Pity in Love's service dwells,
A porter at the rosy temple's gate.
I missed him going: but it is my fate
To come upon him now beside his wells;
Whereby I know that I Love's temple leave,
And that the purple doors have closed behind.
Poor soul! if, in those early days unkind,

The power to sting had been but power to grieve,
We now might with an equal spirit meet,
And not be matched like innocence and vice.   10
She for the Temple's worship has paid price,
And takes the coin of Pity as a cheat.
She sees through simulation to the bone:
What's best in her impels her to the worst:
Never, she cries, shall Pity soothe Love's thirst,
Or foul hypocrisy for truth atone!

XLV

It is the season of the sweet wild rose,
My Lady's emblem in the heart of me!
So golden-crownëd shines she gloriously,
And with that softest dream of blood she glows:
Mild as an evening heaven round Hesper bright!
I pluck the flower, and smell it, and revive
The time when in her eyes I stood alive.
I seem to look upon it out of Night.
Here's Madam, stepping hastily. Her whims
Bid her demand the flower, which I let drop.   10
As I proceed, I feel her sharply stop,
And crush it under heel with trembling limbs.
She joins me in a cat-like way, and talks
Of company, and even condescends
To utter laughing scandal of old friends.
These are the summer days, and these our walks.

XLVI

At last we parley: we so strangely dumb
In such a close communion! It befell
About the sounding of the Matin-bell,
And lo! her place was vacant, and the hum
Of loneliness was round me. Then I rose,
And my disordered brain did guide my foot
To that old wood where our first love-salute
Was interchanged: the source of many throes!
There did I see her, not alone. I moved
Toward her, and made proffer of my arm.   10
She took it simply, with no rude alarm;
And that disturbing shadow passed reproved.
I felt the pained speech coming, and declared
My firm belief in her, ere she could speak.
A ghastly morning came into her cheek,
While with a widening soul on me she stared.

XLVII

We saw the swallows gathering in the sky,
And in the osier-isle we heard them noise.
We had not to look back on summer joys,
Or forward to a summer of bright dye:
But in the largeness of the evening earth
Our spirits grew as we went side by side.
The hour became her husband and my bride.
Love that had robbed us so, thus blessed our dearth!
The pilgrims of the year waxed very loud
In multitudinous chatterings, as the flood   10
Full brown came from the West, and like pale blood
Expanded to the upper crimson cloud.
Love, that had robbed us of immortal things,
This little moment mercifully gave,
Where I have seen across the twilight wave
The swan sail with her young beneath her wings.

XLVIII

Their sense is with their senses all mixed in,
Destroyed by subtleties these women are!
More brain, O Lord, more brain! or we shall mar
Utterly this fair garden we might win.
Behold! I looked for peace, and thought it near.
Our inmost hearts had opened, each to each.
We drank the pure daylight of honest speech.
Alas! that was the fatal draught, I fear.
For when of my lost Lady came the word,
This woman, O this agony of flesh!   10
Jealous devotion bade her break the mesh,
That I might seek that other like a bird.
I do adore the nobleness! despise
The act! She has gone forth, I know not where.
Will the hard world my sentience of her share?
I feel the truth; so let the world surmise.

XLIX

He found her by the ocean's moaning verge,
Nor any wicked change in her discerned;
And she believed his old love had returned,
Which was her exultation, and her scourge.
She took his hand, and walked with him, and seemed
The wife he sought, though shadow-like and dry.

She had one terror, lest her heart should sigh,
And tell her loudly she no longer dreamed.
She dared not say, "This is my breast: look in."
But there's a strength to help the desperate weak.   10
That night he learned how silence best can speak
The awful things when Pity pleads for Sin.
About the middle of the night her call
Was heard, and he came wondering to the bed.
"Now kiss me, dear! it may be, now!" she said.
Lethe had passed those lips, and he knew all.

L

Thus piteously Love closed what he begat:
The union of this ever-diverse pair!
These two were rapid falcons in a snare,
Condemned to do the flitting of the bat.
Lovers beneath the singing sky of May,
They wandered once; clear as the dew on flowers:
But they fed not on the advancing hours:
Their hearts held cravings for the buried day.
Then each applied to each that fatal knife,
Deep questioning, which probes to endless dole.   10
Ah, what a dusty answer gets the soul
When hot for certainties in this our life! —
In tragic hints here see what evermore
Moves dark as yonder midnight ocean's force,
Thundering like ramping hosts of warrior horse,
To throw that faint thin line upon the shore!

[1862; 1892]

PHOEBUS WITH ADMETUS

I

WHEN by Zeus relenting the mandate was revoked,
Sentencing to exile the bright Sun-God,
Mindful were the ploughmen of who the steer had yoked,
Who: and what a track showed the upturned sod!
Mindful were the shepherds as now the noon severe
Bent a burning eyebrow to brown evetide,
How the rustic flute drew the silver to the sphere,
Sister of his own, till her rays fell wide.
God! of whom music
And song and blood are pure,   10
The day is never darkened
That had thee here obscure.

II

Chirping none the scarlet cicalas crouched in ranks:
Slack the thistle-head piled its down-silk grey:
Scarce the stony lizard sucked hollows in his flanks:
Thick on spots of umbrage our drowsed flocks lay.
Sudden bowed the chestnuts beneath a wind unheard,
Lengthened ran the grasses, the sky grew slate:
Then amid a swift flight of winged seed white as curd,
Clear of limb a Youth smote the master's gate.   20
God! of whom music
And song and blood are pure,
The day is never darkened
That had thee here obscure.

III

Water, first of singers, o'er rocky mount and mead,
First of earthly singers, the sun-loved rill,
Sang of him, and flooded the ripples on the reed,
Seeking whom to waken and what ear fill.
Water, sweetest soother to kiss a wound and cool,
Sweetest and divinest, the sky-born brook,   30
Chuckled, with a whimper, and made a mirror-pool
Round the guest we welcomed, the strange hand shook.
God! of whom music
And song and blood are pure,
The day is never darkened
That had thee here obscure.

IV

Many swarms of wild bees descended on our fields:
    Stately stood the wheatstalk with head bent high:
Big of heart we laboured at storing mighty yields,
    Wool and corn, and clusters to make men cry!   40
Hand-like rushed the vintage; we strung the bellied skins
    Plump, and at the sealing the Youth's voice rose:
Maidens clung in circle, on little fists their chins;
    Gentle beasties through pushed a cold long nose.
             God! of whom music
             And song and blood are pure,
             The day is never darkened
             That had thee here obscure.

V

Foot to fire in snowtime we trimmed the slender shaft:
    Often down the pit spied the lean wolf's teeth   50
Grin against his will, trapped by masterstrokes of craft;
    Helpless in his froth-wrath as green logs seethe!
Safe the tender lambs tugged the teats, and winter sped
    Whirled before the crocus, the year's new gold.
Hung the hooky beak up aloft the arrowhead
    Reddened through his feathers for our dear fold.
             God! of whom music
             And song and blood are pure,
             The day is never darkened
             That had thee here obscure.   60

VI

Tales we drank of giants at war with Gods above:
    Rocks were they to look on, and earth climbed air!
Tales of search for simples, and those who sought of love
    Ease because the creature was all too fair.
Pleasant ran our thinking that while our work was good,
    Sure as fruit for sweat would the praise come fast.
He that wrestled stoutest and tamed the billow-brood
    Danced in rings with girls, like a sail-flapped mast.
             God! of whom music
             And song and blood are pure,   70
             The day is never darkened
             That had thee here obscure.

VII

Lo, the herb of healing, when once the herb is known,
    Shines in shady woods bright as new-sprung flame.
Ere the string was tightened we heard the mellow tone,
    After he had taught how the sweet sounds came.
Stretched about his feet, labour done, 'twas as you see
    Red pomegranates tumble and burst hard rind.
So began contention to give delight and be
    Excellent in things aimed to make life kind.   80
           God! of whom music
           And song and blood are pure,
           The day is never darkened
           That had thee here obscure.

VIII

You with shelly horns, rams! and promontory goats,
    You whose browsing beards dip in coldest dew!
Bulls, that walk the pastures in kingly-flashing coats!
    Laurel, ivy, vine, wreathed for feasts not few!
You that build the shade-roof, and you that court the rays,
    You that leap besprinkling the rock stream-rent: 90
He has been our fellow, the morning of our days;
    Us he chose for housemates, and this way went.
           God! of whom music
           And song and blood are pure,
           The day is never darkened
           That had thee here obscure.

                         [*1880;* 1883]

THE LARK ASCENDING

He rises and begins to round,
He drops the silver chain of sound,
Of many links without a break,
In chirrup, whistle, slur and shake,
All intervolved and spreading wide,
Like water-dimples down a tide
Where ripple ripple overcurls
And eddy into eddy whirls;
A press of hurried notes that run
So fleet they scarce are more than one,   10
Yet changeingly the trills repeat

And linger ringing while they fleet,
Sweet to the quick o' the ear, and dear
To her beyond the handmaid ear,
Who sits beside our inner springs,
Too often dry for this he brings,
Which seems the very jet of earth
At sight of sun, her music's mirth,
As up he wings the spiral stair,
A song of light, and pierces air   20
With fountain ardour, fountain play,
To reach the shining tops of day,
And drink in everything discerned
An ecstasy to music turned,
Impelled by what his happy bill
Disperses; drinking, showering still.
Unthinking save that he may give
His voice the outlet, there to live
Renewed in endless notes of glee,
So thirsty of his voice is he,   30
For all to hear and all to know
That he is joy, awake, aglow,
The tumult of the heart to hear
Through pureness filtered crystal-clear,
And know the pleasure sprinkled bright
By simple singing of delight,
Shrill, irreflective, unrestrained,
Rapt, ringing, on the jet sustained
Without a break, without a fall,
Sweet-silvery, sheer lyrical,   40
Perennial, quavering up the chord
Like myriad dews of sunny sward
That trembling into fulness shine,
And sparkle dropping argentine;
Such wooing as the ear receives
From zephyr caught in choric leaves
Of aspens when their chattering net
Is flushed to white with shivers wet;
And such the water-spirit's chime
On mountain heights in morning's prime,   50
Too freshly sweet to seem excess,
Too animate to need a stress;
But wider over many heads
The starry voice ascending spreads,
Awakening, as it waxes thin,
The best in us to him akin;

And every voice to watch him raised
Puts on the light of children praised,
So rich our human pleasure ripes
When sweetness on sincereness pipes,   60
Though nought be promised from the seas,
But only a soft-ruffling breeze
Sweep glittering on a still content,
Serenity in ravishment.

For singing till his heaven fills,
'Tis love of earth that he instils,
And ever winging up and up,
Our valley is his golden cup,
And he the wine which overflows
To lift us with him as he goes: 70
The woods and brooks, the sheep and kine,
He is, the hills, the human line,
The meadows green, the fallows brown,
The dreams of labour in the town;
He sings the sap, the quickened veins;
The wedding song of sun and rains
He is, the dance of children, thanks
Of sowers, shout of primrose-banks,
And eye of violets while they breathe;
All these the circling song will wreathe,   80
And you shall hear the herb and tree,
The better heart of men shall see,
Shall feel celestially, as long
As you crave nothing save the song.

Was never voice of ours could say
Our inmost in the sweetest way,
Like yonder voice aloft, and link
All hearers in the song they drink.
Our wisdom speaks from failing blood,
Our passion is too full in flood,   90
We want the key of his wild note
Of truthful in a tuneful throat,
The song seraphically free
Of taint of personality,
So pure that it salutes the suns,
The voice of one for millions,
In whom the millions rejoice
For giving their one spirit voice.

Yet men have we, whom we revere,
Now names, and men still housing here,   100
Whose lives, by many a battle-dint
Defaced, and grinding wheels on flint,
Yield substance, though they sing not, sweet
For song our highest heaven to greet:
Whom heavenly singing gives us new,
Enspheres them brilliant in our blue,
From firmest base to farthest leap,
Because their love of Earth is deep,
And they are warriors in accord
With life to serve, and pass reward,   110
So touching purest and so heard
In the brain's reflex of yon bird:
Wherefore their soul in me, or mine,
Through self-forgetfulness divine,
In them, that song aloft maintains,
To fill the sky and thrill the plains
With showerings drawn from human stores,
As he to silence nearer soars,
Extends the world at wings and dome,
More spacious making more our home,   120
Till lost on his aërial rings
In light, and then the fancy sings.

[*1881;* 1883]

THE WOODS OF WESTERMAIN

I

ENTER these enchanted woods,
    You who dare.
Nothing harms beneath the leaves
More than waves a swimmer cleaves.
Toss your heart up with the lark,
Foot at peace with mouse and worm,
    Fair you fare.
Only at a dread of dark
Quaver, and they quit their form:
Thousand eyeballs under hoods   10
    Have you by the hair.
Enter these enchanted woods,
    You who dare.

II

Here the snake across your path
Stretches in his golden bath:
Mossy-footed squirrels leap
Soft as winnowing plumes of Sleep:
Yaffles on a chuckle skim
Low to laugh from branches dim:
Up the pine, where sits the star,　　　　　20
Rattles deep the moth-winged jar.
Each has business of his own;
But should you distrust a tone,
　　Then beware.
Shudder all the haunted roods,
All the eyeballs under hoods
　　Shroud you in their glare.
Enter these enchanted woods,
　　You who dare.

III

Open hither, open hence,　　　　　30
Scarce a bramble weaves a fence,
Where the strawberry runs red,
With white star-flower overhead;
Cumbered by dry twig and cone,
Shredded husks of seedlings flown,
Mine of mole and spotted flint:
Of dire wizardry no hint,
Save mayhap the print that shows
Hasty outward-tripping toes,
Heels to terror, on the mould.　　　　　40
These, the woods of Westermain,
Are as others to behold,
Rich of wreathing sun and rain;
Foliage lustreful around
Shadowed leagues of slumbering sound.
Wavy tree-tops, yellow whins,
Shelter eager minikins,
Myriads, free to peck and pipe:
Would you better? would you worse?
You with them may gather ripe　　　　　50
Pleasures flowing not from purse.
Quick and far as Colour flies
Taking the delighted eyes,

You of any well that springs
May unfold the heaven of things;
Have it homely and within,
And thereof its likeness win,
Will you so in soul's desire:
This do sages grant t' the lyre.
This is being bird and more,   60
More than glad musician this;
Granaries you will have a store
Past the world of woe and bliss;
Sharing still its bliss and woe;
Harnessed to its hungers, no.
On the throne Success usurps,
You shall seat the joy you feel
Where a race of water chirps,
Twisting hues of flourished steel:
Or where light is caught in hoop   70
Up a clearing's leafy rise,
Where the crossing deerherds troop
Classic splendours, knightly dyes.
Or, where old-eyed oxen chew
Speculation with the cud,
Read their pool of vision through,
Back to hours when mind was mud;
Nigh the knot, which did untwine
Timelessly to drowsy suns;
Seeing Earth a slimy spine,   80
Heaven a space for winging tons.
Farther, deeper, may you read,
Have you sight for things afield,
Where peeps she, the Nurse of seed,
Cloaked, but in the peep revealed;
Showing a kind face and sweet:
Look you with the soul you see 't.
Glory narrowing to grace,
Grace to glory magnified,
Following that will you embrace   90
Close in arms or aëry wide.
Banished is the white Foam-born
Not from here, nor under ban
Phœbus lyrist, Phœbe's horn,
Pipings of the reedy Pan.
Loved of Earth of old they were,
Loving did interpret her;

And the sterner worship bars
None whom Song has made her stars.
You have seen the huntress moon   100
Radiantly facing dawn,
Dusky meads between them strewn
Glimmering like downy awn:
Argent Westward glows the hunt,
East the blush about to climb;
One another fair they front,
Transient, yet outshine the time;
Even as dewlight off the rose
In the mind a jewel sows.
Thus opposing grandeurs live   110
Here if Beauty be their dower:
Doth she of her spirit give,
Fleetingness will spare her flower.
This is in the tune we play,
Which no spring of strength would quell;
In subduing does not slay;
Guides the channel, guards the well:
Tempered holds the young blood-heat,
Yet through measured grave accord
Hears the heart of wildness beat   120
Like a centaur's hoof on sward.
Drink the sense the notes infuse,
You a larger self will find:
Sweetest fellowship ensues
With the creatures of your kind.
Ay, and Love, if Love it be
Flaming over *I* and *ME*,
Love meet they who do not shove
Cravings in the van of Love.
Courtly dames are here to woo,   130
Knowing love if it be true.
Reverence the blossom-shoot
Fervently, they are the fruit.
Mark them stepping, hear them talk,
Goddess is no myth insane,
You will say of those who walk
In the woods of Westermain.
Waters that from throat and thigh
Dart the sun his arrows back;
Leaves that on a woodland sigh   140

Chat of secret things no lack;
Shadowy branch-leaves, waters clear,
Bare or veiled they move sincere;
Nor by slavish terrors tripped;
Being anew in nature dipped,
Growths of what they step on, these;
With the roots the grace of trees.
Casket-breasts they give, nor hide,
For a tyrant's flattered pride,
Mind, which nourished not by light,   150
Lurks the shuffling trickster sprite:
Whereof are strange tales to tell;
Some in blood writ, tombed in hell.
Here the ancient battle ends,
Joining two astonished friends,
Who the kiss can give and take
With more warmth than in that world
Where the tiger claws the snake,
Snake her tiger clasps infurled,
And the issue of their fight   160
Peoples lands in snarling plight.
Here her splendid beast she leads
Silken-leashed and decked with weeds
Wild as he, but breathing faint
Sweetness of unfelt constraint.
Love, the great volcano, flings
Fires of lower Earth to sky;
Love, the sole permitted, sings
Sovereignly of *ME* and *I*.
Bowers he has of sacred shade,   170
Spaces of superb parade,
Voiceful . . . . But bring you a note
Wrangling, howsoe'er remote,
Discords out of discord spin
Round and round derisive din:
Sudden will a pallor pant
Chill at screeches miscreant;
Owls or spectres, thick they flee;
Nightmare upon horror broods;
Hooded laughter, monkish glee,   180
    Gaps the vital air.
Enter these enchanted woods
    You who dare.

IV

You must love the light so well
That no darkness will seem fell.
Love it so you could accost
Fellowly a livid ghost.
Whish! the phantom wisps away,
Owns him smoke to cocks of day.
In your breast the light must burn   190
Fed of you, like corn in quern
Ever plumping while the wheel
Speeds the mill and drains the meal.
Light to light sees little strange,
Only features heavenly new;
Then you touch the nerve of Change,
Then of Earth you have the clue;
Then her two-sexed meanings melt
Through you, wed the thought and felt.
Sameness locks no scurfy pond   200
Here for Custom, crazy-fond:
Change is on the wing to bud
Rose in brain from rose in blood.
Wisdom, throbbing shall you see
Central in complexity;
From her pasture 'mid the beasts
Rise to her ethereal feasts,
Not, though lightnings track your wit
Starward, scorning them you quit:
For be sure the bravest wing   210
Preens it in our common spring,
Thence along the vault to soar,
You with others, gathering more,
Glad of more, till you reject
Your proud title of elect,
Perilous even here while few
Roam the arched greenwood with you.
      Heed that snare.
Muffled by his cavern-cowl
Squats the scaly Dragon-fowl,   220
Who was lord ere light you drank,
And lest blood of knightly rank
Stream, let not your fair princess
Stray: he holds the leagues in stress,
      Watches keenly there
Oft has he been riven; slain

Is no force in Westermain.
Wait, and we shall forge him curbs,
Put his fangs to uses, tame,
Teach him, quick as cunning herbs,   230
How to cure him sick and lame.
Much restricted, much enringed,
Much he frets, the hooked and winged,
    Never known to spare.
'Tis enough: the name of Sage
Hits no thing in nature, nought;
Man the least, save when grave Age
From yon Dragon guards his thought.
Eye him when you hearken dumb
To what words from Wisdom come.   240
When she says how few are by
Listening to her, eye his eye.
    Self, his name declare.
Him shall Change, transforming late,
Wonderously renovate.
Hug himself the creature may:
What he hugs is loathed decay.
Crying, slip thy scales, and slough!
Change will strip his armour off;
Make of him who was all maw,   250
Inly only thrilling-shrewd,
Such a servant as none saw
Through his days of dragonhood.
Days when growling o'er his bone,
Sharpened he for mine and thine;
Sensitive within alone;
Scaly as in clefts of pine.
Change, the strongest son of Life,
Has the Spirit here to wife.
Lo, their young of vivid breed   260
Bear the lights that onward speed,
Threading thickets, mounting glades,
Up the verdurous colonnades,
Round the fluttered curves, and down,
Out of sight of Earth's blue crown,
Whither, in her central space,
Spouts the Fount and Lure o' the chase.
Fount unresting, Lure divine!
There meet all: too late look most.
Fire in water hued as wine,   270

Springs amid a shadowy host;
Circled: one close-headed mob,
Breathless, scanning divers heaps
Where a Heart begins to throb,
Where it ceases, slow, with leaps.
And 'tis very strange, 'tis said,
How you spy in each of them
Semblance of that Dragon red,
As the oak in bracken-stem.
And, 'tis said, how each and each: 280
Which commences, which subsides:
First my Dragon! doth beseech
Her who food for all provides.
And she answers with no sign;
Utters neither yea nor nay;
Fires the water hued as wine;
Kneads another spark in clay.
Terror is about her hid;
Silence of the thunders locked;
Lightnings lining the shut lid;   290
Fixity on quaking rocked.
Lo, you look at Flow and Drought
Interflashed and interwrought:
Ended is begun, begun
Ended, quick as torrents run.
Young Impulsion spouts to sink;
Luridness and lustre link;
'Tis your come and go of breath;
Mirrored pants the Life, the Death;
Each of either reaped and sown: 300
Rosiest rosy wanes to crone.
See you so? your senses drift;
'Tis a shuttle weaving swift.
Look with spirit past the sense,
Spirit shines in permanence.
That is She, the view of whom
Is the dust within the tomb,
Is the inner blush above,
Look to loathe, or look to love;
Think her Lump, or know her Flame;   310
Dread her scourge, or read her aim;
Shoot your hungers from their nerve;
Or, in her example, serve.
Some have found her sitting grave;

Laughing, some; or, browed with sweat,
Hurling dust of fool and knave
In a hissing smithy's jet.
More it were not well to speak;
Burn to see, you need but seek.
Once beheld she gives the key   320
Airing every doorway, she.
Little can you stop or steer
Ere of her you are the seër.
On the surface she will witch,
Rendering Beauty yours, but gaze
Under, and the soul is rich
Past computing, past amaze.
Then is courage that endures
Even her awful tremble yours.
Then, the reflex of that Fount   330
Spied below, will Reason mount
Lordly and a quenchless force,
Lighting Pain to its mad source,
Scaring Fear till Fear escapes,
Shot through all its phantom shapes.
Then your spirit will perceive
Fleshly seed of fleshly sins;
Where the passions interweave,
How the serpent tangle spins
Of the sense of Earth misprised,   340
Brainlessly unrecognized;
She being Spirit in her clods,
Footway to the God of Gods.
Then for you are pleasures pure,
Sureties as the stars are sure:
Not the wanton beckoning flags
Which, of flattery and delight,
Wax to the grim Habit-Hags
Riding souls of men to night:
Pleasures that through blood run sane,   350
Quickening spirit from the brain.
Each of each in sequent birth,
Blood and brain and spirit, three
(Say the deepest gnomes of Earth),
Join for true felicity.
Are they parted, then expect
Some one sailing will be wrecked:
Separate hunting are they sped,

Scan the morsel coveted.
Earth that Triad is: she hides 360
Joy from him who that divides;
Showers it when the three are one
Glassing her in union.
Earth your haven, Earth your helm,
You command a double realm:
Labouring here to pay your debt,
Till your little sun shall set;
Leaving her the future task:
Loving her too well to ask.
Eglantine that climbs the yew, 370
She her darkest wreathes for those
Knowing her the Ever-new,
And themselves the kin o' the rose.
Life, the chisel, axe and sword,
Wield who have her depths explored:
Life, the dream, shall be their robe,
Large as air about the globe;
Life, the question, hear its cry
Echoed with concordant Why;
Life, the small self-dragon ramped, 380
Thrill for service to be stamped.
Ay, and over every height
Life for them shall wave a wand:
That, the last, where sits affright,
Homely shows the stream beyond.
Love the light and be its lynx,
You will track her and attain;
Read her as no cruel Sphinx
In the woods of Westermain.
Daily fresh the woods are ranged; 390
Glooms which otherwhere appal,
Sounded: here, their worths exchanged,
Urban joins with pastoral:
Little lost, save what may drop
Husk-like, and the mind preserves.
Natural overgrowths they lop,
Yet from nature neither swerves,
Trained or savage: for this cause:
Of our Earth they ply the laws,
Have in Earth their feeding root, 400
Mind of man and bent of brute.
Hear that song; both wild and ruled.

Hear it: is it wail or mirth?
Ordered, bubbled, quite unschooled?
None, and all: it springs of Earth.
O but hear it! 'tis the mind;
Mind that with deep Earth unites,
Round the solid trunk to wind
Rings of clasping parasites.
Music have you there to feed   410
Simplest and most soaring need.
Free to wind, and in desire
Winding, they to her attached
Feel the trunk a spring of fire,
And ascend to heights unmatched,
Whence the tidal world is viewed
As a sea of windy wheat,
Momently black, barren, rude;
Golden-brown, for harvest meet;
Dragon-reaped from folly-sown;   420
Bride-like to the sickle-blade:
Quick it varies, while the moan,
Moan of a sad creature strayed,
Chiefly is its voice. So flesh
Conjures tempest-flails to thresh
Good from worthless. Some clear lamps
Light it; more of dead marsh-damps.
Monster is it still, and blind,
Fit but to be led by Pain.
Glance we at the paths behind,   430
Fruitful sight has Westermain.
There we laboured, and in turn
Forward our blown lamps discern,
As you see on the dark deep
Far the loftier billows leap,
        Foam for beacon bear.
Hither, hither, if you will,
Drink instruction, or instil,
Run the woods like vernal sap,
Crying, hail to luminousness!   440
        But have care.
In yourself may lurk the trap:
On conditions they caress.
Here you meet the light invoked:
Here is never secret cloaked.
Doubt you with the monster's fry

All his orbit may exclude;
Are you of the stiff, the dry,
Cursing the not understood;
Grasp you with the monster's claws;   450
Govern with his truncheon-saws;
Hate, the shadow of a grain;
You are lost in Westermain:
Earthward swoops a vulture sun,
Nighted upon carrion:
Straightway venom winecups shout
Toasts to One whose eyes are out:
Flowers along the reeling floor
Drip henbane and hellebore:
Beauty, of her tresses shorn,   460
Shrieks as nature's maniac:
Hideousness on hoof and horn
Tumbles, yapping in her track:
Haggard Wisdom, stately once,
Leers fantastical and trips:
Allegory drums the sconce,
Impiousness nibblenips.
Imp that dances, imp that flits,
Imp o' the demon-growing girl,
Maddest! whirl with imp o' the pits   470
Round you, and with them you whirl
Fast where pours the fountain-rout
Out of Him whose eyes are out:
Multitudes on multitudes,
Drenched in wallowing devilry:
And you ask where you may be,
    In what reek of a lair
Given to bones and ogre-broods:
    And they yell you Where.
Enter these enchanted woods,   480
    You who dare.

                    [1883]

EARTH AND MAN

I

On her great venture, Man,
Earth gazes while her fingers dint the breast
Which is his well of strength, his home of rest,
And fair to scan.

II

More aid than that embrace,
That nourishment, she cannot give: his heart
Involves his fate; and she who urged the start
Abides the race.

III

For he is in the lists
Contentious with the elements, whose dower
First sprang him; for swift vultures to devour
If he desists.

IV

His breath of instant thirst
Is warning of a creature matched with strife,
To meet it as a bride, or let fall life
On life's accursed.

V

No longer forth he bounds
The lusty animal, afield to roam,
But peering in Earth's entrails, where the gnome
Strange themes propounds.

VI

By hunger sharply sped
To grasp at weapons ere he learns their use,
In each new ring he bears a giant's thews,
An infant's head.

VII

And ever that old task
Of reading what he is and whence he came,
Whither to go, finds wilder letters flame
Across her mask.

VIII

She hears his wailful prayer,
When now to the Invisible he raves   30
To rend him from her, now of his mother craves
Her calm, her care.

IX

The thing that shudders most
Within him is the burden of his cry.
Seen of his dread, she is to his blank eye
The eyeless Ghost.

X

Or sometimes she will seem
Heavenly, but her blush, soon wearing white,
Veils like a gorsebush in a web of blight,
With gold-buds dim.   40

XI

Once worshiped Prime of Powers,
She still was the Implacable: as a beast,
She struck him down and dragged him from the feast
She crowned with flowers.

XII

Her pomp of glorious hues,
Her revelries of ripeness, her kind smile,
Her songs, her peeping faces, lure awhile
With symbol-clues.

XIII

The mystery she holds
For him, inveterately he strains to see,   50
And sight of his obtuseness is the key
Among those folds.

XIV

He may entreat, aspire,
He may despair, and she has never heed.
She drinking his warm sweat will soothe his need,
Not his desire.

XV

She prompts him to rejoice,
Yet scares him on the threshold with the shroud.

He deems her cherishing of her best-endowed
A wanton's choice.   60

XVI

Albeit thereof he has found
Firm roadway between lustfulness and pain;
Has half transferred the battle to his brain,
From bloody ground;

XVII

He will not read her good,
Or wise, but with the passion Self obscures;
Through that old devil of the thousand lures,
Through that dense hood:

XVIII

Through terror, through distrust;
The greed to touch, to view, to have, to live: 70
Through all that makes of him a sensitive
Abhorring dust.

XIX

Behold his wormy home!
And he the wind-whipped, anywhither wave
Crazily tumbled on a shingle-grave
To waste in foam.

XX

Therefore the wretch inclines
Afresh to the Invisible, who, he saith,
Can raise him high: with vows of living faith
For little signs.   80

XXI

Some signs he must demand,
Some proofs of slaughtered nature; some prized few,
To satisfy the senses it is true,
And in his hand,

XXII

This miracle which saves
Himself, himself doth from extinction clutch,
By virtue of his worth, contrasting much
With brutes and knaves.

XXIII

From dust, of him abhorred,
He would be snatched by Grace discovering worth.   90
"Sever me from the hollowness of Earth!
Me take, dear Lord!"

XXIV

She hears him. Him she owes
For half her loveliness a love well won
By work that lights the shapeless and the dun,
Their common foes.

XXV

He builds the soaring spires,
That sing his soul in stone: of her he draws,
Though blind to her, by spelling at her laws,
Her purest fires.   100

XXVI

Through him hath she exchanged,
For the gold harvest-robes, the mural crown,
Her haggard quarry-features and thick frown
Where monsters ranged.

XXVII

And order, high discourse,
And decency, than which is life less dear,
She has of him: the lyre of language clear,
Love's tongue and source.

XXVIII

She hears him, and can hear
With glory in his gains by work achieved: 110
With grief for grief that is the unperceived
In her so near.

XXIX

If he aloft for aid
Imploring storms, her essence is the spur.
His cry to heaven is a cry to her
He would evade.

XXX

Not elsewhere can he tend.
Those are her rules which bid him wash foul sins;

Those her revulsions from the skull that grins
To ape his end.   120

XXXI

And her desires are those
For happiness, for lastingness, for light.
'Tis she who kindles in his haunting night
The hoped dawn-rose.

XXXII

Fair fountains of the dark
Daily she waves him, that his inner dream
May clasp amid the glooms a springing beam,
A quivering lark:

XXXIII

This life and her to know
For Spirit: with awakenedness of glee   130
To feel stern joy her origin: not he
The child of woe.

XXXIV

But that the senses still
Usurp the station of their issue mind,
He would have burst the chrysalis of the blind:
As yet he will;

XXXV

As yet he will, she prays,
Yet will when his distempered devil of Self; —
The glutton for her fruits, the wily elf
In shifting rays; —   140

XXXVI

That captain of the scorned;
The coveter of life in soul and shell,
The fratricide, the thief, the infidel,
The hoofed and horned; —

XXXVII

He singularly doomed
To what he execrates and writhes to shun; —
When fire has passed him vapour to the sun,
And sun relumed,

XXXVIII

Then shall the horrid pall
Be lifted, and a spirit nigh divine,   150
"Live in thy offspring as I live in mine,"
Will hear her call.

XXXIX

Whence looks he on a land
Whereon his labour is a carven page;
And forth from heritage to heritage
Nought writ on sand.

XL

His fables of the Above,
And his gapped readings of the crown and sword,
The hell detested and the heaven adored,
The hate, the love,   160

XLI

The bright wing, the black hoof,
He shall peruse, from Reason not disjoined,
And never unfaith clamouring to be coined
To faith by proof.

XLII

She her just Lord may view,
Not he, her creature, till his soul has yearned
With all her gifts to reach the light discerned
Her spirit through.

XLIII

Then in him time shall run
As in the hour that to young sunlight crows;   170
And — "If thou hast good faith it can repose,"
She tells her son.

XLIV

Meanwhile on him, her chief
Expression, her great word of life, looks she;
Twi-minded of him, as the waxing tree,
Or dated leaf.

[1883]

LUCIFER IN STARLIGHT

On a starred night Prince Lucifer uprose.
Tired of his dark dominion swung the fiend
Above the rolling ball in cloud part screened,
Where sinners hugged their spectre of repose.
Poor prey to his hot fit of pride were those.
And now upon his western wing he leaned,
Now his huge bulk o'er Afric's sands careened,
Now the black planet shadowed Arctic snows.
Soaring through wider zones that pricked his scars
With memory of the old revolt from Awe,   10
He reached a middle height, and at the stars,
Which are the brain of heaven, he looked, and sank.
Around the ancient track marched, rank on rank,
The army of unalterable law.

[1883]

Algernon Charles Swinburne

THE TRIUMPH OF TIME

BEFORE our lives divide for ever,
  While time is with us and hands are free,
(Time, swift to fasten and swift to sever
  Hand from hand, as we stand by the sea)
I will say no word that a man might say
Whose whole life's love goes down in a day;
For this could never have been; and never,
  Though the gods and the years relent, shall be.

Is it worth a tear, is it worth an hour,
  To think of things that are well outworn?   **10**
Of fruitless husk and fugitive flower,   *unrealized love*
  The dream foregone and the deed forborne?
Though joy be done with and grief be vain,
Time shall not sever us wholly in twain;
Earth is not spoilt for a single shower;
  But the rain has ruined the ungrown corn.

It will not grow again, this fruit of my heart,
  Smitten with sunbeams, ruined with rain.
The singing seasons divide and depart,
  Winter and summer depart in twain.   **20**
It will grow not again, it is ruined at root,
The bloodlike blossom, the dull red fruit;

344

Though the heart yet sickens, the lips yet smart,
　　With sullen savour of poisonous pain.

I have given no man of my fruit to eat;　*can't express himself*
　　I trod the grapes, I have drunken the wine.　*love & art*
Had you eaten and drunken and found it sweet,
　　This wild new growth of the corn and vine,
This wine and bread without lees or leaven,
Eden　We had grown as gods, as the gods in heaven,　　　　30
Souls fair to look upon, goodly to greet,
　　One splendid spirit, your soul and mine.

In the change of years, in the coil of things,　*mutability*
　　In the clamour and rumour of life to be,
We, drinking love at the furthest springs,
　　Covered with love as a covering tree,
We had grown as gods, as the gods above,
Filled from the heart to the lips with love,
Held fast in his hands, clothed warm with his wings,
　　O love, my love, had you loved but me!　　　　40

We had stood as the sure stars stand, and moved
　　As the moon moves, loving the world; and seen
Grief collapse as a thing disproved,
　　Death consume as a thing unclean.
Twain halves of a perfect heart, made fast
Soul to soul while the years fell past;
Had you loved me once, as you have not loved;
　　Had the chance been with us that has not been.

I have put my days and dreams out of mind,　*looks to*
　　Days that are over, dreams that are done.　*death*　　50
Though we seek life through, we shall surely find
　　There is none of them clear to us now, not one.
But clear are these things; the grass and the sand,
Where, sure as the eyes reach, ever at hand,
With lips wide open and face burnt blind,
　　The strong sea-daisies feast on the sun.

The low downs lean to the sea; the stream,
　　One loose thin pulseless tremulous vein,
Rapid and vivid and dumb as a dream,
　　Works downward, sick of the sun and the rain;　　60
No wind is rough with the rank rare flowers;

The sweet sea, mother of loves and hours,
Shudders and shines as the grey winds gleam,
    Turning her smile to a fugitive pain.

out of this in Thelassens

Mother of loves that are swift to fade,
    Mother of mutable winds and hours.
A barren mother, a mother-maid,
    Cold and clean as her faint salt flowers.
I would we twain were even as she,
Lost in the night and the light of the sea,
Where faint sounds falter and wan beams wade,
    Break, and are broken, and shed into showers.   **70**

The love and hours of the life of a man,
    They are swift and sad, being born of the sea.
Hours that rejoice and regret for a span,
    Born with a man's breath, mortal as he;
Loves that are lost ere they come to birth,
Weeds of the wave, without fruit upon earth.
I lose what I long for, save what I can,
    My love, my love, and no love for me!   **80**

It is not much that a man can save
    On the sands of life, in the straits of time,
Who swims in sight of the great third wave   *destroyed*
    That never a swimmer shall cross or climb.
Some waif washed up with the strays and spars
That ebb-tide shows to the shore and the stars;
Weed from the water, grass from a grave,
    A broken blossom, a ruined rhyme.

There will no man do for your sake, I think,
    What I would have done for the least word said.   **90**
I had wrung life dry for your lips to drink,
    Broken it up for your daily bread:
Body for body and blood for blood,
As the flow of the full sea risen to flood
That yearns and trembles before it sink,
    I had given, and lain down for you, glad and dead.

Yea, hope at highest and all her fruit,
    And time at fullest and all his dower,
I had given you surely, and life to boot,
    Were we once made one for a single hour.   **100**
But now, you are twain, you are cloven apart,

Flesh of his flesh, but heart of my heart;
And deep in one is the bitter root,
   And sweet for one is the lifelong flower.

To have died if you cared I should die for you, clung
   To my life if you bade me, played my part
As it pleased you — these were the thoughts that stung,
   The dreams that smote with a keener dart
Than shafts of love or arrows of death;
These were but as fire is, dust, or breath,   110
Or poisonous foam on the tender tongue
   Of the little snakes that eat my heart.

I wish we were dead together to-day,
   Lost sight of, hidden away out of sight,
Clasped and clothed in the cloven clay,
   Out of the world's way, out of the light,
Out of the ages of worldly weather,
Forgotten of all men altogether,
As the world's first dead, taken wholly away,
   Made one with death, filled full of the night.   120

How we should slumber, how we should sleep,
   Far in the dark with the dreams and the dews!
And dreaming, grow to each other, and weep,
   Laugh low, live softly, murmur and muse;
Yea, and it may be, struck through by the dream,
Feel the dust quicken and quiver, and seem
Alive as of old to the lips, and leap
   Spirit to spirit as lovers use.

Sick dreams and sad of a dull delight;
   For what shall it profit when men are dead   130
To have dreamed, to have loved with the whole soul's might,
   To have looked for day when the day was fled?
Let come what will, there is one thing worth,
To have had fair love in the life upon earth:
To have held love safe till the day grew night,
   While skies had colour and lips were red.

Would I lose you now? would I take you then,
   If I lose you now that my heart has need?
And come what may after death to men,
   What thing worth this will the dead years breed?   140
Lose life, lose all; but at least I know,

O sweet life's love, having loved you so,
Had I reached you on earth, I should lose not **again**,
In death nor life, nor in dream or deed.

Yea, I know this well: were you once sealed **mine**
Mine in the blood's beat, mine in the breath,
Mixed into me as honey in wine,
Not time, that sayeth and gainsayeth,
Nor all strong things had severed us then;
Not wrath of gods, nor wisdom of men,   150
Nor all things earthly, nor all divine,
Nor joy nor sorrow, nor life nor death.

I had grown pure as the dawn and the dew,
You had grown strong as the sun or the sea.
But none shall triumph a whole life through:
For death is one, and the fates are three.
At the door of life, by the gate of breath,
There are worse things waiting for men than death;
Death could not sever my soul and you,
As these have severed your soul from me.   160

You have chosen and clung to the chance they sent you,
Life sweet as perfume and pure as prayer.
But will it not one day in heaven repent you?
Will they solace you wholly, the days that were?
Will you lift up your eyes between sadness and bliss,
Meet mine, and see where the great love is,
And tremble and turn and be changed? Content you;
The gate is strait; I shall not be there.

But you, had you chosen, had you stretched hand,
Had you seen good such a thing were done,   170
I too might have stood with the souls that stand
In the sun's sight, clothed with the light of the sun;
But who now on earth need care how I live?
Have the high gods anything left to give,
Save dust and laurels and gold and sand?
Which gifts are goodly; but I will none.

O all fair lovers about the world,
There is none of you, none, that shall comfort me.
My thoughts are as dead things, wrecked and whirled
Round and round in a gulf of the sea;   180
And still, through the sound and the straining stream,

Through the coil and chafe, they gleam in a dream,
The bright fine lips so cruelly curled,
    And strange swift eyes where the soul sits free.

Free, without pity, withheld from woe,
    Ignorant; fair as the eyes are fair.
Would I have you change now, change at a blow,
    Startled and stricken, awake and aware?
Yea, if I could, would I have you see
My very love of you filling me,   190
And know my soul to the quick, as I know
    The likeness and look of your throat and hair?

I shall not change you. Nay, though I might,
    Would I change my sweet one love with a word?
I had rather your hair should change in a night,
    Clear now as the plume of a black bright bird;
Your face fail suddenly, cease, turn grey,
Die as a leaf that dies in a day.
I will keep my soul in a place out of sight,
    Far off, where the pulse of it is not heard.   200

Far off it walks, in a bleak blown space,
    Full of the sound of the sorrow of years.
I have woven a veil for the weeping face,
    Whose lips have drunken the wine of tears;
I have found a way for the failing feet,
A place for slumber and sorrow to meet;
There is no rumour about the place,
    Nor light, nor any that sees or hears.

I have hidden my soul out of sight, and said
    "Let none take pity upon thee, none   210
Comfort thy crying: for lo, thou art dead,
    Lie still now, safe out of sight of the sun.
Have I not built thee a grave, and wrought
Thy grave-clothes on thee of grievous thought,
With soft spun verses and tears unshed,
    And sweet light visions of things undone?

"I have given thee garments and balm and myrrh,
    And gold, and beautiful burial things.
But thou, be at peace now, make no stir;
    Is not thy grave as a royal king's?   220
Fret not thyself though the end were sore;

past death

Sleep, be patient, vex me no more.
Sleep; what has thou to do with her?
   The eyes that weep, with the mouth that sings?"

Where the dead red leaves of the years lie rotten,
   The cold old crimes and the deeds thrown by,
The misconceived and the misbegotten,
   I would find a sin to do ere I die,
Sure to dissolve and destroy me all through,
That would set you higher in heaven, serve you   230
And leave you happy, when clean forgotten,
   As a dead man out of mind, am I.

Your lithe hands draw me, your face burns through me,
   I am swift to follow you, keen to see;
But love lacks might to redeem or undo me;
   As I have been, I know I shall surely be;
'What should such fellows as I do?' Nay,
My part were worse if I chose to play;
For the worst is this after all; if they knew me,
   Not a soul upon earth would pity me.   240

And I play not for pity of these; but you,
   If you saw with your soul what man am I,
You would praise me at least that my soul all through
   Clove to you, loathing the lives that lie;
The souls and lips that are bought and sold,
The smiles of silver and kisses of gold,
The lapdog loves that whine as they chew,
   The little lovers that curse and cry.

There are fairer women, I hear; that may be;
   But I, that I love you and find you fair,   250
Who are more than fair in my eyes if they be,
   Do the high gods know or the great gods care?
Though the swords in my heart for one were seven,
Should the iron hollow of doubtful heaven,
That knows not itself whether night-time or day be,
   Reverberate words and a foolish prayer?

I will go back to the great sweet mother,
   Mother and lover of men, the sea.
I will go down to her, I and none other,
   Close with her, kiss her and mix her with me;   260
Cling to her, strive with her, hold her fast:

O fair white mother, in days long past
Born without sister, born without brother,
  Set free my soul as thy soul is free.

O fair green-girdled mother of mine,
  Sea, that art clothed with the sun and the rain,
Thy sweet hard kisses are strong like wine,
  Thy large embraces are keen like pain.
Save me and hide me with all thy waves,
Find me one grave of thy thousand graves,   270
Those pure cold populous graves of thine
  Wrought without hand in a world without stain.

I shall sleep, and move with the moving ships,   *without direction*
  Change as the winds change, veer in the tide;
My lips will feast on the foam of thy lips,
  I shall rise with thy rising, with thee subside;
Sleep, and not know if she be, if she were,
Filled full with life to the eyes and hair,
As a rose is fulfilled to the roseleaf tips
  With splendid summer and perfume and pride.   280

This woven raiment of nights and days,
  Were it once cast off and unwound from me,
Naked and glad would I walk in thy ways,
  Alive and aware of thy ways and thee;
Clear of the whole world, hidden at home,
Clothed with the green and crowned with the foam,
A pulse of the life of thy straits and bays,
  A vein in the heart of the streams of the sea.

Fair mother, fed with the lives of men,
  Thou art subtle and cruel of heart, men say.   290
Thou hast taken, and shalt not render again;
  Thou art full of thy dead, and cold as they.
But death is the worst that comes of thee;
Thou art fed with our dead, O mother, O sea,
But when hast thou fed on our hearts? or when,
  Having given us love, hast thou taken away?

O tender-hearted, O perfect lover,
  Thy lips are bitter, and sweet thine heart.
The hopes that hurt and the dreams that hover,
  Shall they not vanish away and apart?   300
But thou, thou art sure, thou art older than earth;

Thou art strong for death and fruitful of birth;
Thy depths conceal and thy gulfs discover;
    From the first thou wert; in the end thou art.

And grief shall endure not for ever, I know.
    As things that are not shall these things be;
We shall live through seasons of sun and of snow,
    And none be grievous as this to me.
We shall hear, as one in a trance that hears,
The sound of time, the rhyme of the years;   310
Wrecked hope and passionate pain will grow
    As tender things of a spring-tide sea.

Sea-fruit that swings in the waves that hiss,
    Drowned gold and purple and royal rings.
And all time past, was it all for this?
    Times unforgotten, and treasures of things?
Swift years of liking and sweet long laughter,
That wist not well of the years thereafter
Till love woke, smitten at heart by a kiss,
    With lips that trembled and trailing wings?   320

There lived a singer in France of old
    By the tideless dolorous midland sea.
In a land of sand and ruin and gold
    There shone one woman, and none but she.
And finding life for her love's sake fail,
Being fain to see her, he bade set sail,
Touched land, and saw her as life grew cold,
    And praised God, seeing; and so died he.

Died, praising God for his gift and grace:
    For she bowed down to him weeping, and said   330
"Live"; and her tears were shed on his face
    Or ever the life in his face was shed.
The sharp tears fell through her hair, and stung
Once, and her close lips touched him and clung
Once, and grew one with his lips for a space;
    And so drew back, and the man was dead.

O brother, the gods were good to you.
    Sleep, and be glad while the world endures.
Be well content as the years wear through;
    Give thanks for life, and the loves and lures;   340

Give thanks for life, O brother, and death,
For the sweet last sound of her feet, her breath,
For gifts she gave you, gracious and few,
    Tears and kisses, that lady of yours.

Rest, and be glad of the gods; but I,
    How shall I praise them, or how take rest?
There is not room under all the sky
    For me that know not of worst or best,
Dream or desire of the days before,
Sweet things or bitterness, any more.   350
Love will not come to me now though I die,
    As love came close to you, breast to breast.

I shall never be friends again with roses;
    I shall loathe sweet tunes, where a note grown strong
Relents and recoils, and climbs and closes,
    As a wave of the sea turned back by song.
There are sounds where the soul's delight takes fire,
Face to face with its own desire;
A delight that rebels, a desire that reposes;
    I shall hate sweet music my whole life long.   360

The pulse of war and passion of wonder,
    The heavens that murmur, the sounds that shine,
The stars that sing and the loves that thunder,
    The music burning at heart like wine,
An armed archangel whose hands raise up
All senses mixed in the spirit's cup
Till flesh and spirit are molten in sunder —
    These things are over, and no more mine.

These were a part of the playing I heard
    Once, ere my love and my heart were at strife;   370
Love that sings and hath wings as a bird,
    Balm of the wound and heft of the knife.
Fairer than earth is the sea, and sleep
Than overwatching of eyes that weep,
Now time has done with his one sweet word,
    The wine and leaven of lovely life.

I shall go my ways, tread out my measure,
    Fill the days of my daily breath
With fugitive things not good to treasure,

Do as the world doth, say as it saith;   380
But if we had loved each other — O sweet,
Had you felt, lying under the palms of your feet,
The heart of my heart, beating harder with pleasure
To feel you tread it to dust and death —

Ah, had I not taken my life up and given
All that life gives and the years let go,
The wine and honey, the balm and leaven,
The dreams reared high and the hopes brought low?
Come life, come death, not a word be said;
Should I lose you living, and vex you dead?   390
I never shall tell you on earth; and in heaven,
If I cry to you then, will you hear or know?

[1866]

A LEAVE-TAKING

Let us go hence, my songs; she will not hear.
Let us go hence together without fear;
Keep silence now, for singing-time is over,
And over all old things and all things dear.
She loves not you nor me as all we love her.
Yea, though we sang as angels in her ear,
    She would not hear.

Let us rise up and part; she will not know.
Let us go seaward as the great winds go,
Full of blown sand and foam; what help is here?   10
There is no help, for all these things are so,
And all the world is bitter as a tear.
And how these things are, though ye strove to show,
    She would not know.

Let us go home and hence; she will not weep.
We gave love many dreams and days to keep,
Flowers without scent, and fruits that would not grow,
Saying "If thou wilt, thrust in thy sickle and reap."
All is reaped now; no grass is left to mow;
And we that sowed, though all we fell on sleep,   20
    She would not weep.

Let us go hence and rest; she will not love,
She shall not hear us if we sing hereof,
Nor see love's ways, how sore they are and steep.
Come hence, let be, lie still; it is enough.
Love is a barren sea, bitter and deep;
And though she saw all heaven in flower above,
    She would not love.

Let us give up, go down; she will not care.
Though all the stars made gold of all the air, 30
And the sea moving saw before it move
One moon-flower making all the foam-flowers fair;
Though all those waves went over us, and drove
Deep down the stifling lips and drowning hair,
    She would not care.

Let us go hence, go hence; she will not see.
Sing all once more together; surely she,
She too, remembering days and words that were,
Will turn a little toward us, sighing; but we,
We are hence, we are gone, as though we had not been there. 40
Nay, and though all men seeing had pity on me,
    She would not see.

                       [1866]

ITYLUS

Swallow, my sister, O sister swallow,
  How can thine heart be full of the spring?
    A thousand summers are over and dead.
What hast thou found in the spring to follow?
  What hast thou found in thine heart to sing?
    What wilt thou do when the summer is shed?

O swallow, sister, O fair swift swallow,
  Why wilt thou fly after spring to the south,
    The soft south whither thine heart is set?
Shall not the grief of the old time follow? 10
  Shall not the song thereof cleave to thy mouth?
    Hast thou forgotten ere I forget?

Sister, my sister, O fleet sweet swallow,
   Thy way is long to the sun and the south;
     But I, fulfilled of my heart's desire,
Shedding my song upon height, upon hollow,
   From tawny body and sweet small mouth
     Feed the heart of the night with fire.

I the nightingale all spring through,
   O swallow, sister, O changing swallow,   20
     All spring through till the spring be done,
Clothed with the light of the night on the dew,
   Sing, while the hours and the wild birds follow,
     Take flight and follow and find the sun.

Sister, my sister, O soft light swallow,
   Though all things feast in the spring's guest-chamber,
     How hast thou heart to be glad thereof yet?
For where thou fliest I shall not follow,
   Till life forget and death remember,
     Till thou remember and I forget.   30

Swallow, my sister, O singing swallow,
   I know not how thou hast heart to sing.
     Hast thou the heart? is it all past over?
Thy lord the summer is good to follow,
   And fair the feet of thy lover the spring:
     But what wilt thou say to the spring thy lover?

O swallow, sister, O fleeting swallow,
   My heart in me is a molten ember
     And over my head the waves have met.
But thou wouldst tarry or I would follow,   40
   Could I forget or thou remember,
     Couldst thou remember and I forget.

O sweet stray sister, O shifting swallow,
   The heart's division divideth us.
     Thy heart is light as a leaf of a tree;
But mine goes forth among sea-gulfs hollow
   To the place of the slaying of Itylus,
     The feast of Daulis, the Thracian sea.

O swallow, sister, O rapid swallow,
   I pray thee sing not a little space.   50
     Are not the roofs and the lintels wet?

The woven web that was plain to follow,
  The small slain body, the flowerlike face,
    Can I remember if thou forget?

O sister, sister, thy first-begotten!
  The hands that cling and the feet that follow,
    The voice of the child's blood crying yet
Who hath remembered me? who hath forgotten?
  Thou hast forgotten, O summer swallow,
    But the world shall end when I forget.   60

[1866]

HYMN TO PROSERPINE

After the Proclamation in Rome of the Christian Faith

Vicisti, Galilaee.

I HAVE lived long enough, having seen one thing, that love hath an end;
Goddess and maiden and queen, be near me now and befriend.
Thou art more than the day or the morrow, the seasons that laugh or
    that weep;   no progression
For these give joy and sorrow; but thou, Proserpina, sleep.
Sweet is the treading of wine, and sweet the feet of the dove;
But a goodlier gift is thine than foam of the grapes or love.
Yea, is not even Apollo, with hair and harpstring of gold,
A bitter God to follow, a beautiful God to behold?
I am sick of singing: the bays burn deep and chafe: I am fain
To rest a little from praise and grievous pleasure and pain.   10
For the Gods we know not of, who give us our daily breath,
We know they are cruel as love or life, and lovely as death.
O Gods dethroned and deceased, cast forth, wiped out in a day!
From your wrath is the world released, redeemed from your chains,
    men say.
New Gods are crowned in the city; their flowers have broken your rods;
They are merciful, clothed with pity, the young compassionate Gods.
But for me their new device is barren, the days are bare;
Things long past over suffice, and men forgotten that were.
Time and the Gods are at strife; ye dwell in the midst thereof,
Draining a little life from the barren breasts of love.   20
I say to you, cease, take rest; yea, I say to you all, be at peace,
Till the bitter milk of her breast and the barren bosom shall cease.
Wilt thou yet take all, Galilean? but these thou shalt not take,
The laurel, the palms and the paean, the breasts of the nymphs in the
    brake;

Breasts more soft than a dove's, that tremble with tenderer breath;
And all the wings of the Loves, and all the joy before death;
All the feet of the hours that sound as a single lyre,
Dropped and deep in the flowers, with strings that flicker like fire.
More than these wilt thou give, things fairer than all these things?
Nay, for a little we live, and life hath mutable wings.   30
A little while and we die; shall life not thrive as it may?
For no man under the sky lives twice, outliving his day.
And grief is a grievous thing, and a man hath enough of his tears:
Why should he labour, and bring fresh grief to blacken his years?
Thou hast conquered, O pale Galilean; the world has grown grey from
    thy breath;
We have drunken of things Lethean, and fed on the fullness of death.
Laurel is green for a season, and love is sweet for a day;
But love grows bitter with treason, and laurel outlives not May.
Sleep, shall we sleep after all? for the world is not sweet in the end;
For the old faiths loosen and fall, the new years ruin and rend.   40
Fate is a sea without shore, and the soul is a rock that abides;
But her ears are vexed with the roar and her face with the foam of the
    tides.
O lips that the live blood faints in, the leavings of racks and rods!
O ghastly glories of saints, dead limbs of gibbeted Gods!
Though all men abase them before you in spirit, and all knees bend,
I kneel not neither adore you, but standing, look to the end.
All delicate days and pleasant, all spirits and sorrows are cast
Far out with the foam of the present that sweeps to the surf of the
    past:
Waste water washes, and tall ships founder, and deep death waits: 50
Where beyond the extreme sea-wall, and between the remote sea-gates,
Where, mighty with deepening sides, clad about with the seas as with
    wings,
And impelled of invisible tides, and fulfilled of unspeakable things,
White-eyed and poisonous-finned, shark-toothed and serpentine-curled,
Rolls, under the whitening wind of the future, the wave of the world.
The depths stand naked in sunder behind it, the storms flee away;
In the hollow before it the thunder is taken and snared as a prey;
In its sides is the north-wind bound; and its salt is of all men's tears;
With light of ruin, and sound of changes, and pulse of years:
With travail of day after day, and with trouble of hour upon hour;
And bitter as blood is the spray; and the crests are as fangs that
    devour: 60
And its vapour and storm of its steam as the sighing of spirits to be;
And its noise as the noise in a dream; and its depth as the roots of the
    sea:

And the height of its heads as the height of the utmost stars of the air:
And the ends of the earth at the might thereof tremble, and time is made bare.
Will ye bridle the deep sea with reins, will ye chasten the high sea with rods?
Will ye take her to chain her with chains, who is older than all ye Gods?
All ye as a wind shall go by, as a fire shall ye pass and be past;
Ye are Gods, and behold, ye shall die, and the waves be upon you at last.
In the darkness of time, in the deeps of the years, in the changes of things,
Ye shall sleep as a slain man sleeps, and the world shall forget you for kings.   70
Though the feet of thine high priests tread where thy lords and our forefathers trod,
Though these that were Gods are dead, and thou being dead art a God,
Though before thee the throned Cytherean be fallen, and hidden her head,
Yet thy kingdom shall pass, Galilean, thy dead shall go down to thee dead.
Of the maiden thy mother men sing as a goddess with grace clad around;
Thou art crowned where another was king; where another was queen she is crowned.
Yea, once we had sight of another: but now she is queen, say these.
Not as thine, not as thine was our mother, a blossom of flowering seas,
Clothed round with the world's desire as with raiment, and fair as the foam,
And fleeter than kindled fire, and a goddess, and mother of Rome.   80
For thine came pale and a maiden, and sister to sorrow; but ours,
Her deep hair heavily laden with odour and colour of flowers,
White rose of the rose-white water, a silver splendour, a flame,
Bent down unto us that besought her, and earth grew sweet with her name.
For thine came weeping, a slave among slaves, and rejected; but she
Came flushed from the full-flushed wave, and imperial, her foot on the sea.
And the wonderful waters knew her, the winds and the viewless ways,
And the roses grew rosier, and bluer the sea-blue stream of the bays.
Ye are fallen, our lords, by what token? we wist that ye should not fall.
Ye were all so fair that are broken; and one more fair than ye all.   90

But I turn to her still, having seen she shall surely abide in the end;
Goddess and maiden and queen, be near me now and befriend.
O daughter of earth, of my mother, her crown and blossom of birth,
I am also, I also, thy brother; I go as I came unto earth.
In the night where thine eyes are as moons are in heaven, the night
    where thou art,
Where the silence is more than all tunes, where sleep overflows from
    the heart,
Where the poppies are sweet as the rose in our world, and the red rose
    is white,
And the wind falls faint as it blows with the fume of the flowers of the
    night,
And the murmur of spirits that sleep in the shadow of Gods from afar
Grows dim in thine ears and deep as the deep dim soul of a star,   100
In the sweet low light of thy face, under heavens untrod by the sun,
Let my soul with their souls find place, and forget what is done and
    undone.
Thou art more than the Gods who number the days of our temporal
    breath;
For these give labour and slumber; but thou, Proserpina, death.
Therefore now at thy feet I abide for a season in silence. I know
I shall die as my fathers died, and sleep as they sleep; even so.
For the glass of the years is brittle wherein we gaze for a span;
A little soul for a little bears up this corpse which is man.*
So long I endure, no longer; and laugh not again, neither weep.   109
For there is no God found stronger than death; and death is a sleep.

                                      [1866]

* ψυχάριον εἶ βαστάζον νεκρόν. — Epictetus. [SWINBURNE]

THE GARDEN OF PROSERPINE

HERE, where the world is quiet;
    Here, where all trouble seems
Dead winds' and spent waves' riot
    In doubtful dreams of dreams;
I watch the green field growing
For reaping folk and sowing,
For harvest-time and mowing,
    A sleepy world of streams.

I am tired of tears and laughter,
    And men that laugh and weep;   10

Of what may come hereafter
  For men that sow to reap:
I am weary of days and hours,
Blown buds of barren flowers,
Desires and dreams and powers
  And everything but sleep.

Here life has death for neighbour,
  And far from eye or ear
Wan waves and wet winds labour,
  Weak ships and spirits steer;
They drive adrift, and whither
They wot not who make thither;
But no such winds blow hither,
  And no such things grow here.

No growth of moor or coppice,
  No heather-flower or vine,
But bloomless buds of poppies,
  Green grapes of Proserpine,
Pale beds of blowing rushes
Where no leaf blooms or blushes
Save this whereout she crushes
  For dead men deadly wine.

Pale, without name or number,
  In fruitless fields of corn,
They bow themselves and slumber
  All night till light is born;
And like a soul belated,
In hell and heaven unmated,
By cloud and mist abated
  Comes out of darkness morn.

Though one were strong as seven,
  He too with death shall dwell,
Nor wake with wings in heaven,
  Nor weep for pains in hell;
Though one were fair as roses,
His beauty clouds and closes;
And well though love reposes,
  In the end it is not well.

Pale, beyond porch and portal,
  Crowned with calm leaves, she stands

20

30

40

50

Who gathers all things mortal
  With cold immortal hands;
Her languid lips are sweeter
Than love's who fears to greet her
To men that mix and meet her
  From many times and lands.

She waits for each and other,
  She waits for all men born;
Forgets the earth her mother,
  The life of fruits and corn;
And spring and seed and swallow
Take wing for her and follow
Where summer song rings hollow
  And flowers are put to scorn.

There go the loves that wither,
  The old loves with wearier wings;
And all dead years draw thither,
  And all disastrous things;
Dead dreams of days forsaken,
Blind buds that snows have shaken,
Wild leaves that winds have taken,
  Red strays of ruined springs.

We are not sure of sorrow,
  And joy was never sure;
To-day will die to-morrow;
  Time stoops to no man's lure;
And love, grown faint and fretful,
With lips but half regretful
Sighs, and with eyes forgetful
  Weeps that no loves endure.

From too much love of living,
  From hope and fear set free,
We thank with brief thanksgiving
  Whatever gods may be
That no life lives for ever;
That dead men rise up never;
That even the weariest river
  Winds somewhere safe to sea.

Then star nor sun shall waken,
  Nor any change of light:

60

70

80

90

Nor sound of waters shaken,
   Nor any sound or sight:
Nor wintry leaves nor vernal,
Nor days nor things diurnal;
Only the sleep eternal
   In an eternal night.

[1866]

PRELUDE

BETWEEN the green bud and the red
Youth sat and sang by Time, and shed
   From eyes and tresses flowers and tears,
   From heart and spirit hopes and fears,
Upon the hollow stream whose bed
   Is channelled by the foamless years;
And with the white the gold-haired head
   Mixed running locks, and in Time's ears
Youth's dreams hung singing, and Time's truth
Was half not harsh in the ears of Youth.   10

Between the bud and the blown flower
Youth talked with joy and grief an hour,
   With footless joy and wingless grief
   And twin-born faith and disbelief
Who share the seasons to devour;
   And long ere these made up their sheaf
Felt the winds round him shake and shower
   The rose-red and the blood-red leaf,
Delight whose germ grew never grain,
And passion dyed in its own pain.   20

Then he stood up, and trod to dust
Fear and desire, mistrust and trust,
   And dreams of bitter sleep and sweet,
   And bound for sandals on his feet
Knowledge and patience of what must
   And what things may be, in the heat
And cold of years that rot and rust
   And alter; and his spirit's meat
Was freedom, and his staff was wrought
Of strength, and his cloak woven of thought.   30

For what has he whose will sees clear
To do with doubt and faith and fear,
   Swift hopes and slow despondencies?
   His heart is equal with the sea's
And with the sea-wind's, and his ear
   Is level to the speech of these,
And his soul communes and takes cheer
   With the actual earth's equalities,
Air, light, and night, hills, winds, and streams,
And seeks not strength from strengthless dreams.   **40**

His soul is even with the sun
Whose spirit and whose eye are one,
   Who seeks not stars by day, nor light
   And heavy heat of day by night.
Him can no God cast down, whom none
   Can lift in hope beyond the height
Of fate and nature and things done
   By the calm rule of might and right
That bids men be and bear and do,
And die beneath blind skies or blue.   **50**

To him the lights of even and morn
Speak no vain things of love or scorn,
   Fancies and passions miscreate
   By man in things dispassionate.
Nor holds he fellowship forlorn
   With souls that pray and hope and hate,
And doubt they had better not been born,
   And fain would lure or scare off fate
And charm their doomsman from their doom
And make fear dig its own false tomb.   **60**

He builds not half of doubts and half
Of dreams his own soul's cenotaph,
   Whence hopes and fears with helpless eyes,
   Wrapt loose in cast-off cerecloths, rise
And dance and wring their hands and laugh,
   And weep thin tears and sigh light sighs,
And without living lips would quaff
   The living spring in man that lies,
And drain his soul of faith and strength
It might have lived on a life's length.   **70**

He hath given himself and hath not sold
To God for heaven or man for gold,
 Or grief for comfort that it gives,
 Or joy for grief's restoratives.
He hath given himself to time, whose fold
 Shuts in the mortal flock that lives
On its plain pasture's heat and cold
 And the equal year's alternatives.
Earth, heaven, and time, death, life, and he,
Endure while they shall be to be. *(Stoic)*   80

"Yet between death and life are hours
To flush with love and hide in flowers;
 What profit save in these?" men cry:
 "Ah, see, between soft earth and sky,
What only good things here are ours!"
 They say, "what better wouldst thou try,
What sweeter sing of? or what powers
 Serve, that will give thee ere thou die
More joy to sing and be less sad,
More heart to play and grow more glad?"   90

Play then and sing; we too have played,
We likewise, in that subtle shade.
 We too have twisted through our hair
 Such tendrils as the wild Loves wear,
And heard what mirth the Mænads made,
 Till the wind blew our garlands bare
And left their roses disarrayed,
 And smote the summer with strange air,
And disengirdled and discrowned
The limbs and locks that vine-wreaths bound.   100

We too have tracked by star-proof trees
The tempest of the Thyiades *(Closes off stars)*
 Scare the loud night on hills that hid
 The blood-feasts of the Bassarid,
Heard their song's iron cadences
 Fright the wolf hungering from the kid,
Outroar the lion-throated seas,
 Outchide the north-wind if it chid,
And hush the torrent-tongued ravines
With thunders of their tambourines.   110

But the fierce flute whose notes acclaim
Dim goddesses of fiery fame,
    Cymbal and clamorous kettledrum,
    Timbrels and tabrets, all are dumb
That turned the high chill air to flame;
    The singing tongues of fire are numb
That called on Cotys by her name
    Edonian, till they felt her come
And maddened, and her mystic face
Lightened along the streams of Thrace.   120

For Pleasure slumberless and pale,
And Passion with rejected veil,
    Pass, and the tempest-footed throng
    Of hours that follow them with song
Till their feet flag and voices fail,
    And lips that were so loud so long
Learn silence, or a wearier wail;
    So keen is change, and time so strong,
To weave the robes of life and rend
And weave again till life have end.   130

But weak is change, but strengthless time,
To take the light from heaven, or climb
    The hills of heaven with wasting feet.
    Songs they can stop that earth found meet,
But the stars keep their ageless rhyme;
    Flowers they can slay that spring thought sweet,
But the stars keep their spring sublime;
    Passions and pleasures can defeat,
Actions and agonies control,
And life and death, but not the soul.   140

Because man's soul is man's God still,
What wind soever waft his will
    Across the waves of day and night
    To port or shipwreck, left or right,
By shores and shoals of good and ill;
    And still its flame at mainmast height
Through the rent air that foam-flakes fill
    Sustains the indomitable light
Whence only man hath strength to steer
Or helm to handle without fear.   150

Save his own soul's light overhead,
None leads him, and none ever led,
 Across birth's hidden harbour-bar,
 Past youth where shoreward shallows are,
Through age that drives on toward the red
 Vast void of sunset hailed from far,
To the equal waters of the dead;
 Save his own soul he hath no star,
And sinks, except his own soul guide,
Helmless in middle turn of tide.   160

No blast of air or fire of sun
Puts out the light whereby we run
 With girded loins our lamplit race,
 And each from each takes heart of grace
And spirit till his turn be done,
 And light of face from each man's face
In whom the light of trust is one;
 Since only souls that keep their place
By their own light, and watch things roll,
And stand, have light for any soul.   170

A little time we gain from time
To set our seasons in some chime,
 For harsh or sweet or loud or low,
 With seasons played out long ago
And souls that in their time and prime
 Took part with summer or with snow,
Lived abject lives out or sublime,
 And had their chance of seed to sow
For service or disservice done
To those days dead and this their son.   180

A little time that we may fill
Or with such good works or such ill
 As loose the bonds or make them strong
 Wherein all manhood suffers wrong.
By rose-hung river and light-foot rill
 There are who rest not; who think long
Till they discern as from a hill
 At the sun's hour of morning song,
Known of souls only, and those souls free,
The sacred spaces of the sea.   190

[1871]

HERTHA *define force*

I AM that which began;
  Out of me the years roll;
Out of me God and man;
  I am equal and whole;
God changes, and man, and the form of them bodily; I am the soul.

  Before ever land was,
    Before ever the sea,
  Or soft hair of the grass,   *Genesis*
    Or fair limbs of the tree,   *Jo 40L:37*
Or the flesh-coloured fruits of my branches, I was, and thy soul was
  in me.   10

  First life on my sources
    First drifted and swam;
  Out of me are the forces
    That save it or damn;
Out of me man and woman, and wild-beast and bird; before God was,
  I am.

  Beside or above me
    Nought is there to go;   *nothing else*
  Love or unlove me,
    Unknow me or know,
I am that which unloves me and loves; I am stricken, and I am the
  blow.   20

  I the mark that is missed
    And the arrows that miss,
  I the mouth that is kissed
    And the breath in the kiss,
The search, and the sought, and the seeker, the soul and the body
  that is.

  I am that thing which blesses
    My spirit elate;
  That which caresses
    With hands uncreate
My limbs unbegotten that measure the length of the measure of
  fate.   30

But what thing dost thou now,
  Looking Godward, to cry
"I am I, thou art thou,
  I am <u>low</u>, thou art <u>high</u>"?
I am thou, whom thou seekest to find him; find thou but thyself, thou
  art I.

I the grain and the furrow,
  The plough-cloven clod
And the ploughshare drawn thorough,
  The germ and the sod,
The deed and the doer, the seed and the sower, the dust which is
  God.   40

Hast thou known how I fashioned thee,
  Child, underground?
Fire that impassioned thee,
  Iron that bound,
Dim changes of water, what thing of all these hast thou known of or
  found?

Canst thou say in thine heart
  Thou hast seen with thine eyes
With what cunning of art
  Thou wast wrought in what wise,
By what force of what stuff thou wast shapen, and shown on my breast
  to the skies?   50

Who hath given, who hath sold it thee,
  Knowledge of me?
Hath the wilderness told it thee?
  Hast thou learnt of the sea?
Hast thou communed in spirit with night? have the winds taken
  counsel with thee?

Have I set such a star
  To show light on thy brow
That thou sawest from afar
  What I show to thee now?
Have ye spoken as brethren together, the sun and the mountains and
  thou?   60

What is here, dost thou know it?
  What was, hast thou known?

Prophet nor poet
Nor tripod nor throne
Nor spirit nor flesh can make answer, but only thy mother alone.

Mother, not maker,
Born, and not made;
Though her children forsake her,
Allured or afraid,
Praying prayers to the God of their fashion, she stirs not for all that
have prayed.   70

A creed is a rod,
And a crown is of night;
But this thing is God,
To be man with thy might,
To grow straight in the strength of thy spirit, and live out thy life as
the light.

I am in thee to save thee,
As my soul in thee saith;
Give thou as I gave thee,
Thy life-blood and breath,
Green leaves of thy labour, white flowers of thy thought, and red fruit
of thy death.   80

Be the ways of thy giving
As mine were to thee;
The free life of thy living,
Be the gift of it free;
Not as servant to lord, nor as master to slave, shalt thou give thee to me.

O children of banishment,
Souls overcast,
Were the lights ye see vanish meant
Alway to last,
Ye would know not the sun overshining the shadows and stars over-
past.   90

I that saw where ye trod
The dim paths of the night
Set the shadow called God
In your skies to give light;
But the morning of manhood is risen, and the shadowless soul is in
sight.

The tree many-rooted
    That swells to the sky
With frondage red-fruited,
    The life-tree am I; (Yggdrasil)
In the buds of your lives is the sap of my leaves: ye shall live and
    not die.   100

But the Gods of your fashion (destroy)
    That take and that give,
In their pity and passion
    That scourge and forgive,
They are worms that are bred in the bark that falls off; they shall die
    and not live.

My own blood is what stanches
    The wounds in my bark;
Stars caught in my branches
    Make day of the dark,
And are worshipped as suns till the sunrise shall tread out their fires
    as a spark.   110

Where dead ages hide under
    The live roots of the tree,
In my darkness the thunder
    Makes utterance of me;
In the clash of my boughs with each other ye hear the waves sound of
    the sea.

That noise is of Time,
    As his feathers are spread
And his feet set to climb
    Through the boughs overhead,
And my foliage rings round him and rustles, and branches are bent
    with his tread.   120

The storm-winds of ages
    Blow through me and cease,
The war-wind that rages,
    The spring-wind of peace,
Ere the breath of them roughen my tresses, ere one of my blossoms
    increase.

All sounds of all changes,
    All shadows and lights

On the world's mountain-ranges
And stream-riven heights,
Whose tongue is the wind's tongue and language of storm-clouds on
earth-shaking mights;   130

All forms of all faces,
All works of all hands
In unsearchable places
Of time-stricken lands,
All death and all life, and all reigns and all ruins, drop through me as
sands.

Though sore be my burden
And more than ye know,
And my growth have no guerdon
But only to grow,
Yet I fail not of growing for lightnings above me or death-worms
below.   140

These too have their part in me,
As I too in these;
Such fire is at heart in me,
Such sap is this tree's,
Which hath in it all sounds and all secrets of infinite lands and of seas.

In the spring-coloured hours
When my mind was as May's,
There brake forth of me flowers
By centuries of days,
Strong blossoms with perfume of manhood, shot out from my spirit as
rays.   150

And the sound of them springing
And smell of their shoots
Were as warmth and sweet singing
And strength to my roots;
And the lives of my children made perfect with freedom of soul were
my fruits.

I bid you but be;
I have need not of prayer;
I have need of you free
As your mouths of mine air;
That my heart may be greater within me, beholding the fruits of me
fair.   160

More fair than strange fruit is
 Of faiths ye espouse;
In me only the root is
 That blooms in your boughs;
Behold now your God that ye made you, to feed him with faith of your
 vows.

In the darkening and whitening
 Abysses adored,
With dayspring and lightning
 For lamp and for sword,
God thunders in heaven, and his angels are red with the wrath of the
 Lord.   170

O my sons, O too dutiful
 Toward Gods not of me,
Was not I enough beautiful?
 Was it hard to be free?
For behold, I am with you, am in you and of you; look forth now and
 see.

Lo, winged with world's wonders,
 With miracles shod,
With the fires of his thunders
 For raiment and rod,
God trembles in heaven, and his angels are white with the terror of
 God.   180

For his twilight is come on him,
 His anguish is here;
And his spirits gaze dumb on him,
 Grown grey from his fear;
And his hour taketh hold on him stricken, the last of his infinite year.

Thought made him and breaks him,
 Truth slays and forgives;
But to you, as time takes him,
 This new thing it gives,
Even love, the beloved Republic, that feeds upon freedom and
 lives.   190

For truth only is living,
 Truth only is whole,

And the love of his giving
      Man's polestar and pole;
Man, pulse of my centre, and fruit of my body, and seed of my soul.

One birth of my bosom;
      One beam of mine eye;
One topmost blossom
      That scales the sky;
Man, equal and one with me, man that is made of me, man that is I. 200

[1871]

GENESIS

IN the outer world that was before this earth,
      That was before all shape or space was born,
Before the blind first hour of time had birth,
      Before night knew the moonlight or the morn;

Yea, before any world had any light,
      Or anything called God or man drew breath, *life force*
Slowly the strong sides of the heaving night
      Moved, and brought forth the strength of life and death.

And the sad shapeless horror increate
      That was all things and one thing, without fruit,   10
Limit, or law; where love was none, nor hate,
      Where no leaf came to blossom from no root;

The very darkness that time knew not of,
      Nor God laid hand on, nor was man found there,
Ceased, and was cloven in several shapes; above
      Light, and night under, and fire, earth, water, and air.

Sunbeams and starbeams, and all coloured things,
      All forms and all similitudes began;
And death, the shadow cast by life's wide wings,
      And God, the shade cast by the soul of man.   20

Then between shadow and substance, night and light,
      Then between birth and death, and deeds and days,
The illimitable embrace and the amorous fight
      That of itself begets, bears, rears, and slays,

The immortal war of mortal things, that is
    Labour and life and growth and good and ill,
The mild antiphonies that melt and kiss,
    The violent symphonies that meet and kill,

All nature of all things began to be.
    But chiefliest in the spirit (beast or man,
Planet of heaven or blossom of earth or sea)
    The divine contraries of life began.   **30**

For the great labour of growth, being many, is one;
    One thing the white death and the ruddy birth;
The invisible air and the all-beholden sun,
    And barren water and many-childed earth.

And these things are made manifest in men
    From the beginning forth unto this day:
Time writes and life records them, and again
    Death seals them lest the record pass away.   **40**

For if death were not, then should growth not be,
    Change, nor the life of good nor evil things;
Nor were there night at all nor light to see,
    Nor water of sweet nor water of bitter springs.

For in each man and each year that is born
    Are sown the twin seeds of the strong twin powers;
The white seed of the fruitful helpful morn,
    The black seed of the barren hurtful hours.

And he that of the black seed eateth fruit,
    To him the savour as honey shall be sweet;   **50**
And he in whom the white seed hath struck root,
    He shall have sorrow and trouble and tears for meat.

And him whose lips the sweet fruit hath made red
    In the end men loathe and make his name a rod;
And him whose mouth on the unsweet fruit hath fed
    In the end men follow and know for very God.

And of these twain, the black seed and the white,
    All things come forth, endured of men and done;
And still the day is great with child of night,
    And still the black night labours with the sun.   **60**

And each man and each year that lives on earth
　　Turns hither or thither, and hence or thence is fed;
And as a man before was from his birth,
　　So shall a man be after among the dead.

[1871]

AVE ATQUE VALE

In Memory of Charles Baudelaire (redeemed)

> Nous devrions pourtant lui porter quelques fleurs;
> Les morts, les pauvres morts, ont de grandes douleurs,
> Et quand Octobre souffle, émondeur des vieux arbres,
> Son vent mélancolique à l'entour de leurs marbres,
> Certe, ils doivent trouver les vivants bien ingrats.
> **Les Fleurs du Mal.**

I

SHALL I strew on thee rose or rue or laurel,
　　Brother, on this that was the veil of thee?
　　Or quiet sea-flower moulded by the sea,
Or simplest growth of meadow-sweet or sorrel,
　　Such as the summer-sleepy Dryads weave,
　　Waked up by snow-soft sudden rains at eve?
Or wilt thou rather, as on earth before,
　　Half-faded fiery blossoms, pale with heat
　　And full of bitter summer, but more sweet
To thee than gleanings of a northern shore   10
　　Trod by no tropic feet?

II

For always thee the fervid languid glories
　　Allured of heavier suns in mightier skies;
　　Thine ears knew all the wandering watery sighs
Where the sea sobs round Lesbian promontories,
　　The barren kiss of piteous wave to wave
　　That knows not where is that Leucadian grave
Which hides too deep the supreme head of song.
　　Ah, salt and sterile as her kisses were,
　　The wild sea winds her and the green gulfs bear   20
Hither and thither, and vex and work her wrong,
　　Blind gods that cannot spare.

III

Thou sawest, in thine old singing season, brother,
　　Secrets and sorrows unbeheld of us:

Fierce loves, and lovely leaf-buds poisonous,
Bare to thy subtler eye, but for none other
    Blowing by night in some unbreathed-in clime;
    The hidden harvest of luxurious time,
Sin without shape, and pleasure without speech;
    And where strange dreams in a tumultuous sleep   30
    Make the shut eyes of stricken spirits weep;
And with each face thou sawest the shadow on each,
    Seeing as men sow men reap.

IV

O sleepless heart and sombre soul unsleeping,
    That were athirst for sleep and no more life
    And no more love, for peace and no more strife!
Now the dim gods of death have in their keeping
    Spirit and body and all the springs of song,
    Is it well now where love can do no wrong,
Where stingless pleasure has no foam or fang   40
    Behind the unopening closure of her lips?
    Is it not well where soul from body slips
And flesh from bone divides without a pang
    As dew from flower-bell drips?

V

It is enough; the end and the beginning
    Are one thing to thee, who art past the end.
    O hand unclasped of unbeholden friend,
For thee no fruits to pluck, no palms for winning,
    No triumph and no labour and no lust,
    Only dead yew-leaves and a little dust.   50
O quiet eyes wherein the light saith nought,
    Whereto the day is dumb, nor any night
    With obscure finger silences your sight,
Nor in your speech the sudden soul speaks thought,
    Sleep, and have sleep for light.

VI

Now all strange hours and all strange loves are over,
    Dreams and desires and sombre songs and sweet,
    Hast thou found place at the great knees and feet
Of some pale Titan-woman like a lover,
    Such as thy vision here solicited,   60
    Under the shadow of her fair vast head,
The deep division of prodigious breasts,

The solemn slope of mighty limbs asleep,
The weight of awful tresses that still keep
The savour and shade of old-world pine-forests
   Where the wet hill-winds weep?

VII

Hast thou found any likeness for thy vision?
   O gardener of strange flowers, what bud, what bloom,
   Hast thou found sown, what gathered in the gloom?
What of despair, of rapture, of derision,   70
   What of life is there, what of ill or good?
   Are the fruits grey like dust or bright like blood?
Does the dim ground grow any seed of ours,
   The faint fields quicken any terrene root,
   In low lands where the sun and moon are mute
And all the stars keep silence? Are there flowers
   At all, or any fruit?

VIII

Alas, but though my flying song flies after,
   O sweet strange elder singer, thy more fleet
   Singing, and footprints of thy fleeter feet,   80
Some dim derision of mysterious laughter
   From the blind tongueless warders of the dead,
   Some gainless glimpse of Proserpine's veiled head,
Some little sound of unregarded tears
   Wept by effaced unprofitable eyes,
   And from pale mouths some cadence of dead sighs —
These only, these the hearkening spirit hears,
   Sees only such things rise.

IX

Thou art far too far for wings of words to follow,
   Far too far off for thought or any prayer.   90
   What ails us with thee, who art wind and air?
What ails us gazing where all seen is hollow?
   Yet with some fancy, yet with some desire,
   Dreams pursue death as winds a flying fire,
Our dreams pursue our dead and do not find.
   Still, and more swift than they, the thin flame flies,
   The low light fails us in elusive skies,
Still the foiled earnest ear is deaf, and blind
   Are still the eluded eyes.

corporeal bond.

X

Not thee, O never thee, in all time's changes,   100
   Not thee, but this the sound of thy sad soul,
   The shadow of thy swift spirit, this shut scroll
I lay my hand on, and not death estranges
   My spirit from communion of thy song —
   These memories and these melodies that throng
Veiled porches of a Muse funereal —
   These I salute, these touch, these clasp and fold
   As though a hand were in my hand to hold,
Or through mine ears a mourning musical
   Of many mourners rolled.   110

Think about to where he is to reconcile enormous loss.

XI

I among these, I also, in such station
   As when the pyre was charred, and piled the sods,
   And offering to the dead made, and their gods,
The old mourners had, standing to make libation,
   I stand, and to the gods and to the dead
   Do reverence without prayer or praise, and shed
Offering to these unknown, the gods of gloom,
   And what of honey and spice my seedlands bear,
   And what I may of fruits in this chilled air,
And lay, Orestes-like, across the tomb   120
   A curl of severed hair.

XII

But by no hand nor any treason stricken,
   Not like the low-lying head of Him, the King,
   The flame that made of Troy a ruinous thing,
Thou liest, and on this dust no tears could quicken
   There fall no tears like theirs that all men hear
   Fall tear by sweet imperishable tear
Down the opening leaves of holy poets' pages.
   Thee not Orestes, not Electra mourns;
   But bending us-ward with memorial urns   130
The most high Muses that fulfil all ages
   Weep, and our God's heart yearns.

XIII

For, sparing of his sacred strength, not often
   Among us darkling here the lord of light
   Makes manifest his music and his might
In hearts that open and in lips that soften

With the soft flame and heat of songs that shine.
Thy lips indeed he touched with bitter wine,
And nourished them indeed with bitter bread;
Yet surely from his hand thy soul's food came,   140
The fire that scarred thy spirit at his flame
Was lighted, and thine hungering heart he fed
Who feeds our hearts with fame.

XIV

Therefore he too now at thy soul's sunsetting,
God of all suns and songs, he too bends down
To mix his laurel with thy cypress crown,
And save thy dust from blame and from forgetting.
Therefore he too, seeing all thou wert and art,
Compassionate, with sad and sacred heart,
Mourns thee of many his children the last dead,   150
And hallows with strange tears and alien sighs
Thine unmelodious mouth and sunless eyes,
And over thine irrevocable head
Sheds light from the under skies.

XV

And one weeps with him in the ways Lethean,
And stains with tears her changing bosom chill:
That obscure Venus of the hollow hill,
That thing transformed which was the Cytherean,
With lips that lost their Grecian laugh divine
Long since, and face no more called Erycine;   160
A ghost, a bitter and luxurious god.
Thee also with fair flesh and singing spell
Did she, a sad and second prey, compel
Into the footless places once more trod,
And shadows hot from hell.

XVI

And now no sacred staff shall break in blossom,
No choral salutation lure to light
A spirit sick with perfume and sweet night
And love's tired eyes and hands and barren bosom.
There is no help for these things; none to mend   170
And none to mar; not all our songs, O friend,
Will make death clear or make life durable.
Howbeit with rose and ivy and wild vine
And with wild notes about this dust of thine

At least I fill the place where white dreams dwell
   And wreathe an unseen shrine.] *making religion (sanctuary)*
                                               out of poetry

XVII

Sleep; and if life was bitter to thee, pardon,
   If sweet, give thanks; thou hast no more to live;
   And to give thanks is good, and to forgive.
Out of the mystic and the mournful garden   180
   Where all day through thine hands in barren braid
   Wove the sick flowers of secrecy and shade,
Green buds of sorrow and sin, and remnants grey,
   Sweet-smelling, pale with poison, sanguine-hearted,
   Passions that sprang from sleep and thoughts that started,
Shall death not bring us all as thee one day
   Among the days departed?

XVIII

For thee, O now a silent soul, my brother,
   Take at my hands this garland, and farewell.
   Thin is the leaf, and chill the wintry smell,   190
And chill the solemn earth, a fatal mother,
   With sadder than the Niobean womb,
   And in the hollow of her breasts a tomb.
Content thee, howsoe'er, whose days are done;
   There lies not any troublous thing before,
   Nor sight nor sound to war against thee more,
For whom all winds are quiet as the sun,
   All waters as the shore.

                                 [*1868;* 1878]

SONNET

With a copy of "Mademoiselle de Maupin"

This is the golden book of spirit and sense,
   The holy writ of beauty; he that wrought
   Made it with dreams and faultless words and thought
That seeks and finds and loses in the dense
Dim air of life that beauty's excellence
   Wherewith love makes one hour of life distraught
   And all hours after follow and find not aught.
Here is that height of all love's eminence
Where man may breathe but for a breathing-space

And feel his soul burn as an altar-fire 10
To the unknown God of unachieved desire,
And from the middle mystery of the place
Watch lights that break, hear sounds as of a quire,
But see not twice unveiled the veiled God's face.

[1873; 1878]

A FORSAKEN GARDEN

In a coign of the cliff between lowland and highland,
At the sea-down's edge between windward and lee,
Walled round with rocks as an inland island,
The ghost of a garden fronts the sea.
A girdle of brushwood and thorn encloses
The steep square slope of the blossomless bed
Where the weeds that grew green from the graves of its roses
Now lie dead.

The fields fall southward, abrupt and broken,
To the low last edge of the long lone land. 10
If a step should sound or a word be spoken,
Would a ghost not rise at the strange guest's hand?
So long have the grey bare walks lain guestless,
Through branches and briars if a man make way,
He shall find no life but the sea-wind's, restless
Night and day.

The dense hard passage is blind and stifled
That crawls by a track none turn to climb
To the strait waste place that the years have rifled
Of all but the thorns that are touched not of time. 20
The thorns he spares when the rose is taken;
The rocks are left when he wastes the plain.
The wind that wanders, the weeds wind-shaken,
These remain.

Not a flower to be pressed of the foot that falls not;
As the heart of a dead man the seed-plots are dry;
From the thicket of thorns whence the nightingale calls not,
Could she call, there were never a rose to reply.
Over the meadows that blossom and wither
Rings but the note of a sea-bird's song; 30

Only the sun and the rain come hither
    All year long.

The sun burns sere and the rain dishevels
    One gaunt bleak blossom of scentless breath.
Only the wind here hovers and revels
    In a round where life seems barren as death.
Here there was laughing of old, there was weeping,
    Haply, of lovers none ever will know,
Whose eyes went seaward a hundred sleeping
    Years ago.   40

Heart handfast in heart as they stood, "Look thither,"
    Did he whisper? "look forth from the flowers to the sea;
For the foam-flowers endure when the rose-blossoms wither,
    And men that love lightly may die — but we?"
And the same wind sang and the same waves whitened,
    And or ever the garden's last petals were shed,
In the lips that had whispered, the eyes that had lightened,
    Love was dead.

Or they loved their life through, and then went whither?
    And were one to the end — but what end who knows?   50
Love deep as the sea as a rose must wither,
    As the rose-red seaweed that mocks the rose.
Shall the dead take thought for the dead to love them?
    What love was ever as deep as a grave?
They are loveless now as the grass above them
    Or the wave.

All are at one now, roses and lovers,
    Not known of the cliffs and the fields and the sea.
Not a breath of the time that has been hovers
    In the air now soft with a summer to be.   60
Not a breath shall there sweeten the seasons hereafter
    Of the flowers or the lovers that laugh now or weep,
When as they that are free now of weeping and laughter
    We shall sleep.

Here death may deal not again for ever;
    Here change may come not till all change end.
From the graves they have made they shall rise up never,
    Who have left nought living to ravage and rend.
Earth, stones, and thorns of the wild ground growing,

While the sun and the rain live, these shall be;   70
Till a last wind's breath upon all these blowing
    Roll the sea.

Till the slow sea rise and the sheer cliff crumble,
    Till terrace and meadow the deep gulfs drink,
Till the strength of the waves of the high tides humble
    The fields that lessen, the rocks that shrink,
Here now in his triumph where all things falter,
    Stretched out on the spoils that his own hand spread,
As a god self-slain on his own strange altar,
      Death lies dead.   80

                [*1876; 1878*]

A VISION OF SPRING IN WINTER

I

O TENDER time that love thinks long to see,
    Sweet foot of spring that with her footfall sows
    Late snowlike flowery leavings of the snows,
Be not too long irresolute to be;
    O mother-month, where have they hidden thee?
    Out of the pale time of the flowerless rose
I reach my heart out toward the springtime lands,
    I stretch my spirit forth to the fair hours,
      The purplest of the prime;
I lean my soul down over them, with hands   10
    Made wide to take the ghostly growths of flowers;
      I send my love back to the lovely time.

II

Where has the greenwood hid thy gracious head?
    Veiled with what visions while the grey world grieves,
    Or muffled with what shadows of green leaves,
What warm intangible green shadows spread
To sweeten the sweet twilight for thy bed?
    What sleep enchants thee? what delight deceives?
Where the deep dreamlike dew before the dawn
    Feels not the fingers of the sunlight yet   20
      Its silver web unweave,
Thy footless ghost on some unfooted lawn
    Whose air the unrisen sunbeams fear to fret
      Lives a ghost's life of daylong dawn and eve.

III

Sunrise it sees not, neither set of star,
  Large nightfall, nor imperial plenilune,
  Nor strong sweet shape of the full-breasted noon;
But where the silver-sandalled shadows are,
Too soft for arrows of the sun to mar,
  Moves with the mild gait of an ungrown moon: 30
Hard overhead the half-lit crescent swims,
  The tender-coloured night draws hardly breath,
      The light is listening;
They watch the dawn of slender-shapen limbs,
  Virginal, born again of doubtful death,
      Chill foster-father of the weanling spring.

IV

As sweet desire of day before the day,
  As dreams of love before the true love born,
  From the outer edge of winter overworn
The ghost arisen of May before the May   40
Takes through dim air her unawakened way,
  The gracious ghost of morning risen ere morn.
With little unblown breasts and child-eyed looks
  Following, the very maid, the girl-child spring,
      Lifts windward her bright brows,
Dips her light feet in warm and moving brooks,
  And kindles with her own mouth's colouring
      The fearful firstlings of the plumeless boughs.

V

I seek thee sleeping, and awhile I see,
  Fair face that art not, how thy maiden breath   50
  Shall put at last the deadly days to death
And fill the fields and fire the woods with thee
And seaward hollows where my feet would be
  When heaven shall hear the word that April saith
To change the cold heart of the weary time,
  To stir and soften all the time to tears,
      Tears joyfuller than mirth;
As even to May's clear height the young days climb
  With feet not swifter than those fair first years
      Whose flowers revive not with thy flowers on earth.   60

VI

I would not bid thee, though I might, give back
  One good thing youth has given and borne away;

I crave not any comfort of the day
That is not, nor on time's retrodden track
Would turn to meet the white-robed hours or black
    That long since left me on their mortal way;
Nor light nor love that has been, nor the breath
    That comes with morning from the sun to be
        And sets light hope on fire;
No fruit, no flower thought once too fair for death,   70
    No flower nor hour once fallen from life's green tree,
        No leaf once plucked or once fulfilled desire.

VII

The morning song beneath the stars that fled
    With twilight through the moonless mountain air,
    While youth with burning lips and wreathless hair
Sang toward the sun that was to crown his head,
Rising; the hopes that triumphed and fell dead,
    The sweet swift eyes and songs of hours that were;
These may'st thou not give back for ever; these,
    As at the sea's heart all her wrecks lie waste,   80
        Lie deeper than the sea;
But flowers thou may'st, and winds, and hours of ease,
    And all its April to the world thou may'st
        Give back, and half my April back to me.

[1875; 1878]

A BALLAD OF DREAMLAND

I HID my heart in a nest of roses,
    Out of the sun's way, hidden apart;
In a softer bed than the soft white snow's is,
    Under the roses I hid my heart.
    Why would it sleep not? why should it start,
When never a leaf of the rose-tree stirred?
    What made sleep flutter his wings and part?
Only the song of a secret bird.

Lie still, I said, for the wind's wing closes,
    And mild leaves muffle the keen sun's dart;   10
Lie still, for the wind on the warm sea dozes,
    And the wind is unquieter yet than thou art.
    Does a thought in thee still as a thorn's wound smart?

Does the fang still fret thee of hope deferred?
  What bids the lids of thy sleep dispart?
Only the song of a secret bird.

The green land's name that a charm encloses,
  It never was writ in the traveller's chart,
And sweet on its trees as the fruit that grows is,
  It never was sold in the merchant's mart.   20
    The swallows of dreams through its dim fields dart,
And sleep's are the tunes in its tree-tops heard;
    No hound's note wakens the wildwood hart,
Only the song of a secret bird.

Envoi

In the world of dreams I have chosen my part,
  To sleep for a season and hear no word
Of true love's truth or of light love's art,
  Only the song of a secret bird.

[1876; 1878]

A BALLAD OF FRANÇOIS VILLON

Prince of all Ballad-makers

BIRD of the bitter bright grey golden morn
  Scarce risen upon the dusk of dolorous years,
First of us all and sweetest singer born
  Whose far shrill note the world of new men hears
  Cleave the cold shuddering shade as twilight clears;
When song new-born put off the old world's attire
And felt its tune on her changed lips expire,
  Writ foremost on the roll of them that came
Fresh girt for service of the latter lyre,
  Villon, our sad bad glad mad brother's name!   10

Alas the joy, the sorrow, and the scorn,
  That clothed thy life with hopes and sins and fears,
And gave thee stones for bread and tares for corn
  And plume-plucked gaol-birds for thy starveling peers
  Till death clipt close their flight with shameful shears;
Till shifts came short and loves were hard to hire,
When lilt of song nor twitch of twangling wire
  Could buy thee bread or kisses; when light fame

Spurned like a ball and haled through brake and briar,
  Villon, our sad bad glad mad brother's name!   **20**

Poor splendid wings so frayed and soiled and torn!
  Poor kind wild eyes so dashed with light quick tears!
Poor perfect voice, most blithe when most forlorn,
    That rings athwart the sea whence no man steers
    Like joy-bells crossed with death-bells in our ears!
What far delight has cooled the fierce desire
That like some ravenous bird was strong to tire
    On that frail flesh and soul consumed with flame,
But left more sweet than roses to respire,
  Villon, our sad bad glad mad brother's name?   **30**

          Envoi

Prince of sweet songs made out of tears and fire,
A harlot was thy nurse, a God thy sire;
  Shame soiled thy song, and song assoiled thy shame.
But from thy feet now death has washed the mire,
Love reads out first at head of all our quire,
  Villon, our sad bad glad mad brother's name.

                          [1877; 1878]

THE BALLAD OF VILLON AND FAT MADGE

    'Tis no sin for a man to labour in his vocation. — FALSTAFF.
        The night cometh, when no man can work.

WHAT though the beauty I love and serve be cheap,
  Ought you to take me for a beast or fool?
All things a man could wish are in her keep;
    For her I turn swashbuckler in love's school.
    When folk drop in, I take my pot and stool
And fall to drinking with no more ado.
I fetch them bread, fruit, cheese, and water, too;
  I say all's right so long as I'm well paid;
"Look in again when your flesh troubles you,
  Inside this brothel where we drive our trade."   **10**

But soon the devil's among us flesh and fell,
  When penniless to bed comes Madge my whore;
I loathe the very sight of her like hell.
  I snatch gown, girdle, surcoat, all she wore,
  And tell her, these shall stand against her score.

She grips her hips with both hands, cursing God,
Swearing by Jesus' body, bones, and blood,
   That they shall not. Then I, no whit dismayed,
Cross her cracked nose with some stray shiver of wood
   Inside this brothel where we drive our trade.   **20**

When all's made up she drops me a windy word,
   Bloat like a beetle puffed and poisonous:
Grins, thumps my pate, and calls me dickey-bird,
   And cuffs me with a fist that's ponderous.
   We sleep like logs, being drunken both of us;
Then when we wake her womb begins to stir;
To save her seed she gets me under her
   Wheezing and whining, flat as planks are laid:
And thus she spoils me for a whoremonger
   Inside this brothel where we drive our trade.   **30**

Blow, hail or freeze, I've bread here baked rent-free!
Whoring's my trade, and my whore pleases me;
   Bad cat, bad rat; we're just the same if weighed.
We that love filth, filth follows us, you see;
Honour flees from us, as from her we flee
   Inside this brothel where we drive our trade.

                                [*1910*; 1964]

THE COMPLAINT OF THE FAIR ARMOURESS

1

Meseemeth I heard cry and groan
   That sweet who was the armourer's maid;
For her young years she made sore moan,
   And right upon this wise she said;
   "Ah fierce old age with foul bald head,
To spoil fair things thou art over fain;
   Who holdeth me? who? would God I were dead
Would God I were well dead and slain!

2

"Lo, thou hast broken the sweet yoke
   That my high beauty held above   **10**
All priests and clerks and merchant-folk;
   There was not one but for my love

Would give me gold and gold enough,
Though sorrow his very heart had riven,
To win from me such wage thereof
As now no thief would take if given.

3

"I was right chary of the same,
God wot it was my great folly,
For love of one sly knave of them,
Good store of that same sweet had he;   20
For all my subtle wiles, perdie,
God wot I loved him well enow;
Right evilly he handled me,
But he loved well my gold, I trow.

4

"Though I gat bruises green and black,
I loved him never the less a jot;
Though he bound burdens on my back,
If he said "Kiss me and heed it not"
Right little pain I felt, God wot,
When that foul thief's mouth, found so sweet,   30
Kissed me — Much good thereof I got!
I keep the sin and the shame of it.

5

"And he died thirty year agone.
I am old now, no sweet thing to see;
By God, though, when I think thereon,
And of that good glad time, woe's me,
And stare upon my changed body
Stark naked, that has been so sweet,
Lean, wizen, like a small dry tree,
I am nigh mad with the pain of it.   40

6

"Where is my faultless forehead's white
The lifted eyebrows, soft gold hair,
Eyes wide apart and keen of sight,
With subtle skill in the amorous air;
The straight nose, great nor small, but fair,
The small carved ears of shapeliest growth,
Chin dimpling, colour good to wear,
And sweet red splendid kissing mouth?

7

"The shapely slender shoulders small,
  Long arms, hands wrought in glorious wise,   50
Round little breasts, the hips withal
  High, full of flesh, not scant of size,
  Fit for all amorous masteries;
The large loins and the flower that was
  Planted above my strong, round thighs
In a small garden of soft grass?

8

"A writhled forehead, hair gone grey,
  Fallen eyebrows, eyes gone blind and red,
Their laughs and looks all fled away,
  Yea, all that smote mens' hearts are fled;   60
  The bowed nose, fallen from goodlihead;
Foul flapping ears like water-flags;
  Peaked chin, and cheeks all waste and dead,
And lips that are two skinny rags:

9

"Thus endeth all the beauty of us.
  The arms made short, the hands made lean,
The shoulders bowed and ruinous,
  The breasts, alack! all fallen in;
  The flanks too, like the breasts, grown thin
As for the sweet place, out on it!   70
  For the lank thighs, no thighs but skin,
They are specked with spots like sausage-meat.

10

"So we make moan for the old sweet days,
  Poor old light women, two or three
Squatting about the straw-fire's blaze,
  The bosom crushed against the knee,
  Like fagots on a heap we be,
Round fires soon lit, soon quenched and done;
  And we were once so sweet, even we!
Thus fareth many and many an one."   80

[1878]

love, hate, hope & fear
apollo & Cymothoe
give birth to Thal.
creative

THALASSIUS

UPON the flowery forefront of the year,
One wandering by the grey-green April sea
Found on a reach of shingle and shallower sand
Inlaid with starrier glimmering jewellery
Left for the sun's love and the light wind's cheer
Along the foam-flowered strand
Breeze-brightened, something nearer sea than land
Though the last shoreward blossom-fringe was near,
A babe asleep with flower-soft face that gleamed
To sun and seaward as it laughed and dreamed,   10
Too sure of either love for either's fear,
Albeit so birdlike slight and light, it seemed
Nor man nor mortal child of man, but fair
As even its twin-born tenderer spray-flowers were,
That the wind scatters like an Oread's hair.

For when July strewed fire on earth and sea
The last time ere that year,
Out of the flame of morn Cymothoe
Beheld one brighter than the sunbright sphere
Move toward her from its fieriest heart, whence trod   20
The live sun's very God,
Across the foam-bright water-ways that are
As heavenlier heavens with star for answering star,
And on her eyes and hair and maiden mouth
Felt a kiss falling fierier than the South
And heard above afar
A noise of songs and wind-enamoured wings
And lutes and lyres of milder and mightier strings,
And round the resonant radiance of his car
Where depth is one with height,   30
Light heard as music, music seen as light.
And with that second moondawn of the spring's
That fosters the first rose,
A sun-child whiter than the sunlit snows
Was born out of the world of sunless things
That round the round earth flows and ebbs and flows.

But he that found the sea-flower by the sea
And took to foster like a graft of earth

Was born of man's most highest and heavenliest birth,
Free-born as winds and stars and waves are free;   40
A warrior grey with glories more than years,
Though more of years than change the quick to dead
Had rained their light and darkness on his head;
A singer that in time's and memory's ears
Should leave such words to sing as all his peers
Might praise with hallowing heat of rapturous tears
Till all the days of human flight were fled.
And at his knees his fosterling was fed
Not with man's wine and bread
Nor mortal mother-milk of hopes and fears,   50
But food of deep memorial days long sped;
For bread with wisdom and with song for wine
Clear as the full calm's emerald hyaline.
And from his grave glad lips the boy would gather
Fine honey of song-notes goldener than gold,
More sweet than bees make of the breathing heather,
That he, as glad and bold,
Might drink as they, and keep his spirit from cold.
And the boy loved his laurel-laden hair
As his own father's risen on the eastern air,   60
And that less white brow-binding bayleaf bloom
More than all flowers his father's eyes relume;
And those high songs he heard,
More than all notes of any landward bird,
More than all sounds less free
Than the wind's quiring to the choral sea.

    High things the high song taught him; how the breath
Too frail for life may be more strong than death;
And this poor flash of sense in life, that gleams
As a ghost's glory in dreams,   70
More stabile than the world's own heart's root seems,
By that strong faith of lordliest love which gives
To death's own sightless-seeming eyes a light
Clearer, to death's bare bones a verier might,
Than shines or strikes from any man that lives.
How he that loves life overmuch shall die
The dog's death, utterly:
And he that much less loves it than he hates
All wrongdoing that is done
Anywhere always underneath the sun   80
Shall live a mightier life than time's or fate's.

One fairer thing he shewed him, and in might
More strong than day and night
Whose strengths build up time's towering period:
Yea, one thing stronger and more high than God,
Which if man had not, then should God not be:
And that was Liberty.
And gladly should man die to gain, he said,
Freedom; and gladlier, having lost, lie dead.
For man's earth was not, nor the sweet sea-waves   90
His, nor his own land, nor its very graves,
Except they bred not, bore not, hid not slaves:
But all of all that is,
Were one man free in body and soul, were his.

And the song softened, even as heaven by night
Softens, from sunnier down to starrier light,
And with its moonbright breath
Blessed life for death's sake, and for life's sake death.
Till as the moon's own beam and breath confuse
In one clear hueless haze of glimmering hues   100
The sea's line and the land's line and the sky's,
And light for love of darkness almost dies,
As darkness only lives for light's dear love,
Whose hands the web of night is woven of,
So in that heaven of wondrous words were life
And death brought out of strife;
Yea, by that strong spell of serene increase
Brought out of strife to peace.

And the song lightened, as the wind at morn
Flashes, and even with lightning of the wind   110
Night's thick-spun web is thinned
And all its weft unwoven and overworn
Shrinks, as might love from scorn.
And as when wind and light on water and land
Leap as twin gods from heavenward hand in hand,
And with the sound and splendour of their leap
Strike darkness dead, and daunt the spirit of sleep,
And burn it up with fire;
So with the light that lightened from the lyre
Was all the bright heat in the child's heart stirred   120
And blown with blasts of music into flame
Till even his sense became
Fire, as the sense that fires the singing bird

Whose song calls night by name.
And in the soul within the sense began
The manlike passion of a godlike man,
And in the sense within the soul again
Thoughts that make men of gods and gods of men.

For love the high song taught him: love that turns
God's heart toward man as man's to Godward; love   **130**
That life and death and life are fashioned of,
From the first breath that burns
Half kindled on the flowerlike yeanling's lip,
So light and faint that life seems like to slip,
To that yet weaklier drawn
When sunset dies of night's devouring dawn.
But the man dying not wholly as all men dies
If aught be left of his in live men's eyes
Out of the dawnless dark of death to rise;
If aught of deed or word   **140**
Be seen for all time or of all time heard.
Love, that though body and soul were overthrown
Should live for love's sake of itself alone,
Though spirit and flesh were one thing doomed and dead,
Not wholly annihilated.
Seeing even the hoariest ash-flake that the pyre
Drops, and forgets the thing was once afire
And gave its heart to feed the pile's full flame
Till its own heart its own heat overcame,
Outlives its own life, though by scarce a span,   **150**
As such men dying outlive themselves in man,
Outlive themselves for ever; if the heat
Outburn the heart that kindled it, the sweet
Outlast the flower whose soul it was, and flit
Forth of the body of it
Into some new shape of a strange perfume
More potent than its light live spirit of bloom,
How shall not something of that soul relive,
That only soul that had such gifts to give
As lighten something even of all men's doom   **160**
Even from the labouring womb
Even to the seal set on the unopening tomb?
And these the loving light of song and love
Shall wrap and lap round and impend above,
Imperishable; and all springs born illume
Their sleep with brighter thoughts than wake the dove

To music, when the hillside winds resume
The marriage-song of heather-flower and broom
And all the joy thereof.

And hate the song too taught him: hate of all   170
That brings or holds in thrall
Of spirit or flesh, freeborn ere God began,
The holy body and sacred soul of man.
And wheresoever a curse was or a chain,
A throne for torment or a crown for bane
Rose, moulded out of poor men's molten pain,
There, said he, should man's heaviest hate be set
Inexorably, to faint not or forget
Till the last warmth bled forth of the last vein
In flesh that none should call a king's again,   180
Seeing wolves and dogs and birds that plague-strike air
Leave the last bone of all the carrion bare.

And hope the high song taught him: hope whose eyes
Can sound the seas unsoundable, the skies
Inaccessible of eyesight; that can see
What earth beholds not, hear what wind and sea
Hear not, and speak what all these crying in one
Can speak not to the sun.
For in her sovereign eyelight all things are
Clear as the closest seen and kindlier star   190
That marries morn and even and winter and spring
With one love's golden ring.
For she can see the days of man, the birth
Of good and death of evil things on earth
Inevitable and infinite, and sure
As present pain is, or herself is pure,
Yea, she can hear and see, beyond all things
That lighten from before Time's thunderous wings
Through the awful circle of wheel-winged periods,
The tempest of the twilight of all Gods: 200
And higher than all the circling course they ran
The sundawn of the spirit that was man.

And fear the song too taught him; fear to be
Worthless the dear love of the wind and sea
That bred him fearless, like a sea-mew reared
In rocks of man's foot feared,
Where nought of wingless life may sing or shine.

Fear to wax worthless of that heaven he had
When all the life in all his limbs was glad
And all the drops in all his veins were wine   210
And all the pulses music; when his heart,
Singing, bade heaven and wind and sea bear part
In one live song's reiterance, and they bore:
Fear to go crownless of the flower he wore
When the winds loved him and the waters knew,
The blithest life that clove their blithe life through
With living limbs exultant, or held strife
More amorous than all dalliance aye anew
With the bright breath and strength of their large life,
With all strong wrath of all sheer winds that blew,   220
All glories of all storms of the air that fell
Prone, ineluctable,
With roar from heaven of revel, and with hue
As of a heaven turned hell.
For when the red blast of their breath had made
All heaven aflush with light more dire than shade,
He felt it in his blood and eyes and hair
Burn as if all the fires of the earth and air
Had laid strong hold upon his flesh, and stung
The soul behind it as with serpent's tongue,   230
Forked like the loveliest lightnings: nor could bear
But hardly, half distraught with strong delight,
The joy that like a garment wrapped him round
And lapped him over and under
With raiment of great light
And rapture of great sound
At every loud leap earthward of the thunder
From heaven's most furthest bound:
So seemed all heaven in hearing and in sight,
Alive and mad with glory and angry joy,   240
That something of its marvellous mirth and might
Moved even to madness, fledged as even for flight,
The blood and spirit of one but mortal boy.

So, clothed with love and fear that love makes great,
And armed with hope and hate,
He set first foot upon the spring-flowered ways
That all feet pass and praise.
And one dim dawn between the winter and spring,
In the sharp harsh wind harrying heaven and earth
To put back April that had borne his birth   250

From sunward on her sunniest shower-struck wing,
With tears and laughter for the dew-dropt thing,
Slight as indeed a dew-drop, by the sea
One met him lovelier than all men may be,
God-featured, with god's eyes; and in their might
Somewhat that drew men's own to mar their sight,
Even of all eyes drawn toward him: and his mouth
Was as the very rose of all men's youth,
One rose of all the rose-beds in the world:
But round his brows the curls were snakes that curled,   260
And like his tongue a serpent's; and his voice
Speaks death, and bids rejoice.
Yet then he spake no word, seeming as dumb,
A dumb thing mild and hurtless; nor at first
From his bowed eyes seemed any light to come,
Nor his meek lips for blood or tears to thirst:
But as one blind and mute in mild sweet wise
Pleading for pity of piteous lips and eyes,
He strayed with faint bare lily-lovely feet
Helpless, and flowerlike sweet: 270
Nor might man see, not having word hereof,
That this of all gods was the great god Love.

And seeing him lovely and like a little child
That wellnigh wept for wonder that it smiled
And was so feeble and fearful, with soft speech
The youth bespake him softly; but there fell
From the sweet lips no sweet word audible
That ear or thought might reach:
No sound to make the dim cold silence glad,
No breath to thaw the hard harsh air with heat;   280
Only the saddest smile of all things sweet,
Only the sweetest smile of all things sad.

And so they went together one green way
Till April dying made free the world for May;
And on his guide suddenly Love's face turned,
And in his blind eyes burned
Hard light and heat of laughter; and like flame
That opens in a mountain's ravening mouth
To blear and sear the sunlight from the south,
His mute mouth opened, and his first word came: 290
"Knowest thou me now by name?"
And all his stature waxed immeasurable,

As of one shadowing heaven and lightening hell;
And statelier stood he than a tower that stands
And darkens with its darkness far-off sands
Whereon the sky leans red;
And with a voice that stilled the winds he said:
"I am he that was thy lord before thy birth,
I am he that is thy lord till thou turn earth:
I make the night more dark, and all the morrow   300
Dark as the night whose darkness was my breath:
O fool, my name is sorrow;
Thou fool, my name is death."

And he that heard spake not, and looked right on
Again, and Love was gone.

Through many a night toward many a wearier day
His spirit bore his body down its way.
Through many a day toward many a wearier night
His soul sustained his sorrows in her sight.
And earth was bitter, and heaven, and even the sea   310
Sorrowful even as he.
And the wind helped not, and the sun was dumb;
And with too long strong stress of grief to be
His heart grew sere and numb.

And one bright eve ere summer in autumn sank
At stardawn standing on a grey sea-bank
He felt the wind fitfully shift and heave
As toward a stormier eve;
And all the wan wide sea shuddered; and earth
Shook underfoot as toward some timeless birth,   320
Intolerable and inevitable; and all
Heaven, darkling, trembled like a stricken thrall.
And far out of the quivering east, and far
From past the moonrise and its guiding star,
Began a noise of tempest and a light
That was not of the lightning; and a sound
Rang with it round and round
That was not of the thunder; and a flight
As of blown clouds by night,
That was not of them; and with songs and cries   330
That sang and shrieked their soul out at the skies
A shapeless earthly storm of shapes began
From all ways round to move in on the man,

Clamorous against him silent; and their feet
Were as the wind's are fleet,
And their shrill songs were as wild birds' are sweet.

And as when all the world of earth was wronged
And all the host of all men driven afoam
By the red hand of Rome,
Round some fierce amphitheatre overthronged   340
With fair clear faces full of bloodlier lust
Than swells and stings the tiger when his mood
Is fieriest after blood
And drunk with trampling of the murderous must
That soaks and stains the tortuous close-coiled wood
Made monstrous with its myriad-mustering brood,
Face by fair face panted and gleamed and pressed,
And breast by passionate breast
Heaved hot with ravenous rapture, as they quaffed
The red ripe full fume of the deep live draught,   350
The sharp quick reek of keen fresh bloodshed, blown
Through the dense deep drift up to the emperor's throne
From the under steaming sands
With clamour of all-applausive throats and hands,
Mingling in mirthful time
With shrill blithe mockeries of the lithe-limbed mime:
So from somewhence far forth of the unbeholden,
Dreadfully driven from over and after and under,
Fierce, blown through fifes of brazen blast and golden,
With sound of chiming waves that drown the thunder   360
Or thunder that strikes dumb the sea's own chimes,
Began the bellowing of the bull-voiced mimes,
Terrible; firs bowed down as briars or palms
Even at the breathless blast as of a breeze
Fulfilled with clamour and clangour and storms of psalms;
Red hands rent up the roots of old-world trees,
Thick flames of torches tossed as tumbling seas
Made mad the moonless and infuriate air
That, ravening, revelled in the riotous hair
And raiment of the furred Bassarides.   370

So came all those in on him; and his heart,
As out of sleep suddenly struck astart,
Danced, and his flesh took fire of theirs, and grief
Was as a last year's leaf
Blown dead far down the wind's way; and he set

His pale mouth to the brightest mouth it met
That laughed for love against his lips, and bade
Follow; and in following all his blood grew glad
And as again a sea-bird's; for the wind
Took him to bathe him deep round breast and brow   380
Not as it takes a dead leaf drained and thinned,
But as the brightest bay-flower blown on bough,
Set springing toward it singing: and they rode
By many a vine-leafed, many a rose-hung road,
Exalt with exultation; many a night
Set all its stars upon them as for spies
On many a moon-bewildering mountain-height
Where he rode only by the fierier light
Of his dread lady's hot sweet hungering eyes.
For the moon wandered witless of her way,   390
Spell-stricken by strong magic in such wise
As wizards use to set the stars astray.
And in his ears the music that makes mad
Beat always; and what way the music bade,
That alway rode he; nor was any sleep
His, nor from height nor deep.
But heaven was as red iron, slumberless,
And had no heart to bless;
And earth lay sere and darkling as distraught,
And help in her was nought.   400

Then many a midnight, many a morn and even,
His mother, passing forth of her fair heaven,
With goodlier gifts than all save gods can give
From earth or from the heaven where sea-things live,
With shine of sea-flowers through the bay-leaf braid
Woven for a crown her foam-white hands had made
To crown him with land's laurel and sea-dew,
Sought the sea-bird that was her boy: but he
Sat panther-throned beside Erigone,
Riding the red ways of the revel through   410
Midmost of pale-mouthed passion's crownless crew.
Till on some winter's dawn of some dim year
He let the vine-bit on the panther's lip
Slide, and the green rein slip,
And set his eyes to seaward, nor gave ear
If sound from landward hailed him, dire or dear;
And passing forth of all those fair fierce ranks
Back to the grey sea-banks,

Against a sea-rock lying, aslant the steep,
Fell after many sleepless dreams on sleep.   420

And in his sleep the dun green light was shed
Heavily round his head
That through the veil of sea falls fathom-deep,
Blurred like a lamp's that when the night drops dead
Dies; and his eyes gat grace of sleep to see
The deep divine dark dayshine of the sea,
Dense water-walls and clear dusk water-ways,
Broad-based, or branching as a sea-flower sprays
That side or this dividing; and anew
The glory of all her glories that he knew.   430
And in sharp rapture of recovering tears
He woke on fire with yearnings of old years,
Pure as one purged of pain that passion bore,
Ill child of bitter mother; for his own
Looked laughing toward him from her midsea throne,
Up toward him there ashore.

Thence in his heart the great same joy began,
Of child that made him man:
And turned again from all hearts else on quest,
He communed with his own heart, and had rest.   440
And like sea-winds upon loud waters ran
His days and dreams together, till the joy
Burned in him of the boy.
Till the earth's great comfort and the sweet sea's breath
Breathed and blew life in where was heartless death,
Death spirit-stricken of soul-sick days, where strife
Of thought and flesh made mock of death and life.
And grace returned upon him of his birth
Where heaven was mixed with heavenlike sea and earth;
And song shot forth strong wings that took the sun   450
From inward, fledged with might of sorrow and mirth
And father's fire made mortal in his son.
Nor was not spirit of strength in blast and breeze
To exalt again the sun's child and the sea's;
For as wild mares in Thessaly grow great
With child of ravishing winds, that violate
Their leaping length of limb with manes like fire
And eyes outburning heaven's
With fires more violent than the lightning levin's
And breath drained out and desperate of desire,   460

Even so the spirit in him, when winds grew strong,
Grew great with child of song.
Nor less than when his veins first leapt for joy
To draw delight in such as burns a boy,
Now too the soul of all his senses felt
The passionate pride of deep sea-pulses dealt
Through nerve and jubilant vein
As from the love and largess of old time,
And with his heart again
The tidal throb of all the tides keep rhyme   470
And charm him from his own soul's separate sense
With infinite and invasive influence
That made strength sweet in him and sweetness strong,
Being now no more a singer, but a song.

Till one clear day when brighter sea-wind blew
And louder sea-shine lightened, for the waves
Were full of godhead and the light that saves,
His father's, and their spirit had pierced him through,
He felt strange breath and light all round him shed
That bowed him down with rapture; and he knew   480
His father's hand, hallowing his humbled head,
And the old great voice of the old good time, that said:

"Child of my sunlight and the sea, from birth
A fosterling and fugitive on earth;
Sleepless of soul as wind or wave or fire,
A manchild with an ungrown God's desire;
Because thou hast loved nought mortal more than me,
Thy father, and thy mother-hearted sea;
Because thou hast set thine heart to sing, and sold
Life and life's love for song, God's living gold;   490
Because thou hast given thy flower and fire of youth
To feed men's hearts with visions, truer than truth;
Because thou hast kept in those world-wandering eyes
The light that makes me music of the skies;
Because thou hast heard with world-unwearied ears
The music that puts light into the spheres;
Have therefore in thine heart and in thy mouth
The sound of song that mingles north and south,
The song of all the winds that sing of me,
And in thy soul the sense of all the sea."   500

[1880]

THE HIGHER PANTHEISM IN A NUTSHELL

ONE, who is not, we see: but one, whom we see not, is:
Surely this is not that: but that is assuredly this.

What, and wherefore, and whence? for under is over and under:
If thunder could be without lightning, lightning could be without
 thunder.

Doubt is faith in the main: but faith, on the whole, is doubt:
We cannot believe by proof: but could we believe without?

Why, and whither, and how? for barley and rye are not clover:
Neither are straight lines curves: yet over is under and over.

Two and two may be four: but four and four are not eight:
Fate and God may be twain: but God is the same thing as fate.   10

Ask a man what he thinks, and get from a man what he feels:
God, once caught in the fact, shews you a fair pair of heels.

Body and spirit are twins: God only knows which is which:
The soul squats down in the flesh, like a tinker drunk in a ditch.

More is the whole than a part: but half is more than the whole:
Clearly, the soul is the body: but is not the body the soul?

One and two are not one: but one and nothing is two:
Truth can hardly be false, if falsehood cannot be true.

Once the mastodon was: pterodactyls were common as cocks:
Then the mammoth was God: now is He a prize ox.   20

Parallels all things are: yet many of these are askew:
You are certainly I: but certainly I am not you.

Springs the rock from the plain, shoots the stream from the rock:
Cocks exist for the hen: but hens exist for the cock.

God, whom we see not, is: and God, who is not, we see:
Fiddle, we know, is diddle: and diddle, we take it, is dee.

[1880]

SONNET FOR A PICTURE

THAT nose is out of drawing. With a gasp,
   She pants upon the passionate lips that ache
   With the red drain of her own mouth, and make
A monochord of colour. Like an asp,
One lithe lock wriggles in his rutilant grasp.
   Her bosom is an oven of myrrh, to bake
   Love's white warm shewbread to a browner cake.
The lock his fingers clench has burst its hasp.
The legs are absolutely abominable.
   Ah! what keen overgust of wild-eyed woes   **10**
   Flags in that bosom, flushes in that nose?
Nay! Death sets riddles for desire to spell,
   Responsive. What red hem earth's passion sews,
But may be ravenously unripped in hell?

                                   [1880]

POETA LOQUITUR

IF a person conceives an opinion
   That my verses are stuff that will wash,
Or my Muse has one plume on her pinion,
   That person's opinion is bosh.
My philosophy, politics, free-thought!
   Are worth not three skips of a flea,
And the emptiest of thoughts that can be thought
   Are mine on the sea.

In a maze of monotonous murmur
   Where reason roves ruined by rhyme,   **10**
In a voice neither graver nor firmer
   Than the bells on a fool's cap chime,
A party pretentiously pensive,
   With a Muse that deserves to be skinned,
Makes language and metre offensive
   With rhymes on the wind.

A perennial procession of phrases
   Pranked primly, though pruriently prime,

Precipitates preachings on praises
  In a ruffianly riot of rhyme   20
Through the pressure of print on my pages:
  But reckless the reader must be
Who imagines me one of the sages
  That steer through Time's sea.

Mad mixtures of Frenchified offal
  With insults to Christendom's creed,
Blind blasphemy, schoolboylike scoff, all
  These blazon me blockhead indeed.
I conceive myself obviously some one
  Whose audience will never be thinned,   30
But the pupil must needs be a rum one
  Whose teacher is wind.

In my poems, with ravishing rapture
  Storm strikes me and strokes me and stings:
But I'm scarcely the bird you might capture
  Out of doors in the thick of such things.
I prefer to be well out of harm's way
  When tempest makes tremble the tree,
And the wind with omnipotent arm-sway
  Makes soap of the sea.   40

Hanging hard on the rent rags of others,
  Who before me did better, I try
To believe them my sisters and brothers,
  Though I know what a low lot am I.
The mere sight of a church sets me yelping
  Like a boy that at football is shinned!
But the cause must indeed be past helping
  Whose gospel is wind!

All the pale past's red record of history
  Is dusty with damnable deeds;   50
But the future's mild motherly mystery
  Peers pure of all crowns and all creeds.
Truth dawns on time's resonant ruin,
  Frank, fulminant, fragrant, and free:
And apparently this is the doing
  Of wind on the sea.

Fame flutters in front of pretension
  Whose flagstaff is flagrantly fine:

And it cannot be needful to mention
    That such beyond question is mine.   60
Some singers indulging in curses,
    Though sinful, have splendidly sinned:
But my would-be maleficent verses
    Are nothing but wind.

[For freedom to swagger and scribble,
    In a style that's too silly for school,
At the heels of his betters to nibble,
    While flaunting the flag of a fool,
May to me seem the part of a poet,
    But where out of Bedlam is he   70
Who can think that in struggling to show it
    I am not at sea?]

[I may think to get honour and glory at
    The rate of a comet or star,
By maligning the Muse of a Laureate,
    Or denouncing the deeds of a Czar.
But such rollicking rhymsters get duly
    (As schoolboys at football say) shinned,
When their Muse, as such trollops will truly,
    Sails too near the wind.]   80

            [1918]

A BALLAD OF SARK

HIGH beyond the granite portal arched across
    Like the gateway of some godlike giant's hold
Sweep and swell the billowy breasts of moor and moss
    East and westward, and the dell their slopes enfold
    Basks in purple, glows in green, exults in gold.
Glens that know the dove and fells that hear the lark
Fill with joy the rapturous island, as an ark
    Full of spicery wrought from herb and flower and tree.
None would dream that grief even here may disembark
    On the wrathful woful marge of earth and sea.   10

Rocks emblazoned like the mid shield's royal boss
    Take the sun with all their blossom broad and bold.
None would dream that all this moorland's glow and gloss
    Could be dark as tombs that strike the spirit acold

Even in eyes that opened here, and here behold
Now no sun relume from hope's belated spark
Any comfort, nor may ears of mourners hark
　　Though the ripe woods ring with golden-throated glee,
While the soul lies shattered, like a stranded bark
　　On the wrathful woful marge of earth and sea.　　　　20

Death and doom are they whose crested triumphs toss
　　On the proud plumed waves whence mourning notes are toiled.
Wail of perfect woe and moan for utter loss
Raise the bride-song through the graveyard on the wold
Where the bride-bed keeps the bridegroom fast in mould,
Where the bride, with death for priest and doom for clerk,
Hears for choir the throats of waves like wolves that bark,
　　Sore anhungered, off the drear Eperquerie,
Fain to spoil the strongholds of the strength of Sark
　　On the wrathful woful marge of earth and sea.　　　　30

Prince of storm and tempest, lord whose ways are dark,
Wind whose wings are spread for flight that none may mark,
　　Lightly dies the joy that lives by grace of thee.
Love through thee lies bleeding, hope lies cold and stark,
　　On the wrathful woful marge of earth and sea.

　　　　　　　　　　　　　　　　　　[*1884; 1884*]

THE TYNESIDE WIDOW

　　THERE's mony a man loves land and life,
　　　　Loves life and land and fee;
　　And mony a man loves fair women,
　　　　But never a man loves me, my love,
　　　　But never a man loves me.

　　O weel and weel for a' lovers,
　　　　I wot weel may they be;
　　And weel and weel for a' fair maidens,
　　　　But aye mair woe for me, my love,
　　　　But aye mair woe for me.　　　　　　10

　　O weel be wi' you, ye sma' flowers,
　　　　Ye flowers and every tree;
　　And weel be wi' you, a' birdies,

But teen and tears wi' me, my love,
But teen and tears wi' me.

O weel be yours, my three brethren,
  And ever weel be ye;
Wi' deeds for doing and loves for wooing,
  But never a love for me, my love,
  But never a love for me.   20

And weel be yours, my seven sisters,
  And good love-days to see,
And long life-days and true lovers,
  But never a day for me, my love,
  But never a day for me.

Good times wi' you, ye bauld riders,
  By the hieland and the lee;
And by the leeland and by the hieland
  It's weary times wi' me, my love,
  It's weary times wi' me.   30

Good days wi' you, ye good sailors,
  Sail in and out the sea;
And by the beaches and by the reaches
  It's heavy days wi' me, my love,
  It's heavy days wi' me.

I had his kiss upon my mouth,
  His bairn upon my knee;
I would my soul and body were twain,
  And the bairn and the kiss wi' me, my love,
  And the bairn and the kiss wi' me.   40

The bairn down in the mools, my dear,
  O saft and saft lies she;
I would the mools were ower my head,
  And the young bairn fast wi' me, my love,
  And the young bairn fast wi' me.

The father under the faem, my dear,
  O sound and sound sleeps he;
I would the faem were ower my face,
  And the father lay by me, my love,
  And the father lay by me.   50

I would the faem were ower my face,
  Or the mools on my ee-bree;
And waking-time with a' lovers,
  But sleeping-time wi' me, my love,
  But sleeping-time wi' me.

I would the mools were meat in my mouth,
  The saut faem in my ee;
And the land-worm and the water-worm
  To feed fu' sweet on me, my love,
  To feed fu' sweet on me.   60

My life is sealed with a seal of love,
  And locked with love for a key;
And I lie wrang and I wake lang,
  But ye tak' nae thought for me, my love,
  But ye tak' nae thought for me.

We were weel fain of love, my dear,
  O fain and fain were we;
It was weel with a' the weary world,
  But O, sae weel wi' me, my love,
  But O, sae weel wi' me.   70

We were nane ower mony to sleep, my dear,
  I wot we were but three;
And never a bed in the weary world
  For my bairn and my dear and me, my love,
  For my bairn and my dear and me.

                          [*1877; 1888;* 1889]

TO A SEAMEW

Whˢᴺ I had wings, my brother,
  Such wings were mine as thine:
Such life my heart remembers
In all as wild Septembers
As this when life seems other,
  Though sweet, than once was mine;
When I had wings, my brother,
  Such wings were mine as thine.

Such life as thrills and quickens
   The silence of thy flight,
Or fills thy note's elation
With lordlier exultation
Than man's, whose faint heart sickens
   With hopes and fears that blight
Such life as thrills and quickens
   The silence of thy flight.

Thy cry from windward clanging
   Makes all the cliffs rejoice;
Though storm clothe seas with sorrow,
Thy call salutes the morrow;
While shades of pain seem hanging
   Round earth's most rapturous voice,
Thy cry from windward clanging
   Makes all the cliffs rejoice.

We, sons and sires of seamen,
   Whose home is all the sea,
What place man may, we claim it;
But thine — whose thought may name it?
Free birds live higher than freemen,
   And gladlier ye than we —
We, sons and sires of seamen,
   Whose home is all the sea.

For you the storm sounds only
   More notes of more delight
Than earth's in sunniest weather:
When heaven and sea together
Join strengths against the lonely
   Lost bark borne down by night,
For you the storm sounds only
   More notes of more delight.

With wider wing, and louder
   Long clarion-call of joy,
Thy tribe salutes the terror
Of darkness, wild as error,
But sure as truth, and prouder
   Than waves with man for toy;
With wider wing, and louder
Long clarion-call of joy.

10

20

30

40

The wave's wing spreads and flutters,
   The wave's heart swells and breaks;   50
One moment's passion thrills it,
One pulse of power fulfils it
And ends the pride it utters
   When, loud with life that quakes,
The wave's wing spreads and flutters,
   The wave's heart swells and breaks.

But thine and thou, my brother,
   Keep heart and wing more high
Than aught may scare or sunder;
The waves whose throats are thunder   60
Fall hurtling each on other,
   And triumph as they die;
But thine and thou, my brother,
   Keep heart and wing more high.

More high than wrath or anguish,
   More strong than pride or fear,
The sense or soul half hidden
In thee, for us forbidden,
Bids thee nor change nor languish,
   But live thy life as here,   70
More high than wrath or anguish,
   More strong than pride or fear.

We are fallen, even we, whose passion
   On earth is nearest thine;
Who sing, and cease from flying;
Who live, and dream of dying:
Grey time, in time's grey fashion,
   Bids wingless creatures pine:
We are fallen, even we, whose passion
   On earth is nearest thine.   80

The lark knows no such rapture,
   Such joy no nightingale,
As sways the songless measure
Wherein thy wings take pleasure:
Thy love may no man capture,
   Thy pride may no man quail;
The lark knows no such rapture,
   Such joy no nightingale.

And we, whom dreams embolden,
    We can but creep and sing   90
And watch through heaven's waste hollow
The flight no sight may follow
To the utter bourne beholden
    Of none that lack thy wing:
And we, whom dreams embolden,
    We can but creep and sing.

Our dreams have wings that falter;
    Our hearts bear hopes that die;
For thee no dream could better
A life no fears may fetter,   100
A pride no care can alter,
    That wots not whence or why
Our dreams have wings that falter,
    Our hearts bear hopes that die.

With joy more fierce and sweeter
    Than joys we deem divine
Their lives, by time untarnished,
Are girt about and garnished,
Who match the wave's full metre
    And drink the wind's wild wine   110
With joy more fierce and sweeter
    Than joys we deem divine.

Ah, well were I for ever,
    Wouldst thou change lives with me,
And take my song's wild honey,
And give me back thy sunny
Wide eyes that weary never,
    And wings that search the sea;
Ah, well were I for ever,
    Wouldst thou change lives with me.   120

Beachy Head: September 1886.   [1889]

THE LAKE OF GAUBE

THE sun is lord and god, sublime, serene,
    And sovereign on the mountains: earth and air
Lie prone in passion, blind with bliss unseen
    By force of sight and might of rapture, fair
    As dreams that die and know not what they were.
The lawns, the gorges, and the peaks, are one
Glad glory, thrilled with sense of unison
In strong compulsive silence of the sun.

Flowers dense and keen as midnight stars aflame
    And living things of light like flames in flower   10
That glance and flash as though no hand might tame
    Lightnings whose life outshone their stormlit hour
    And played and laughed on earth, with all their power
Gone, and with all their joy of life made long
And harmless as the lightning life of song,
Shine sweet like stars when darkness feels them strong.

The deep mild purple flaked with moonbright gold
    That makes the scales seem flowers of hardened light,
The flamelike tongue, the feet that noon leaves cold,
    The kindly trust in man, when once the sight   20
    Grew less than strange, and faith bade fear take flight,
Outlive the little harmless life that shone
And gladdened eyes that loved it, and was gone
Ere love might fear that fear had looked thereon.

Fear held the bright thing hateful, even as fear,
    Whose name is one with hate and horror, saith
That heaven, the dark deep heaven of water near,
    Is deadly deep as hell and dark as death.
    The rapturous plunge that quickens blood and breath
With pause more sweet than passion, ere they strive   30
To raise again the limbs that yet would dive
Deeper, should there have slain the soul alive.

As the bright salamander in fire of the noonshine exults and is glad of
    his day,
The spirit that quickens my body rejoices to pass from the sunlight
    away,

To pass from the glow of the mountainous flowerage, the high multi-
 tudinous bloom,
Far down through the fathomless night of the water, the gladness of
 silence and gloom.
Death-dark and delicious as death in the dream of a lover and dreamer
 may be,
It clasps and encompasses body and soul with delight to be living and
 free:
Free utterly now, though the freedom endure but the space of a peri-
 lous breath,
And living, though girdled about with the darkness and coldness and
 strangeness of death: 40
Each limb and each pulse of the body rejoicing, each nerve of the spirit
 at rest,
All sense of the soul's life rapture, a passionate peace in its blindness
 blest.
So plunges the downward swimmer, embraced of the water unfath-
 omed of man,
The darkness unplummeted, icier than seas in midwinter, for blessing
 or ban;
And swiftly and sweetly, when strength and breath fall short, and the
 dive is done,
Shoots up as a shaft from the dark depth shot, sped straight into sight
 of the sun;
And sheer through the snow-soft water, more dark than the roof of
 the pines above,
Strikes forth, and is glad as a bird whose flight is impelled and sus-
 tained of love.
As a sea-mew's love of the sea-wind breasted and ridden for rapture's
 sake
Is the love of his body and soul for the darkling delight of the soundless
 lake: 50
As the silent speed of a dream too living to live for a thought's space
 more
Is the flight of his limbs through the still strong chill of the darkness
 from shore to shore.
Might life be as this is and death be as life that casts off time as a robe,
The likeness of infinite heaven were a symbol revealed of the lake of
 Gaube.

> Whose thought has fathomed and measured
> The darkness of life and of death,
> The secret within them treasured,
> The spirit that is not breath?

Whose vision has yet beholden
    The splendour of death and of life?   60
Though sunset as dawn be golden,
    Is the word of them peace, not strife?
Deep silence answers: the glory
    We dream of may be but a dream,
And the sun of the soul wax hoary
    As ashes that show not a gleam.
But well shall it be with us ever
    Who drive through the darkness here,
If the soul that we live by never,
    For aught that a lie saith, fear.   70

              [*1899; 1904*]

ATALANTA IN CALYDON

A TRAGEDY

The Argument

Althaea, daughter of Thestius and Eurythemis, queen of Calydon, being with child of Meleager her first-born son, dreamed that she brought forth a brand burning; and upon his birth came the three Fates and prophesied of him three things, namely these; that he should have great strength of his hands, and good fortune in this life, and that he should live no longer when the brand then in the fire were consumed: wherefore his mother plucked it forth and kept it by her. And the child being a man grown sailed with Jason after the fleece of gold, and won himself great praise of all men living; and when the tribes of the north and west made war upon Aetolia, he fought against their army and scattered it. But Artemis, having at first stirred up these tribes to war against Oeneus king of Calydon, because he had offered sacrifice to all the gods saving her alone, but her he had forgotten to honour, was yet more wroth because of the destruction of this army, and sent upon the land of Calydon a wild boar which slew many and wasted all their increase, but him could none slay, and many went against him and perished. Then were all the chief men of Greece gathered together, and among them Atalanta daughter of Iasius the Arcadian, a virgin; for whose sake Artemis let slay the boar, seeing she favoured the maiden greatly; and Meleager having dispatched it gave the spoil thereof to Atalanta, as one beyond measure enamoured of her; but the brethren of Althaea his mother, Toxeus and Plexippus, with such others as misliked that she only should bear off the praise whereas many had borne the labour, laid wait for her to take away her spoil; but Meleager fought against them and slew them: whom when Althaea their sister beheld and knew to be slain of her son, she waxed for wrath and sorrow like as one mad, and taking the brand whereby the measure of her son's life was meted to him, she cast it upon a fire; and with the wasting thereof his life likewise wasted away, that being brought back to his father's house he died in a brief space; and his mother also endured not long after for very sorrow; and this was his end, and the end of that hunting.

[handwritten annotation:] quest for unity · Meleager questing for Atalanta · male & female, gods & men · Meleager (active) althaea (passive) · search for value & permanence in a chaotic world.

The Persons

Chief Huntsman	Atalanta
Chorus	Toxeus
Althaea	Plexippus
Meleager	Herald
Oeneus	Messenger
Second Messenger	

ἴστω δ' ὅστις οὐχ ὑπόπτερος
φροντίσιν δαείς,
τὰν ἁ παιδολύμας τάλαινα Θεστιὰς μήσατο
πυρδαῆ τινα πρόνοιαν,
καταίθουσα παιδὸς δαφοινὸν
δαλὸν ἥλικ', ἐπεὶ μολὼν
ματρόθεν κελάδησε;
σύμμετρόν τε διαὶ βίου
μοιρόκραντον ἐς ἆμαρ.[1]

AESCH. *Cho.* 602–11.

CHIEF HUNTSMAN

Maiden, and mistress of the months and stars
Now folded in the flowerless fields of heaven,
Goddess whom all gods love with threefold heart,
Being treble in thy divided deity,
A light for dead men and dark hours, a foot
Swift on the hills as morning, and a hand
To all things fierce and fleet that roar and range
Mortal, with gentler shafts than snow or sleep;
Hear now and help and lift no violent hand,
But favourable and fair as thine eye's beam   10
Hidden and shown in heaven; for I all night
Amid the king's hounds and the hunting men
Have wrought and worshipped toward thee; nor shall man
See goodlier hounds or deadlier edge of spears;
But for the end, that lies unreached at yet
Between the hands and on the knees of gods.
O fair-faced sun, killing the stars and dews
And dreams and desolation of the night!
Rise up, shine, stretch thine hand out, with thy bow
Touch the most dimmest height of trembling heaven,   20

[1] If any there be who is not light-minded in his understanding, let him
know this, when he hath learned of the device of a lighted brand, planned
by Thestius' heartless daughter, who wrought the ruin of her own child,
when she consumed the charred brand, which was to be like-aged with him
from the hour when he came forth from his mother's womb and cried aloud,
and which kept pace with him throughout his life unto the day foredoomed
of fate. [H. Weir Smyth, Loeb Classical Library]

And burn and break the dark about thy ways,
Shot through and through with arrows; let thine hair
Lighten as flame above that flameless shell
Which was the moon, and thine eyes fill the world
And thy lips kindle with swift beams; let earth
Laugh, and the long sea fiery from thy feet
Through all the roar and ripple of streaming springs
And foam in reddening flakes and flying flowers
Shaken from hands and blown from lips of nymphs
Whose hair or breast divides the wandering wave   30
With salt close tresses cleaving lock to lock,
All gold, or shuddering and unfurrowed snow;
And all the winds about thee with their wings,
And fountain-heads of all the watered world;
Each horn of Acheloüs, and the green
Euenus, wedded with the straitening sea.
For in fair time thou comest; come also thou,
Twin-born with him, and virgin, Artemis,
And give our spears their spoil, the wild boar's hide,
Sent in thine anger against us for sin done   40
And bloodless altars without wine or fire.
Him now consume thou; for thy sacrifice
With sanguine-shining steam divides the dawn,
And one, the maiden rose of all thy maids,
Arcadian Atalanta, snowy-souled,
Fair as the snow and footed as the wind,
From Ladon and well-wooded Maenalus
Over the firm hills and the fleeting sea
Hast thou drawn hither, and many an armèd king,
Heroes, the crown of men, like gods in fight.   50
Moreover out of all the Aetolian land,
From the full-flowered Lelantian pasturage
To what of fruitful field the son of Zeus
Won from the roaring river and labouring sea
When the wild god shrank in his horn and fled
And foamed and lessened through his wrathful fords,
Leaving clear lands that steamed with sudden sun,
These virgins with the lightening of the day
Bring thee fresh wreaths and their own sweeter hair,
Luxurious locks and flower-like mixed with flowers,   60
Clean offering, and chaste hymns; but me the time
Divides from these things; whom do thou not less
Help and give honour, and to mine hounds good speed,
And edge to spears, and luck to each man's hand.

420 • *Algernon Charles Swinburne*

CHORUS

When the hounds of spring are on winter's traces,
    The mother of months in meadow or plain
Fills the shadows and windy places
    With lisp of leaves and ripple of rain;
And the brown bright nightingale amorous
Is half assuaged for Itylus,   70
For the Thracian ships and the foreign faces,
    The tongueless vigil, and all the pain.

Come with bows bent and with emptying of quivers,
    Maiden most perfect, lady of light,
With a noise of winds and many rivers,
    With a clamour of waters, and with might;
Bind on thy sandals, O thou most fleet,
Over the splendour and speed of thy feet;
For the faint east quickens, the wan west shivers,
    Round the feet of the day and the feet of the night.   80

Where shall we find her, how shall we sing to her,
    Fold our hands round her knees, and cling?
O that man's heart were as fire and could spring to her,
    Fire, or the strength of the streams that spring!
For the stars and the winds are unto her
As raiment, as songs of the harp-player;
For the risen stars and the fallen cling to her,
    And the southwest-wind and the west-wind sing.

For winter's rains and ruins are over,
    And all the season of snows and sins;
The days dividing lover and lover,   90
    The light that loses, the night that wins;
And time remembered is grief forgotten,
And frosts are slain and flowers begotten,
And in green underwood and cover
    Blossom by blossom the spring begins.

The full streams feed on flower of rushes,
    Ripe grasses trammel a travelling foot,
The faint fresh flame of the young year flushes
    From leaf to flower and flower to fruit;   100
And fruit and leaf are as gold and fire,
And the oat is heard above the lyre,

And the hoofèd heel of a satyr crushes
   The chestnut-husk at the chestnut-root.

And Pan by noon and Bacchus by night,
   Fleeter of foot than the fleet-foot kid,
Follows with dancing and fills with delight
   The Maenad and the Bassarid;
And soft as lips that laugh and hide
The laughing leaves of the trees divide,   110
And screen from seeing and leave in sight
   The god pursuing, the maiden hid.

The ivy falls with the Bacchanal's hair
   Over her eyebrows hiding her eyes;
The wild vine slipping down leaves bare
   Her bright breast shortening into sighs;
The wild vine slips with the weight of its leaves,
But the berried ivy catches and cleaves
To the limbs that glitter, the feet that scare
   The wolf that follows, the fawn that flies.   120

ALTHAEA *puts down hopefulness*
What do ye singing? what is this ye sing? *pleasure & pain*

CHORUS

Flowers bring we, and pure lips that please the gods.
And raiment meet for service: lest the day
Turn sharp with all its honey in our lips.

ALTHAEA

Night, a black hound, follows the white fawn day,
Swifter than dreams the white flown feet of sleep;
Will ye pray back the night with any prayers?
And though the spring put back a little while   *gods are higher than man*
Winter, and snows that plague all men for sin,   *& it's no use aspiring*
And the iron time of cursing, yet I know   130
Spring shall be ruined with the rain, and storm
Eat up like fire the ashen autumn days.
I marvel what men do with prayers awake
Who dream and die with dreaming; any god,
Yea the least god of all things called divine,
Is more than sleep and waking; yet we say,
Perchance by praying a man shall match his god.
For if sleep have no mercy, and man's dreams

Bite to the blood and burn into the bone,
What shall this man do waking? By the gods,   140
He shall not pray to dream sweet things to-night,
Having dreamt once more bitter things than death.

CHORUS

Queen, but what is it that hath burnt thine heart?
For thy speech flickers like a blown-out flame.

ALTHAEA

Look, ye say well, and know not what ye say;
For all my sleep is turned into a fire,
And all my dreams to stuff that kindles it.

CHORUS

Yet one doth well being patient of the gods.

ALTHAEA

Yea, lest they smite us with some four-foot plague.

CHORUS

But when time spreads find out some herb for it.   150

ALTHAEA

And with their healing herbs infect our blood.

CHORUS

What ails thee to be jealous of their ways?

ALTHAEA

What if they give us poisonous drinks for wine?

CHORUS

They have their will; much talking mends it not.

ALTHAEA

And gall for milk, and cursing for a prayer?

CHORUS

Have they not given life, and the end of life?

ALTHAEA

Lo, where they heal, they help not; thus they do,
They mock us with a little piteousness,

And we say prayers, and weep; but at the last,
Sparing awhile, they smite and spare no whit.   160

CHORUS

Small praise man gets dispraising the high gods:
What have they done that thou dishonourest them?

ALTHAEA

First Artemis for all this harried land
I praise not, and for wasting of the boar
That mars with tooth and tusk and fiery feet
Green pasturage and the grace of standing corn
And meadow and marsh with springs and unblown leaves,
Flocks and swift herds and all that bite sweet grass,
I praise her not; what things are these to praise?

CHORUS

But when the king did sacrifice, and gave   170
Each god fair dues of wheat and blood and wine,
Her not with bloodshed nor burnt-offering
Revered he, nor with salt or cloven cake;
Wherefore being wroth she plagued the land; but now
Takes off from us fate and her heavy things.
Which deed of these twain were not good to praise?
For a just deed looks always either way
With blameless eyes, and mercy is no fault.

ALTHAEA

Yea, but a curse she hath sent above all these
To hurt us where she healed us; and hath lit   180
Fire where the old fire went out, and where the wind
Slackened, hath blown on us with deadlier air.

CHORUS

What storm is this that tightens all our sail?

ALTHAEA

Love, a thwart sea-wind full of rain and foam.

CHORUS

Whence blown, and born under what stormier star?

ALTHAEA

Southward across Euenus from the sea.

CHORUS

Thy speech turns toward Arcadia like blown wind.

ALTHAEA

Sharp as the north sets when the snows are out.

CHORUS

Nay, for this maiden hath no touch of love.

Atlanta

ALTHAEA

I would she had sought in some cold gulf of sea   190
Love, or in dens where strange beasts lurk, or fire,
Or snows on the extreme hills, or iron land
Where no spring is; I would she had sought therein
And found, or ever love had found her here.   *jealous of her son's love for Atalanta*

CHORUS

She is holier than all holy days or things,
The sprinkled water or fume of perfect fire;
Chaste, dedicated to pure prayers, and filled
With higher thoughts than heaven; a maiden clean,
Pure iron, fashioned for a sword; and man
She loves not; what should one such do with love?   200

ALTHAEA

Look you, I speak not as one light of wit,
But as a queen speaks, being heart-vexed; for oft
I hear my brothers wrangling in mid hall,
And am not moved; and my son chiding them,
And these things nowise move me, but I know
Foolish and wise men must be to the end,
And feed myself with patience; but this most,
This moves me, that for wise men as for fools
Love is one thing, an evil thing, and turns
Choice words and wisdom into fire and air.   *love is monster*   210
And in the end shall no joy come, but grief,
Sharp words and soul's division and fresh tears
Flower-wise upon the old root of tears brought forth,
Fruit-wise upon the old flower of tears sprung up,
Pitiful sighs, and much regrafted pain.
These things are in my presage, and myself
Am part of them and know not; but in dreams
The gods are heavy on me, and all the fates
Shed fire across my eyelids mixed with night,

And burn me blind, and disilluminate   220
My sense of seeing, and my perspicuous soul
Darken with vision; seeing I see not, hear
And hearing am not holpen, but mine eyes
Stain many tender broideries in the bed
Drawn up about my face that I may weep
And the king wake not; and my brows and lips
Tremble and sob in sleeping, like swift flames
That tremble, or water when it sobs with heat
Kindled from under; and my tears fill my breast
And speck the fair dyed pillows round the king   230
With barren showers and salter than the sea,
Such dreams divide me dreaming; for long since
I dreamed that out of this my womb had sprung *what happened*
Fire and a firebrand; this was ere my son,
Meleager, a goodly flower in fields of fight,
Felt the light touch him coming forth, and wailed
Childlike; but yet he was not; and in time
I bare him, and my heart was great; for yet
So royally was never strong man born,
Nor queen so nobly bore as noble a thing   240
As this my son was: such a birth God sent
And such a grace to bear it. Then came in
Three weaving women, and span each a thread,
Saying This for strength and That for luck, and one
Saying Till the brand upon the hearth burn down,
So long shall this man see good days and live.
And I with gathered raiment from the bed
Sprang, and drew forth the brand, and cast on it
Water, and trod the flame bare-foot, and crushed
With naked hand spark beaten out of spark   250
And blew against and quenched it; for I said,
These are the most high Fates that dwell with us,
And we find favour a little in their sight,
A little, and more we miss of, and much time
Foils us; howbeit they have pitied me, O son,
And thee most piteous, thee a tenderer thing
Than any flower of fleshly seed alive.
Wherefore I kissed and hid him with my hands,
And covered under arms and hair, and wept,
And feared to touch him with my tears, and laughed;   260
So light a thing was this man, grown so great
Men cast their heads back, seeing against the sun
Blaze the armed man carven on his shield, and hear

The laughter of little bells along the brace
Ring, as birds singing or flutes blown, and watch,
High up, the cloven shadow of either plume
Divide the bright light of the brass, and make
His helmet as a windy and wintering moon
Seen through blown cloud and plume-like drift, when ships
Drive, and men strive with all the sea, and oars   270
Break, and the beaks dip under, drinking death;
Yet was he then but a span long, and moaned
With inarticulate mouth inseparate words,
And with blind lips and fingers wrung my breast
Hard, and thrust out with foolish hands and feet,
Murmuring; but those grey women with bound hair
Who fright the gods frighted not him; he laughed
Seeing them, and pushed out hands to feel and haul
Distaff and thread, intangible; but they
Passed, and I hid the brand, and in my heart   280
Laughed likewise, having all my will of heaven.
But now I know not if to left or right
The gods have drawn us hither; for again
I dreamt, and saw the black brand burst on fire
As a branch bursts in flower, and saw the flame
Fade flower-wise, and Death came and with dry lips
Blew the charred ash into my breast; and Love
Trampled the ember and crushed it with swift feet.
This I have also at heart; that not for me,
Not for me only or son of mine, O girls,   *Althaea*   290
The gods have wrought life, and desire of life,
Heart's love and heart's division; but for all
There shines one sun and one wind blows till night.
And when night comes the wind sinks and the sun,
And there is no light after, and no storm,
But sleep and much forgetfulness of things.
In such wise I gat knowledge of the gods
Years hence, and heard high sayings of one most wise,
Eurythemis my mother, who beheld
With eyes alive and spake with lips of these   300
As one on earth disfleshed and disallied
From breath or blood corruptible; such gifts
Time gave her, and an equal soul to these
And equal face to all things; thus she said.
But whatsoever intolerable or glad
The swift hours weave and unweave, I go hence
Full of mine own soul, perfect of myself,

Toward mine and me sufficient; and what chance
The gods cast lots for and shake out on us,
That shall we take, and that much bear withal. *jealous*   310
And now, before these gather to the hunt,
I will go arm my son and bring him forth,
Lest love or some man's anger work him harm.

CHORUS

Before the beginning of years
    There came to the making of man
Time, with a gift of tears;
    Grief, with a glass that ran;
Pleasure, with pain for leaven;
    Summer, with flowers that fell;
Remembrance fallen from heaven,   320
    And madness risen from hell;
Strength without hands to smite;
    Love that endures for a breath:
Night, the shadow of light,
    And life, the shadow of death.

And the high gods took in hand
    Fire, and the falling of tears,
And a measure of sliding sand
    From under the feet of the years;
And froth and drift of the sea;   330
    And dust of the labouring earth;
And bodies of things to be
    In the houses of death and of birth;
And wrought with weeping and laughter,
    And fashioned with loathing and love,
With life before and after
    And death beneath and above,
For a day and a night and a morrow,
    That his strength might endure for a span
With travail and heavy sorrow,
    The holy spirit of man.   340

From the winds of the north and the south
    They gathered as unto strife;
They breathed upon his mouth,
    They filled his body with life;
Eyesight and speech they wrought
    For the veils of the soul therein,

A time for labour and thought,
   A time to serve and to sin;
They gave him light in his ways,   350
   And love, and a space for delight,
And beauty and length of days,
   And night, and sleep in the night.
His speech is a burning fire;
   With his lips he travaileth;
In his heart is a blind desire,
   In his eyes foreknowledge of death;
He weaves, and is clothed with derision;
   Sows, and he shall not reap;
His life is a watch or a vision   360
   Between a sleep and a sleep.

MELEAGER

O sweet new heaven and air without a star,
Fair day, be fair and welcome, as to men
With deeds to do and praise to pluck from thee.
Come forth a child, born with clear sound and light,
With laughter and swift limbs and prosperous looks;
That this great hunt with heroes for the hounds
May leave thee memorable and us well sped.

ALTHAEA

Son, first I praise thy prayer, then bid thee speed;
But the gods hear men's hands before their lips,   370
And heed beyond all crying and sacrifice
Light of things done and noise of labouring men.
But thou, being armed and perfect for the deed,
Abide; for like rain-flakes in a wind they grow,
The men thy fellows, and the choice of the world,
Bound to root out the tuskèd plague, and leave
Thanks and safe days and peace in Calydon.

MELEAGER

For the whole city and all the low-lying land
Flames, and the soft air sounds with them that come;
The gods give all these fruit of all their works.   380

ALTHAEA

Set thine eye thither and fix thy spirit and say
Whom there thou knowest; for sharp mixed shadow and wind
Blown up between the morning and the mist,

With steam of steeds and flash of bridle or wheel,
And fire, and parcels of the broken dawn,
And dust divided by hard light, and spears
That shine and shift as the edge of wild beasts' eyes,
Smite upon mine; so fiery their blind edge
Burns, and bright points break up and baffle day.

MELEAGER

The first, for many I know not, being far off,   390
Peleus the Larissaean, couched with whom
Sleeps the white sea-bred wife and silver-shod,
Fair as fled foam, a goddess; and their son
Most swift and splendid of men's children born,
Most like a god, full of the future fame.

ALTHAEA

Who are these shining like one sundered star?

MELEAGER

Thy sister's sons a double flower of men.

ALTHAEA

O sweetest kin to me in all the world,
O twin-born blood of Leda, gracious heads
Like kindled lights in untempestuous heaven,   400
Fair flower-like stars on the iron foam of fight,
With what glad heart and kindliness of soul,
Even to the staining of both eyes with tears
And kindling of warm eyelids with desire,
A great way off I greet you, and rejoice
Seeing you so fair, and moulded like as gods.
Far off ye come, and least in years of these,
But lordliest, but worth love to look upon.

MELEAGER

Even such (for sailing hither I saw far hence,
And where Eurotas hollows his moist rock   410
Nigh Sparta with a strenuous-hearted stream)
Even such I saw their sisters; one swan-white,
The little Helen, and less fair than she
Fair Clytaemnestra, grave as pasturing fawns
Who feed and fear some arrow; but at whiles,
As one smitten with love or wrung with joy,
She laughs and lightens with her eyes, and then

Weeps; whereat Helen, having laughed, weeps too,
And the other chides her, and she being chid speaks nought,
But cheeks and lips and eyelids kisses her,   420
Laughing; so fare they, as in their bloomless bud
And full of unblown life, the blood of gods.

ALTHAEA

Sweet days befall them and good loves and lords,
And tender and temperate honours of the hearth,
Peace, and a perfect life and blameless bed.
But who shows next an eagle wrought in gold,
That flames and beats broad wings against the sun
And with void mouth gapes after emptier prey?

MELEAGER

Know by that sign the reign of Telamon
Between the fierce mouths of the encountering brine   430
On the strait reefs of twice-washed Salamis.

ALTHAEA

For like one great of hand he bears himself,
Vine-chapleted, with savours of the sea,
Glittering as wine and moving as a wave.
But who girt round there roughly follows him?

MELEAGER

Ancaeus, great of hand, an iron bulk,
Two-edged for fight as the axe against his arm,
Who drives against the surge of stormy spears
Full-sailed; him Cepheus follows, his twin-born,
Chief name next his of all Arcadian men.   440

ALTHAEA

Praise be with men abroad; chaste lives with us,
Home-keeping days and household reverences.

MELEAGER

Next by the left unsandalled foot know thou
The sail and oar of this Aetolian land,
Thy brethren, Toxeus and the violent-souled
Plexippus, over-swift with hand and tongue;
For hands are fruitful, but the ignorant mouth
Blows and corrupts their work with barren breath.

ALTHAEA

Speech too bears fruit, being worthy; and air blows down
Things poisonous, and high-seated violences,   450
And with charmed words and songs have men put out
Wild evil, and the fire of tyrannies.

MELEAGER

Yea, all things have they, save the gods and love.

ALTHAEA

Love thou the law and cleave to things ordained. *Conservative*

MELEAGER

Law lives upon their lips whom these applaud.

ALTHAEA

How sayest thou these? what god applauds new things?

MELEAGER

Zeus, who hath fear and custom under foot.

ALTHAEA

But loves not laws thrown down and lives awry.

MELEAGER

Yet is not less himself than his own law.

ALTHAEA

Nor shifts and shuffles old things up and down.   460

MELEAGER *or recreate from Winter*

But what he will remoulds and discreates.

ALTHAEA

Much, but not this, that each thing live its life.

MELEAGER

Nor only live, but lighten and lift up higher. *elevate*

ALTHAEA

Pride breaks itself, and too much gained is gone.

MELEAGER

Things gained are gone, but great things done endure.

Med. restrain your
love (not adventure)
Spirit

ALTHAEA

Child, if a man serve law through all his life
And with his whole heart worship, him all gods
Praise; but who loves it only with his lips,
And not in heart and deed desiring it
Hides a perverse will with obsequious words,   470
Him heaven infatuates and his twin-born fate
Tracks, and gains on him, scenting sins far off,
And the swift hounds of violent death devour.
Be man at one with equal-minded gods,
So shall he prosper; not through laws torn up,
Violated rule and a new face of things.
A woman armed makes war upon herself,
Unwomanlike, and treads down use and wont
And the sweet common honour that she hath,
Love, and the cry of children, and the hand   480
Trothplight and mutual mouth of marriages,
This doth she, being unloved; whom if one love,
Not fire nor iron and the wide-mouthed wars
Are deadlier than her lips or braided hair.
For of the one comes poison, and a curse
Falls from the other and burns the lives of men.
But thou, son, be not filled with evil dreams,
Nor with desire of these things; for with time
Blind love burns out; but if one feed it full
Till some discolouring stain dyes all his life,   490
He shall keep nothing praiseworthy, nor die
The sweet wise death of old men honourable,
Who have lived out all the length of all their years
Blameless, and seen well-pleased the face of gods,
And without shame and without fear have wrought
Things memorable, and while their days held out
In sight of all men and the sun's great light
Have gat them glory and given of their own praise
To the earth that bare them and the day that bred,
Home friends and far-off hospitalities,   500
And filled with gracious and memorial fame
Lands loved of summer or washed by violent seas,
Towns populous and many unfooted ways,
And alien lips and native with their own.
But when white age and venerable death
Mow down the strength and life within their limbs,
Drain out the blood and darken their clear eyes,
Immortal honour is on them, having past

Through splendid life and death desirable
To the clear seat and remote throne of souls,   510
Lands indiscoverable in the unheard-of west,
Round which the strong stream of a sacred sea
Rolls without wind for ever, and the snow
There shows not her white wings and windy feet,
Nor thunder nor swift rain saith anything,
Nor the sun burns, but all things rest and thrive;
And these, filled full of days, divine and dead,
Sages and singers fiery from the god,
And such as loved their land and all things good
And, best beloved of best men, liberty,   520
Free lives and lips, free hands of men free-born,
And whatsoever on earth was honourable
And whosoever of all the ephemeral seed,
Live there a life no liker to the gods
But nearer than their life of terrene days.
Love thou such life and look for such a death.
But from the light and fiery dreams of love
Spring heavy sorrows and a sleepless life,
Visions not dreams, whose lids no charm shall close
Nor song assuage them waking; and swift death   530
Crushes with sterile feet the unripening ear,
Treads out the timeless vintage; whom do thou
Eschewing embrace the luck of this thy life,
Not without honour; and it shall bear to thee
Such fruit as men reap from spent hours and wear,
Few men, but happy; of whom be thou, O son,
Happiest, if thou submit thy soul to fate,
And set thine eyes and heart on hopes high-born
And divine deeds and abstinence divine.   *sterility—winter*
So shalt thou be toward all men all thy days   540
As light and might communicable, and burn
From heaven among the stars above the hours,
And break not as a man breaks nor burn down:
For to whom other of all heroic names
Have the gods given his life in hand as thine?
And gloriously hast thou lived, and made thy life
To me that bare thee and to all men born
Thankworthy, a praise for ever; and hast won fame
When wild wars broke all round thy father's house,
And the mad people of windy mountain ways   550
Laid spears against us like a sea, and all
Aetolia thundered with Thessalian hoofs;

Yet these, as wind baffles the foam, and beats
Straight back the relaxed ripple, didst thou break
And loosen all their lances, till undone
And man from man they fell; for ye twain stood
God against god, Ares and Artemis,
And thou the mightier; wherefore she unleashed
A sharp-toothed curse thou too shalt overcome;
For in the greener blossom of thy life   560
Ere the full blade caught flower, and when time gave
Respite, thou didst not slacken soul nor sleep,
But with great hand and heart seek praise of men
Out of sharp straits and many a grievous thing,
Seeing the strange foam of undivided seas
On channels never sailed in, and by shores
Where the old winds cease not blowing, and all the night
Thunders, and day is no delight to men.

CHORUS

Meleager, a noble wisdom and fair words
The gods have given this woman; hear thou these.   570

MELEAGER

O mother, I am not fain to strive in speech
Nor set my mouth against thee, who art wise
Even as they say and full of sacred words.
But one thing I know surely, and cleave to this;
That though I be not subtle of wit as thou
Nor womanlike to weave sweet words, and melt
Mutable minds of wise men as with fire,
I too, doing justly and reverencing the gods,
Shall not want wit to see what things be right.
For whom they love and whom reject, being gods,   580
There is no man but seeth, and in good time
Submits himself, refraining all his heart.
And I too as thou sayest, have seen great things;
Seen otherwhere, but chiefly when the sail
First caught between stretched ropes the roaring west,
And all our oars smote eastward, and the wind
First flung round faces of seafaring men
White splendid snow-flakes of the sundering foam,
And the first furrow in virginal green sea
Followed the plunging ploughshare of hewn pine,   590
And closed, as when deep sleep subdues man's breath
Lips close and heart subsides; and closing, shone

Sunlike with many a Nereid's hair, and moved
Round many a trembling mouth of doubtful gods,
Risen out of sunless and sonorous gulfs
Through waning water and into shallow light,
That watched us; and when flying the dove was snared
As with men's hands, but we shot after and sped
Clear through the irremeable Symplegades;
And chiefliest when hoar beach and herbless cliff   600
Stood out ahead from Colchis, and we heard
Clefts hoarse with wind, and saw through narrowing reefs
The lightning of the intolerable wave
Flash, and the white wet flame of breakers burn
Far under a kindling south wind, as a lamp
Burns and bends all its blowing flame one way;
Wild heights untravelled of the wind, and vales
Cloven seaward by their violent streams, and white
With bitter flowers and bright salt scurf of brine;
Heard sweep their sharp swift gales, and bowing birdwise   610
Shriek with birds' voices, and with furious feet
Tread loose the long skirts of a storm; and saw
The whole white Euxine clash together and fall
Full-mouthed, and thunderous from a thousand throats:
Yet we drew thither and won the fleece and won
Medea, deadlier than the sea; but there
Seeing many a wonder and fearful things to men
I saw not one thing like this one seen here,
Most fair and fearful, feminine, a god,
Faultless; whom I that love not, being unlike,   620
Fear, and give honour, and choose from all the gods.

OENEUS

Lady, the daughter of Thestius, and thou, son,
Not ignorant of your strife nor light of wit,
Scared with vain dreams and fluttering like spent fire,
I come to judge between you, but a king
Full of past days and wise from years endured.
Nor thee I praise, who art fain to undo things done:
Nor thee, who art swift to esteem them overmuch.
For what the hours have given is given, and this
Changeless; howbeit these change, and in good time   630
Devise new things and good, not one thing still.
Us have they sent now at our need for help
Among men armed a woman, foreign born,
Virgin, not like the natural flower of things

That grows and bears and brings forth fruit and dies;
Unlovable, no light for a husband's house,
Espoused; a glory among unwedded girls,
And chosen of gods who reverence maidenhood.
These too we honour in honouring her; but thou,
Abstain thy feet from following, and thine eyes   640
From amorous touch; nor set toward hers thine heart,
Son, lest hate bear no deadlier fruit than love.

ALTHAEA

O king, thou art wise, but wisdom halts; and just,
But the gods love not justice more than fate,
And smite the righteous and the violent mouth,
And mix with insolent blood the reverent man's,
And bruise the holier as the lying lips.
Enough; for wise words fail me, and my heart
Takes fire and trembles flamewise, O my son,
O child, for thine head's sake; mine eyes wax thick,   650
Turning toward thee, so goodly a weaponed man,
So glorious; and for love of thine own eyes
They are darkened, and tears burn them, fierce as fire,
And my lips pause and my soul sinks with love.
But by thine hand, by thy sweet life and eyes,
By thy great heart and these clasped knees, O son,
I pray thee that thou slay me not with thee.
For there was never a mother woman-born
Loved her sons better; and never a queen of men
More perfect in her heart toward whom she loved.   660
For what lies light on many and they forget,
Small things and transitory as a wind o' the sea,
I forget never; I have seen thee all thine years
A man in arms, strong and a joy to men
Seeing thine head glitter and thine hand burn its way
Through a heavy and iron furrow of sundering spears;
But always also a flower of three suns old,
The small one thing that lying drew down my life
To lie with thee and feed thee; a child and weak,
Mine, a delight to no man, sweet to me.   670
Who then sought to thee? who gat help? who knew
If thou wert goodly? nay, no man at all.
Or what sea saw thee, or sounded with thine oar,
Child? or what strange land shone with war through thee?
But fair for me thou wert, O little life,
Fruitless, the fruit of mine own flesh, and blind,

More than much gold, ungrown, a foolish flower.
For silver nor bright snow nor feather of foam
Was whiter, and no gold yellower than thine hair,
O child, my child; and now thou art lordlier grown,   680
Not lovelier, not a new thing in mine eyes,
I charge thee by thy soul and this my breast,
Fear thou the gods and me and thine own heart,
Lest all these turn against thee; for who knows
What wind upon what wave of altering time
Shall speak a storm and blow calamity?
And there is nothing stabile in the world
But the gods break it; yet not less, fair son,
If but one thing be stronger, if one endure,
Surely the bitter and the rooted love   690
That burns between us, going from me to thee,
Shall more endure than all things. What dost thou,
Following strange loves? why wilt thou kill mine heart?
Lo, I talk wild and windy words, and fall
From my clear wits, and seem of mine own self
Dethroned, dispraised, disseated; and my mind,
That was my crown, breaks, and mine heart is gone,
And I am naked of my soul, and stand
Ashamed, as a mean woman; take thou thought:
Live if thou wilt, and if thou wilt not, look,   700
The gods have given thee life to lose or keep,
Thou shalt not die as men die, but thine end
Fallen upon thee shall break me unaware.

MELEAGER

Queen, my whole heart is molten with thy tears,
And my limbs yearn with pity of thee, and love
Compels with grief mine eyes and labouring breath;
For what thou art I know thee, and this thy breast
And thy fair eyes I worship, and am bound
Toward thee in spirit and love thee in all my soul.
For there is nothing terribler to men   710
Than the sweet face of mothers, and the might.
But what shall be let be; for us the day
Once only lives a little, and is not found.
Time and the fruitful hour are more than we,
And these lay hold upon us; but thou, God,
Zeus, the sole steersman of the helm of things,
Father, be swift to see us, and as thou wilt
Help: or if adverse, as thou wilt, refrain.

CHORUS

We have seen thee, O Love, thou art fair; thou art goodly, O Love;
Thy wings make light in the air as the wings of a dove.   720
Thy feet are as winds that divide the stream of the sea;
Earth is thy covering to hide thee, the garment of thee.
Thou art swift and subtle and blind, as a flame of fire;
Before thee the laughter, behind thee the tears of desire;
And twain go forth beside thee, a man with a maid;
Her eyes are the eyes of a bride whom delight makes afraid;
As the breath in the buds that stir is her bridal breath:
But Fate is the name of her; and his name is Death.

    For an evil blossom was born
      Of sea-foam and the frothing of blood,   730
        Blood-red and bitter of fruit,
          And the seed of it laughter and tears,
    And the leaves of it madness and scorn;
      A bitter flower from the bud,
        Sprung of the sea without root,
          Sprung without graft from the years.

    The weft of the world was untorn
      That is woven of the day on the night,
      The hair of the hours was not white
    Nor the raiment of time overworn,   740
      When a wonder, a world's delight,
    A perilous goddess was born;
      And the waves of the sea as she came
    Clove, and the foam at her feet,
        Fawning, rejoiced to bring forth
      A fleshly blossom, a flame
    Filling the heavens with heat
        To the cold white ends of the north.

    And in air the clamorous birds,
      And men upon earth that hear   750
    Sweet articulate words
        Sweetly divided apart,
      And in shallow and channel and mere
    The rapid and footless herds,
        Rejoiced, being foolish of heart.

    For all they said upon earth,
      She is fair, she is white like a dove,

And the life of the world in her breath
Breathes, and is born at her birth;
   For they knew thee for mother of love,   760
   And knew thee not mother of death.

What hadst thou to do being born,
   Mother, when winds were at ease,
As a flower of the springtime of corn,
   A flower of the foam of the seas?
For bitter thou wast from thy birth,
   Aphrodite, a mother of strife;
For before thee some rest was on earth,
     A little respite from tears,
   A little pleasure of life;   770
For life was not then as thou art,
     But as one that waxeth in years
Sweet-spoken, a fruitful wife;
     Earth had no thorn, and desire
No sting, neither death any dart;
   What hadst thou to do amongst these,
     Thou, clothed with a burning fire,
Thou, girt with sorrow of heart,
   Thou, sprung of the seed of the seas
As an ear from a seed of corn,   780
     As a brand plucked forth of a pyre,
As a ray shed forth of the morn,
   For division of soul and disease,
For a dart and a sting and a thorn?
What ailed thee then to be born?

Was there not evil enough,
   Mother, and anguish on earth
   Born with a man at his birth,
Wastes underfoot, and above
   Storm out of heaven, and dearth   790
Shaken down from the shining thereof,
     Wrecks from afar overseas
   And peril of shallow and firth,
     And tears that spring and increase
     In the barren places of mirth,
That thou, having wings as a dove,
   Being girt with desire for a girth,
     That thou must come after these,
That thou must lay on him love?

Thou shouldst not so have been born: 800
But death should have risen with thee,
Mother, and visible fear,
Grief, and the wringing of hands,
And noise of many that mourn;
The smitten bosom, the knee
Bowed, and in each man's ear
A cry as of perishing lands,
A moan as of people in prison,
A tumult of infinite griefs;
And thunder of storm on the sands,   810
And wailing of wives on the shore;
And under thee newly arisen
Loud shoals and shipwrecking reefs,
Fierce air and violent light;
Sail rent and sundering oar,
Darkness, and noises of night;
Clashing of streams in the sea,
Wave against wave as a sword,
Clamour of currents, and foam;
Rains making ruin on earth,   820
Winds that wax ravenous and roam
As wolves in a wolfish horde;
Fruits growing faint in the tree,
And blind things dead in their birth;
Famine, and blighting of corn,
When thy time was come to be born.

All these we know of; but thee
Who shall discern or declare?
In the uttermost ends of the sea
The light of thine eyelids and hair,   830
The light of thy bosom as fire
Between the wheel of the sun
And the flying flames of the air?
Wilt thou turn thee not yet nor have pity,
But abide with despair and desire
And the crying of armies undone,
Lamentation of one with another
And breaking of city by city;
The dividing of friend against friend,
The severing of brother and brother;   840
Wilt thou utterly bring to an end?
Have mercy, mother!

For against all men from of old
  Thou hast set thine hand as a curse,
    And cast out gods from their places.
      These things are spoken of thee.
Strong kings and goodly with gold
  Thou hast found out arrows to pierce,
    And made their kingdoms and races
      As dust and surf of the sea.   850
All these, overburdened with woes
  And with length of their days waxen weak,
    Thou slewest; and sentest moreover
      Upon Tyro an evil thing,
Rent hair and a fetter and blows
  Making bloody the flower of the cheek,
    Though she lay by a god as a lover,
      Though fair, and the seed of a king.

For of old, being full of thy fire,
  She endured not longer to wear   860
    On her bosom a saffron vest,
      On her shoulder an ashwood quiver;
Being mixed and made one through desire
  With Enipeus, and all her hair
    Made moist with his mouth, and her breast
      Filled full of the foam of the river.

ATALANTA

Sun, and clear light among green hills, and day
Late risen and long sought after, and you just gods
Whose hands divide anguish and recompense,
But first the sun's white sister, a maid in heaven,   870
On earth of all maids worshipped — hail, and hear,
And witness with me if not without sign sent,
Not without rule and reverence, I a maid
Hallowed, and huntress holy as whom I serve,
Here in your sight and eyeshot of these men
Stand, girt as they toward hunting, and my shafts
Drawn; wherefore all ye stand up on my side,
If I be pure and all ye righteous gods,
Lest one revile me, a woman, yet no wife,
That bear a spear for spindle, and this bow strung   880
For a web woven; and with pure lips salute
Heaven, and the face of all the gods, and dawn
Filling with maiden flames and maiden flowers

The starless fold o' the stars, and making sweet
The warm wan heights of the air, moon-trodden ways
And breathless gates and extreme hills of heaven.
Whom, having offered water and bloodless gifts,
Flowers, and a golden circlet of pure hair,
Next Artemis I bid be favourable
And make this day all golden, hers and ours,   890
Gracious and good and white to the unblamed end.
But thou, O well-beloved, of all my days
Bid it be fruitful, and a crown for all,
To bring forth leaves and bind round all my hair
With perfect chaplets woven for thine of thee.
For not without the word of thy chaste mouth,
For not without law given and clean command,
Across the white straits of the running sea
From Elis even to the Acheloïan horn,
I with clear winds came hither and gentle gods,   900
Far off my father's house, and left uncheered
Iasius, and uncheered the Arcadian hills
And all their green-haired waters, and all woods
Disconsolate, to hear no horn of mine
Blown, and behold no flash of swift white feet.

MELEAGER

For thy name's sake and awe toward thy chaste head,
O holiest Atalanta, no man dares
Praise thee, though fairer than whom all men praise,
And godlike for thy grace of hallowed hair
And holy habit of thine eyes, and feet   910
That make the blown foam neither swift nor white
Though the wind winnow and whirl it; yet we praise
Gods, found because of thee adorable
And for thy sake praiseworthiest from all men:
Thee therefore we praise also, thee as these,
Pure, and a light lit at the hands of gods.

TOXEUS

How long will ye whet spears with eloquence,
Fight, and kill beasts dry-handed with sweet words?
Cease, or talk still and slay thy boars at home.

PLEXIPPUS

Why, if she ride among us for a man,   920
Sit thou for her and spin; a man grown girl
Is worth a woman weaponed; sit thou here.

MELEAGER

Peace, and be wise; no gods love idle speech.

PLEXIPPUS

Nor any man a man's mouth woman-tongued.

MELEAGER

For my lips bite not sharper than mine hands.

PLEXIPPUS

Nay, both bite soft, but no whit softly mine.

MELEAGER

Keep thine hands clean; they have time enough to stain.

PLEXIPPUS

For thine shall rest and wax not red to-day.

MELEAGER

Have all thy will of words; talk out thine heart.

ALTHAEA

Refrain your lips, O brethren, and my son,   930
Lest words turn snakes and bite you uttering them.

TOXEUS

Except she give her blood before the gods,
What profit shall a maid be among men?

PLEXIPPUS

Let her come crowned and stretch her throat for a knife,
Bleat out her spirit and die, and so shall men
Through her too prosper and through prosperous gods,
But nowise through her living; shall she live
A flower-bud of the flower-bed, or sweet fruit
For kisses and the honey-making mouth,
And play the shield for strong men and the spear?   940
Then shall the heifer and her mate lock horns,
And the bride overbear the groom, and men
Gods; for no less division sunders these;
Since all things made are seasonable in time,
But if one alter unseasonable are all.
But thou, O Zeus, hear me that I may slay
This beast before thee and no man halve with me
Nor woman, lest these mock thee, though a god,

Who hast made men strong, and thou being wise be held
Foolish; for wise is that thing which endures.   950

ATALANTA

Men, and the chosen of all this people, and thou,
King, I beseech you a little bear with me.
For if my life be shameful that I live,
Let the gods witness and their wrath; but these
Cast no such word against me. Thou, O mine,
O holy, O happy goddess, if I sin
Changing the words of women and the works
For spears and strange men's faces, hast not thou
One shaft of all thy sudden seven that pierced
Seven through the bosom or shining throat or side,   960
All couched about one mother's loosening knees,
All holy born, engraffed of Tantalus?
But if toward any of you I am overbold
That take thus much upon me, let him think
How I, for all my forest holiness,
Fame, and this armed and iron maidenhood,
Pay thus much also; I shall have no man's love
For ever, and no face of children born
Or feeding lips upon me or fastening eyes
For ever, nor being dead shall kings my sons   970
Mourn me and bury, and tears on daughters' cheeks
Burn; but a cold and sacred life, but strange,
But far from dances and the back-blowing torch,
Far off from flowers or any bed of man,
Shall my life be for ever: me the snows
That face the first o' the morning, and cold hills
Full of the land-wind and sea-travelling storms
And many a wandering wing of noisy nights
That know the thunder and hear the thickening wolves —
Me the utmost pine and footless frost of woods   980
That talk with many winds and gods, the hours
Re-risen, and white divisions of the dawn,
Springs thousand-tongued with the intermitting reed
And streams that murmur of the mother snow —
Me these allure, and know me; but no man
Knows, and my goddess only. Lo now, see
If one of all you these things vex at all.
Would God that any of you had all the praise
And I no manner of memory when I die,
So might I show before her perfect eyes   990

Pure, whom I follow, a maiden to my death.
But for the rest let all have all they will;
For is it a grief to you that I have part,
Being woman merely, in your male might and deeds
Done by main strength? yet in my body is throned
As great a heart, and in my spirit, O men,
I have not less of godlike. Evil it were
That one a coward should mix with you, one hand
Fearful, one eye abase itself; and these
Well might ye hate and well revile, not me.   1000
For not the difference of the several flesh
Being vile or noble or beautiful or base
Makes praiseworthy, but purer spirit and heart
Higher than these meaner mouths and limbs, that feed,
Rise, rest, and are and are not; and for me,
What should I say? but by the gods of the world
And this my maiden body, by all oaths
That bind the tongue of men and the evil will,
I am not mighty-minded, nor desire
Crowns, nor the spoil of slain things nor the fame;   1010
Feed ye on these, eat and wax fat; cry out,
Laugh, having eaten, and leap without a lyre,
Sing, mix the wind with clamour, smite and shake
Sonorous timbrels and tumultuous hair,
And fill the dance up with tempestuous feet,
For I will none; but having prayed my prayers
And made thank-offering for prosperities,
I shall go hence and no man see me more.
What thing is this for you to shout me down,
What, for a man to grudge me this my life   1020
As it were envious of all yours, and I
A thief of reputations? nay, for now,
If there be any highest in heaven, a god
Above all thrones and thunders of the gods
Throned, and the wheel of the world roll under him,
Judge he between me and all of you, and see
If I trangress at all: but ye, refrain
Transgressing hands and reinless mouths, and keep
Silence, lest by much foam of violent words
And proper poison of your lips ye die.   1030

OENEUS

O flower of Tegea, maiden, fleetest foot
And holiest head of women, have good cheer

Of thy good words: but ye, depart with her
In peace and reverence, each with blameless eye
Following his fate; exalt your hands and hearts,
Strike, cease not, arrow on arrow and wound on wound,
And go with gods and with the gods return.

CHORUS

Who hath given man speech? or who hath set therein
A thorn for peril and a snare for sin?
For in the word his life is and his breath,   1040
   And in the word his death,
That madness and the infatuate heart may breed
   From the word's womb the deed
And life bring one thing forth ere all pass by,
Even one thing which is ours yet cannot die —
Death. Hast thou seen him ever anywhere,
Time's twin-born brother, imperishable as he
Is perishable and plaintive, clothed with care
   And mutable as sand,
But death is strong and full of blood and fair   1050
And perdurable and like a lord of land?
Nay, time thou seest not, death thou wilt not see
Till life's right hand be loosened from thine hand
   And thy life-days from thee.

For the gods very subtly fashion
   Madness with sadness upon earth:
Not knowing in any wise compassion,
   Nor holding pity of any worth;
And many things they have given and taken,
   And wrought and ruined many things;   1060
The firm land have they loosed and shaken,
   And sealed the sea with all her springs;
They have wearied time with heavy burdens
   And vexed the lips of life with breath:
Set men to labour and given them guerdons,
   Death, and great darkness after death:
Put moans into the bridal measure
   And on the bridal wools a stain;
And circled pain about with pleasure,
   And girdled pleasure about with pain;   1070
And strewed one marriage-bed with tears and fire
For extreme loathing and supreme desire.

What shall be done with all these tears of ours?
 Shall they make watersprings in the fair heaven
To bathe the brows of morning? or like flowers
Be shed and shine before the starriest hours,
 Or made the raiment of the weeping Seven?
Or rather, O our masters, shall they be
Food for the famine of the grievous sea,
 A great well-head of lamentation   1080
Satiating the sad gods? or fall and flow
Among the years and seasons to and fro,
 And wash their feet with tribulation
And fill them full with grieving ere they go?
 Alas, our lords, and yet alas again,
Seeing all your iron heaven is gilt as gold
 But all we smite thereat in vain;
Smite the gates barred with groanings manifold,
 But all the floors are paven with our pain.
Yea, and with weariness of lips and eyes,   1090
With breaking of the bosom, and with sighs,
 We labour, and are clad and fed with grief
And filled with days we would not fain behold
And nights we would not hear of; we wax old,
 All we wax old and wither like a leaf.
We are outcast, strayed between bright sun and moon;
 Our light and darkness are as leaves of flowers,
Black flowers and white, that perish; and the noon
 As midnight, and the night as daylight hours.
 A little fruit a little while is ours,   1100
  And the worm finds it soon.

But up in heaven the high gods one by one
 Lay hands upon the draught that quickeneth,
Fulfilled with all tears shed and all things done,
 And stir with soft imperishable breath
 The bubbling bitterness of life and death,
And hold it to our lips and laugh; but they
Preserve their lips from tasting night or day,
 Lest they too change and sleep, the fates that spun,
The lips that made us and the hands that slay; 1110
 Lest all these change, and heaven bow down to none,
Change and be subject to the secular sway
 And terrene revolution of the sun.
Therefore they thrust it from them, putting time away.

I would the wine of time, made sharp and sweet
   With multitudinous days and nights and tears
   And many mixing savours of strange years,
Were no more trodden of them under feet,
   Cast out and spilt about their holy places:
That life were given them as a fruit to eat   1120
And death to drink as water; that the light
Might ebb, drawn backward from their eyes, and night
   Hide for one hour the imperishable faces.
That they might rise up sad in heaven, and know
Sorrow and sleep, one paler than young snow,
   One cold as blight of dew and ruinous rain;
Rise up and rest and suffer a little, and be
Awhile as all things born with us and we,
   And grieve as men, and like slain men be slain.

For now we know not of them; but one saith   1130
   The gods are gracious, praising God; and one,
When hast thou seen? or hast thou felt his breath
   Touch, nor consume thine eyelids as the sun,
Nor fill thee to the lips with fiery death?
   None hath beheld him, none
Seen above other gods and shapes of things,
Swift without feet and flying without wings,
Intolerable, not clad with death or life,
   Insatiable, not known of night or day,
The lord of love and loathing and of strife   1140
   Who gives a star and takes a sun away;
Who shapes the soul, and makes her a barren wife
   To the earthly body and grievous growth of clay;
Who turns the large limbs to a little flame
   And binds the great sea with a little sand;
Who makes desire, and slays desire with shame;
   Who shakes the heaven as ashes in his hand;
Who, seeing the light and shadow for the same,
   Bids day waste night as fire devours a brand,
Smites without sword, and scourges without rod;   1150
   The supreme evil, God.
Yea, with thine hate, O God, thou hast covered us,
   One saith, and hidden our eyes away from sight,
And made us transitory and hazardous,
   Light things and slight;
Yet have men praised thee, saying, He hath made man thus,
   And he doeth right.

Thou hast kissed us, and hast smitten; thou hast laid
Upon us with thy left hand life, and said,
Live: and again thou hast said, Yield up your breath,   **1160**
And with thy right hand laid upon us death.
Thou hast sent us sleep, and stricken sleep with dreams,
    Saying, Joy is not, but love of joy shall be;
Thou hast made sweet springs for all the pleasant streams,
    In the end thou hast made them bitter with the sea.
Thou hast fed one rose with dust of many men;
    Thou hast marred one face with fire of many tears;
Thou hast taken love, and given us sorrow again;
    With pain thou hast filled us full to the eyes and ears.
Therefore because thou art strong, our father, and we   **1170**
    Feeble; and thou art against us, and thine hand
Constrains us in the shallows of the sea
    And breaks us at the limits of the land;
Because thou hast bent thy lightnings as a bow,
    And loosed the hours like arrows; and let fall
Sins and wild words and many a wingèd woe
    And wars among us, and one end of all;
Because thou hast made the thunder, and thy feet
    Are as a rushing water when the skies
Break, but thy face as an exceeding heat   **1180**
    And flames of fire the eyelids of thine eyes;
Because thou art over all who are over us;
    Because thy name is life and our name death;
Because thou art cruel and men are piteous,
    And our hands labour and thine hand scattereth;
Lo, with hearts rent and knees made tremulous,
    Lo, with ephemeral lips and casual breath,
        At least we witness of thee ere we die
That these things are not otherwise, but thus;
    That each man in his heart sigheth, and saith,   **1190**
        That all men even as I,
All we are against thee, against thee, O God most high.

    But ye, keep ye on earth
    Your lips from over-speech,
Loud words and longing are so little worth;
    And the end is hard to reach.
For silence after grievous things is good,
    And reverence, and the fear that makes men whole,
And shame, and righteous governance of blood,
    And lordship of the soul.   **1200**

But from sharp words and wits men pluck no fruit,
And gathering thorns they shake the tree at root;
For words divide and rend;
But silence is most noble till the end.

ALTHAEA

I heard within the house a cry of news
And came forth eastward hither, where the dawn
Cheers first these warder gods that face the sun
And next our eyes unrisen; for unaware
Came clashes of swift hoofs and trampling feet
And through the windy pillared corridor   1210
Light sharper than the frequent flames of day
That daily fill it from the fiery dawn;
Gleams, and a thunder of people that cried out,
And dust and hurrying horsemen; lo their chief,
That rode with Oeneus rein by rein, returned.
What cheer, O herald of my lord the king?

HERALD

Lady, good cheer and great; the boar is slain.

CHORUS

Praised be all gods that look toward Calydon.

ALTHAEA

Good news and brief; but by whose happier hand?

HERALD

A maiden's and a prophet's and thy son's.   1220

ALTHAEA

Well fare the spear that severed him and life.

HERALD

Thine own, and not an alien, hast thou blest.

ALTHAEA

Twice be thou too for my sake blest and his.

HERALD

At the king's word I rode afoam for thine.

ALTHAEA

Thou sayest he tarrieth till they bring the spoil?

HERALD

Hard by the quarry, where they breathe, O queen.

ALTHAEA

Speak thou their chance; but some bring flowers and crown
These gods and all the lintel, and shed wine,
Fetch sacrifice and slay; for heaven is good.

HERALD

Some furlongs northward where the brakes begin   1230
West of that narrowing range of warrior hills
Whose brooks have bled with battle when thy son
Smote Acarnania, there all they made halt,
And with keen eye took note of spear and hound,
Royally ranked; Laertes island-born,
The young Gerenian Nestor, Panopeus,
And Cepheus and Ancaeus, mightiest thewed,
Arcadians; next, and evil-eyed of these,
Arcadian Atalanta, with twain hounds
Lengthening the leash, and under nose and brow   1240
Glittering with lipless tooth and fire-swift eye;
But from her white braced shoulder the plumed shafts
Rang, and the bow shone from her side; next her
Meleager, like a sun in spring that strikes
Branch into leaf and bloom into the world,
A glory among men meaner; Iphicles,
And following him that slew the biform bull
Pirithous, and divine Eurytion,
And, bride-bound to the gods, Aeacides.
Then Telamon his brother, and Argive-born   1250
The seer and sayer of visions and of truth,
Amphiaraus; and a four-fold strength,
Thine, even thy mother's and thy sister's sons.
And recent from the roar of foreign foam
Jason, and Dryas twin-begot with war,
A blossom of bright battle, sword and man
Shining; and Idas, and the keenest eye
Of Lynceus, and Admetus twice-espoused,
And Hippasus and Hyleus, great in heart.
These having halted bade blow horns, and rode   1260
Through woods and waste lands cleft by stormy streams,
Past yew-trees and the heavy hair of pines,
And where the dew is thickest under oaks,
This way and that; but questing up and down
They saw no trail nor scented; and one said,

Plexippus, Help, or help not, Artemis,
And we will flay thy boarskin with male hands;
But saying, he ceased and said not that he would,
Seeing where the green ooze of a sun-struck marsh
Shook with a thousand reeds untunable,   1270
And in their moist and multitudinous flower
Slept no soft sleep, with violent visions fed,
The blind bulk of the immeasurable beast.
And seeing, he shuddered with sharp lust of praise
Through all his limbs, and launched a double dart.
And missed; for much desire divided him,
Too hot of spirit and feebler than his will,
That his hand failed, though fervent; and the shaft,
Sundering the rushes, in a tamarisk stem
Shook, and stuck fast; then all abode save one,   1280
The Arcadian Atalanta; from her side
Sprang her hounds, labouring at the leash, and slipped,
And plashed ear-deep with plunging feet; but she
Saying, Speed it as I send it for thy sake,
Goddess, drew bow and loosed; the sudden string
Rang, and sprang inward, and the waterish air
Hissed, and the moist plumes of the songless reeds
Moved as a wave which the wind moves no more.
But the boar heaved half out of ooze and slime
His tense flank trembling round the barbèd wound,   1290
Hateful; and fiery with invasive eyes
And bristling with intolerable hair
Plunged, and the hounds clung, and green flowers and white
Reddened and broke all round them where they came.
And charging with sheer tusk he drove, and smote
Hyleus; and sharp death caught his sudden soul,
And violent sleep shed night upon his eyes.
Then Peleus, with strong strain of hand and heart,
Shot; but the sidelong arrow slid, and slew
His comrade born and loving countryman,   1300
Under the left arm smitten, as he no less
Poised a like arrow; and bright blood brake afoam,
And falling, and weighed back by clamorous arms,
Sharp rang the dead limbs of Eurytion.
Then one shot happier, the Cadmean seer,
Amphiaraus; for his sacred shaft
Pierced the red circlet of one ravening eye
Beneath the brute brows of the sanguine boar,
Now bloodier from one slain; but he so galled

Sprang straight, and rearing cried no lesser cry   1310
Than thunder and the roar of wintering streams
That mix their own foam with the yellower sea;
And as a tower that falls by fire in fight
With ruin of walls and all its archery,
And breaks the iron flower of war beneath,
Crushing charred limbs and molten arms of men;
So through crushed branches and the reddening brake
Clamoured and crashed the fervour of his feet,
And trampled, springing sideways from the tusk,
Too tardy a moving mould of heavy strength,   1320
Ancaeus; and as flakes of weak-winged snow
Break, all the hard thews of his heaving limbs
Broke, and rent flesh fell every way, and blood
Flew, and fierce fragments of no more a man.
Then all the heroes drew sharp breath, and gazed,
And smote not; but Meleager, but thy son,
Right in the wild way of the coming curse
Rock-rooted, fair with fierce and fastened lips,
Clear eyes, and springing muscle and shortening limb —
With chin aslant indrawn to a tightening throat,   1330
Grave, and with gathered sinews, like a god, —
Aimed on the left side his well-handled spear
Grasped where the ash was knottiest hewn, and smote,
And with no missile wound, the monstrous boar
Right in the hairiest hollow of his hide
Under the last rib, sheer through bulk and bone,
Deep in; and deeply smitten, and to death,
The heavy horror with his hanging shafts
Leapt, and fell furiously, and from raging lips
Foamed out the latest wrath of all his life.   1340
And all they praised the gods with mightier heart,
Zeus and all gods, but chiefliest Artemis,
Seeing; but Meleager bade whet knives and flay,
Strip and stretch out the splendour of the spoil;
And hot and horrid from the work all these
Sat, and drew breath and drank and made great cheer
And washed the hard sweat off their calmer brows.
For much sweet grass grew higher than grew the reed,
And good for slumber, and every holier herb,
Narcissus, and the low-lying melilote,   1350
And all of goodliest blade and bloom that springs
Where, hid by heavier hyacinth, violet buds
Blossom and burn; and fire of yellower flowers

And light of crescent lilies, and such leaves
As fear the Faun's and know the Dryad's foot;
Olive and ivy and poplar dedicate,
And many a well-spring overwatched of these.
There now they rest; but me the king bade bear
Good tidings to rejoice this town and thee.
Wherefore be glad, and all ye give much thanks,   1360
For fallen is all the trouble of Calydon.

ALTHAEA

Laud ye the gods; for this they have given is good,
And what shall be they hide until their time.
Much good and somewhat grievous hast thou said,
And either well; but let all sad things be,
Till all have made before the prosperous gods
Burnt-offering, and poured out the floral wine.
Look fair, O gods, and favourable; for we
Praise you with no false heart or flattering mouth,
Being merciful, but with pure souls and prayer.   1370

HERALD

Thou hast prayed well; for whoso fears not these,
But once being prosperous waxes huge of heart,
Him shall some new thing unaware destroy.

CHORUS

O that I now, I too were
By deep wells and water-floods,
Streams of ancient hills, and where
All the wan green places bear
Blossoms cleaving to the sod,
Fruitless fruit, and grasses fair,
Or such darkest ivy-buds   1380
As divide thy yellow hair,
Bacchus, and their leaves that nod
Round thy fawnskin brush the bare
Snow-soft shoulders of a god;
There the year is sweet, and there
Earth is full of secret springs,
And the fervent rose-cheeked hours,
Those that marry dawn and noon,
There are sunless, there look pale
In dim leaves and hidden air,   1390
Pale as grass or latter flowers

Or the wild vine's wan wet rings
Full of dew beneath the moon,
And all day the nightingale
Sleeps, and all night sings;
There in cold remote recesses
That nor alien eyes assail,
Feet, nor imminence of wings,
Nor a wind nor any tune,
Thou, O queen and holiest,   1400
Flower the whitest of all things,
With reluctant lengthening tresses
And with sudden splendid breast
Save of maidens unbeholden,
There art wont to enter, there
Thy divine swift limbs and golden
Maiden growth of unbound hair,
Bathed in waters white,
Shine, and many a maid's by thee
In moist woodland or the hilly   1410
Flowerless brakes where wells abound
Out of all men's sight;
Or in lower pools that see
All their marges clothed all round
With the innumerable lily,
Whence the golden-girdled bee
Flits through flowering rush to fret
White or duskier violet,
Fair as those that in far years
With their buds left luminous   1420
And their little leaves made wet,
From the warmer dew of tears,
Mother's tears in extreme need,
Hid the limbs of Iamus,
Of thy brother's seed;
For his heart was piteous
Toward him, even as thine heart now
Pitiful toward us;
Thine, O goddess, turning hither
A benignant blameless brow;   1430
Seeing enough of evil done
And lives withered as leaves wither
In the blasting of the sun;
Seeing enough of hunters dead,
Ruin enough of all our year,

Herds and harvests slain and shed,
Herdsmen stricken many an one,
Fruits and flocks consumed together,
And great length of deadly days.
Yet with reverent lips and fear   1440
Turn we toward thee, turn and praise
For this lightening of clear weather
And prosperities begun.
For not seldom, when all air
As bright water without breath
Shines, and when men fear not, fate
Without thunder unaware
Breaks, and brings down death.
Joy with grief ye great gods give,
Good with bad, and overbear   1450
All the pride of us that live,
All the high estate,
As ye long since overbore,
As in old time long before,
Many a strong man and a great,
All that were.
But do thou, sweet, otherwise,
Having heed of all our prayer,
Taking note of all our sighs;
We beseech thee by thy light,   1460
By thy bow, and thy sweet eyes,
And the kingdom of the night,
Be thou favourable and fair;
Be thine arrows and thy might
And Orion overthrown;
By the maiden thy delight,
By the indissoluble zone
And the sacred hair.

MESSENGER

Maidens, if ye will sing now, shift your song,
Bow down, cry, wail for pity; is this a time   1470
For singing? nay, for strewing of dust and ash,
Rent raiment, and for bruising of the breast.

CHORUS

What new thing wolf-like lurks behind thy words?
What snake's tongue in thy lips? what fire in the eyes?

MESSENGER

Bring me before the queen and I will speak.

CHORUS

Lo, she comes forth as from thank-offering made.

MESSENGER

A barren offering for a bitter gift.

ALTHAEA

What are these borne on branches, and the face
Covered? no mean men living, but now slain
Such honour have they, if any dwell with death.   1480

MESSENGER

Queen, thy twain brethren and thy mother's sons.

ALTHAEA

Lay down your dead till I behold their blood
If it be mine indeed, and I will weep.

MESSENGER

Weep if thou wilt, for these men shall no more.

ALTHAEA

O brethren, O my father's sons, of me
Well loved and well reputed, I should weep
Tears dearer than the dear blood drawn from you
But that I know you not uncomforted,
Sleeping no shameful sleep, however slain,
For my son surely hath avenged you dead.   1490

MESSENGER

Nay, should thine own seed slay himself, O queen?

ALTHAEA

Thy double word brings forth a double death.

MESSENGER

Know this then singly, by one hand they fell.

ALTHAEA

What mutterest thou with thine ambiguous mouth?

MESSENGER

Slain by thy son's hand; is that saying so hard?

ALTHAEA

Our time is come upon us: it is here.

CHORUS

O miserable, and spoiled at thine own hand.

ALTHAEA

Wert thou not called Meleager from this womb?

CHORUS

A grievous huntsman hath it bred to thee.

ALTHAEA

Wert thou born fire, and shalt thou not devour?   1500

CHORUS

The fire thou madest, will it consume even thee?

ALTHAEA

My dreams are fallen upon me; burn thou too.

CHORUS

Not without God are visions born and die.

ALTHAEA

The gods are many about me; I am one.

CHORUS

She groans as men wrestling with heavier gods.

ALTHAEA

They rend me, they divide me, they destroy.

CHORUS

Or one labouring in travail of strange births.

ALTHAEA

They are strong, they are strong; I am broken, and these prevail.

CHORUS

The god is great against her; she will die.

ALTHAEA

Yea, but not now; for my heart too is great.   1510
I would I were not here in sight of the sun.
But thou, speak all thou sawest, and I will die.

MESSENGER

O queen, for queenlike hast thou borne thyself,
A little word may hold so great mischance.
For in division of the sanguine spoil
These men thy brethren wrangling bade yield up
The boar's head and the horror of the hide
That this might stand a wonder in Calydon,
Hallowed; and some drew toward them; but thy son
With great hands grasping all that weight of hair   1520
Cast down the dead heap clanging and collapsed
At female feet, saying This thy spoil not mine,
Maiden, thine own hand for thyself hath reaped,
And all this praise God gives thee: she thereat
Laughed, as when dawn touches the sacred night
The sky sees laugh and redden and divide
Dim lips and eyelids virgin of the sun,
Hers, and the warm slow breasts of morning heave,
Fruitful, and flushed with flame from lamp-lit hours,
And maiden undulation of clear hair   1530
Colour the clouds; so laughed she from pure heart,
Lit with a low blush to the braided hair,
And rose-coloured and cold like very dawn,
Golden and godlike, chastely with chaste lips,
A faint grave laugh; and all they held their peace,
And she passed by them. Then one cried Lo now,
Shall not the Arcadian shoot out lips at us,
Saying all we were despoiled by this one girl?
And all they rode against her violently
And cast the fresh crown from her hair, and now   1540
They had rent her spoil away, dishonouring her,
Save that Meleager, as a tame lion chafed,
Bore on them, broke them, and as fire cleaves wood
So clove and drove them, smitten in twain; but she
Smote not nor heaved up hand; and this man first,
Plexippus, crying out This for love's sake, sweet,
Drove at Meleager, who with spear straightening
Pierced his cheek through; then Toxeus made for him,
Dumb, but his spear spake; vain and violent words.
Fruitless; for him too stricken through both sides   1550
The earth felt falling, and his horse's foam

Blanched thy son's face, his slayer; and these being slain,
None moved nor spake; but Oeneus bade bear hence
These made of heaven infatuate in their deaths,
Foolish; for these would baffle fate, and fell.
And they passed on, and all men honoured her,
Being honourable, as one revered of heaven.

ALTHAEA

What say you, women? is all this not well done?

CHORUS

No man doth well but God hath part in him.

ALTHAEA

But no part here; for these my brethren born   1560
Ye have no part in, these ye know not of
As I that was their sister, a sacrifice
Slain in their slaying. I would I had died for these;
For this man dead walked with me, child by child,
And made a weak staff for my feebler feet
With his own tender wrist and hand, and held
And led me softly and showed me gold and steel
And shining shapes of mirror and bright crown
And all things fair; and threw light spears, and brought
Young hounds to huddle at my feet and thrust   1570
Tame heads against my little maiden breasts
And please me with great eyes; and those days went
And these are bitter and I a barren queen
And sister miserable, a grievous thing
And mother of many curses; and she too,
My sister Leda, sitting overseas
With fair fruits round her, and her faultless lord,
Shall curse me, saying A sorrow and not a son,
Sister, thou barest, even a burning fire,
A brand consuming thine own soul and me.   1580
But ye now, sons of Thestius, make good cheer,
For ye shall have such wood to funeral fire
As no king hath; and flame that once burnt down
Oil shall not quicken or breath relume or wine
Refresh again; much costlier than fine gold,
And more than many lives of wandering men.

CHORUS

O queen, thou hast yet with thee love-worthy things,
Thine husband, and the great strength of thy son.

ALTHAEA

Who shall get brothers for me while I live?
Who bear them? who bring forth in lieu of these?   1590
Are not our fathers and our brethren one,
And no man like them? are not mine here slain?
Have we not hung together, he and I,
Flowerwise feeding as the feeding bees,
With mother-milk for honey? and this man too,
Dead, with my son's spear thrust between his sides,
Hath he not seen us, later born than he,
Laugh with lips filled, and laughed again for love?
There were no sons then in the world, nor spears,   1600
Nor deadly births of women; but the gods
Allowed us, and our days were clear of these.
I would I had died unwedded, and brought forth
No swords to vex the world; for these that spake
Sweet words long since and loved me will not speak
Nor love nor look upon me; and all my life
I shall not hear nor see them living men.
But I too living, how shall I now live?
What life shall this be with my son, to know
What hath been and desire what will not be,
Look for dead eyes and listen for dead lips,   1610
And kill mine own heart with remembering them,
And with those eyes that see their slayer alive
Weep, and wring hands that clasp him by the hand?
How shall I bear my dreams of them, to hear
False voices, feel the kisses of false mouths
And footless sound of perished feet, and then
Wake and hear only it may be their own hounds
Whine masterless in miserable sleep,
And see their boar-spears and their beds and seats
And all the gear and housings of their lives   1620
And not the men? shall hounds and horses mourn,
Pine with strange eyes, and prick up hungry ears,
Famish and fail at heart for their dear lords,
And I not heed at all? and those blind things
Fall off from life for love's sake, and I live?
Surely some death is better than some life,
Better one death for him and these and me.
For if the gods had slain them it may be
I had endured it; if they had fallen by war
Or by the nets and knives of privy death   1630
And by hired hands while sleeping, this thing too
I had set my soul to suffer; or this hunt,

Had this dispatched them, under tusk or tooth
Torn, sanguine, trodden, broken; for all deaths
Or honourable or with facile feet avenged
And hands of swift gods following, all save this,
Are bearable; but not for their sweet land
Fighting, but not a sacrifice, lo these
Dead; for I had not then shed all mine heart   1640
Out at mine eyes; then either with good speed,
Being just, I had slain their slayer atoningly,
Or strewn with flowers their fire and on their tombs
Hung crowns, and over them a song, and seen
Their praise outflame their ashes: for all men,
All maidens, had come thither, and from pure lips
Shed songs upon them, from heroic eyes
Tears; and their death had been a deathless life;
But now, by no man hired nor alien sword,
By their own kindred are they fallen, in peace,
After much peril, friendless among friends,   1650
By hateful hands they loved; and how shall mine
Touch these returning red and not from war,
These fatal from the vintage of men's veins,
Dead men my brethren? how shall these wash off
No festal stains of undelightful wine,
How mix the blood, my blood on them, with me,
Holding mine hand? or how shall I say, son,
That am no sister? but by night and day
Shall we not sit and hate each other, and think
Things hate-worthy? not live with shamefast eyes,   1660
Brow-beaten, treading soft with fearful feet,
Each unupbraided, each without rebuke
Convicted, and without a word reviled
Each of another? and I shall let thee live
And see thee strong and hear men for thy sake
Praise me, but these thou wouldest not let live
No man shall praise for ever? these shall lie
Dead, unbeloved, unholpen, all through thee?
Sweet were they toward me living, and mine heart
Desired them, but was then well satisfied,   1670
That now is as men hungered; and these dead
I shall want always to the day I die.
For all things else and all men may renew;
Yea, son for son the gods may give and take.
But never a brother or sister any more.

CHORUS

Nay, for the son lies close about thine heart,
Full of thy milk, warm from thy womb, and drains
Life and the blood of life and all thy fruit,
Eats thee and drinks thee as who breaks bread and eats,
Treads wine and drinks, thyself, a sect of thee;   1680
And if he feed not, shall not thy flesh faint?
Or drink not, are not thy lips dead for thirst?
This thing moves more than all things, even thy son,
That thou cleave to him; and he shall honour thee,
Thy womb that bare him and the breasts he knew,
Reverencing most for thy sake all his gods.

ALTHAEA

But these the gods too gave me, and these my son,
Not reverencing his gods nor mine own heart
Nor the old sweet years nor all venerable things,
But cruel, and in his ravin like a beast,   1690
Hath taken away to slay them: yea, and she,
She the strange woman, she the flower, the sword,
Red from spilt blood, a mortal flower to men,
Adorable, detestable — even she
Saw with strange eyes and with strange lips rejoiced,
Seeing these mine own slain of mine own, and me
Made miserable above all miseries made,
A grief among all women in the world,
A name to be washed out with all men's tears.

CHORUS   1700

Strengthen thy spirit; is this not also a god,
Chance, and the wheel of all necessities?
Hard things have fallen upon us from harsh gods,
Whom lest worse hap rebuke we not for these.

ALTHAEA

My spirit is strong against itself, and I
For these things' sake cry out on mine own soul
That it endures outrage, and dolorous days,
And life, and this inexpiable impotence.
Weak am I, weak and shameful; my breath drawn
Shames me, and monstrous things and violent gods.
What shall atone? what heal me? what bring back   1710
Strength to the foot, light to the face? what herb
Assuage me? what restore me? what release?

What strange thing eaten or drunken, O great gods,
Make me as you or as the beasts that feed,
Slay and divide and cherish their own hearts?
For these ye show us; and we less than these
Have not wherewith to live as all these things
Which all their lives fare after their own kind
As who doth well rejoicing; but we ill,
Weeping or laughing, we whom eyesight fails,   1720
Knowledge and light of face and perfect heart,
And hands we lack, and wit; and all our days
Sin, and have hunger, and die infatuated.
For madness have ye given us and not health,
And sins whereof we know not; and for these
Death, and sudden destruction unaware.
What shall we say now? what thing comes of us?

CHORUS

Alas, for all this all men undergo.

ALTHAEA

Wherefore I will not that these twain, O gods,
Die as a dog dies, eaten of creeping things,   1730
Abominable, a loathing; but though dead
Shall they have honour and such funereal flame
As strews men's ashes in their enemies' face
And blinds their eyes who hate them: lest men say,
"Lo how they lie, and living had great kin,
And none of these hath pity of them, and none
Regards them lying, and none is wrung at heart,
None moved in spirit for them, naked and slain,
Abhorred, abased, and no tears comfort them":
And in the dark this grieve Eurythemis,   1740
Hearing how these her sons come down to her
Unburied, unavenged, as kinless men,
And had a queen their sister. That were shame
Worse than this grief. Yet how to atone at all
I know not; seeing the love of my born son,
A new-made mother's new-born love, that grows
From the soft child to the strong man, now soft
Now strong as either, and still one sole same love,
Strives with me, no light thing to strive withal;
This love is deep, and natural to man's blood,   1750
And ineffaceable with many tears.
Yet shall not these rebuke me though I die,

Nor she in that waste world with all her dead,
My mother, among the pale flocks fallen as leaves,
Folds of dead people, and alien from the sun;
Nor lack some bitter comfort, some poor praise,
Being queen, to have borne her daughter like a queen,
Righteous; and though mine own fire burn me too,
She shall have honour and these her sons, though dead.
But all the gods will, all they do, and we   1760
Not all we would, yet somewhat; and one choice
We have, to live and do just deeds and die.

CHORUS

Terrible words she communes with, and turns
Swift fiery eyes in doubt against herself,
And murmurs as who talks in dreams with death.

ALTHAEA

For the unjust also dieth, and him all men
Hate, and himself abhors the unrighteousness,
And seeth his own dishonour intolerable.
But I being just, doing right upon myself,
Slay mine own soul, and no man born shames me.   1770
For none constrains nor shall rebuke, being done,
What none compelled me doing; thus these things fare.
Ah, ah, that such things should so fare; ah me,
That I am found to do them and endure,
Chosen and constrained to choose, and bear myself
Mine own wound through mine own flesh to the heart
Violently stricken, a spoiler and a spoil,
A ruin ruinous, fallen on mine own son.
Ah, ah, for me too as for these; alas,
For that is done that shall be, and mine hand   1780
Full of the deed, and full of blood mine eyes,
That shall see never nor touch anything
Save blood unstanched and fire unquenchable.

CHORUS

What wilt thou do? what ails thee? for the house
Shakes ruinously; wilt thou bring fire for it?

ALTHAEA

Fire in the roofs, and on the lintels fire.
Lo ye, who stand and weave, between the doors,
There; and blood drips from hand and thread, and stains

Threshold and raiment and me passing in
Flecked with the sudden sanguine drops of death.   **1790**

CHORUS

Alas that time is stronger than strong men,
Fate than all gods: and these are fallen on us.

ALTHAEA

A little since and I was glad; and now
I never shall be glad or sad again.

CHORUS

Between two joys a grief grows unaware.

ALTHAEA

A little while and I shall laugh; and then
I shall weep never and laugh not any more.

CHORUS

What shall be said? for words are thorns to grief.
Withhold thyself a little and fear the gods.

ALTHAEA

Fear died when these were slain; and I am as dead,   **1800**
And fear is of the living; these fear none.

CHORUS

Have pity upon all people for their sake.

ALTHAEA

It is done now; shall I put back my day?

CHORUS

An end is come, an end; this is of God.

ALTHAEA

I am fire, and burn myself; keep clear of fire.

CHORUS

The house is broken, is broken; it shall not stand.

ALTHAEA

Woe, woe for him that breaketh; and a rod
Smote it of old, and now the axe is here.

CHORUS

Not as with sundering of the earth
    Nor as with cleaving of the sea   1810
Nor fierce foreshadowings of a birth
    Nor flying dreams of death to be
Nor loosening of the large world's girth
And quickening of the body of night,
    And sound of thunder in men's ears
And fire of lightning in men's sight,
    Fate, mother of desires and fears,
    Bore unto men the law of tears;
But sudden, an unfathered flame,
    And broken out of night, she shone,   1820
She, without body, without name,
    In days forgotten and foregone;
And heaven rang round her as she came
Like smitten cymbals, and lay bare;
    Clouds and great stars, thunders and snows,
The blue sad fields and folds of air,
    The life that breathes, the life that grows,
    All wind, all fire, that burns or blows,
Even all these knew her: for she is great;
    The daughter of doom, the mother of death,   1830
The sister of sorrow; a lifelong weight
    That no man's finger lighteneth,
Nor any god can lighten fate;
A landmark seen across the way
    Where one race treads as the other trod;
An evil sceptre, an evil stay,
    Wrought for a staff, wrought for a rod,
    The bitter jealousy of God.

For death is deep as the sea,
    And fate as the waves thereof.   1840
Shall the waves take pity on thee
    Or the southwind offer thee love?
Wilt thou take the night for thy day
Or the darkness for light on thy way,
    Till thou say in thine heart Enough?
Behold, thou art over fair, thou art over wise;
The sweetness of spring in thine hair, and the light in thine eyes.
The light of the spring in thine eyes, and the sound in thine ears;
Yet thine heart shall wax heavy with sighs and thine eyelids with tears.
Wilt thou cover thine hair with gold, and with silver thy feet?   1850

Hast thou taken the purple to fold thee, and made thy mouth sweet?
Behold, when thy face is made bare, he that loved thee shall hate;
Thy face shall be no more fair at the fall of thy fate.
For thy life shall fall as a leaf and be shed as the rain,
And the veil of thine head shall be grief; and the crown shall be pain.

ALTHAEA

Ho, ye that wail, and ye that sing, make way
Till I be come among you. Hide your tears,
Ye little weepers, and your laughing lips,
Ye laughers for a little; lo mine eyes
That outweep heaven at rainiest, and my mouth   1860
That laughs as gods laugh at us. Fate's are we,
Yet fate is ours a breathing-space; yea, mine,
Fate is made mine for ever; he is my son,
My bedfellow, my brother. You strong gods,
Give place unto me; I am as any of you,
To give life and to take life. Thou, old earth,
That hast made man and unmade; thou whose mouth
Looks red from the eaten fruits of thine own womb;
Behold me with what lips upon what food
I feed and fill my body; even with flesh   1870
Made of my body. Lo, the fire I lit
I burn with fire to quench it; yea, with flame
I burn up even the dust and ash thereof.

CHORUS

Woman, what fire is this thou burnest with?

ALTHAEA

Yea to the bone, yea to the blood and all.

CHORUS

For this thy face and hair are as one fire.

ALTHAEA

A tongue that licks and beats upon the dust.

CHORUS

And in thine eyes are hollow light and heat.

ALTHAEA

Of flame not fed with hand or frankincense.

CHORUS

I fear thee for the trembling of thine eyes.   1880

ALTHAEA

Neither with love they tremble nor for fear.

CHORUS

And thy mouth shuddering like a shot bird.

ALTHAEA

Not as the bride's mouth when man kisses it.

CHORUS

Nay, but what thing is this thing thou hast done?

ALTHAEA

Look, I am silent, speak your eyes for me.

CHORUS

I see a faint fire lightening from the hall.

ALTHAEA

Gaze, stretch your eyes, strain till the lids drop off.

CHORUS

Flushed pillars down the flickering vestibule.

ALTHAEA

Stretch with your necks like birds: cry, chirp as they.

CHORUS

And a long brand that blackens: and white dust.   1890

ALTHAEA

O children, what is this ye see? your eyes
Are blinder than night's face at fall of moon.
That is my son, my flesh, my fruit of life,
My travail, and the year's weight of my womb,
Meleager, a fire enkindled of mine hands
And of mine hands extinguished; this is he.

CHORUS

O gods, what word has flown out at thy mouth?

ALTHAEA

I did this and I say this and I die.

CHORUS

Death stands upon the doorway of thy lips,
And in thy mouth has death set up his house.   1900

ALTHAEA

O death, a little, a little while, sweet death,
Until I see the brand burnt down and die.

CHORUS

She reels as any reed under the wind,
And cleaves unto the ground with staggering feet.

ALTHAEA

Girls, one thing will I say and hold my peace.
I that did this will weep not nor cry out,
Cry ye and weep: I will not call on gods,
Call ye on them; I will not pity man,
Shew ye your pity. I know not if I live;
Save that I feel the fire upon my face   1910
And on my cheek the burning of a brand.
Yea the smoke bites me, yea I drink the steam
With nostril and with eyelid and with lip
Insatiate and intolerant; and mine hands
Burn, and fire feeds upon mine eyes; I reel
As one made drunk with living, whence he draws
Drunken delight; yet I, though mad for joy,
Loathe my long living and am waxen red
As with the shadow of shed blood; behold,
I am kindled with the flames that fade in him,   1920
I am swollen with subsiding of his veins,
I am flooded with his ebbing; my lit eyes
Flame with the falling fire that leaves his lids
Bloodless; my cheek is luminous with blood
Because his face is ashen. Yet, O child,
Son, first-born, fairest — O sweet mouth, sweet eyes,
That drew my life out through my suckling breast,
That shone and clove mine heart through — O soft knees
Clinging, O tender treadings of soft feet,
Cheeks warm with little kissings — O child, child,   1930
What have we made each other? Lo, I felt
Thy weight cleave to me, a burden of beauty, O son,

Thy cradled brows and loveliest loving lips,
The floral hair, the little lightening eyes,
And all thy goodly glory; with mine hands
Delicately I fed thee, with my tongue
Tenderly spake, saying, Verily in God's time,
For all the little likeness of thy limbs,
Son, I shall make thee a kingly man to fight,
A lordly leader; and hear before I die,   1940
"She bore the goodliest sword of all the world."
Oh! oh! For all my life turns round on me;
I am severed from myself, my name is gone,
My name that was a healing, it is changed,
My name is a consuming. From this time,
Though mine eyes reach to the end of all these things,
My lips shall not unfasten till I die.

SEMICHORUS

She has filled with sighing the city,
   And the ways thereof with tears;
She arose, she girdled her sides,   1950
She set her face as a bride's;
She wept, and she had no pity;
   Trembled, and felt no fears.

SEMICHORUS

Her eyes were clear as the sun,
   Her brows were fresh as the day;
She girdled herself with gold,
Her robes were manifold;
But the days of her worship are done,
   Her praise is taken away.

SEMICHORUS

For she set her hand to the fire,   1960
   With her mouth she kindled the same;
As the mouth of a flute-player,
So was the mouth of her;
With the might of her strong desire
   She blew the breath of the flame.

SEMICHORUS

She set her hand to the wood,
   She took the fire in her hand;
As one who is nigh to death,

She panted with strange breath;
She opened her lips unto blood,   **1970**
  She breathed and kindled the brand.

SEMICHORUS

As a wood-dove newly shot,
  She sobbed and lifted her breast;
She sighed and covered her eyes,
Filling her lips with sighs;
She sighed, she withdrew herself not,
  She refrained not, taking not rest;

SEMICHORUS

But as the wind which is drouth,
  And as the air which is death,
As storm that severeth ships,   **1980**
Her breath severing her lips,
The breath came forth of her mouth
  And the fire came forth of her breath.

SECOND MESSENGER

Queen, and you maidens, there is come on us
A thing more deadly than the face of death;
Meleager the good lord is as one slain.

SEMICHORUS

Without sword, without sword is he stricken;
  Slain, and slain without hand.

SECOND MESSENGER

For as keen ice divided of the sun
His limbs divide, and as thawed snow the flesh   **1990**
Thaws from all his body to the hair.

SEMICHORUS

He wastes as the embers quicken;
  With the brand he fades as a brand.

SECOND MESSENGER

Even while they sang and all drew hither and he
Lifted both hands to crown the Arcadian's hair
And fix the looser leaves, both hands fell down.

SEMICHORUS

With rending of cheek and of hair
Lament ye, mourn for him, weep.

SECOND MESSENGER

Straightway the crown slid off and smote on earth,
First fallen; and he, grasping his own hair, groaned   2000
And cast his raiment round his face and fell.

SEMICHORUS

Alas for visions that were,
And soothsayings spoken in sleep.

SECOND MESSENGER

But the king twitched his reins in and leapt down
And caught him, crying out twice "O child" and thrice,
So that men's eyelids thickened with their tears.

SEMICHORUS

Lament with a long lamentation,
Cry, for an end is at hand.

SECOND MESSENGER

O son, he said, son, lift thine eyes, draw breath,
Pity me; but Meleager with sharp lips   2010
Gasped, and his face waxed like as sunburnt grass.

SEMICHORUS

Cry aloud, O thou kingdom, O nation,
O stricken, a ruinous land.

SECOND MESSENGER

Whereat King Oeneus, straightening feeble knees,
With feeble hands heaved up a lessening weight,
And laid him sadly in strange hands, and wept.

SEMICHORUS

Thou art smitten, her lord, her desire,
Thy dear blood wasted as rain.

SECOND MESSENGER

And they with tears and rendings of the beard
Bear hither a breathing body, wept upon   2020
And lightening at each footfall, sick to death.

SEMICHORUS

Thou madest thy sword as a fire,
With fire for a sword thou art slain.

SECOND MESSENGER

And lo, the feast turned funeral, and the crowns
Fallen; and the huntress and the hunter trapped;
And weeping and changed faces and veiled hair.

MELEAGER

Let your hands meet
Round the weight of my head;
Lift ye my feet
As the feet of the dead;   2030

For the flesh of my body is molten, the limbs of it molten as lead.

CHORUS

O thy luminous face,
Thine imperious eyes!
O the grief, O the grace,
As of day when it dies!

Who is this bending over thee, lord, with tears and suppression of
  sighs?

MELEAGER

Is a bride so fair?
Is a maid so meek?
With unchapleted hair,
With unfilleted cheek,   2040

Atalanta, the pure among women, whose name is as blessing to speak.

ATALANTA

I would that with feet
Unsandalled, unshod,
Overbold, overfleet,
I had swum not nor trod

From Arcadia to Calydon northward, a blast of the envy of God.

MELEAGER

Unto each man his fate;
Unto each as he saith
In whose fingers the weight
Of the world is as breath;   2050

Yet I would that in clamour of battle mine hands had laid hold upon
  death.

CHORUS

Not with cleaving of shields
And their clash in thine ear,
When the lord of fought fields
Breaketh spearshaft from spear,
Thou art broken, our lord, thou art broken, with travail and labour and fear.

MELEAGER

Would God he had found me
Beneath fresh boughs!
Would God he had bound me
Unawares in mine house,   2060
With light in mine eyes, and songs in my lips, and a crown on my brows!

CHORUS

Whence art thou sent from us?
Whither thy goal?
How art thou rent from us,
Thou that wert whole,
As with severing of eyelids and eyes, as with sundering of body and soul!

MELEAGER

My heart is within me
As an ash in the fire;
Whosoever hath seen me,
Without lute, without lyre,   2070
Shall sing of me grievous things, even things that were ill to desire.

CHORUS

Who shall raise thee
From the house of the dead?
Or what man praise thee
That thy praise may be said?
Alas thy beauty! alas thy body! alas thine head!

MELEAGER

But thou, O mother,
The dreamer of dreams,
Wilt thou bring forth another
To feel the sun's beams   2080
When I move among shadows a shadow, and wail by impassable streams?

OENEUS

What thing wilt thou leave me
  Now this thing is done?
A man wilt thou give me,
  A son for my son,
For the light of mine eyes, the desire of my life, the desirable one?

CHORUS

Thou wert glad above others,
  Yea, fair beyond word;
Thou wert glad among mothers;
  For each man that heard   2090
Of thee, praise there was added unto thee, as wings to the feet of a
  bird.

OENEUS

Who shall give back
  Thy face of old years,
With travail made black,
  Grown grey among fears,
Mother of sorrow, mother of cursing, mother of tears?

MELEAGER

Though thou art as fire
  Fed with fuel in vain,
My delight, my desire,
  Is more chaste than the rain,   2100
More pure than the dewfall, more holy than stars are that live without
  stain.

ATALANTA

I would that as water
  My life's blood had thawn,
Or as winter's wan daughter
  Leaves lowland and lawn
Spring-stricken, or ever mine eyes had beheld thee made dark in thy
  dawn.

CHORUS

When thou dravest the men
  Of the chosen of Thrace,
None turned him again
  Nor endured he thy face   2110
Clothed round with the blush of the battle, with light from a terrible
  place.

OENEUS

Thou shouldst die as he dies
For whom none sheddeth tears;
Filling thine eyes
And fulfilling thine ears
With the brilliance of battle, the bloom and the beauty, the splendour
of spears.

CHORUS

In the ears of the world
It is sung, it is told,
And the light thereof hurled
And the noise thereof rolled   2120
From the Acroceraunian snow to the ford of the fleece of gold.

MELEAGER

Would God ye could carry me
Forth of all these;
Heap sand and bury me
By the Chersonese
Where the thundering Bosphorus answers the thunder of Pontic seas.

OENEUS

Dost thou mock at our praise
And the singing begun
And the men of strange days
Praising my son   2130
In the folds of the hills of home, high places of Calydon?

MELEAGER

For the dead man no home is;
Ah, better to be
What the flower of the foam is
In fields of the sea,
That the sea-waves might be as my raiment, the gulf-stream a garment
for me.

CHORUS

Who shall seek thee and bring
And restore thee thy day,
When the dove dipt her wing
And the oars won their way   2140
Where the narrowing Symplegades whitened the straits of Propontis
with spray?

MELEAGER

Will ye crown me my tomb
Or exalt me my name,
Now my spirits consume,
Now my flesh is a flame?
Let the sea slake it once, and men speak of me sleeping to praise **me**
or shame.

CHORUS

Turn back now, turn thee,
As who turns him to wake;
Though the life in thee burn thee,
Couldst thou bathe it and slake 2150
Where the sea-ridge of Helle hangs heavier, and east upon west waters
break?

MELEAGER

Would the winds blow me back
Or the waves hurl me home?
Ah, to touch in the track
Where the pine learnt to roam
Cold girdles and crowns of the sea-gods, cool blossoms of water and
foam!

CHORUS

The gods may release
That they made fast;
Thy soul shall have ease
In thy limbs at the last; 2160
But what shall they give thee for life, sweet life that is overpast?

MELEAGER

Not the life of men's veins,
Not of flesh that conceives;
But the grace that remains,
The fair beauty that cleaves
To the life of the rains in the grasses, the life of the dews on the leaves.

CHORUS

Thou wert helmsman and chief;
Wilt thou turn in an hour,
Thy limbs to the leaf,
Thy face to the flower, 2170
Thy blood to the water, thy soul to the gods who divide and devour?

MELEAGER

The years are hungry,
They wail all their days;
The gods wax angry
And weary of praise;
And who shall bridle their lips? and who shall straiten their ways?

CHORUS

The gods guard over us
With sword and with rod;
Weaving shadow to cover us,
Heaping the sod,   2180
That law may fulfil herself wholly, to darken man's face before God.

MELEAGER

O holy head of Oeneus, lo thy son
Guiltless, yet red from alien guilt, yet foul
With kinship of contaminated lives,
Lo, for their blood I die; and mine own blood
For bloodshedding of mine is mixed therewith,
That death may not discern me from my kin.
Yet with clean heart I die and faultless hand,
Not shamefully; thou therefore of thy love
Salute me, and bid fare among the dead   2190
Well, as the dead fare; for the best man dead
Fares sadly; nathless I now faring well
Pass without fear where nothing is to fear
Having thy love about me and thy goodwill,
O father, among dark places and men dead.

OENEUS

Child, I salute thee with sad heart and tears,
And bid thee comfort, being a perfect man
In fight, and honourable in the house of peace.
The gods give thee fair wage and dues of death,
And me brief days and ways to come at thee.   2200

MELEAGER *to mother*

Pray thou thy days be long before thy death,
And full of ease and kingdom; seeing in death
There is no comfort and none aftergrowth,
Nor shall one thence look up and see day's dawn
Nor light upon the land whither I go.
Live thou and take thy fill of days and die

When thy day comes; and make not much of death
Lest ere thy day thou reap an evil thing.
Thou too, the bitter mother and mother-plague
Of this my weary body — thou too, queen,   2210
The source and end, the sower and the scythe,
The rain that ripens and the drought that slays,
The sand that swallows and the spring that feeds,
To make me and unmake me — thou, I say,
Althaea, since my father's ploughshare, drawn
Through fatal seedland of a female field,
Furrowed thy body, whence a wheaten ear
Strong from the sun and fragrant from the rains
I sprang and cleft the closure of thy womb,
Mother, I dying with unforgetful tongue   2220
Hail thee as holy and worship thee as just
Who art unjust and unholy; and with my knees
Would worship, but thy fire and subtlety,
Dissundering them, devour me; for these limbs
Are as light dust and crumblings from mine urn
Before the fire has touched them; and my face
As a dead leaf or dead foot's mark on snow,
And all this body a broken barren tree
That was so strong, and all this flower of life
Disbranched and desecrated miserably,   2230
And minished all that god-like muscle and might
And lesser than a man's: for all my veins
Fail me, and all mine ashen life burns down.
I would thou hadst let me live; but gods averse,
But fortune, and the fiery feet of change,
And time, these would not, these tread out my life,
These and not thou; me too thou hast loved, and I
Thee; but this death was mixed with all my life,
Mine end with my beginning: and this law,
This only, slays me, and not my mother at all.   2240
And let no brother or sister grieve too sore,
Nor melt their hearts out on me with their tears,
Since extreme love and sorrowing overmuch
Vex the great gods, and overloving men
Slay and are slain for love's sake; and this house
Shall bear much better children; why should these
Weep? but in patience let them live their lives
And mine pass by forgotten: thou alone,
Mother, thou sole and only, thou not these,
Keep me in mind a little when I die   2250

Because I was thy first-born; let thy soul
Pity me, pity even me gone hence and dead,
Though thou wert wroth, and though thou bear again
Much happier sons, and all men later born
Exceedingly excel me; yet do thou
Forget not, nor think shame; I was thy son.
Time was I did not shame thee; and time was
I thought to live and make thee honourable
With deeds as great as these men's; but they live,
These, and I die; and what thing should have been   2260
Surely I know not; yet I charge thee, seeing
I am dead already, love me not the less,
Me, O my mother; I charge thee by these gods,
My father's, and that holier breast of thine,
By these that see me dying, and that which nursed,
Love me not less, thy first-born: though grief come,
Grief only, of me, and of all these great joy,
And shall come always to thee; for thou knowest,
O mother, O breasts that bare me, for ye know,
O sweet head of my mother, sacred eyes,   2270
Ye know my soul albeit I sinned, ye know
Albeit I kneel not neither touch thy knees,
But with my lips I kneel, and with my heart
I fall about thy feet and worship thee.
And ye farewell now, all my friends; and ye,
Kinsmen, much younger and glorious more than I,
Sons of my mother's sister; and all farewell
That were in Colchis with me, and bare down
The waves and wars that met us: and though times
Change, and though now I be not anything,   2280
Forget not me among you, what I did
In my good time; for even by all those days,
Those days and this, and your own living souls,
And by the light and luck of you that live,
And by this miserable spoil, and me
Dying, I beseech you, let my name not die.
But thou, dear, touch me with thy rose-like hands,
And fasten up mine eyelids with thy mouth,
A bitter kiss; and grasp me with thine arms,
Printing with heavy lips my light waste flesh,   2290
Made light and thin by heavy-handed fate,
And with thine holy maiden eyes drop dew,
Drop tears for dew upon me who am dead,
Me who have loved thee; seeing without sin done

I am gone down to the empty weary house
Where no flesh is nor beauty nor swift eyes
Nor sound of mouth nor might of hands and feet.
But thou, dear, hide my body with thy veil,
And with thy raiment cover foot and head,
And stretch thyself upon me and touch hands   2300
With hands and lips with lips: be pitiful
As thou art maiden perfect; let no man
Defile me to despise me, saying, This man
Died woman-wise, a woman's offering, slain
Through female fingers in his woof of life,
Dishonourable; for thou hast honoured me.
And now for God's sake kiss me once and twice
And let me go; for the night gathers me,
And in the night shall no man gather fruit.

                    ATALANTA

Hail thou: but I with heavy face and feet   2310
Turn homeward and am gone out of thine eyes.

                    CHORUS
Who shall contend with his lords
    Or cross them or do them wrong?
Who shall bind them as with cords?
    Who shall tame them as with song?
Who shall smite them as with swords?
    For the hands of their kingdom are strong.

                              [1865]

THE LEPER

NOTHING is better, I well think,
　　Than love; the hidden well-water
Is not so delicate to drink:
　　This was well seen of me and her.

I served her in a royal house;
　　I served her wine and curious meat.
For will to kiss between her brows,
　　I had no heart to sleep or eat.

Mere scorn God knows she had of me,
　　A poor scribe, nowise great or fair,　　　　10
Who plucked his clerk's hood back to see
　　Her curled-up lips and amorous hair.

I vex my head with thinking this.
　　Yea, though God always hated me,
And hates me now that I can kiss
　　Her eyes, plait up her hair to see

How she then wore it on the brows,
　　Yet am I glad to have her dead
Here in this wretched wattled house
　　Where I can kiss her eyes and head.　　　　20

Nothing is better, I well know,
　　Than love; no amber in cold sea
Or gathered berries under snow:
　　That is well seen of her and me.

Three thoughts I make my pleasure of:
　　First I take heart and think of this:
That knight's gold hair she chose to love,
　　His mouth she had such will to kiss.

Then I remember that sundawn
　　I brought him by a privy way　　　　30
Out at her lattice, and thereon
　　What gracious words she found to say.

(Cold rushes for such little feet —
    Both feet could lie into my hand.
A marvel was it of my sweet
    Her upright body could so stand.)

"Sweet friend, God give you thank and grace;
    Now am I clean and whole of shame,
Nor shall men burn me in the face
    For my sweet fault that scandals them."   40

I tell you over word by word.
    She, sitting edgewise on her bed,
Holding her feet, said thus. The third,
    A sweeter thing than these, I said.

God, that makes time and ruins it
    And alters not, abiding God,
Changed with disease her body sweet,
    The body of love wherein she abode.

Love is more sweet and comelier
    Than a dove's throat strained out to sing.   50
All they spat out and cursed at her
    And cast her forth for a base thing.

They cursed her, seeing how God had wrought
    This curse to plague her, a curse of his.
Fools were they surely, seeing not
    How sweeter than all sweet she is.

He that had held her by the hair,
    With kissing lips blinding her eyes,
Felt her bright bosom, strained and bare,
    Sigh under him, with short mad cries   60

Out of her throat and sobbing mouth
    And body broken up with love,
With sweet hot tears his lips were loth
    Her own should taste the savour of,

Yea, he inside whose grasp all night
    Her fervent body leapt or lay,

Stained with sharp kisses red and white,
    Found her a plague to spurn away.

I hid her in this wattled house,
    I served her water and poor bread.   70
For joy to kiss between her brows
    Time upon time I was nigh dead.

Bread failed; we got but well-water
    And gathered grass with dropping seed.
I had such joy of kissing her,
    I had small care to sleep or feed.

Sometimes when service made me glad
    The sharp tears leapt between my lids,
Falling on her, such joy I had
    To do the service God forbids.   80

"I pray you let me be at peace,
    Get hence, make room for me to die."
She said that: her poor lip would cease,
    Put up to mine, and turn to cry.

I said, "Bethink yourself how love
    Fared in us twain, what either did;
Shall I unclothe my soul thereof?
    That I should do this, God forbid."

Yea, though God hateth us, he knows
    That hardly in a little thing   90
Love faileth of the work it does
    Till it grow ripe for gathering.

Six months, and now my sweet is dead
    A trouble takes me; I know not
If all were done well, all well said,
    No word or tender deed forgot.

Too sweet, for the least part in her,
    To have shed life out by fragments; yet,
Could the close mouth catch breath and stir,
    I might see something I forget.   100

Six months, and I sit still and hold
   In two cold palms her cold two feet.
Her hair, half grey half ruined gold,
   Thrills me and burns me in kissing it.

Love bites and stings me through, to see
   Her keen face made of sunken bones.
Her worn-off eyelids madden me,
   That were shot through with purple once.

She said, "Be good with me; I grow
   So tired for shame's sake, I shall die   110
If you say nothing:" even so.
   And she is dead now, and shame put by.

Yea, and the scorn she had of me
   In the old time, doubtless vexed her then.
I never should have kissed her. See
   What fools God's anger makes of men!

She might have loved me a little too,
   Had I been humbler for her sake.
But that new shame could make love new
   She saw not — yet her shame did make.   120

I took too much upon my love,
   Having for such mean service done
Her beauty and all the ways thereof,
   Her face and all the sweet thereon.

Yea, all this while I tended her,
   I know the old love held fast his part:
I know the old scorn waxed heavier,
   Mixed with sad wonder, in her heart.

It may be all my love went wrong —
   A scribe's work writ awry and blurred,   130
Scrawled after the blind evensong —
   Spoilt music with no perfect word.

But surely I would fain have done
   All things the best I could. Perchance

Because I failed, came short of one,
  She kept at heart that other man's.

I am grown blind with all these things:
  It may be now she hath in sight
Some better knowledge; still there clings
  The old question. Will not God do right?*   140

---

* En ce temps-là estoyt dans ce pays grand nombre de ladres et de meseaulx, ce dont le roy eut grand desplaisir, veu que Dieu dust en estre moult griefvement courroucé. Ores il advint qu'une noble damoyselle appelée Yolande de Sallières estant atteincte et touste guastée de ce vilain mal, tous ses amys et ses parens ayant devant leurs yeux la paour de Dieu la firent issir fors de leurs maisons et oncques ne voulurent recepvoir ni reconforter chose mauldicte de Dieu et à tous les hommes puante et abhominable. Ceste dame avoyt esté moult belle et gracieuse de formes, et de son corps elle estoyt large et de vie lascive. Pourtant nul des amans qui l'avoyent souventesfois accollée et baisée moult tendrement ne voulust plus héberger si laide femme et si détestable pescheresse. Ung seul clerc qui feut premièrement son lacquays et son entremetteur en matière d'amour la reçut chez luy et la récéla dans une petite cabane. Là mourut la meschinette de grande misère et de male mort : et après elle décéda ledist clerc qui pour grand amour l'avoyt six mois durant soignée, lavée, habillée et deshabillée tous les jours de ses mains propres. Mesme dist-on que ce meschant homme et mauldict clerc se remémourant de la grande beauté passée et guastée de ceste femme se délectoyt maintesfois à la baiser sur sa bouche orde et lépreuse et l'accoller doulcement de ses mains amoureuses. Aussy est-il mort de ceste mesme maladie abhominable. Cecy advint près Fontainebellant en Gastinois. Et quand ouyt le roy Philippe ceste adventure moult en estoyt esmerveillé.

          Grandes Chroniques de France, 1505.

[1861]   [1865]

ANACTORIA

τίνος αὖ τὺ πειθοῖ
μὰψ σαγηνεύσας φιλότατα;
          SAPPHO.

My life is bitter with thy love; thine eyes
Blind me, thy tresses burn me, thy sharp sighs
Divide my flesh and spirit with soft sound,
And my blood strengthens, and my veins abound.

I pray thee sigh not, speak not, draw not breath;
Let life burn down, and dream it is not death.
I would the sea had hidden us, the fire
(Wilt thou fear that, and fear not my desire?)
Severed the bones that bleach, the flesh that cleaves,
And let our sifted ashes drop like leaves.   10
I feel thy blood against my blood: my pain
Pains thee, and lips bruise lips, and vein stings vein,
Let fruit be crushed on fruit, let flower on flower,
Breast kindle breast, and either burn one hour.
Why wilt thou follow lesser loves? are thine
Too weak to bear these hands and lips of mine?
I charge thee for my life's sake, O too sweet
To crush love with thy cruel faultless feet,
I charge thee keep thy lips from hers or his,
Sweetest, till theirs be sweeter than my kiss: 20
Lest I too lure, a swallow for a dove,
Erotion or Erinna to my love.
I would my love could kill thee; I am satiated
With seeing thee live, and fain would have thee dead.
I would earth had thy body as fruit to eat,
And no mouth but some serpent's found thee sweet.
I would find grievous ways to have thee slain,
Intensive device, and superflux of pain;
Vex thee with amorous agonies, and shake
Life at thy lips, and leave it there to ache;   30
Strain out thy soul with pangs too soft to kill,
Intolerable interludes, and infinite ill;
Relapse and reluctation of the breath,
Dumb tunes and shuddering semitones of death.
I am weary of all thy words and soft strange ways,
Of all love's fiery nights and all his days,
And all the broken kisses salt as brine
That shuddering lips make moist with waterish wine,
And eyes the bluer for all those hidden hours
That pleasure fills with tears and feeds from flowers,   40
Fierce at the heart with fire that half comes through,
But all the flowerlike white stained round with blue;
The fervent underlid, and that above
Lifted with laughter or abashed with love;
Thine amorous girdle, full of thee and fair,
And leavings of the lilies in thine hair.

Yea, all sweet words of thine and all thy ways,
And all the fruit of nights and flower of days,
And stinging lips wherein the hot sweet brine
That Love was born of burns and foams like wine,   50
And eyes insatiable of amorous hours,
Fervent as fire and delicate as flowers,
Coloured like night at heart, but cloven through
Like night with flame, dyed round like night with blue,
Clothed with deep eyelids under and above —
Yea, all thy beauty sickens me with love;
Thy girdle empty of thee and now not fair,
And ruinous lilies in thy languid hair.
Ah, take no thought for Love's sake; shall this be,
And she who loves thy lover not love thee?   60
Sweet soul, sweet mouth of all that laughs and lives,
Mine is she, very mine; and she forgives.
For I beheld in sleep the light that is
In her high place in Paphos, heard the kiss
Of body and soul that mix with eager tears
And laughter stinging through the eyes and ears;
Saw Love, as burning flame from crown to feet,
Imperishable, upon her storied seat;
Clear eyelids lifted toward the north and south,
A mind of many colours, and a mouth   70
Of many tunes and kisses; and she bowed,
With all her subtle face laughing aloud,
Bowed down upon me, saying, "Who doth thee wrong,
Sappho?" but thou — thy body is the song,
Thy mouth the music; thou art more than I,
Though my voice die not till the whole world die;
Though men that hear it madden; though love weep,
Though nature change, though shame be charmed to sleep.
Ah, wilt thou slay me lest I kiss thee dead?
Yet the queen laughed from her sweet heart and said: 80
"Even she that flies shall follow for thy sake,
And she shall give thee gifts that would not take,
Shall kiss that would not kiss thee" (yea, kiss me)
"When thou wouldst not" — when I would not kiss thee!
Ah, more to me than all men as thou art,
Shall not my songs assuage her at the heart?
Ah, sweet to me as life seems sweet to death,
Why should her wrath fill thee with fearful breath?

Nay, sweet, for is she God alone? hath she
Made earth and all the centuries of the sea,   90
Taught the sun ways to travel, woven most fine
The moonbeams, shed the starbeams forth as wine,
Bound with her myrtles, beaten with her rods,
The young men and the maidens and the gods?
Have we not lips to love with, eyes for tears,
And summer and flower of women and of years?
Stars for the foot of morning, and for noon
Sunlight, and exaltation of the moon;
Waters that answer waters, fields that wear
Lilies, and languor of the Lesbian air?   100
Beyond those flying feet of fluttered doves,
Are there not other gods for other loves?
Yea, though she scourge thee, sweetest, for my sake,
Blossom not thorns and flowers not blood should break.
Ah that my lips were tuneless lips, but pressed
To the bruised blossom of thy scourged white breast!
Ah that my mouth for Muses' milk were fed
On the sweet blood thy sweet small wounds had bled!
That with my tongue I felt them, and could taste
The faint flakes from thy bosom to the waist!   110
That I could drink thy veins as wine, and eat
Thy breasts like honey! that from face to feet
Thy body were abolished and consumed,
And in my flesh thy very flesh entombed!
Ah, ah, thy beauty! like a beast it bites,
Stings like an adder, like an arrow smites,
Ah sweet, and sweet again, and seven times sweet,
The paces and the pauses of thy feet!
Ah sweeter than all sleep or summer air
The fallen fillets fragrant from thine hair!   120
Yea, though their alien kisses do me wrong,
Sweeter thy lips than mine with all their song;
Thy shoulders whiter than a fleece of white,
And flower-sweet fingers, good to bruise or bite
As honeycomb of the inmost honey-cells,
With almond-shaped and roseleaf-coloured shells
And blood like purple blossom at the tips
Quivering; and pain made perfect in thy lips
For my sake when I hurt thee; O that I
Durst crush thee out of life with love, and die,   130

Die of thy pain and my delight, and be
Mixed with thy blood and molten into thee!
Would I not plague thee dying overmuch?
Would I not hurt thee perfectly? not touch
Thy pores of sense with torture, and make bright
Thine eyes with bloodlike tears and grievous light?
Strike pang from pang as note is struck from note,
Catch the sob's middle music in thy throat,
Take thy limbs living, and new-mould with these
A lyre of many faultless agonies?   140
Feed thee with fever and famine and fine drouth,
With perfect pangs convulse thy perfect mouth,
Make thy life shudder in thee and burn afresh,
And wring thy very spirit through the flesh?
Cruel? but love makes all that love him well
As wise as heaven and crueller than hell.
Me hath love made more bitter toward thee
Than death toward man; but were I made as he
Who hath made all things to break them one by one,
If my feet trod upon the stars and sun   150
And souls of men as his have alway trod,
God knows I might be crueller than God.
For who shall change with prayers or thanksgivings
The mystery of the cruelty of things?
Or say what God above all gods and years
With offering and blood-sacrifice of tears,
With lamentation from strange lands, from graves
Where the snake pastures, from scarred mouths of slaves,
From prison, and from plunging prows of ships
Through flamelike foam of the sea's closing lips —   160
With thwartings of strange signs, and wind-blown hair
Of comets, desolating the dim air,
When darkness is made fast with seals and bars,
And fierce reluctance of disastrous stars,
Eclipse, and sound of shaken hills, and wings
Darkening, and blind inexpiable things —
With sorrow of labouring moons, and altering light
And travail of the planets of the night,
And weeping of the weary Pleiads seven,
Feeds the mute melancholy lust of heaven?   170
Is not his incense bitterness, his meat
Murder? his hidden face and iron feet

Hath not man known, and felt them on their way
Threaten and trample all things and every day?
Hath he not sent us hunger? who hath cursed
Spirit and flesh with longing? filled with thirst
Their lips who cried unto him? who bade exceed
The fervid will, fall short the feeble deed,
Bade sink the spirit and the flesh aspire,
Pain animate the dust of dead desire,   180
And life yield up her flower to violent fate?
Him would I reach, him smite, him desecrate,
Pierce the cold lips of God with human breath,
And mix his immortality with death.
Why hath he made us? what had all we done
That we should live and loathe the sterile sun,
And with the moon wax paler as she wanes,
And pulse by pulse feel time grow through our veins?
Thee too the years shall cover; thou shalt be
As the rose born of one same blood with thee,   190
As a song sung, as a word said, and fall
Flower-wise, and be not any more at all,
Nor any memory of thee anywhere;
For never Muse has bound above thine hair
The high Pierian flower whose graft outgrows
All summer kinship of the mortal rose
And colour of deciduous days, nor shed
Reflex and flush of heaven about thine head,
Nor reddened brows made pale by floral grief
With splendid shadow from that lordlier leaf.   200
Yea, thou shalt be forgotten like spilt wine,
Except these kisses of my lips on thine
Brand them with immortality; but me —
Men shall not see bright fire nor hear the sea,
Nor mix their hearts with music, nor behold
Cast forth of heaven, with feet of awful gold
And plumeless wings that make the bright air blind,
Lightning, with thunder for a hound behind
Hunting through fields unfurrowed and unsown,
But in the light and laughter, in the moan   210
And music, and in grasp of lip and hand
And shudder of water that makes felt on land
The immeasurable tremor of all the sea,
Memories shall mix and metaphors of me.

Like me shall be the shuddering calm of night,
When all the winds of the world for pure delight
Close lips that quiver and fold up wings that ache;
When nightingales are louder for love's sake,
And leaves tremble like lute-strings or like fire;
Like me the one star swooning with desire   220
Even at the cold lips of the sleepless moon,
As I at thine; like me the waste white noon,
Burnt through with barren sunlight; and like me
The land-stream and the tide-stream in the sea.
I am sick with time as these with ebb and flow,
And by the yearning in my veins I know
The yearning sound of waters; and mine eyes
Burn as that beamless fire which fills the skies
With troubled stars and travailing things of flame;
And in my heart the grief consuming them   230
Labours, and in my veins the thirst of these,
And all the summer travail of the trees
And all the winter sickness; and the earth,
Filled full with deadly works of death and birth,
Sore spent with hungry lusts of birth and death,
Has pain like mine in her divided breath;
Her spring of leaves is barren, and her fruit
Ashes; her boughs are burdened, and her root
Fibrous and gnarled with poison; underneath
Serpents have gnawn it through with tortuous teeth   240
Made sharp upon the bones of all the dead,
And wild birds rend her branches overhead.
These, woven as raiment for his word and thought,
These hath God made, and me as these, and wrought
Song, and hath lit it at my lips; and me
Earth shall not gather though she feed on thee.
As a shed tear shalt thou be shed; but I —
Lo, earth may labour, men live long and die,
Years change and stars, and the high God devise
New things, and old things wane before his eyes   250
Who wields and wrecks them, being more strong than they —
But, having made me, me he shall not slay.
Nor slay nor satiate, like those herds of his
Who laugh and live a little, and their kiss
Contents them, and their loves are swift and sweet,
And sure death grasps and gains them with slow feet,

Love they or hate they, strive or bow their knees —
And all these end; he hath his will of these.
Yea, but albeit he slay me, hating me —
Albeit he hide me in the deep dear sea   260
And cover me with cool wan foam, and ease
This soul of mine as any soul of these,
And give me water and great sweet waves, and make
The very sea's name lordlier for my sake,
The whole sea sweeter — albeit I die indeed
And hide myself and sleep and no man heed,
Of me the high God hath not all his will.
Blossom of branches, and on each high hill
Clear air and wind, and under in clamorous vales
Fierce noises of the fiery nightingales,   270
Buds burning in the sudden spring like fire,
The wan washed sand and the waves' vain desire,
Sails seen like blown white flowers at sea, and words
That bring tears swiftest, and long notes of birds
Violently singing till the whole world sings —
I Sappho shall be one with all these things,
With all high things for ever; and my face
Seen once, my songs once heard in a strange place,
Cleave to men's lives, and waste the days thereof
With gladness and much sadness and long love.   280
Yea, they shall say, earth's womb has borne in vain
New things, and never this best thing again;
Borne days and men, borne fruits and wars and wine,
Seasons and songs, but no song more like mine.
And they shall know me as ye who have known me here,
Last year when I loved Atthis, and this year
When I love thee; and they shall praise me, and say
"She hath all time as all we have our day,
Shall she not live and have her will" — even I?
Yea, though thou diest, I say I shall not die.   290
For these shall give me of their souls, shall give
Life, and the days and loves wherewith I live,
Shall quicken me with loving, fill with breath,
Save me and serve me, strive for me with death.
Alas, that neither moon nor snow nor dew
Nor all cold things can purge me wholly through,
Assuage me nor allay me nor appease,
Till supreme sleep shall bring me bloodless ease;

Till time wax faint in all his periods;
Till fate undo the bondage of the gods,   300
And lay, to slake and satiate me all through,
Lotus and Lethe on my lips like dew,
And shed around and over and under me
Thick darkness and the insuperable sea.

[1863–65]   [1866]

BIBLIOGRAPHICAL NOTE
(1975)

The one indispensable book remains W. E. Fredeman's *Pre-Raphaelitism, A Bibliocritical Study* (1965), a volume that has made it possible to study Pre-Raphaelitism systematically. Its usefulness, as anyone who tried to work the field Before Fredeman will recognize, cannot be overemphasized, and nineteenth-century scholarship will always be in his debt. As the Preface states, it is a "critical reference guide to the whole subject of Pre-Raphaelitism," and its thorough, concise, authoritative coverage makes it unnecessary for me to include bibliographical lists here, other than the most basic texts and titles for each author.

Pre-Raphaelite studies have so proliferated recently that it is impracticable to mention everything, or even most things, deserving notice. Ifor Evans, *English Poetry in the Later Nineteenth Century* (revised, 1966) and Lionel Stevenson, *The Pre-Raphaelite Poets* (1972) are useful surveys. The best books with reproductions of Pre-Raphaelite pictures are the Phaidon Press *Pre-Raphaelite Painters,* ed. Robin Ironside, with a Descriptive Catalogue by John Gere (1948) and, more recently, Raymond Watkinson's *Pre-Raphaelite Art and Design* (Studio Vista, 1970). Reproductions of Pre-Raphaelite pictures have also appeared in volumes edited by John Nicoll, Timothy Hilton, Martin Harrison, and Graham Ovenden (photography) and individually, poster-size, by Portal Publications, and there are many in G. H. Fleming's *Rossetti and the Pre-Raphaelite Brotherhood* and *That Ne'er Shall Meet Again* (1967, 1971). Allen Staley's *The Pre-Raphaelite Landscape* (1973) is an original, valuable newcomer. J. D. Hunt's *The Pre-Raphaelite Imagination* (1968) and *Pre-Raphaelitism, A Collection of Critical Essays* (1974), ed. James Sambrook, are useful. All the poets here are dealt with in *The Victorian Poets, A Guide to Research,* ed. F. E. Faverty (revised, 1968), and the file of *Victorian Poetry* is of course a mother lode.

Virginia Surtees's *The Paintings and Drawings of Dante Gabriel Rossetti (1828–1882): A Catalogue Raisonné* (2 vols., 1971) is a milestone; Marina Henderson's *Dante Gabriel Rossetti* (1973) has over a hundred reproductions, eleven in color. In Morris studies *The Critical Heritage,* ed. Peter Faulkner (1973), Ray Watkinson's *William Morris as Designer* (1967), *The Unpublished Lectures,* ed. E. D. LeMire (1969), and Paul Meir, *La Pensée Utopique de William Morris* (1974), are all worthy, and A. C. Sewter's *The Stained Glass of William Morris and*

His Circle (1974, vol. 2 forthcoming) is a landmark. Any serious student of Morris must belong to the William Morris Society. C. L. Cline's exemplary edition of Meredith's letters (3 vols.) appeared in 1970, and J. B. Rodenbeck's study of "Love in the Valley" in *Victorian Poetry* (Spring, 1973) is first rate. Valuable editions of Swinburne's criticism and of reviews have been edited by C. K. Hyder, *Swinburne Replies* (1966), *Swinburne as Critic* (1972), and *The Critical Heritage* (1970). J. O. Fuller's biography (1968) is vulgar, pretentious, and inaccurate; Philip Henderson's (1974) is an admirable synthesis. A double number of *Victorian Poetry*, Spring–Summer, 1971, was devoted wholly to Swinburne, and Jerome McGann's *Swinburne, An Experiment in Criticism* (1972) is an important, exciting *experience*.

The texts of the poems in this anthology are from the standard editions, as noted for each author. At the end of a poem a date on the left is the date of composition; on the right, the date of publication (italicized if printed in a periodical, or elsewhere, before publication in a book).

NOTES ON THE POEMS

❖

DANTE GABRIEL ROSSETTI (1828–82)

The salient facts of Rossetti's life are discussed in the Introduction, pp. xvi–xviii. See also, below, the note on *The House of Life* (pp. 504–506). He published only three books: *The Early Italian Poets from Ciullo d'Alcamo to Dante Alighieri (1100–1200–1300) in the Original Metres together with Dante's Vita Nuova* (1861; the second edition, 1874, was called *Dante and His Circle*); *Poems* (1870; A New Edition, 1881); and *Ballads and Sonnets* (1881).

The standard edition of his poetry is *The Works of Dante Gabriel Rossetti*, ed. W. M. Rossetti (1911; Fredeman, 23:27), but the need for a modern scholarly edition is urgent. The best biographies are Oswald Doughty's *A Victorian Romantic* (1949; second edition, 1960; Fredeman, 25:92) and Rosalie Glynn Grylls's *Portrait of Rossetti* (1964). Both are scholarly and reliable. Doughty's volume is fuller, *Portrait of Rossetti* much more sympathetic and readable. Of *The Letters of Dante Gabriel Rossetti*, ed. Oswald Doughty and J. R. Wahl, two volumes appeared in 1965 and two more in 1967. This edition is standard, *faute de mieux*, but no other commendation is possible. A *catalogue raisonné* of Rossetti's paintings and drawings being prepared by Virginia Surtees will correct and supersede the now standard work by H. C. Marillier, *Dante Gabriel Rossetti, An Illustrated Memorial of His Art and Life* (1899; Fredeman, 30:24). Two general articles are noteworthy: Wendell Stacy Johnson's "D. G. Rossetti as Painter and Poet," *Victorian Poetry*, III (Winter, 1965), 9–18, and Jerome McGann's "Rossetti's Significant Details," to be published in *Victorian Poetry*, VII (Spring, 1969).

Page 1: "The Blessed Damozel," written in 1847, was first published in *The Germ* (1850); with some alterations it next appeared in *The Oxford and Cambridge Magazine* (1856); with still more revisions it was included in Rossetti's *Poems* (1870), and continued to be touched up in subsequent editions until it reached its final form in *Poems*, A New Edition (1881). For the whole story see *The Blessed Damozel, The Unpublished Manuscript, Texts and Collation*, with an Introduction, ed. Paull Franklin Baum (Chapel Hill, 1937).

The "sources" of the poem are as complex, and have been as carefully studied, as its publishing history. Several decades after it was written, Rossetti himself said that it had originated "out of his love for 'The Raven.'" Poe, he said, "had done the utmost it was possible to do with the grief of the lover on earth, and so I determined to reverse the conditions, and give utterance to the yearning of the loved one in heaven" (T. Hall Caine, *Recollections of Dante Gabriel Rossetti*, 1882, p. 284). Others have found in it echoes of Revelation, Dante, especially the *Vita Nuova*, "Purgatorio," and "Paradiso," Coleridge, Keats, Shelley, Goethe, and Philip James Bailey's *Festus* (1839), an overwhelming poem, unreadable though we now find it, that flowed into the genius of so much Victorian literature, including *Jane Eyre* and *Wuthering Heights*. In fact, if chronology did not forbid it, one could hardly help assuming that these two novels had something to do with Rossetti's poem, instead of arising (partly) from the same source.

Page 5: "My Sister's Sleep," written in 1847, was printed first in *The Germ* (1850) and later, condensed and revised, in *Poems* (1870). According to Rossetti, its composition had "no relation to actual fact." Rossetti is not the speaker. As Jerome McGann brilliantly demonstrates, (*VP*, VII, 1969), Rossetti, in deliberately making the religious imagery non-symbolic, forces us to "recognize the purely sensational value of the lines" and in this way intensifies the "emotional drama, and ultimately the fundamentally affective quality of the mother's and son's thoughts."

Page 7: "Mary's Girlhood (*For a Picture*)," written in 1848. The first was revised for *Poems* (1870); the second was printed by Rossetti only on gilded paper affixed to the frame of the painting "The Girlhood of Mary Virgin." The closing lines of the first probably refer to the painting "Ecce Ancilla Domini." See Plates 2 and 3.

Page 8: "Ave," first published in *Poems* (1870). An early version, written in 1847 and titled "Mater Pulchrae Delectionis," is printed in Rossetti's *Works* (1911), 661–62.

Page 11: "Jenny," much expanded and altered, both structurally and conceptually, from an early version (about 1847) now lost, was rewritten in 1858–59 and again revised for publication in *Poems* (1870).

Page 20: "The Portrait," first published in *Poems* (1870), is a kind of transmutation of "On Mary's Portrait Which I Painted Six Years Ago," written in 1846 and 1847 and first published in *Dante Gabriel Rossetti, An Analytical List of Manuscripts in the Duke University Library, with Hitherto Unpublished Verse and Prose*, ed. P. F. Baum (Durham, N. C., 1931). The "adaptation" was made in the autumn, 1869. Associations with Rossetti's painting "Beata Beatrix," and therefore with his dead wife, are irresistible.

Page 23: "The Burden of Nineveh," written in 1850 and first printed in *The Oxford and Cambridge Magazine* (1856), was extensively revised before its inclusion in *Poems* (1870). In the title (Nahum 1:1) the word *Burden* is a deliberate pun. Much of the concrete detail comes from the description by Sir Austen Henry Layard of his excavations, *Nineveh and Its Remains* (1849) and *A Popular Account of Discoveries at Nineveh* (1851).

Page 28: "The Staff and Scrip," based on a story in a translation of the *Gesta Romanorum*, was written in 1851–52, first published in *The Oxford and Cambridge Magazine* (1856), and collected in *Poems* (1870).

Page 34: "Sister Helen," written in 1851 or 1852, was first published in *The Düsseldorf Artist's Album*, in 1854. A scrupulous record of its myriad revisions, in manuscript, galley proofs, page proofs, trial books, *Poems* (1870) in various editions (including Tauchnitz) up to *Poems, A New Edition* (1881), is set forth in *Rossetti's Sister Helen*, ed. Janet Camp Troxell (New Haven, 1939).

Page 42: "The Woodspurge," written in 1856, was published in *Poems* (1870). The "point" of the trinitarian evocation of the "three cups in one" lies precisely in its irrelevance, as Jerome McGann points out (*VP, VII*, 1969): "When the three-in-one detail is completely freed of its possible religious connotations we suddenly realize the enormous relevance of the flower's unsymbolic fact. At that time and in that place this poet gained a measure of relief from a simple act of observation. . . . The poem hints at the mystery which Rossetti felt in the mere fact of precise sensory perception and in the hidden resources of the simple human organism."

Page 42: "Even So," written in 1859, was published in *Poems* (1870).

Page 43: "The Song of the Bower," written in 1860, was published in *Poems* (1870). The second stanza was added in 1869. No one supposes that the situation is merely imaginary or that the references are generalized, though no further agreement has been reached. The nomination by Rossetti's brother, William Michael, of Rossetti's wife, Elizabeth Siddal, is so preposterous that it must have been intended as a joke. The only possible candidates are Fanny Cornforth and (conceivably) Janey Morris. An early version, in Swinburne's holograph and lacking the second stanza, is printed in James Pope-Hennessy's *Monckton Milnes, The Flight of Youth, 1851–1885* (London, 1951), p. 256.

Page 44: "The Stream's Secret," begun in 1869, published in *Poems* (1870), is simultaneously the poem of Rossetti's that reveals most and conceals most. It is hardly too much to say that this monody epitomizes his whole adult inner life, and the fact that most of the factual basis of the secret is now common knowledge has in no way affected its heavy-lidded subtlety.

Page 51: "After the French Liberation of Italy," written in 1859, was, though privately printed, withheld from publication till more than two decades after Rossetti's death.

Page 51: All three translations from Villon date from 1869–70 and were first collected in *Poems* (1870).

Page 54: "The Bride's Prelude," begun in 1848 or 1849, was published, still unfinished, in *Ballads and Sonnets* (1881). Rossetti's prose synopsis of the conclusion, written about 1878, is printed in his *Works* (1911), p. 648: "Urscelyn has become celebrated as a soldier of fortune, selling his sword to the highest bidder, and in this character reports reach Aloÿse and her family respecting him. Aloÿse now becomes enamoured of a young knight who loves her deeply; this leads, after fears and hesitations, to her confessing to him the stain on her life; he still remains devoted to her. Urscelyn now reappears; his influence as a soldier renders a lasting bond with him desirable to the brothers of Aloÿse, much as they hate him; and he, on his side, is bent on assuming an important position in the family to which he as yet only half belongs. He therefore offers marriage to Aloÿse, supported by the will of her brothers, who moreover are well aware of the blot they have to efface, which would thus disappear. At a tournament Urscelyn succeeds in treacherously slaying the knight to whom Aloÿse has betrothed herself; and this death is followed in due course by the bridal to which the poem relates. It winds up with the description of the last preparations preceding the bridal procession. Amelotte would draw attention to the passing of the time. Aloÿse then says: 'There is much now that you remember; how we heard that Urscelyn had become a soldier of fortune, and how he returned here, etc. You must also remember well the death of that young knight at the tourney.' Amelotte should then describe the event, and say how well she remembers Urscelyn's bitter grief at the mischance. Aloÿse would then tell her how she herself was betrothed secretly to the young knight, and how Urscelyn slew him intentionally. As the bridal procession appears, perhaps it might become apparent that the brothers mean to kill Urscelyn when he has married her."

Page 79: *The House of Life.* Every aspect of this work is so complex that a mere note can only call attention to some of the problems, which begin with the title. The word *House* has been taken by most critics in its astrological sense, though Swinburne, Rossetti's most intimate friend, reviewing the 1870 volume, unhesitatingly construed it in its familiar architectural sense.

The poem is a collection of sonnets forming (perhaps) a sequence or a series or a cycle. The number of sonnets is either 101, 102 (counting the prefatory sonnet), or 103 (counting No. VIa, "Nuptial

Sleep"). They range in date of composition from 1848 to 1881, in date of publication from 1863 to 1881. Some of them (sixteen) were first published as a *group* in the *Fortnightly Review,* March, 1869; a larger group (fifty) was first published in book form in *Poems,* 1870, under the title "Sonnets and Songs, towards a work to be called 'The House of Life,' " though this volume had been preceded by at least five complete sets of proof sheets with deletions, additions, revisions, and rearrangements. Rossetti's final version, called "The House of Life; A Sonnet-Sequence," appeared in *Ballads and Sonnets,* 1881.

Many of the sonnets are addressed, or refer, to Rossetti's wife, Elizabeth Siddal, who committed suicide in 1862 and to whose grave he remorsefully consigned his manuscripts, there to moulder until their disinterment in October, 1869. Moreover, though the case is not yet absolutely proved, it seems equally clear that the "Innominata" of many others was Janey Morris (Mrs. William Morris), whom Rossetti — pathetically unable to be off with the old love before he was on with the new — had known (before her marriage or his own) since the late fifties. In addition, the superlatively voluptuous Fanny Cornforth, his housekeeper and mistress, whom, also, he had come to know in the late fifties, hovers in the background poetically as, in real life, she loomed domestically, and nothing could be neater, or more revealing, than Rossetti's conception of this triad as Beata Beatrix, Proserpine-Pandora, and Lilith.

Another kind of complication that once thickened the murk can now be dismissed as a historical curiosity — the charge of "fleshliness," exploded with deliberate malice by the poetaster Robert Buchanan in a notorious essay "The Fleshly School of Poetry" (*1871,* 1872) — but several observations must be made. For one thing, though the attack was a foul blow, in several senses of the phrase, Rossetti himself, already ill, was so far from regarding it as a curiosity that the damage to his health, physical as well as mental, was irreparable. Moreover, it resulted in the absurd removal of the sonnet "Nuptial Sleep," a necessary chamber in this house, and, finally, the charge so fogged the issue for more than half a century that only recently has criticism been able to approach the poems as poetry. By now, of course, the whole affair is simply irrelevant, and if the word *fleshly* happened to be used of the sonnets, it would be intended as praise.

No poetry has been subjected to more insistent biographical probing than Rossetti's, but, though I am not sure one wants to do so, I believe it is easier to read his work without reference to biography than Arnold's or Tennyson's (Wordsworth and Byron being special cases). And it is certain that the most rewarding initial approach to *The House of Life* is the direct one that Rossetti intended — a poetic examination in the form of a sonnet-sequence, not of "The House of

Love," as some have claimed, but of "The House of Life," the steady progression from "Youth and Change" to "Change and Fate," the relentless movement from the initial view of "Love enthroned" far above Truth, Hope, Fame, and Life itself to the awful conclusion compelling us to recognize that the "one Hope's one name" is neither Love nor the name of any person but a mocking pun, *wanhope.*

The indispensable works to be consulted are *The House of Life, A Sonnet-Sequence,* ed. Paull Franklin Baum (Cambridge, Mass., 1928); *The Kelmscott Love Sonnets of Dante Gabriel Rossetti,* ed. John Robert Wahl (Cape Town and Amsterdam, 1954); W. E. Fredeman's article, "Rossetti's 'In Memoriam': An Elegiac Reading of *The House of Life,*" *Bulletin of the John Rylands Library* XLVII (March, 1965), 298–341; and Henri Talon's two studies, "Dante Gabriel Rossetti, peintre-poète dans *La Maison de Vie,*" *Etudes anglaises,* XIX (Jan.–March, 1966), 1–14, and *D. G. Rossetti: The House of Life* (Archives des Lettres Modernes, Paris, 1966).

CHRISTINA GEORGINA ROSSETTI (1830–94)

Christina Rossetti's principal volumes of verse were *Goblin Market and Other Poems* (1862), *The Prince's Progress and Other Poems* (1866), *Sing-Song* (1872), *Goblin Market, The Prince's Progress, and Other Poems* (1875), *A Pageant and Other Poems* (1881), and *Verses* (1893). Posthumous additions were made to the canon in two volumes edited by her brother, William Michael Rossetti, *New Poems* (1896) and *Poetical Works* (1904). An intensely devout Anglican, she published also a number of tracts for the Society for Promoting Christian Knowledge in which a few of her poems first appeared.

With one exception these three sentences tell us nearly everything essential that is *known* about her life. She was apparently in love with the Pre-Raphaelite painter James Collinson but, unable to accommodate her scrupulous Anglicanism to the Roman Catholicism that he turned to, she terminated their engagement in 1850. A dozen years later another affair, this time with Charles Bagot Cayley, the translator of Dante, was ended for similar, though not identical, reasons. Her most recent biographer, the late Lona Mosk Packer, argued that the great love of her life was the painter-poet William Bell Scott, a married man, and believed that this fearsome passion was, with her religion, one of the major sources of her poetic inspiration, a theory that William E. Fredeman has largely discredited (see *Victorian Studies,* VIII, Sept. 1964, 71–77).

The standard edition of her poetry is *The Poetical Works,* ed. William Michael Rossetti (1904; Fredeman, 44:14), which is scandalously bad from every point of view. Some of her letters are in *The Family Letters of Christina Georgina Rossetti, with Some Supplementary Letters and Appendices,* ed. William Michael Rossetti (1908; Fredeman, 44:15), but a complete edition is needed. The best biography is Lona Mosk Packer's *Christina Rossetti* (1963; Fredeman, 44:94).

Page 130: "Goblin Market" was first published in *Goblin Market and Other Poems* (1862). The author's brother, William Michael Rossetti, who edited several collected editions of his sister's poems, assures us that Christina Rossetti "did not mean anything profound by this fairy tale," though he himself found the incidents "suggestive." It will be a very eccentric reader indeed who reads this poem merely for the "story." The best discussions are in B. Ifor Evans's article, "The Sources of Christina Rossetti's 'Goblin Market,'" *Modern Language Review,* XXVIII (April, 1933), 156–65, and in Lona Mosk Packer's *Christina Rossetti* (1963).

Page 144: "Monna Innominata" was first published in *A Pageant and Other Poems* (1881). No one, except their author, has ever pretended that these sonnets were anything but intensely personal. The only problem is that of the identity of the lover, generally supposed to be Charles Cayley, though Lona Mosk Packer's biography *Christina Rossetti* (pp. 232–39) argues persuasively for William Bell Scott.

William Michael Rossetti translated the epigraphs from Dante and Petrarch as follows:

1a. The day that they have said adieu to their sweet friends.
1b. Love, with how great a stress dost thou vanquish me to-day!
2a. It was already the hour which turns back the desire.
2b. I recur to the time when I first saw thee.
3a. Oh shades, empty save in semblance!
3b. An imaginary guide conducts her.
4a. A small spark fosters a great flame.
4b. Every other thing, every thought, goes off, and love alone remains there with you.
5a. Love, who exempts no loved one from loving.
5b. Love led me into such joyous hope.
6a. Now canst thou comprehend the quantity of the love which glows in me towards thee.
6b. I do not choose that Love should release me from such a tie.
7a. Here always Spring and every fruit.
7b. Conversing with me, and I with him.
8a. As if he were to say to God, "I care for nought else."
8b. I hope to find pity, and not only pardon.
9a. O dignified and pure conscience!
9b. Spirit more lit with burning virtues.

10a. With better course and with better star.
10b. Life flees, and stays not an hour.
11a. Come after me, and leave folk to talk.
11b. Relating the casualties of our life.
12a. Love, who speaks within my mind.
12b. Love comes in the beautiful face of this lady.
13a. And we will direct our eyes to the Primal Love.
13b. But I find a burden to which my arms suffice not.
14a. And His will is our peace.
14b. Only with these thoughts, with different locks.

Page 151: "Advent" was first published in *Time Flies* (1885) reprinted in *Verses* (1893).

Page 152: "Paradise," written in 1854, was first published in *Goblin Market, The Prince's Progress, and Other Poems* (1875). The original title was "Easter Even."

Page 153: "Old and New Year Ditties," first published in *Goblin Market and Other Poems* (1862). The original titles were "The End of the Year," "New Year's Eve," "The Knell of the Year."

Page 155: "The Lowest Place" was first published in *The Prince's Progress* (1866). The second stanza was inscribed on Christina Rossetti's tombstone.

Page 155: "Bitter for Sweet" first appeared in *Goblin Market and Other Poems* (1862).

Page 155: "Song" ("When I am dead my dearest"), written in 1848, was first published in *Goblin Market and Other Poems* (1862).

Page 156: "Song" ("Oh roses for the flush of youth") was first published in *The Germ*, February, 1850, reprinted in *Goblin Market and Other Poems* (1862).

Page 156: "Rest," written in 1849, was first published in *Goblin Market and Other Poems* (1862).

Page 157: "Remember" was first published in *Goblin Market and Other Poems* (1862).

Page 157: "Echo," written in 1854, was first published in *Goblin Market and Other Poems* (1862). Four canceled stanzas are printed in Lona Mosk Packer's *Christina Rossetti*, p. 91.

Page 158: "A Birthday" was first published in *Goblin Market and Other Poems* (1862). No one has been able to relate this "outburst of exuberant joy," as William Rossetti called it, to any definite event.

Page 158: "Up-hill," first published in *Macmillan's Magazine*, February, 1861, was reprinted in *Goblin Market and Other Poems* (1862).

The author had this poem printed next to "Amor Mundi" — a "significant juxtaposition," according to her brother, "done no doubt with intention."

Page 159: "Amor Mundi" was first published in *Goblin Market, The Prince's Progress, and Other Poems* (1875). See the note on "Uphill."

Page 159: "De Profundis" first appeared in *Called To Be Saints* (1881).

Page 160: "Ash Wednesday" was first published in *Time Flies* (1885), reprinted in *Verses* (1893).

Page 160: "Sleeping at Last," first published, posthumously, in *New Poems* (1896), was thought by the author's brother to be the last verses she ever wrote.

WILLIAM MORRIS (1834–96)

Morris's life, as far as it was visible to the world, is a chronicle of his incredibly multifarious activities, of which something has been said in the Introduction (pp. xix–xx). Of his inner life, though we can guess or suppose much, we *know* next to nothing.

The standard edition of his writings is *The Collected Works of William Morris,* ed. May Morris (24 vols., 1910–15; Fredeman, 43:21, but see also 43:24), recently reprinted. The standard biography, J. W. Mackail's *Life of William Morris* (2 vols., 1899; Fredeman, 43:45), has been corrected and brought up to date by Philip Henderson's *William Morris, His Life, Work and Friends* (1967). Some of his letters are in Henderson's excellent volume, *The Letters of William Morris to His Family and Friends* (1950; Fredeman 43:25); a presumably complete edition has been announced by Norman Kelvin. Paul Thompson's *The Work of William Morris* (1967) is an excellent attempt to survey his life, work, and ideas in one volume.

Pages 161–278: *The Defence of Guenevere and Other Poems* (1858) was, as has already been said, the first (as well as the most) Pre-Raphaelite volume of poems published. Rossetti's influence is apparent, but Morris's special achievement was to cross Pre-Raphaelitism (or Rossetti-ism) plus "Browning-ism" with his own poetic being in such a way as to produce poems like no others in the language, before or since, even in his own works. Browning can be seen in the dramatic technique (abrupt openings, omitted transitions, harsh meter, etc.), Rossetti in the vivid, concrete detail. The poems have been described as "Dramatic Lyrics and Dramatic Romances" of the fourteenth and fifteenth centuries. The inspiration for them derives not only from Malory's *Morte Darthur* but also from the *Chroniques* of Jean Froissart (the Canon of Chimay of "Concerning Geffray Teste Noire"), a record, as Lord Berners, whose fifteenth-century translation was Morris's source, put it, of "the honourable and noble aventures of featis of armes, done and achyved by the warres of France and Inglande" — in other words, a history of his own times, during the Hundred Years War.

Morris's contribution to his hybrid of Rossetti and Browning was in the directness, bluntness, and violence — the brutality — with which he rendered his pictures of the Middle Ages. English poetry had seen nothing like it. Thus, the claim that "The Haystack in the Floods," for instance, "comes nearer the cruelty and courage of the Middle Ages than anything else written in the nineteenth century" (*William Morris*, ed. Ronald Fuller, Oxford, 1956, p. 39) is, though accurate enough, entirely beside the point. It was not merely nineteenth-century poetic views of the Middle Ages that had been deficient, and a more relevant statement would be that his poetry came nearer the "courage and cruelty of the Middle Ages" than any poetry written in any century preceding, including the Middle Ages. Only myopic book-ishness and selective evidence could persuade generations familiar with Buchenwald, Algiers, and Vietnam that medieval times were crueler — or more courageous — than nineteenth- or twentieth-century life, and the real point is that Morris was a revisionist not in respect of the Middle Ages, significant though this was, but in respect of the nature of poetry. Morris demonstrated how verse could be both poetic and brutal —

> that was all the fight
> Except a spout of blood on the hot land.
> ("The Defence of Guenevere," ll. 213–14)

> see how white
> The skull is, loose within the coif!
> ("Concerning Geffray Teste Noire," ll. 82–83)

or the last twenty-five lines of "The Haystack in the Floods."

Of the short lyrics in *The Defence of Guenevere and Other Poems* from neither Malory nor Froissart we know little, and need to know more, of the background, sources, and poetic quiddity, but the sensitive reader will assume, as the alert reader will find, that no line is mere decoration, every verse has its poetic logic. The effect of the whole volume is so cumulative that — with Morris referring to the Duc de Berry as casually and familiarly as, nowadays, one might mention J. P. Morgan or Andrew Mellon — the final impression is of a kind of *patria mei creatrix, patria mea genetrix*.

Page 161: "The Defence of Guenevere,"
Page 170: "King Arthur's Tomb."

The two poems acquire an extra dimension if read as pendants. In the former, a dramatic monologue in all but the strictest sense, Guenevere is guilty of everything except the indictments — she is "something better than innocent" — and the text will support the view that she is stalling for time, for the rescue in the last stanza. "King Arthur's Tomb" was suggested partly by Rossetti's watercolor (1854; Marillier, pp. 61–62), owned for a while by Morris, whom Lancelot's features are thought to resemble. A replica of the watercolor is in the Tate Gallery; the original version was sold at Sotheby's in 1962 (Fredeman 19:39).

Page 182: "Sir Galahad: A Christmas Mystery,"
Page 188: "The Chapel in Lyoness."

Like the two poems preceding, these can be viewed as a kind of diptych.

Page 252: "The Blue Closet,"
Page 255: "The Tune of Seven Towers."

Each poem was inspired by a Rossetti watercolor (Marillier 65 and 66, reproduced pp. 78–81; both now in the Tate Gallery). Marillier's contention that the poems and pictures "have nothing in common but their names" is controverted by his own descriptions (p. 81), and it is difficult to see how these poems — or Rossetti's watercolors — could be dismissed as mere decoration or dreamy atmosphere for its own sake. Behind "The Blue Closet," for instance, can be seen Perrault's "Barbe Bleue" or an analogue, and no fantastic leaps of imagination are required to view *towers* in a traditional or mythic context or, more specifically, to relate the subject-matter of "The Tune of Seven Towers" to Browning's "Childe Roland" and the Charlemagne cycle.

Page 267: "Two Red Roses across the Moon." The refrain is not only the lady's song and a battle-cry but also, according to Morris (*The Defence of Guenevere and Other Poems*, ed. Robert Steele, 1904, p. 251), the device pictured on the knight's shield or banner.

Page 279: *The Earthly Paradise* (1868–70), of which only the "Apology," the opening lines of the Prologue, and the Envoy can be included here, is another story in every possible meaning of the phrase. It is, in fact, another set of stories, two dozen of them, two for each month of the year, each month having, as its own special lyric, the poet speaking in his own voice. The Norse wanderers of the Argument, despairing of their quest for the earthly paradise, settle in the "nameless city in a distant sea," and exchange stories with the Elders of the City — classical legends from the hosts (descendants of the ancient Greeks), tales from Norse and other medieval sources from the Wanderers, all alike cast in the medieval mold. (The first narrative outgrew itself and was published separately as *The Life and Death of Jason*, 1867.)

Morris's model for *The Earthly Paradise* was the *Canterbury Tales*, and Chaucer, the only narrative poet in the language superior to him, he acknowledged as Master. "Pardon me," he wrote at the beginning of the last book of *Jason*,

> if yet in vain
> Thou art my Master, and I fail to bring
> Before men's eyes the image of the thing
> My heart is filled with. . . .

Since long poems and narrative for its own sake are no longer prized as they once were, it ought to be noted that all these poems are not in fact "long," that the narrative mode is necessarily more leisurely and relaxed (and diffuse) than the lyric or dramatic, and that Morris, like all other poets, wrote from the spirit breathed into him.

Page 285: "French Noel" first appeared in Edmund Sedding's *Antient Christmas Carols* (1860). It was reprinted in *A Christmas Garland, Carols and Poems from the Fifteenth Century to the Present Time*, ed. A. H. Bullen (1885). The source of the present text is *William Morris: Artist, Writer, Socialist*, ed. May Morris (1936), p. 532.

Page 287: "Thunder in the Garden" was first published in *Poems by the Way* (1891).

Page 288: "Love's Gleaning-tide" first appeared in the *Athenaeum*, April, 1874, and was reprinted in *Poems by the Way* (1891). It is said to be from a "fragment of a poem in dramatic form written about 1872" (Morris's *Works*, IX, xxxv).

Page 289: "Spring's Bedfellow," of which the manuscript is dated "March 8th 1873" (Morris's *Works*, IX, xxxiv), was first published in *Poems by the Way* (1891).

Page 289: "A Garden by the Sea" first appeared in *The Life and Death of Jason* (1867), Book IV, ll. 577–608, and was reprinted, revised, in *Poems by the Way* (1891).

Page 290: "For the Bed at Kelmscott," written for "the embroidered hangings that furnish the carved oak bedstead" at Morris's home, Kelmscott Manor (see the photograph in Morris's *Works*, XVI, frontispiece), appeared first in the *Catalogue of the Arts and Crafts Exhibition* (1893) and then in J. W. Mackail's *Life of William Morris*, chap. 20. See Edmund Penning-Rowsell's article, "Kelmscott Manor Restored," *Country Life*, Nov. 9, 1967, pp. 1190–92.

GEORGE MEREDITH (1828–1909)

Meredith is more famous for his dozen-odd novels than for his poetry, a fact that he himself recognized and deplored, especially since even his fiction, partly because of a difficult, mannered prose style, was uncommonly slow in winning acceptance. His novels were never *popular,* but their rejection by such latter-day intellectuals as Virginia Woolf and E. M. Forster was clearly patricidal. He has nine volumes of poetry: *Poems* (1851); *Modern Love and Poems of the English Roadside* (1862); *Poems and Lyrics of the Joy of Earth* (1883); *Ballads and Poems of Tragic Life* (1887); *A Reading of Earth* (1888); *Poems, the Empty Purse, with Odes* (1892); *Odes in Contribution to the Song of French History* (1898); *A Reading of Life* (1901); and *Last Poems* (1909). Probably his verse, though it seems to be gaining favor now, will always attract the few rather than the many.

There are two authoritative editions of Meredith's works, the Memorial Edition (27 vols., 1909–11) and the De Luxe Edition (37 vols., 1898–1910). The edition of his poetry being edited by Phyllis Bartlett, nearly ready for publication by Yale University Press, will supersede all other editions, and for his letters the same can be said of the edition, also nearly ready for publication (Oxford), being prepared by C. L. Cline. The best biography is Lionel Stevenson's *The Ordeal of George Meredith* (1953); the standard edition of the poetry, at present, is *The Poetical Works of George Meredith* (1912), ed. G. M. Trevelyan; the standard study of the poetry, Trevelyan's *The Poetry and Philosophy of George Meredith* (1906).

Page 293: "Love in the Valley," first published in *Poems* (1851), was much revised, and more than doubled in length, for republication in its present form in *Macmillan's Magazine,* October, 1878. The meter (wittily, but not decently, expropriated in W. H. Auden's "The Geography of the House" in *About the House*) is clearly a *tour de force,* and any special lyric simplicity or spontaneity that may have been lost is more than made up for by the sensuous showing off of exuberance. "Happy in herself is the maiden that I love" ran line 16 of the first version, and the rhythm and dwelling upon words here seem, similarly, to be happy in themselves. The effect, which is almost unique but can perhaps best be compared with that of "sprung rhythm," is the direct (and deliberate) opposite of the stately melancholy usually associated with a succession of stressed syllables. The progression of seasons in the poem is both structural and thematic.

Page 299: "Modern Love" was first published in 1862, slightly revised in 1892. A holograph version of most of the work shows many interesting variant readings, all to be recorded in Phyllis Bartlett's forthcoming edition of Meredith's poetry. The best discussion of the poem is C. Day Lewis's introduction to a separate edition published in 1948. Some notes can be found in *Selected Poetical Works of George Meredith*, ed. G. M. Trevelyan (1955), as well as in his standard edition of the poetical works.

The poem anatomizes, in fifty 16-line "sonnets," the failure of a marriage. Sometimes the poet speaks, referring to husband and wife in the third person, sometimes the husband speaks in the first person. "Madam" is always the wife, the "Lady" or "my lady" always the Other Woman, as "the man" referred to in the third sonnet is the Other Man. In Sonnet 49 the "strength to help the desperate weak" is suicide, by means of a poison potion — "Lethe had passed those lips" (l. 16).

Meredith is to some extent debunking the sonnet tradition, but in the background are not only the familiar sonnet-sequences but also such poems as Tennyson's "Locksley Hall," *The Princess,* and *Maud,* Mrs. Browning's *Aurora Leigh,* and Coventry Patmore's *Angel in the House.* It is also worth while to remember — Meredith being a novelist and satirist — that the reliability of the speaker is not necessarily immaculate.

Obviously, as C. Day Lewis observes, this is an intensely personal poem in which actual "experience has, for the sake of art and decorum, been given a fictional disguise." Meredith had barely reached his legal majority when he married Mary Nicolls, who was not only a widow and six and a half years older than he was but was also the daughter of Thomas Love Peacock and as brilliant, witty, sensitive (and self-centered) as Meredith himself — in other words, about the last woman in England he ought to have married. In 1858, abandoning husband and child, she ran away to Capri with a painter who, after a short liaison, abandoned her. She died in 1861.

The poem may properly be called bitter but not unfair. Meredith *anatomizes,* and nothing is more remote from his method than self-pity. Indeed, the portrait of the husband has more in common with that of Sir Willoughby Patterne, in Meredith's novel *The Egoist* (1879), than has been generally recognized, and it is surely not straining to recognize in parts, especially Sonnet 7, another debt owed by *The Waste Land* to Victorian poetry.

Page 320: "Phoebus with Admetus," first published in *Macmillan's Magazine,* December, 1881, reprinted in *Poems and Lyrics of the Joy of Earth* (1883). Phoebus Apollo, as we learn in the opening lines of Euripides' *Alcestis,* having slain the Cyclops, was exiled by Zeus to serve a mortal, Admetus, for a year.

Page 322: "The Lark Ascending," first published in the *Fortnightly Review,* May, 1881, reprinted in *Poems and Lyrics of the Joy of Earth*

(1883). The "taint of personality" in line 94 is much the same as the "scaly Dragon-fowl" ("Self") in "The Woods of Westermain." The metrical effects here are equaled, perhaps surpassed, in the songs of the nightingales in "Night of Frost in May."

Page 325: "The Woods of Westermain" was first published in *Poems and Lyrics of the Joy of Earth* (1883). The title of the volume is the most succinct commentary on this poem, in which Meredith uses for a philosophical lyric the same *ideas* he had shaped into a comedy of manners in his novel *The Egoist* (1879). The enchanted woods are a *selva oscura,* though in no other dimension is the poem Dantesque. The "scaly Dragon-fowl" of l. 220, named "Self" (l. 243), is to be not slain but "renovated" by Change. The "Fount and Lure o' the chase" (l. 267), as G. M. Trevelyan points out (*Selected Poetical Works of George Meredith*), is Love, and she "who food for all provides" (l. 283) is Mother Earth or Nature; the "Triad" of l. 360 is the "Blood and brain and spirit" of l. 353. Only those who have explored Earth's "depths" (l. 375) can wield "the chisel, axe, and sword" and know the meaning of life; others, trapped by self and lost in Westermain, know only how to find Death, "One whose eyes are out" (l. 457).

Page 337: "Earth and Man" was first published in *Poems and Lyrics of the Joys of Earth* (1883). The poem makes explicit what is metaphorical and allegorical, or mythopoeic, in "The Woods of Westermain." The "Invisible" (ll. 30, 78) is the *super*natural god — the god of formal or revealed religion — as opposed to Earth or Nature.

ALGERNON CHARLES SWINBURNE (1837–1909)

Swinburne, like all great writers, pushed back the horizons of literature, and he did it in three areas, drama, poetry, and criticism. He ranges with Dryden, Coleridge, Poe, Arnold, and Eliot among the great poet-critics in English. He extended the boundaries of poetry both in subject matter (most notably in his poems on the psychology of sex) and in meter, and he was, simultaneously, a scholar, an antiquary, and a fierce, confident propagandist — whose taste and intuitions were virtually infallible — for the literature of his own century. Altogether he published over three dozen volumes, including a novel. His finest drama, *Atalanta in Calydon,* is given here complete, and his best volumes of verse are all represented, except two long narrative poems, *Tristram of Lyonesse* (1882) and *The Tale of Balen* (1896).

The standard edition of his poetry and dramas is the collected edition in eleven volumes, 1904–05 (see Fredeman, 62:6), but for the prose and much early and some posthumous poetry there is, regrettably, no alternative to *The Complete Works*, Bonchurch Edition (20 vols., 1925–27; Fredeman, 62:6). For his correspondence see *The Swinburne Letters*, ed. C. Y. Lang (6 vols., 1959–62; Fredeman, 62:12). Edmund Gosse's *Life of Algernon Charles Swinburne* (1917, reprinted in Bonchurch Edition) is standard, but should be supplemented by Georges Lafourcade's *La Jeunesse de Swinburne, 1837–67* (2 vols., 1928; Fredeman, 62:28) and his *Swinburne: A Literary Biography* (1932; Fredeman, 62:31). The time is ripe, however, for a new biography. John D. Rosenberg's "Swinburne," *Victorian Studies,* XI (Dec., 1967), 131–52, is by all odds the best general essay.

Page 344: "The Triumph of Time." Published in *Poems and Ballads* (1866), this autobiographical poem undoubtedly tells the story of an overwhelming disappointment in love in the early sixties. The older books had it that Swinburne proposed marriage to a girl named Jane Faulkner, who was so startled that she nervously laughed in his face, but it is now known that "Boo" Faulkner was in fact only ten years old at the time and is generally supposed that the girl he loved was his double first-cousin, Mary Gordon, who in 1865 married General Disney Leith, a man many years her senior. See John S. Mayfield, "Swinburne's Boo," *English Miscellany*, IV (1953), and Cecil Y. Lang, "Swinburne's Lost Love," *PMLA*, LXXIV (March, 1959). Whatever the poem is or is not, it will not be called diffuse by anyone aware of its density. It cries out for close critical study, as (on one level) the echoes of *Hamlet* (ll. 33, 126, 237), *A Midsummer Night's Dream* (l. 149), *Wuthering Heights*, chap. 15 (ll. 113–14) and chap. 12 (ll. 391–92), Jaufré Rudel (ll. 321 ff.), *Iliad* (ll. 382–83), and the conclusion of the *Republic* (Shorey's Loeb Classics translation cites and uses l. 83 for the *Republic* 472a), not to mention Genesis, Isaiah, Job, Ecclesiastes, the Synoptic Gospels, the Pauline Epistles, and many others, all abundantly witness, or as (on another level) these words from John Heath-Stubbs's *Darkling Plain* (1950) richly suggest (p. 33): "The image of the drowned man is one of peculiar poignancy which haunts English poetry whenever the poet envisages the possibilities of failure, through the overreaching of his powers. While he remains master of his own creative impulse, the poet may be said to ride that sea, which is at once the welter of his subconscious emotions, and the surge of impersonal hostile forces which surround him in the world. Should his genius fail him, he may at any time be sucked under, and become the sport and prey of unco-ordinated passion within, and the world's cruelty without."

Materials to support such study are in the variant readings recorded in Lafourcade's *La Jeunesse de Swinburne*, II, 566–67, and the present editor's article in the *Yale University Library Gazette*, XXXI (April,

1957), 163–71, which also includes manuscript variants of "A Leave-taking."

Page 354: "A Leave-taking," published, like "The Triumph of Time," with which it must be associated, in *Poems and Ballads* (1866). Pulsing behind the lines one hears, or ought to hear, Theocritus' second Idyll and Virgil's eighth Eclogue.

Page 355: "Itylus." Published in *Poems and Ballads* (1866). In the familiar myth King Tereus, married to Procne, fell in love with her sister Philomela, raped her, and cut out her tongue; but Philomela, though mute, wove the story into a tapestry and revealed the truth to Procne, who for revenge slew her own son Itys (Itylus) and served his flesh to Tereus. To escape his wrath Philomela was changed into a swallow, Procne into a nightingale (or, as in the later, Latin authors, invariably the source of the English versions, Philomela became the nightingale, Procne the swallow). In this poem Philomela, the nightingale-victim, addresses Procne, the swallow-mother. The old myth is alluded to in the first chorus of *Atalanta in Calydon,* and it is worth noting that in that drama, as in this poem, a mother is responsible for the death of her son.

Page 357: "Hymn to Proserpine." First published in *Poems and Ballads* (1866). The speaker is a Roman pagan of the fourth century — after the Edict of Milan, in 313, establishing the separate but equal status of Christianity. Julian the Apostate, Roman emperor A.D. 361–363, though reared a Christian, proclaimed himself a pagan on becoming emperor. According to the wonderful old legend used here, he was slain by a Christian and died exclaiming "Vicisti, Galilaee" (Thou hast conquered, Galilean). The best discussion of the poem is in W. R. Rutland's *Swinburne, A Nineteenth Century Hellene* (Oxford, 1931), pp. 274–76.

Page 360: "The Garden of Proserpine." First published in *Poems and Ballads* (1866). The symbolic garden here, in Swinburne's most familiar poem, is to be compared with the literal one in "A Forsaken Garden."

Page 363: "Prelude." Of the volume *Songs before Sunrise* (1871) Swinburne said: "My other books are books; that one is myself." In fact, it is becoming clear that all of Swinburne's books were himself and that *Songs before Sunrise* is different because he was himself different. The volume can be traced directly to a specific emotional, spiritual, and intellectual crisis, his meeting with Mazzini, the Italian patriot and revolutionary, in March, 1867. (The confrontation, far from being accidental or coincidental, was deliberately staged, with a *mise-en-scène* and principals so Jamesian that one can hardly read

The Princess Cassimassima free of the suspicion that to Turgeniev James applied an overlay of Swinburne and Mazzini.)

The "Prelude" shows Swinburne in the middle of the road of his life, looking before and after. Its calm, proud humanism is to be read both as a generalized credo and as a specific *mea culpa* or *amende honorable,* thrusting forward to the future of the poet as an individual (and of "all manhood"), backward, in direct and implied allusions, to the self of *Poems and Ballads* and *Atalanta in Calydon.*

Page 368: "Hertha," first published in *Songs before Sunrise* (1871), is a philosophical poem, and its development, like that of Job, Ecclesiastes, *De rerum natura,* the *Essay on Man, In Memoriam,* and *The Rubáiyát of Omar Khayyám,* is therefore additive rather than organic. Part of its effect thus derives from the fact that it is a static poem about growth. Another part depends on another paradox — "Nature" speaking in the very language and rhythm of that which she controverts (rather, of which she assumes the non-existence).

"Of all that I have done," Swinburne once remarked, "I rate 'Hertha' highest as a single piece, finding in it the most of lyric force and music combined with the most of condensed and clarified thought." The difficulty of the poem arises neither from the language, which is lucid and precise, nor from the meter, which is perfectly tuned to its function, but from the fact that the *ideas* are difficult and their vehicle is an unfamiliar mythology.

The ideas are those of nineteenth-century evolutionary science and positivism, their vehicle is that of Norse mythology. Hertha, identified by Tacitus as the Teutonic goddess of earth, or the earth-mother, speaks to man. The "tree many-rooted," the "life-tree," in lines 96 ff., is Yggdrasil, the world-tree linking together heaven, earth, and hell.

Reverberations of Emerson ("The Oversoul"), Blake, Whitman, and Job are audible, and to this traditional list I would add Bressac's harangue in Sade's *La Nouvelle Justine* (Sceaux, 1953), I, 136 ff., and Gwynplaine's address to the House of Lords in Hugo's *L'Homme qui rit,* Bk. VIII, chap. 7. The best explication of details in this poem is in the eccentric misreading in E. M. W. Tillyard's *Five Poems, 1470–1870* (London, 1948).

Page 374: "Genesis." First published in *Songs before Sunrise* (1871), this poem, one of the least sentimental ever written by any poet, is Shelleyan in its agnostic honesty, in its reliance on myth to deny revelation, and in its refusal either to collapse into despair or to retreat into vagueness. The poem is Lucretian, both generally and particularly (see *De rerum natura,* especially Bk. II).

Page 376: "Ave atque Vale." With this poem Swinburne enlarged the trio of great English elegies to a quartet, and a comparative study of them all, and of their relation to the elegiac tradition, would be both edifying and interesting. Baudelaire, the "sweet strange elder singer," born sixteen years before Swinburne, died in August, 1867, at the age of 46. As the poem suggests, the two poets never met, though they were very much aware of each other and had some slight correspondence occasioned by Swinburne's essay on *Les Fleurs du mal* in 1862. The elegy, begun when a false report of Baudelaire's death appeared in the papers, was first published in the *Fortnightly Review,* January, 1868, and collected in *Poems and Ballads,* Second Series (1878). It will be read with pleasure by any reasonably well-informed person, but the choicest appreciation is reserved for those who can take the elegiac tradition for granted and whose pulses beat, like Swinburne's own, with the poetry of Aeschylus, Dante, and Baudelaire. An excellent introduction to the poem is the discussion in Samuel C. Chew's *Swinburne* (1929).

The title is from the last line of Catullus' lament (*Carmen* 101): "Atque in perpetuum, frater, ave atque vale" ("And now forever, brother, hail and farewell"). The epigraph is from Baudelaire's "La Servante au grand coeur" and, among many echoes of *Les Fleurs du mal,* the sixth stanza is something between a translation and an accommodation of "La Géante."

Page 381: "Sonnet (With a copy of 'Mademoiselle de Maupin')." Théophile Gautier, poet, novelist, and critic, died in October, 1872, and to a memorial volume published in his honor in 1873, *Le Tombeau de Théophile Gautier,* Swinburne contributed not only this sonnet and "Memorial Verses" but also an ode and a sonnet in French, a poem of eighteen lines in Latin, and fifty-six lines of Greek verses. All these were collected in *Poems and Ballads,* Second Series (1878), except the Greek verses, which are printed and translated in W. R. Rutland's *Swinburne, A Nineteenth Century Hellene* (Oxford, 1931).

One of the strengths of the sonnet is in the deliberate, audacious near-blasphemy with which Swinburne makes Pauline diction suggest that his own most intimate compulsions are, after all, hallowed because Greek.

Page 382: "A Forsaken Garden." Published in the *Athenaeum* in 1876 and in *Poems and Ballads,* Second Series (1878). Perhaps the only adverse criticism that could be leveled against this poem is that (for an earlier generation, at least) it has been staled by familiarity. It should be read as a very Swinburnian New Jerusalem, but no further comment is required beyond the remark that it is intensely personal and can be profitably viewed as a kind of counterpart of "The Triumph of Time." The landscape is that of East Dene, in the Isle of Wight, home of Swinburne's cousin, Mary Gordon (compare the "Dedication" to Swinburne's tragedy, *The Sisters,* 1892).

Page 384: "A Vision of Spring in Winter." Published in *Poems and Ballads*, Second Series (1878). The poem is very characteristic and very personal — and deliberately Keatsian.

Page 386: "A Ballad of Dreamland." This poem, first collected in *Poems and Ballads*, Second Series (1878), should be read in conjunction with "The Triumph of Time" and "A Forsaken Garden."

Page 387: "A Ballad of François Villon, Prince of All Ballad Makers,"
Page 388: "The Ballad of Villon and Fat Madge,"
Page 389: "The Complaint of the Fair Armouress."

As the first stanza of the first poem suggests, Swinburne regarded François Villon (1431–?65) as the first modern poet, and in the early 1860's he and Rossetti made plans to translate all of Villon's work. "The Ballad of Villon and Fat Madge" probably dates from this period. In *Poems and Ballads*, Second Series (1878) Swinburne published ten of his translations together with his own tribute, "A Ballad of François Villon, Prince of all Ballad Makers." He did not include here, however, his rendering of the "Ballade de Villon et de la Grosse Margot," because, as he noted (*Letters*, III, 270–71), "it has not six decent lines (nor a single bad or weak one) in it from beginning to end." The translation was privately printed after his death and was first published in book form in *New Writings by Swinburne*, ed. Cecil Y. Lang (1964). In 1878 it was considered necessary to suppress six verses (lines 54–56, 70–72) of "The Complaint of the Fair Armouress," two of which were restored in the six-volume collected *Poems* (1904), the others in T. J. Wise's *Bibliography* some years later.

Page 392: "Thalassius." Published in *Songs of the Springtides* (1880). Swinburne conceived it as "a symbolical quasi-autobiographical poem after the fashion of Shelley or of Hugo, concerning the generation, birth and rearing of a by-blow of Amphitrite's . . . reared like Ion in the temple-service of Apollo" (*Letters*, IV, 106). See Richard D. McGhee's excellent study, " 'Thalassius': Swinburne's Poetic Myth," *Victorian Poetry*, V (Summer, 1967), 127–36.

The title means "of the sea" (i.e., "born of the sea"); ll. 88–89 are an adaptation of Landor's Latin inscription for the Spanish patriots slain in resisting the Napoleonic invasion, 1811–12.

Page 404: "The Higher Pantheism in a Nutshell,"

Page 405: "Sonnet for a Picture,"

Page 405: "Poeta Loquitur."

The first two parodies here come from Swinburne's anonymous volume *The Heptalogia, or the Seven against Sense. A Cap with Seven Bells* (1880). One of them makes merry with Tennyson's poem "The Higher Pantheism," the other with Rossetti's mannerisms in *The House of Life.* The five remaining pieces in the volume were in the manner of Coventry Patmore, the two Brownings, "Owen Meredith" (the second Lord Lytton), and, in a poem called "Nephelidia," of Swinburne himself. "John Jones," the original parody of Browning's "James Lee," was revised to "John Jones' Wife" after Swinburne learned (tardily) that Browning had revised *his* poem to "James Lee's Wife," and ll. 15–16 of "The Higher Pantheism" were first published in 1904. All the revisions are recorded in Robert A. Greenberg's fine article, "Swinburne's Revision of *The Heptalogia,*" to be published in *Studies in Bibliography,* XXII (1969).

"Poeta Loquitur" (The Poet Speaks), another essay in auto-criticism, first appeared in *Posthumous Poems* (1917). The last two (extra) stanzas are transcribed from T. J. Wise's *A Swinburne Library.*

Swinburne was the greatest parodist that English poetry has ever seen. It is his special distinction that he not only caught his victims' manner and mannerisms but also exposed the very matter, so skillfully that at their best the relation of his parodies to the originals is like that of anti-matter to matter.

Page 407: "A Ballad of Sark." Published in the *English Illustrated Magazine,* 1884, and reprinted in *A Midsummer Holiday and Other Poems,* in the same year. Swinburne visited the Channel island Sark in 1876 and 1882, and, as can be seen from letters written on the spot, recorded his impressions, both visual and philosophical, in this poem and in "The Garden of Cymodoce." See *The Swinburne Letters,* III, 187–88, 190, 193, 210, and IV, 142.

Page 408: "The Tyneside Widow." Published in *Poems and Ballads,* Third Series (1889). Swinburne's knowledge of balladry was that of a connoisseur, both scholarly and esthetic. He could reconstruct genuine old ballads with his head and compose new ones with his heart. When writing of Northumberland or the Scottish border, he was writing of what he knew and loved best, and there are those who believe that in his own compositions even the modern touches (usually considered inevitable and unavoidable in a modern ballad) were deliberately planted. See C. K. Hyder, "Swinburne and the Popular Ballad," *PMLA,* XLIX, (March, 1934), 295–309, and Anne Henry Ehrenpreis, "Swinburne's Edition of Popular Ballads," *PMLA,* LXXVIII (December, 1963), 559–71, and *The Literary Ballad* (1966).

Page 410: "To a Seamew." First published in *Poems and Ballads,* Third Series, 1889. The poem was written when Swinburne was nearly fifty years old, but the intense identification with the seamew dates from his childhood, as many references and an extraordinary letter, probably written late in life but recounting a youthful experience, make clear (*Letters,* VI, 251–53).

Page 414: "The Lake of Gaube." First collected in *A Channel Passage and Other Poems* (1904). The autobiographical aspect of the poem recalls Swinburne's actual experience of the Lac de Gaube, high up in the Pyrenees, near Cauterets, in the early sixties.

Page 417: *Atalanta in Calydon,* Swinburne's third volume, published in July, 1865, established his reputation as a poet, and it has been said that if he had published no other work "his name would still be sure of a place among the major poets of the language" (W. R. Rutland, *Swinburne, A Nineteenth Century Hellene,* Oxford, 1931, p. 93).

Discussion and appraisal of the dramatic poem will be more economical if certain claims, intended as purely descriptive, not evaluative, can be attended to. It is a drama cast in the Greek mold and written, like everything else worth reading, to say something that its author thought and felt: it is in no sense a mere artifact, like Arnold's *Merope.* Formally, it is closer to the Greek models than anything else in English except Milton's *Samson Agonistes* and Swinburne's other Greek drama *Erechtheus* (1876), and, apart from technicalities of structure, is far more Greek in matter and spirit even than Milton's great poem, much less Shelley's *Prometheus Unbound.* Its admixture of exclusively modern thought is no denser than that of *Samson* and incomparably less dense than that of Shelley's poem or of Arnold's *Empedocles on Etna.*

Swinburne's sources are considered in detail in Georges Lafourcade's *La Jeunesse de Swinburne,* II, 382–416, and in W. R. Rutland's study (cited above), Part Two. The classical echoes that so enrich the poem also impede appreciation for a generation not nurtured on the classics. They are an integral part of the design, however, precisely as they are in Pope's "Imitations of Horace" and Johnson's "London" and "Vanity of Human Wishes," and no one reared on Yeats, Joyce, Pound, and Eliot will be intimidated by the labor of looking up Swinburne's allusions.

No reductive reading could do justice to the subtlety and complexity of the drama, but a few generalizations may be worth while. Swinburne's bone-bred antitheses (unity and division, pleasure and pain, desire and restraint, growth and stasis, etc.) combined with the traditional Greek problem of fate *vs* free will shadow forth the dark ambiguities of existence — in the imagery and in the very characters as well as in the subject matter. As the governing symbol of the burning brand shows, neither fate nor free will is quite absolute (Fate imposes, man disposes); Althaea ("Mother and lover," like the sea in "The Triumph of Time") is both right and wrong; Meleager's sense of the "generation gap" is natural, but his love for Atalanta is (to say the least) unrealistic; and, as Althaea observes, Atalanta herself is "adorable, detestable."

Page 483: "The Leper" was first published in *Poems and Ballads* (1866). The prose note — a hoax composed by Swinburne himself (*Letters*, VI, 150, 156) — may be literally rendered as follows:

At that time there was in this country a large number of lepers, which greatly displeased the king, since because of them God must have been grievously angered. Now it happened that a noble damsel named Yolande de Sallières, being afflicted and utterly ravaged by this evil malady, all her friends and relatives, having before their eyes the fear of God, drove her out of their houses and never were willing to receive or comfort a thing accursed by God and stinking and abominable to all men. That Lady had been very beautiful and of graceful figure, goodly in stature and lascivious in her life. However, none of the lovers who had often embraced and kissed her very tenderly was willing to harbor any longer so ugly a woman and so detestable a sinner. Only a clerk who had been at first her servant and go-between in matters of love took her with him and hid her in a small hut. There the wicked woman died an evil death in great misery. And after her died the clerk aforesaid, who out of his great love had for six months cared for her, washed her, dressed and undressed her every day with his own hands. People even say that this wicked man and cursed clerk, remembering this woman's former great beauty, [now] ravaged, often delighted in kissing her foul and leprous mouth and in caressing her gently with his loving hands. Therefore, he died of this same abominable disease. This happened near Fontainebellant in Gastinois. And when King Philip heard the story he marveled greatly.

C. K. Hyder's useful study, "The Medieval Background of Swinburne's 'The Leper,' " *PMLA*, XLVI (Dec. 1931), 1280–8, should be consulted. An early version of the poem, called "A Vigil," inaccurately transcribed in T. J. Wise, *A Swinburne Library*, and in Lafourcade, *La Jeunesse de Swinburne*, II, 63–4, 572–3, is fascinating, and in T. E. Welby, *A Study of Swinburne*, a facsimile of the original holograph manuscript of ll. 1–16 reveals that l. 8 first aimed at the present tense — "Ay, the flesh stiffens to the bone" (cf. "The Leper," l. 93, and also l. 106, where "keen" is a visual image).

"The Leper" descends from Browning (e.g., "Porphyria's Lover"), Morris ("The Wind"), and Tennyson (*Maud*), in all of which (among other resemblances) the speaker is demented and autistic, like the clerk here, as seen in the opening stanza (cf. "well" and "well-begotten" in *Maud*, I, 6, 119, 683). The language is studiedly quaint, sounding occasionally as if translated from the French. Line 12 means initially, "Her scornful lips and lovable (or lovely) hair," though it has other reverberations. In l. 41 "you" refers to the stanza preceding, "tell" suggesting the telling of beads in a rosary. Line 46: "And does not change, continuing to be God." In l. 63 "sweet hot tears" parallels "short mad cries" l. 60). And in ll. 121–4 the grammar is precise, the signification resonant: "beauty," "ways," "face," and "sweet" are the objects of "Having," and the phrase "for such mean service done" is to be read parenthetically.

Swineburne's ambiguity, here as elsewhere, is always functional, an essential part of his poetic strategy, and the language and structure of this poem, together with its ancestry and fraudulent "source," are all part of a conspiracy luring the willing reader to interpretations that can neither be wholly sustained nor comfortably dismissed — among them homicide, voyeurism, necrophilia. To cite a "safe" example: "blind" in l. 137 may (or may not) suggest that the clerk "died of this same abominable disease."

Page 487: "Anactoria" first appeared in *Poems and Ballads* (1866). The primary sources (Sappho and Catullus) are dealt with in Rutland's *Swinburne, A Nineteenth Century Hellene,* but Pope's "Eloisa to Abelard" and two of *his* sources, Ovid's "Sappho to Phaon" and *Letters from a Portuguese Nun,* also belong in the genealogy. Indispensable are Swinburne's own defense of the poem in *Notes on Poems and Reviews* and David A. Cook's explicit article, "The Content and Meaning of Swinburne's "Anactoria," *Victorian Poetry,* IX (Spring-Summer, 1971), 73–93. The poem remains, what it has always been, the most notorious of the Swinburnian "shockers" of unchallenged merit. It is not English poetry's first indictment of the irreconcilability of good and the means of good, but it is the first time that the vehicle has been, straightforwardly, homosexual love (with glancing blows at cunnilingus), which was not, a century ago, a literary staple of this happy breed of men.

Formally, "Anactoria" is a dramatic monologue; effectively and intentionally, it is a symphonic poem: Anactoria has forsaken Sappho — perhaps, as in Fragment 38, "To Anactoria," has "gone with a soldier husband to Lydia" (*Lyra Graeca,* I, 209 n., Loeb Classical Library) — whom we may visualize contemplating her beloved's abandoned cincture and, in two magnificent surges of identical protraction, four grand modulations of accelerating intensity (ll. 1–58, 59–152, 153–88, 189–304), giving utterance to her passion (frustrate) and despair (animate), of which the ontological septicaemia of the third section is the culmination and, in the fourth, the redemptive therapy of her all-consoling esthetic conscience the resolution. Only the conclusion of "Adonais" rivals the sublimity of the last of these, a perverse Magnificat — "Thee too the years shall cover," which (in Hardy's words) are "the finest drama of Death and Oblivion . . . in our tongue."

Prosodically, Swinburne's special genius was for instinctive artifice. With the pentameter couplet, an instrument admitting a range of subtle variations, he here achieves effects never surpassed even by himself (though equaled in *Tristram of Lyonesse*) in a "scheme of movement and modulation" that he called "original in structure and combination" (*Letters*, II, 74). Dryden, assuredly, was not his model, as Lafourcade oddly suggests, but Shelley, in "Epipsychidion." The rhymes are not muffled by *enjambement* to a sort of blanched verse (as in "Endymion" or "My Last Duchess") — of the fifty-odd sentences, lengthening from a single line to eighteen, all end on the rhyme—but they never ring epigrammatically like Pope's. That Swinburne strove for another sonority is evident in the opening verses, where the assonance of "Blind" (which first read "Sting") and "Divide" pulls magnetically on the rhymes, as the double stress of "sharp sighs" and "soft sound" mutes them. The manipulation of caesura is better appreciated than demonstrated, as are the vowel patterns (e. g., "Severed . . . bleach, . . . flesh . . . cleaves" in l. 9; the incredible orchestration of the conclusion) and the precise counterpoint of ll. 35–46, 47–58 (a feat twice duplicated in *Tristram of Lyonesse*).

No poet before him deployed language with more precision or awareness than Swinburne, the peer in this respect of Milton and Pope, and no poem uses language more cunningly than this one, as a few glosses will perhaps indicate. In the epigraph (from a corrupt text of Sappho's Fragment I, "Ode to Aphrodite") Aphrodite asks Sappho "Of whom by persuasion hast thou vainly caught love?" now amended to read, "Whom shall I make to give thee room in her heart's love?" Her question is continued in "Anactoria," ll. 73–4, 81–4 (see Rutland, pp. 285–6, for the other echoes of Sappho). In l. 22 "Erotion" is a Swinburnian diminutive of Eros, "Erinna" was a Greek poetess formerly thought to be from Lesbos and a friend of Sappho's. In ll. 28–34, a remarkable passage, "intense" means "keen," but also has its Latin sense of "strained" or "stretched"; "device" means "pleasure" or "desire," "superflux" means "overflowing"; "vex" is a double pun, with its usual meaning as well as *two* Latin significations, "shake" or "agitate" and also (as in Petronius and Martial) with sexual implications; "strain," another pun, suggests "stretch" or "make taut" (as on the rack, in torture) and also the musical sense of tightening strings for raising pitch; "relapse" means "falling or sinking back again" and "reluctation" means "struggle," and the lines describes exhalation and gasping inhalation, with the signification echoed in "Dumb tunes and shuddering semitones." In l. 40 "flowers" are eyes, with an implied pun on "irises," and in l. 52 "fervent" means "boiling" or "glowing."

In ll. 59–103 "Love" (upper-case), "queen," "she," and "her" always refer to Aphrodite (except in ll. 81–2, where "she" is Anactoria). Aphrodite, whose very name was supposed to mean "foamborn" (cf. ll. 37 f., 49 f.), arose from the sea after Kronos "cut off the genitals of his father [Uranos], and cast the bleeding member behind him far away into the sea" (cf. *Letters,* I, 75 n., and *Atalanta in Calydon,* ll. 729 ff.). "Mixed" (l. 132) should be understood in its obsolete (and Latin) sexual sense. "Lyre" (l. 140) is a (meta) physical conceit, specifically visual as well as metaphorical generally and also symbolic, and in "perfect pangs" (l. 142) the adjective suggests sexual completion, as in Martial, *Epigrams,* III. lxxix. 2, or Ovid, *Art of Love,* I. 389. In ll. 162–4: etymologically "comet" means "long-haired," "disastrous" means "ill-starred." Lines 171 ff. Lafourcade (*La Jeunesse de Swinburne,* II, 356 ff., 432) traces to the Marquis de Sade. Line 237: cf. Ovid, "Sappho to Phaon," 151 f. "Even the branches have laid aside their leafage" (Loeb).

NOTES ON THE ILLUSTRATIONS

✧

FRONTISPIECE

The P.R.B.'s and Their Associates*

DANTE GABRIEL ROSSETTI (1853), etching, by William Bell Scott (*British Museum*). Reproduced in *Autobiographical Notes of the Life of William Bell Scott,* ed. W. Minto (2 vols., 1892), I, 288. (Photograph, Copyright British Museum)

CHRISTINA ROSSETTI (1849?), oil, by James Collinson (*Coll. Helen Rossetti Angeli*). Reproduced in Rosalie Glynn Grylls, *Portrait of Rossetti* (1964), p. 33. (Photograph, Courtesy of Mrs. Angeli and Lady Mander)

WILLIAM MICHAEL ROSSETTI (1848), drawing, by D. G. Rossetti (*Coll. Helen Rossetti Angeli*). Reproduced in *Dante Gabriel Rossetti, His Family-Letters, with a Memoir,* by W. M. Rossetti (2 vols., 1895), II, 39. (Photograph, Copyright British Museum)

F. G. STEPHENS (1853), pencil drawing, by J. E. Millais (*National Portrait Gallery*). Reproduced in *Frederic George Stephens and the Pre-Raphaelite Brothers,* with notes by J. B. Manson (privately printed, 1920), and in Richard Ormond's article, "Portraits to Australia, a group of Pre-Raphaelite drawings," *Apollo,* LXXXV (Jan., 1967), 25–27. (Photograph, Copyright National Portrait Gallery, London)

JOHN EVERETT MILLAIS (1850), pencil drawing, by Charles Allston Collins (*Ashmolean Museum*). Collins was *not* a member of the Brotherhood, despite the initials after his signature. (Photograph, Copyright The University of Oxford, Ashmolean Museum, Department of Western Art)

THOMAS WOOLNER (1852), pencil drawing, by D. G. Rossetti (*National Portrait Gallery*). Reproduced in Amy Woolner, *Thomas Woolner, R.A.* (1917). See Richard Ormond's article in *Apollo,* cited above. (Photograph, Copyright National Portrait Gallery, London)

WILLIAM HOLMAN HUNT (1854), pencil, sepia, and colored wash, by J. E. Millais (*Ashmolean Museum*). Hitherto reproduced only

---

* No portrait of James Collinson is known.

in the catalogue *Millais, PRB, PRA:* An Exhibition organized by the Walker Art Gallery, Liverpool, and the Royal Academy of Arts, London, January–April, 1967, Plate 15. A self-portrait of Hunt, aged 17 (1848), is reproduced in Hunt's *Pre-Raphaelitism and the Pre-Raphaelite Brotherhood* (2 vols., 1905–06), II, 55, and a pencil drawing by D. G. Rossetti (1853) is included in Richard Ormond's *Apollo* article, cited above, but no other likenesses *imberbes* are known to me. (Photograph, Copyright The University of Oxford, Ashmolean Museum, Department of Western Art)

WILLIAM MORRIS (about 1857), pencil, self-portrait *(Victoria and Albert Museum).* Apparently hitherto unreproduced but similar to the early self-portrait (also in the Victoria and Albert) in Morris's *Collected Works* (24 vols., 1910–15), I, frontispiece, and of the same period as the photograph (1857), at age 23, in XXIV, frontispiece, and in Georgiana Burne-Jones, *Memorials of Edward Burne-Jones* (2 vols., 1904), I, 96. (Photograph, Courtesy of Victoria and Albert Museum)

EDWARD BURNE-JONES (1859), pencil drawing, by Simeon Solomon *(Ashmolean Museum.)* Apparently hitherto unreproduced, though early likenesses are far from common. That Burne-Jones (not, as commonly supposed, Meredith) posed for the head of Christ in Rossetti's "Mary Magdalen at the Door of Simon the Pharisee" (1858; Fitzwilliam Museum), I am assured by Professor C. L. Cline, who had it from Sir Sydney Cockerell, whose sources were Meredith himself and Philip Webb. See also H. C. Marillier, *Dante Gabriel Rossetti, An Illustrated Memorial of His Art and Life* (Second Edition, 1904), p. 74. (It is worth recording — in an obscure footnote — that Pharisees persist in identifying the Christ as W. J. Stillman.)

FORD MADOX BROWN (1850–53), self-portrait *(Coll. Sir Frank Soskice).* Reproduced in Ford M. Hueffer, *Ford Madox Brown, A Record of His Life and Work* (1896), facing p. 67. Compare the very similar sketch by D. G. Rossetti (1852) reproduced in Lionel Cust, *The National Portrait Gallery* (2 vols., 1901–02), II, 276, and in many memoirs and studies. (Photograph, Copyright British Museum)

ALGERNON CHARLES SWINBURNE (1860), etching, by W. B. Scott *(Balliol College).* Reproduced in *Autobiographical Notes of the Life of William Bell Scott,* II, 18.

WILLIAM BELL SCOTT (1852), crayon, by D. G. Rossetti *(Coll. Evelyn Courtney-Boyd, Penkill Castle).* Reproduced in Lona Mosk

Packer, *Christina Rossetti* (Berkeley and Los Angeles, 1963), tenth page after p. 172. (Photograph, Courtesy of Miss Evelyn Courtney-Boyd)

GEORGE MEREDITH (1862), photograph in S. M. Ellis, *George Meredith* (1920), p. 204. See the note on Burne-Jones, above. (Photograph, Courtesy of Yale University Library)

JOHN RUSKIN (1853), pencil, with touches of sepia, by J. E. Millais (*The Ruskin Galleries,* Bembridge School). Reproduced in James Dearden's article, "Some Portraits of Ruskin," *Apollo,* LXXII (Dec., 1960), 190–95. This is a study for the familiar, famous, and notorious oil portrait (1854). See the catalogue for the Millais exhibition (cited above), Nos. 42, 293, 294. (Photograph, Courtesy of J. S. Dearden, Curator, The Ruskin Galleries, Bembridge School, Isle of Wight)

PLATES 1–16

(Between pages 160–161)

PLATE 1.   Three drawings by D. G. Rossetti

a. ELIZABETH SIDDAL (about 1854; *Tate Gallery*). Likenesses of Mrs. Rossetti are numerous and have been frequently reproduced. Representative examples are in H. C. Marillier, *Dante Gabriel Rossetti, An Illustrated Memorial of His Art and Life; Pre-Raphaelite Painters,* ed. Robin Ironside, with a Descriptive Catalogue by John Gere (1948); *The Pre-Raphaelites and Their Contemporaries,* catalogue of an exhibition, Maas Gallery, London, Nov.–Dec., 1961; catalogue of the Pre-Raphaelite exhibition, Herron Museum of Art, Indianapolis, Feb.–March, Huntington Hartford Museum, April–May, 1964; and of course in nearly all the relevant memoirs and standard studies. She was not only Ophelia for Millais and Arthur Hughes, but also Viola for Walter Deverell's "Twelfth Night" and Sylvia in Hunt's "Valentine Rescuing Sylvia from Proteus" (and also in his "Christian Missionary Persecuted by Druids"), and, apart from portraits, appears in about two dozen of Rossetti's oils and watercolors. See William Michael Rossetti's article, "Dante Gabriel Rossetti and Elizabeth Siddal," *Burlington Magazine,* I (May, 1903), 273–95, which reproduces five Rossetti drawings of her (four of which reappear in Violet Hunt's *The Wife of Rossetti,* 1932) and her self-portrait. See also Rosalie Mander's article "Rossetti's Models," *Apollo,* LXXVIII (July, 1963), 18–22. (Photograph, Copyright The Tate Gallery, London)

b. JANE MORRIS (1860; Pierpont Morgan Library). Compare, among many other early likenesses, Rossetti's first drawing of her, in pencil, as he knew her (age 17) at Oxford in 1857 in Georgiana Burne-Jones's *Memorials of Edward Burne-Jones*, I, facing page 168; his pen-and-ink drawing of her (age 18) in J. W. Mackail's *Life of William Morris* (2 vols., 1899), I, facing p. 138; and a third one, at about the same age, in *The Letters of William Morris to His Family and Friends*, ed. Philip Henderson (1950), facing p. 16; and the pencil drawings by Morris (1858) and Rossetti (1861) in Morris's *Collected Works*, II, facing p. xxvi, and XVII, facing p. xx. See, below, the note on "La Pia," Plate 6. (Photograph, Courtesy of the Pierpont Morgan Library)

c. FANNY CORNFORTH (about 1865; *National Gallery of Scotland*). Compare the likenesses in the Birmingham crayon study reproduced in *Rossetti's Letters to Fanny Cornforth*, ed. Paull Franklin Baum (Baltimore, 1940), frontispiece, and, facing p. 24, the crayon study for "Lady with a Fan," as well as Rossetti's paintings "Aurelia (Fazio's Mistress)" and "The Blue Bower" (Marillier, Nos. 144, 163). (Photograph, Courtesy of the National Galleries of Scotland)

PLATE 2. D. G. Rossetti, THE GIRLHOOD OF MARY VIRGIN (1849), oil (*Tate Gallery*). "The scene shown is a room in the Virgin's home, with an open carved balcony at which her father, St. Joachim, is tending a symbolically fruitful vine. On the right of the picture, shown against an olive-green curtain, are the figures of the Virgin and her mother, St. Anna, seated at an embroidery frame. The latter, clothed in dark green and brown, with a nun-like head-dress of dull red, sits watching with clasped hands the work before her, whilst the young girl, a most untypical Madonna, in simple grey dress with pale green at the wrists, pauses with the needle in her hand and gazes with a rapt ascetic look at the room before her, where, as if visible to her eyes, a child-angel is tending a tall white lily. Beneath the pot in which the lily grows are six large books in heavy bindings, bearing the names of the six cardinal virtues. These, and a white dove perching on the trellis, are amongst the peaceful symbols of the picture, whilst the tragedy also is foreshadowed in a figure of the cross formed by the young vine-tendrils and in some strips of palm and 'seven-thorned briar' laid across the floor. Each of the figures, and the dove, bears a halo, the name being inscribed within it. Rossetti painted the calm face of his mother for St. Anna, and his sister Christina for the Virgin." — H. C. Marillier, *Dante Gabriel Rossetti, An Illustrated Memorial of His Art and Life* (1899), pp. 22–23. Compare the two sonnets "Mary's Girlhood (*For a Picture*)," p. 7, above. (Photograph, Copyright The Tate Gallery, London)

PLATE 3. D. G. Rossetti, Ecce Ancilla Domini (1850), oil (*Tate Gallery*), also known as "The Annunciation," illustrating Luke 1:26–38, with the concluding words of Mary to Gabriel, "Ecce ancilla Domini, fiat mihi secundum verbum tuum." William Michael and Christina Rossetti were the models.

"It is . . . difficult for anyone of this generation to see what in the quiet, shrinking girl-like figure of Rossetti's Virgin, in the handsome human-looking angel, or the simple entourage of that Eastern room, could infuriate and outrage the so-called critical opinions of the mid-Victorian age. To us . . . there seems an especial charm in this new conception of the oft-depicted scene: the angel, not as usual gay with peacock wings and trappings, but grave and simply clad; the Virgin, not raised triumphant on a throne, nor impossibly bedecked with jewels, but waked from slumber in the early dawn, and crouching half in fear and awe upon a pallet couch. The white painting, too, is a masterpiece, skilfully relieved by touches of bright colour, the red embroidery at the bed foot, the soft blue curtain at the Virgin's head, and through the open window the blue sky and bright sun of a Syrian morning streaming into the room." (Marillier, pp. 25–26)
(Photograph, Copyright The Tate Gallery, London)

PLATE 4. D. G. Rossetti, The Wedding of St. George (1864), watercolor, with additions in oil and pencil (*Coll. Jerrold N. Moore, New Haven, Conn.*). Compare the earlier watercolor, "The Wedding of St. George and Princess Sabra" (1857; Tate Gallery), reproduced in color in *Pre-Raphaelite Painters*, ed. Robin Ironside.

Except for a detail of the two central figures in Kerrison Preston's *Blake and Rossetti* (1944), this watercolor has been reproduced earlier only in the catalogue of the Pre-Raphaelite exhibition, Herron Museum of Art, Indianapolis, and Huntington Hartford Museum, New York, 1964. The following note is quoted from Mr. Moore's catalogue:

"The design of this picture was originally conceived as the last of a series of six stained glass windows illustrating the story of St. George and the dragon, designed for Morris, Marshall, Faulkner, and Co. in 1861–62. These designs figure as No. 119 in Marillier's Catalogue, and are reproduced in his book between pp. 112 and 113, where they are discussed. The second of the series, 'The Princess drawing the fatal lot,' was painted over in watercolors, and the fourth design, 'Saint George slaying the dragon,' was rendered in watercolors in 1863 (Marillier catalogue, No. 140), the year before Rossetti painted the present work. Perhaps because of the long single-family provenance, however, 'The Wedding of St. George' remained apparently unknown to all early commentators, including the artist's brother.

"It is in fact one of Rossetti's most interesting and evocative works, for the Saint George seems clearly to be a self-portrait, the face of the Princess is a reminiscence of Elizabeth Eleanor Siddal, and the King and Queen may probably have been painted from William Michael and Christina Rossetti. The right-hand trumpeter may be William Morris."

PLATE 5. D. G. Rossetti, THE BLESSED DAMOZEL (1876–77), oil (*Fogg Art Museum*). In a replica painted in 1879, now in the Lady Lever Gallery, Port Sunlight, Rossetti substituted two angel heads for the background lovers and (thereby) lost much of the "poetry." The description in the catalogue (p. 89) of the Pre-Raphaelite exhibition in the Fogg Museum (1946) reads: "A young woman in blue and white drapery, with stars in her red-brown hair and white lilies in her arms, leans on a rose-colored parapet and looks down; three angels with blue wings folded behind haloes of pink flame are below her; numerous pairs of embracing lovers clad in blue are in the background. In the predella the earthly lover lies beneath a spreading tree beside a stream, and looks up toward the evening sky." (Photograph, Courtesy of the Fogg Art Museum, Harvard University, Grenville L. Winthrop Bequest)

PLATE 6. D. G. Rossetti, LA PIA DE' TOLOMEI (1868–81), oil (*University of Kansas Museum of Art*). The model was Mrs. William Morris. On her association with Rossetti, and the relevance of this painting to their relations, see the brilliant, learned, suggestive study by W. D. Paden, *Register of the Museum of Art* (University of Kansas), II (Nov., 1958). I borrow from his conclusion the description of the painting by F. G. Stephens in the *Athenaeum*, Feb. 26, 1881: ". . . The subject is taken from the passage in the fifth canto of the 'Purgatorio,' in which Dante describes his meeting with Pia de' Tolomei among those whose opportunity of repentance was only at the last moment, and who dies without absolution. She had been done to death by her husband, Nello della Pietra, who confined her causelessly in a fortress of the Maremma, where she pined and died of malaria, or, as some say, by poison. The words which her spirit speaks to Dante run thus: —

> Deh quando tu sarai tornato al mondo
>   E riposato della lunga via,
> (Seguitò il terzo spirito al secondo,)
>   Ricorditi di me che son la Pia.
> Siena me fe', disfecemi Maremma:
>   Salsi colui che inanellata pria
> Disposando m'avea colla sua gemma.

A translation by Mr. Rossetti of these lines is placed on the frame of the picture: —

> Ah! when on earth thy voice again is heard,
>   And thou from the long road hast rested thee
> (After the second spirit said the third),
>   Remember me who am La Pia; me
> Siena, me Maremma, made, unmade.
>   This in his inmost heart well knoweth he
> With whose fair jewel I was ringed and wed.

"It is the evening, just before the gloaming, of a hot and languid autumn day. The lady reclines on the ramparts beside the grey stonework of a cylindrical tower. This tower is covered with the dense foliage of a climbing fig tree, which grows above and about the lady's seat. Dividing on our left, and thus opening before the face of La Pia, the foliage gives glimpses of the distant part of the ramparts and outer chapel. On these lie a bundle of lances, and the red banner of her husband drapes the battlements. The stone path of the rampart ends in a hollow *tourelle,* which forms the summit of a staircase, and its conical tiled roof stands out against the sky of wind-driven ashy clouds and their interspaces of white, which have a wannish lustre; a swarm of rooks wheels in evening flight to the turret. The lady languidly stoops a little forward. Her hands reach along her knees; some of her fingers are interlocked, while one thumb and forefinger clasp tightly, even to the whitening of the nail and knuckle, the "fair jewel" on the other hand. She is looking at the landscape, yet hardly seems to see the stunted clumps of wood that stand in the unwholesome pools, or the grey mists that gather about them, or the scarcely distinguishable slopes of heather which end at the level horizon, and are broken only by dense belts of bluish vapour and ghastly streaks of light reflected from distant ponds. On her features are no signs of animation, or hope, or care for existence, still less of a desire to battle for life. Their melancholy is meditative and habitual. And yet the face is at once fair and noble, because the large eyes and their lids have a massive character; and although the cheeks have lost their colour and their fulness is gone, their sculpturesque contours retain a look of high breeding, and the lips, which have a tinge of hectic red, are slightly parted with the languors of decline. Her dark hair hangs loose on her shoulders and expands about her head.

"The lady's dress is of blue embroidered with gold, and dashed with greenish hues and warm reflections of the light; over that is a robe of semi-transparent lustrous silk tissue with the colour of tarnished silver, through parts of which the darker tint of the undergarment shows itself. At her knee lies a breviary, and on it is a rosary of black and silver beads; by these is a bundle of the letters of her husband, written while he was yet her lover. . . ."

PLATE 7. D. G. Rossetti, THE SERMON ON THE MOUNT (1863), cartoon for stained glass (*William Morris Gallery*). Designed for All Saints Church, Selsley, Gloucestershire, but also used, in 1869, in Christ Church, Albany Street, London, N. W. 1, as a memorial to Rossetti's aunt, Miss Polidori, who died in 1867. Identification of the likenesses is an amusing diversion, and some have supposed them to be as follows: Christ (George Meredith), St. John (Swinburne), St. James (Simeon Solomon), Virgin Mary (Christina Rossetti), Mary Magdalen (Fanny Cornforth), Judas (Ernest Gambart, the picture dealer), St. Peter (William Bell Scott). May Morris (*William Morris: Artist, Writer, Socialist*, 1936, p. 17) names Christina Rossetti as the Virgin, Morris (her father) as Christ, Janey Morris (her mother) as Mary Magdalen. I myself would nominate Burne-Jones as Christ, Ruth Herbert as Mary Magdalen, and William Morris as St. Peter. (Photograph, Courtesy of William Morris Gallery, Walthamstow)

PLATE 8. William Holman Hunt, THE HIRELING SHEPHERD (1851), oil (*Manchester City Art Gallery*). The picture was exhibited with this quotation from *King Lear* (III.vi.44–47):

> Sleepest or wakest thou, jolly shepherd:
> Thy sheep be in the corn;
> And for one blast of thy minikin mouth,
> Thy sheep shall take no harm.

"Hunt's first picture with a moral: in his own words, it was intended to be 'a rebuke to the sectarian vanities and vital negligencies of the day.' The shepherd is a type of the 'muddle-headed pastors who instead of performing their services to their flock — which is in constant peril — discuss vain questions of no value to any human soul. My fool has found a Death's Head Moth, and this fills his little mind with forebodings of evil, and he takes it to an equally sage counsellor for her opinion. She scorns his anxiety from ignorance rather than profundity, but only the more distracts his faithfulness. While she feeds her lamb with sour apples, his sheep have burst bounds and got into the corn.'" (John Gere's Descriptive Catalogue in *Pre-Raphaelite Painters*, ed. Robin Ironside, p. 28)

(Photograph, Copyright City Art Gallery, Manchester, England)

PLATE 9. W. H. Hunt, MAY MORNING ON MAGDALEN TOWER (1889–91), oil (*Birmingham City Museum and Art Gallery*). The picture, in Hunt's words, shows "the ceremony of May morning, Magdalen Tower, Oxford, at sunrise, when the choristers, in perpetuation of a service which is a survival of primitive sun-worship, — perhaps Druidical, — sing a hymn as the sun appears above the horizon. . . . I ascended the Tower, making observations and sketches, and a few days later I returned to settle to work. For several weeks I mounted to the Tower roof about four in the morning with my small canvas to watch for the first rays of the rising sun, and to choose the sky which was most suitable for the subject." (*Pre-Raphaelitism and the Pre-Raphaelite Brotherhood, II,* 378) A much better description of the service than Hunt's is in Compton Mackenzie's *Sinister Street,* Bk. III, chap. 5, "Youth's Domination." On the painting see H. T. Kirby's article, "May Morning on Magdalen Tower," *Country Life,* April 27, 1951, pp. 1284–86. (Photograph, Copyright City of Birmingham, England)

PLATE 10. John Everett Millais, CHRIST IN THE HOUSE OF HIS PARENTS (1850), oil (*Tate Gallery*), also derisively known as "The Carpenter's Shop." It was exhibited at the Royal Academy in 1850 with these lines from Zachariah 12:6: "And one shall say unto him, What are these wounds in thine hands? Then he shall answer, Those with which I was wounded in the house of my friends." Studies for the picture, of which several were included in the Millais exhibition at the Royal Academy, 1967 (one reproduced in the catalogue), show that the child John the Baptist, carrying a basin of water, was not part of the original conception. The other female figure is presumably St. Elizabeth, his mother.

Critical reception of the picture was extraordinarily violent, and it is customary to cite Dickens's description from *Household Words,* June 15, 1850:

"You behold the interior of a carpenter's shop. In the foreground of that carpenter's shop is a hideous, wry-necked, blubbering, redheaded boy, in a bed-gown; who appears to have received a poke in the hand, from the stick of another boy with whom he has been playing in an adjacent gutter, and to be holding it up for the contemplation of a kneeling woman, so horrible in her ugliness, that (supposing it were possible for any human creature to exist for a moment with that dislocated throat) she would stand out from the rest of the company as a Monster, in the vilest cabaret in France or the lowest gin-shop in England."

The excellent catalogue, cited above, from which I have drawn these remarks, should be consulted for further details.

(Photograph, Copyright The Tate Gallery, London)

PLATE 11. John Everett Millais, OPHELIA (1852), oil (*Tate Gallery*). The background was painted outdoors in accordance with the strictest Pre-Raphaelite tenets, but Ophelia was done in Millais's studio. "Miss Siddal had a trying experience whilst acting as a model for 'Ophelia.' In order that the artist might get the proper set of the garments in water and the right atmosphere and aqueous effects, she had to lie in a large bath filled with water, which was kept at an even temperature by lamps placed beneath. One day, just as the picture was nearly finished, the lamps went out unnoticed by the artist, who was so intensely absorbed in his work that he thought of nothing else, and the poor lady was kept floating in the cold water till she was quite benumbed. She herself never complained of this, but the result was that she contracted a severe cold, and her father (an auctioneer at Oxford) wrote to Millais, threatening him with an action for £50 damages for his carelessness. Eventually the matter was satisfactorily compromised. Millais paid the doctor's bill; and Miss Siddal, quickly recovering, was none the worse for her cold bath." (John Guille Millais, *The Life and Letters of Sir John Everett Millais*, 2 vols., 1899, I, 144) Elizabeth Siddal was in fact the daughter of a Sheffield cutler.

The picture illustrates these lines from *Hamlet* (IV.iv.167–84):

> There is a willow grows aslant a brook,
> That shows his hoar leaves in the glassy stream;
> There with fantastic garlands did she come,
> Of crow-flowers, nettles, daisies, and long purples,
> That liberal shepherds give a grosser name,
> But our cold maids do dead men's fingers call them:
> There, on the pendent boughs her coronet weeds
> Clambering to hang, an envious sliver broke,
> When down her weedy trophies and herself
> Fell in the weeping brook. Her clothes spread wide,
> And, mermaid-like, awhile they bore her up;
> Which time she chanted snatches of old tunes,
> As one incapable of her own distress,
> Or like a creature native and indu'd
> Unto that element; but long it could not be
> Till that her garments, heavy with their drink,
> Pull'd the poor wretch from her melodious lay
> To muddy death.

See also Hunt's *Pre-Raphaelitism and the Pre-Raphaelite Brotherhood*, I, 262–64, 269.

(Photograph, The Tate Gallery, London)

PLATE 12. Ford Madox Brown, AN ENGLISH AUTUMN AFTERNOON (1852–54), oil (*Birmingham City Museum and Art Gallery*). Brown's own comment on his picture is the best one known to me:
"It is a literal transcript of the scenery round London, as looked at from Hampstead. The smoke is seen rising half way above the fantastic shaped, small distant cumuli which accompany particularly fine weather. The upper portion of the sky would be blue, as seen reflected in the youth's hat, the grey mist of autumn only rising a certain height. The time is 3 P.M., when late in October the shadows already lie long, and the sun's rays (coming from behind us in this work) are preternaturally glowing, as in rivalry of the foliage. The figures are peculiarly English — they are hardly lovers — mere boy and girl neighbours and friends. In no other country would they be so allowed out together, save in America, where (if report says true) the young ladies all carry latchkeys; both of us true inheritors from the Norsemen of Iceland, whose ladies would take horse and ride for three months about the island, without so much as a presumptuous question on their return from the much tolerating husbands of the period." (Ford Madox Hueffer, *Ford Madox Brown: A Record of His Life and Work*, 1896, p. 83)
(Photograph, Copyright City of Birmingham, England)

PLATE 13. John Ruskin, STUDY OF TREES (1847), sepia wash and ink over pencil (*The Ruskin Galleries, Bembridge School*), probably made at Ambleside, according to James S. Dearden, Curator of The Ruskin Galleries. The inscription in the lower left-hand corner reads: "Best way of studying Trees with a view to knowledge of their leafage. Young shoots of the Oak and Ash in Spring. J. R. 1847. (Unfinished)." (Photograph, Courtesy of J. S. Dearden, Curator, The Ruskin Galleries, Bembridge School, Isle of Wight)

PLATE 14: Edward Burne-Jones, THE CHESS PLAYERS (1862), watercolor (*Birmingham City Museum and Art Gallery*). I have retained the traditional title of the picture, though the game is clearly backgammon. (Photograph, Copyright City of Birmingham, England)

PLATE 15. Edward Burne-Jones, THE BUILDING OF THE BRAZEN TOWER (1872), oil (*Ashmolean Museum*). This is the earliest of three versions of this picture. The large upright version painted in 1888, now in the City Art Gallery, Glasgow, is reproduced in all editions of Malcolm Bell's *Edward Burne-Jones: A Record and Review* (1892–98) and, recently, in Graham Reynolds's *Victorian Painting* (1966), Plate 46. The small oblong version (1876), now in the Fogg Art Museum, is reproduced in the catalogue of the Pre-Raphaelite exhibition, *Paint-*

ings and Drawings of the Pre-Raphaelites and Their Circle, No. 20. The Ashmolean version, in my opinion the best of the three, has been hitherto reproduced only in *A Catalogue of the Pictures and Drawings in the Collection of Frederick John Nettlefold,* by C. Reginald Grundy (4 vols., London and Derby, 1933), I, 42 — an excellent reproduction in color.

The painting is based on Morris's poem "The Doom of King Acrisius," the third tale of *The Earthly Paradise,* of which the prose Argument is as follows:

"Acrisius, King of Argos, being warned by an oracle that the son of his daughter Danaë should slay him, shut her up in a brazen tower built for that end beside the sea: there, though no man could come nigh her, she nevertheless bore a son [Perseus] to Jove, and she and her new-born son, set adrift on the sea, came to the island of Seriphos. Thence her son, grown to manhood, set out to win the Gorgon's Head, and accomplished that end by the help of Minerva; and afterwards rescued Andromeda, daughter of Cepheus, from a terrible doom, and wedded her. Coming back to Seriphos he took his mother thence, and made for Argos, but by stress of weather came to Thessaly, and there, at Larissa, accomplished the prophecy, by unwittingly slaying Acrisius. In the end he founded the city of Mycenae, and died there."

The picture illustrates lines 38–43:

> Now thither oft would maiden Danaë stray,
> And watch its strange walls growing day by day,
> Because, poor soul! she knew not anything
> Of these forebodings of the fearful King,
> Nor how he meted out for her this doom,
> Therein to dwell as in a living tomb.

Burne-Jones also did a series of pictures based on the story of Perseus, Danaë's son. See the Pre-Raphaelite catalogue, Fogg Museum, cited above, from which I have drawn many of these details.

(Photograph, Copyright The University of Oxford, Ashmolean Museum, Department of Western Art)

PLATE 16. William Morris and Edward Burne-Jones, Kelmscott Press *Chaucer,* p. 129 (*William Morris Gallery*). Of the 53 books issued by the Kelmscott Press, the *Chaucer,* Number 40, is the most important and most famous. Here, the woodcut illustration is by Burne-Jones; all the rest, including the type (known as "Chaucer," though used several years before this book), by Morris. Page 58 of the *Chaucer* is reproduced in Morris's *Collected Works,* XXIV, facing p. xiii. See H. Halliday Sparling, *The Kelmscott Press and William Morris* (1924), which includes Morris's "Note on His Aim in Founding the Kelmscott Press" and Sydney Cockerell's articles "A Short Description of the Kelmscott Press" and "An Annotated List of Books Printed at the Press."

Many Morris designs, including pages from *King Floris and Fair Jehane* and *The Golden Legend*, stained glass, the decorated St. George cabinet, carpets, tapestries, embroidery, wallpaper, and even an illuminated manuscript, are conveniently reproduced in *William Morris, Selected Writings and Designs*, ed. Asa Briggs (Pelican, 1962) and in *William Morris*, Victoria and Albert Museum, Small Picture Book No. 43 (1958).

(Photograph, Courtesy of William Morris Gallery, Walthamstow)

Additions
(1975)

Page 526. Morris's self-portrait is reproduced in Ray Watkinson's *William Morris as Designer*, No. 27

Pages 527–37. Plate 1a, Surtees, No. 501; 1b, not in Surtees; 1c, Surtees, No. 292. Plate 2, Surtees, No. 40. Plate 3, Surtees, No. 44. Plate 4, Surtees, No. 150, R.1. Plate 5, Surtees, No. 244. Plate 6, Surtees, No. 207. Plate 7, Surtees, No. 142. Plates 8 and 9, see the marvelous catalogue by Mary Bennett of the Hunt Exhibition, Walker Art Gallery and Victoria and Albert Museum, March–June, 1969. (The singers on Magdalen Tower, identified in the catalogue, Nos. 59–60, include "a Parsee, a sun-worshipper, at the right," and Sir Herbert Warren, President of Magdalen and author of a sonnet on the picture in the *Oxford Book of Victorian Verse*, p. 749.) Plate 15, reproduced in David Cecil's *Visionary & Dreamer* (1969) and in Martin Harrison and Bill Waters, *Burne-Jones* (1973), No. 121.

INDEX OF POEMS